Mastering Java Machine Learning

Mastering and implementing advanced techniques in machine learning

Dr. Uday Kamath

Krishna Choppella

D1710835

Mastering Java Machine Learning

First published: June 2017

Production reference: 1290617

Published by Packt Publishing Ltd.
Livery Place
35 Livery Street
Birmingham B3 2PB, UK.

ISBN 978-1-78588-051-3

www.packtpub.com

Credits

Authors
  Dr. Uday Kamath

  Krishna Choppella

Reviewers
  Samir Sahli

  Prashant Verma

Commissioning Editor
  Veena Pagare

Acquisition Editor
  Divya Poojari

Content Development Editor
  Mayur Pawanikar

Technical Editor
  Vivek Arora

Copy Editor
  Safis Editing

Project Coordinator
  Nidhi Joshi

Proofreader
  Safis Editing

Indexer
  Francy Puthiry

Graphics
  Tania Dutta

Production Coordinator
  Arvindkumar Gupta

Cover Work
  Arvindkumar Gupta

Foreword

Dr. Uday Kamath is a volcano of ideas. Every time he walked into my office, we had fruitful and animated discussions. I have been a professor of computer science at George Mason University (GMU) for 15 years, specializing in machine learning and data mining. I have known Uday for five years, first as a student in my data mining class, then as a colleague and co-author of papers and projects on large-scale machine learning. While a chief data scientist at BAE Systems Applied Intelligence, Uday earned his PhD in evolutionary computation and machine learning. As if having two high-demand jobs was not enough, Uday was unusually prolific, publishing extensively with four different people in the computer science faculty during his tenure at GMU, something you don't see very often. Given this pedigree, I am not surprised that less than four years since Uday's graduation with a PhD, I am writing the foreword for his book on mastering advanced machine learning techniques with Java. Uday's thirst for new stimulating challenges has struck again, resulting in this terrific book you now have in your hands.

This book is the product of his deep interest and knowledge in sound and well-grounded theory, and at the same time his keen grasp of the practical feasibility of proposed methodologies. Several books on machine learning and data analytics exist, but Uday's book closes a substantial gap—the one between theory and practice. It offers a comprehensive and systematic analysis of classic and advanced learning techniques, with a focus on their advantages and limitations, practical use and implementations. This book is a precious resource for practitioners of data science and analytics, as well as for undergraduate and graduate students keen to master practical and efficient implementations of machine learning techniques.

The book covers the classic techniques of machine learning, such as classification, clustering, dimensionality reduction, anomaly detection, semi-supervised learning, and active learning. It also covers advanced and recent topics, including learning with stream data, deep learning, and the challenges of learning with big data. Each chapter is dedicated to a topic and includes an illustrative case study, which covers state-of-the-art Java-based tools and software, and the entire knowledge discovery cycle: data collection, experimental design, modeling, results, and evaluation. Each chapter is self-contained, providing great flexibility of usage. The accompanying website provides the source code and data. This is truly a gem for both students and data analytics practitioners, who can experiment first-hand with the methods just learned or deepen their understanding of the methods by applying them to real-world scenarios.

As I was reading the various chapters of the book, I was reminded of the enthusiasm Uday has for learning and knowledge. He communicates the concepts described in the book with clarity and with the same passion. I am positive that you, as a reader, will feel the same. I will certainly keep this book as a personal resource for the courses I teach, and strongly recommend it to my students.

Dr. Carlotta Domeniconi

Associate Professor of Computer Science, George Mason University

About the Authors

Dr. Uday Kamath is the chief data scientist at BAE Systems Applied Intelligence. He specializes in scalable machine learning and has spent 20 years in the domain of AML, fraud detection in financial crime, cyber security, and bioinformatics, to name a few. Dr. Kamath is responsible for key products in areas focusing on the behavioral, social networking and big data machine learning aspects of analytics at BAE AI. He received his PhD at George Mason University, under the able guidance of Dr. Kenneth De Jong, where his dissertation research focused on machine learning for big data and automated sequence mining.

I would like to thank my friend, Krishna Choppella, for accepting the offer to co-author this book and being an able partner on this long but satisfying journey.

Heartfelt thanks to our reviewers, especially Dr. Samir Sahli for his valuable comments, suggestions, and in-depth review of the chapters. I would like to thank Professor Carlotta Domeniconi for her suggestions and comments that helped us shape various chapters in the book. I would also like to thank all the Packt staff, especially Divya Poojari, Mayur Pawanikar, and Vivek Arora, for helping us complete the tasks in time. This book required making a lot of sacrifices on the personal front and I would like to thank my wife, Pratibha, and our nanny, Evelyn, for their unconditional support. Finally, thanks to all my lovely teachers and professors for not only teaching the subjects, but also instilling the joy of learning.

Krishna Choppella builds tools and client solutions in his role as a solutions architect for analytics at BAE Systems Applied Intelligence. He has been programming in Java for 20 years. His interests are data science, functional programming, and distributed computing.

About the Reviewers

Samir Sahli was awarded a BSc degree in applied mathematics and information sciences from the University of Nice Sophia-Antipolis, France, in 2004. He received MSc and PhD degrees in physics (specializing in optics/photonics/image science) from University Laval, Quebec, Canada, in 2008 and 2013, respectively. During his graduate studies, he worked with Defence Research and Development Canada (DRDC) on the automatic detection and recognition of targets in aerial imagery, especially in the context of uncontrolled environment and sub-optimal acquisition conditions. He has worked since 2009 as a consultant for several companies based in Europe and North America specializing in the area of Intelligence, Surveillance, and Reconnaissance (ISR) and in remote sensing.

Dr. Sahli joined McMaster Biophotonics in 2013 as a postdoctoral fellow. His research was in the field of optics, image processing, and machine learning. He was involved in several projects, such as the development of a novel generation of gastrointestinal tract imaging device, hyperspectral imaging of skin erythema for individualized radiotherapy treatment, and automatic detection of the precancerous Barrett's esophageal cell using fluorescence lifetime imaging microscopy and multiphoton microscopy.

Dr. Sahli joined BAE Systems Applied Intelligence in 2015. He has since worked as a data scientist to develop analytics models to detect complex fraud patterns and money laundering schemes for insurance, banking, and governmental clients using machine learning, statistics, and social network analysis tools.

Prashant Verma started his IT career in 2011 as a Java developer in Ericsson, working in the telecom domain. After a couple of years of Java EE experience, he moved into the big data domain and has worked on almost all of the popular big data technologies such as Hadoop, Spark, Flume, Mongo, Cassandra, and so on. He has also played with Scala. Currently, he works with QA Infotech as a lead data engineer, working on solving e-learning problems with analytics and machine learning.

Prashant has worked for many companies, such as Ericsson and QA Infotech, with domain knowledge of telecom and e-learning. He has also worked as a freelance consultant in his free time.

I want to thank Packt Publishing for giving me the chance to review the book, as well as my employer and my family for their patience while I was busy working on this book.

www.PacktPub.com

eBooks, discount offers, and more

Did you know that Packt offers eBook versions of every book published, with PDF and ePub files available? You can upgrade to the eBook version at www.PacktPub.com and as a print book customer, you are entitled to a discount on the eBook copy. Get in touch with us at customercare@packtpub.com for more details.

At www.PacktPub.com, you can also read a collection of free technical articles, sign up for a range of free newsletters and receive exclusive discounts and offers on Packt books and eBooks.

https://www.packtpub.com/mapt

Get the most in-demand software skills with Mapt. Mapt gives you full access to all Packt books and video courses, as well as industry-leading tools to help you plan your personal development and advance your career.

Why subscribe?

- Fully searchable across every book published by Packt
- Copy and paste, print, and bookmark content
- On demand and accessible via a web browser

Customer Feedback

Thanks for purchasing this Packt book. At Packt, quality is at the heart of our editorial process. To help us improve, please leave us an honest review on this book's Amazon page at https://www.amazon.com/dp/1785880519.

If you'd like to join our team of regular reviewers, you can e-mail us at customerreviews@packtpub.com. We award our regular reviewers with free eBooks and videos in exchange for their valuable feedback. Help us be relentless in improving our products!

Dedicated to my parents, Krishna Kamath and Bharathi Kamath, my wife, Pratibha Shenoy, and the kids, Aaroh and Brandy

- Dr. Uday Kamath

To my parents

Krishna Choppella

Table of Contents

Preface

There are many notable books on machine learning, from pedagogical tracts on the theory of learning from data; to standard references on specializations in the field, such as clustering and outlier detection or probabilistic graph modeling; to cookbooks that offer practical advice on the use of tools and libraries in a particular language. The books that tend to be broad in coverage are often short on theoretical detail, while those with a focus on one topic or tool may not, for example, have much to say about the difference in approach in a streaming as opposed to a batch environment. Besides, for the non-novices with a preference for tools in Java who wish to reach for a single volume that will extend their knowledge—simultaneously, on the essential aspects—there are precious few options.

Finding in one place

- The pros and cons of different techniques given any data availability scenario—when data is labeled or unlabeled, streaming or batch, local, or distributed, structured or unstructured

- A ready reference for the most important mathematical results related to those very techniques for a better appreciation of the underlying theory

- An introduction to the most mature Java-based frameworks, libraries, and visualization tools with descriptions and illustrations on how to put these techniques into practice is not possible today, as far as we know

The core idea of this book, therefore, is to address this gap while maintaining a balance between treatment of theory and practice with the aid of probability, statistics, basic linear algebra, and rudimentary calculus in the service of one, and emphasizing methodology, case studies, tools and code in support of the other.

According to the KDnuggets 2016 software poll, Java, at 16.8%, has the second highest share in popularity among languages used in machine learning, after Python. What's more is that this marks a 19% increase from the year before! Clearly, Java remains an important and effective vehicle to build and deploy systems involving machine learning, despite claims of its decline in some quarters. With this book, we aim to reach professionals and motivated enthusiasts with some experience in Java and a beginner's knowledge of machine learning. Our goal is to make *Mastering Java Machine Learning* the next step on their path to becoming advanced practitioners in data science. To guide them on this path, the book covers a veritable arsenal of techniques in machine learning—some which they may already be familiar with, others perhaps not as much, or only superficially—including methods of data analysis, learning algorithms, evaluation of model performance, and more in supervised and semi-supervised learning, clustering and anomaly detection, and semi-supervised and active learning. It also presents special topics such as probabilistic graph modeling, text mining, and deep learning. Not forgetting the increasingly important topics in enterprise-scale systems today, the book also covers the unique challenges of learning from evolving data streams and the tools and techniques applicable to real-time systems, as well as the imperatives of the world of Big Data:

- How does machine learning work in large-scale distributed environments?
- What are the trade-offs?
- How must algorithms be adapted?
- How can these systems interoperate with other technologies in the dominant Hadoop ecosystem?

This book explains how to apply machine learning to real-world data and real-world domains with the right methodology, processes, applications, and analysis. Accompanying each chapter are case studies and examples of how to apply the newly learned techniques using some of the best available open source tools written in Java. This book covers more than 15 open source Java tools supporting a wide range of techniques between them, with code and practical usage. The code, data, and configurations are available for readers to download and experiment with. We present more than ten real-world case studies in Machine Learning that illustrate the data scientist's process. Each case study details the steps undertaken in the experiments: data ingestion, data analysis, data cleansing, feature reduction/selection, mapping to machine learning, model training, model selection, model evaluation, and analysis of results. This gives the reader a practical guide to using the tools and methods presented in each chapter for solving the business problem at hand.

What this book covers

Chapter 1, Machine Learning Review, is a refresher of basic concepts and techniques that the reader would have learned from Packt's *Learning Machine Learning in Java* or a similar text. This chapter is a review of concepts such as data, data transformation, sampling and bias, features and their importance, supervised learning, unsupervised learning, big data learning, stream and real-time learning, probabilistic graphic models, and semi-supervised learning.

Chapter 2, Practical Approach to Real-World Supervised Learning, cobwebs dusted, dives straight into the vast field of supervised learning and the full spectrum of associated techniques. We cover the topics of feature selection and reduction, linear modeling, logistic models, non-linear models, SVM and kernels, ensemble learning techniques such as bagging and boosting, validation techniques and evaluation metrics, and model selection. Using WEKA and RapidMiner, we carry out a detailed case study, going through all the steps from data analysis to analysis of model performance. As in each of the other chapters, the case study is presented as an example to help the reader understand how the techniques introduced in the chapter are applied in real life. The dataset used in the case study is UCI HorseColic.

Chapter 3, Unsupervised Machine Learning Techniques, presents many advanced methods in clustering and outlier techniques, with applications. Topics covered are feature selection and reduction in unsupervised data, clustering algorithms, evaluation methods in clustering, and anomaly detection using statistical, distance, and distribution techniques. At the end of the chapter, we perform a case study for both clustering and outlier detection using a real-world image dataset, MNIST. We use the Smile API to do feature reduction and ELKI for learning.

Chapter 4, Semi-Supervised Learning and Active Learning, gives details of algorithms and techniques for learning when only a small amount labeled data is present. Topics covered are self-training, generative models, transductive SVMs, co-training, active learning, and multi-view learning. The case study involves both learning systems and is performed on the real-world UCI Breast Cancer Wisconsin dataset. The tools introduced are JKernelMachines ,KEEL and JCLAL.

Chapter 5, Real-Time Stream Machine Learning, covers data streams in real-time present unique circumstances for the problem of learning from data. This chapter broadly covers the need for stream machine learning and applications, supervised stream learning, unsupervised cluster stream learning, unsupervised outlier learning, evaluation techniques in stream learning, and metrics used for evaluation. A detailed case study is given at the end of the chapter to illustrate the use of the MOA framework. The dataset used is Electricity (ELEC).

Chapter 6, Probabilistic Graph Modeling, shows that many real-world problems can be effectively represented by encoding complex joint probability distributions over multi-dimensional spaces. Probabilistic graph models provide a framework to represent, draw inferences, and learn effectively in such situations. The chapter broadly covers probability concepts, PGMs, Bayesian networks, Markov networks, Graph Structure Learning, Hidden Markov Models, and Inferencing. A detailed case study on a real-world dataset is performed at the end of the chapter. The tools used in this case study are OpenMarkov and WEKA's Bayes network. The dataset is UCI Adult (Census Income).

Chapter 7, Deep Learning, if there is one super-star of machine learning in the popular imagination today it is deep learning, which has attained a dominance among techniques used to solve the most complex AI problems. Topics broadly covered are neural networks, issues in neural networks, deep belief networks, restricted Boltzman machines, convolutional networks, long short-term memory units, denoising autoencoders, recurrent networks, and others. We present a detailed case study showing how to implement deep learning networks, tuning the parameters and performing learning. We use DeepLearning4J with the MNIST image dataset.

Chapter 8, Text Mining and Natural Language Processing, details the techniques, algorithms, and tools for performing various analyses in the field of text mining. Topics broadly covered are areas of text mining, components needed for text mining, representation of text data, dimensionality reduction techniques, topic modeling, text clustering, named entity recognition, and deep learning. The case study uses real-world unstructured text data (the Reuters-21578 dataset) highlighting topic modeling and text classification; the tools used are MALLET and KNIME.

Chapter 9, Big Data Machine Learning – The Final Frontier, discusses some of the most important challenges of today. What learning options are available when data is either big or available at a very high velocity? How is scalability handled? Topics covered are big data cluster deployment frameworks, big data storage options, batch data processing, batch data machine learning, real-time machine learning frameworks, and real-time stream learning. In the detailed case study for both big data batch and real-time we select the UCI Covertype dataset and the machine learning libraries H2O, Spark MLLib and SAMOA.

Appendix A, Linear Algebra, covers concepts from linear algebra, and is meant as a brief refresher. It is by no means complete in its coverage, but contains a whirlwind tour of some important concepts relevant to the machine learning techniques featured in the book. It includes vectors, matrices and basic matrix operations and properties, linear transformations, matrix inverse, eigen decomposition, positive definite matrix, and singular value decomposition.

Appendix B, Probability, provides a brief primer on probability. It includes the axioms of probability, Bayes' theorem, density estimation, mean, variance, standard deviation, Gaussian standard deviation, covariance, correlation coefficient, binomial distribution, Poisson distribution, Gaussian distribution, central limit theorem, and error propagation.

What you need for this book

This book assumes you have some experience of programming in Java and a basic understanding of machine learning concepts. If that doesn't apply to you, but you are curious nonetheless and self-motivated, fret not, and read on! For those who do have some background, it means that you are familiar with simple statistical analysis of data and concepts involved in supervised and unsupervised learning. Those who may not have the requisite math or must poke the far reaches of their memory to shake loose the odd formula or funny symbol, do not be disheartened. If you are the sort that loves a challenge, the short primer in the appendices may be all you need to kick-start your engines—a bit of tenacity will see you through the rest! For those who have never been introduced to machine learning, the first chapter was equally written for you as for those needing a refresher—it is your starter-kit to jump in feet first and find out what it's all about. You can augment your basics with any number of online resources. Finally, for those innocent of Java, here's a secret: many of the tools featured in the book have powerful GUIs. Some include wizard-like interfaces, making them quite easy to use, and do not require any knowledge of Java. So if you are new to Java, just skip the examples that need coding and learn to use the GUI-based tools instead!

Who this book is for

The primary audience of this book is professionals who works with data and whose responsibilities may include data analysis, data visualization or transformation, the training, validation, testing and evaluation of machine learning models—presumably to perform predictive, descriptive or prescriptive analytics using Java or Java-based tools. The choice of Java may imply a personal preference and therefore some prior experience programming in Java. On the other hand, perhaps circumstances in the work environment or company policies limit the use of third-party tools to only those written in Java and a few others. In the second case, the prospective reader may have no programming experience in Java. This book is aimed at this reader just as squarely as it is at their colleague, the Java expert (who came up with the policy in the first place).

A secondary audience can be defined by a profile with two attributes alone: an intellectual curiosity about machine learning and the desire for a single comprehensive treatment of the concepts, the practical techniques, and the tools. A specimen of this type of reader can opt to skip the math and the tools and focus on learning the most common supervised and unsupervised learning algorithms alone. Another might skim over *Chapters 1, 2, 3,* and *7*, skip the others entirely, and jump headlong into the tools—a perfectly reasonable strategy if you want to quickly make yourself useful analyzing that dataset the client said would be here any day now. Importantly, too, with some practice reproducing the experiments from the book, it'll get you asking the right questions of the gurus! Alternatively, you might want to use this book as a reference to quickly look up the details of the algorithm for affinity propagation (*Chapter 3, Unsupervised Machine Learning Techniques*), or remind yourself of an LSTM architecture with a brief review of the schematic (*Chapter 7, Deep Learning*), or dog-ear the page with the list of pros and cons of distance-based clustering methods for outlier detection in stream-based learning (*Chapter 5, Real-Time Stream Machine Learning*). All specimens are welcome and each will find plenty to sink their teeth into.

Conventions

In this book, you will find a number of text styles that distinguish between different kinds of information. Here are some examples of these styles and an explanation of their meaning.

Code words in text, database table names, folder names, filenames, file extensions, pathnames, dummy URLs, user input, and Twitter handles are shown as follows: "The algorithm calls the eliminate function in a loop, as shown here."

A block of code is set as follows:

```
DataSource source = new DataSource(trainingFile);
Instances data = source.getDataSet();
if (data.classIndex() == -1)
   data.setClassIndex(data.numAttributes() - 1);
```

Any command-line input or output is written as follows:

```
Correctly Classified Instances       53        77.9412 %
Incorrectly Classified Instances     15        22.0588 %
```

New terms and **important words** are shown in bold.

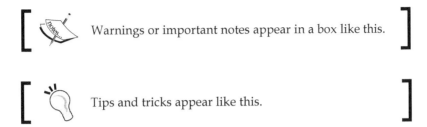

[Warnings or important notes appear in a box like this.]

[Tips and tricks appear like this.]

Reader feedback

Feedback from our readers is always welcome. Let us know what you think about this book—what you liked or disliked. Reader feedback is important for us as it helps us develop titles that you will really get the most out of.

To send us general feedback, simply e-mail feedback@packtpub.com, and mention the book's title in the subject of your message.

If there is a topic that you have expertise in and you are interested in either writing or contributing to a book, see our author guide at www.packtpub.com/authors.

Customer support

Now that you are the proud owner of a Packt book, we have a number of things to help you to get the most from your purchase.

You can download the code files by following these steps:

1. Log in or register to our website using your e-mail address and password.
2. Hover the mouse pointer on the **SUPPORT** tab at the top.
3. Click on **Code Downloads & Errata**.
4. Enter the name of the book in the **Search** box.
5. Select the book for which you're looking to download the code files.
6. Choose from the drop-down menu where you purchased this book from.
7. Click on **Code Download**.

You can also download the code files by clicking on the **Code Files** button on the book's webpage at the Packt Publishing website. This page can be accessed by entering the book's name in the **Search** box. Please note that you need to be logged in to your Packt account.

Once the file is downloaded, please make sure that you unzip or extract the folder using the latest version of:

- WinRAR / 7-Zip for Windows
- Zipeg / iZip / UnRarX for Mac
- 7-Zip / PeaZip for Linux

The code bundle for the book is also hosted on GitHub at `https://github.com/mjmlbook/mastering-java-machine-learning`. We also have other code bundles from our rich catalog of books and videos available at `https://github.com/PacktPublishing/`. Check them out!

Errata

Although we have taken every care to ensure the accuracy of our content, mistakes do happen. If you find a mistake in one of our books — maybe a mistake in the text or the code — we would be grateful if you could report this to us. By doing so, you can save other readers from frustration and help us improve subsequent versions of this book. If you find any errata, please report them by visiting `http://www.packtpub.com/submit-errata`, selecting your book, clicking on the **Errata Submission Form** link, and entering the details of your errata. Once your errata are verified, your submission will be accepted and the errata will be uploaded to our website or added to any list of existing errata under the Errata section of that title.

To view the previously submitted errata, go to `https://www.packtpub.com/books/content/support` and enter the name of the book in the search field. The required information will appear under the **Errata** section.

Piracy

Piracy of copyrighted material on the Internet is an ongoing problem across all media. At Packt, we take the protection of our copyright and licenses very seriously. If you come across any illegal copies of our works in any form on the Internet, please provide us with the location address or website name immediately so that we can pursue a remedy.

Please contact us at copyright@packtpub.com with a link to the suspected pirated material.

We appreciate your help in protecting our authors and our ability to bring you valuable content.

Questions

If you have a problem with any aspect of this book, you can contact us at questions@packtpub.com, and we will do our best to address the problem.

Machine Learning Review

Recent years have seen the revival of **artificial intelligence** (**AI**) and machine learning in particular, both in academic circles and the industry. In the last decade, AI has seen dramatic successes that eluded practitioners in the intervening years since the original promise of the field gave way to relative decline until its re-emergence in the last few years.

What made these successes possible, in large part, was the impetus provided by the need to process the prodigious amounts of ever-growing data, key algorithmic advances by dogged researchers in deep learning, and the inexorable increase in raw computational power driven by Moore's Law. Among the areas of AI leading the resurgence, machine learning has seen spectacular developments, and continues to find the widest applicability in an array of domains. The use of machine learning to help in complex decision making at the highest levels of business and, at the same time, its enormous success in improving the accuracy of what are now everyday applications, such as searches, speech recognition, and personal assistants on mobile phones, have made its effects commonplace in the family room and the board room alike. Articles breathlessly extolling the power of deep learning can be found today not only in the popular science and technology press but also in mainstream outlets such as *The New York Times* and *The Huffington Post*. Machine learning has indeed become ubiquitous in a relatively short time.

An *ordinary* user encounters machine learning in many ways in their day-to-day activities. Most e-mail providers, including Yahoo and Gmail, give the user automated sorting and categorization of e-mails into headings such as Spam, Junk, Promotions, and so on, which is made possible using text mining, a branch of machine learning. When shopping online for products on e-commerce websites, such as https://www.amazon.com/, or watching movies from content providers, such as Netflix, one is offered recommendations for other products and content by so-called recommender systems, another branch of machine learning, as an effective way to retain customers.

Forecasting the weather, estimating real estate prices, predicting voter turnout, and even election results — all use some form of machine learning to see into the future, as it were.

The ever-growing availability of data and the promise of systems that can enrich our lives by learning from that data place a growing demand on the skills of the limited workforce of professionals in the field of data science. This demand is particularly acute for well-trained experts who know their way around the landscape of machine learning techniques in the more popular languages, such as Java, Python, R, and increasingly, Scala. Fortunately, thanks to the thousands of contributors in the open source community, each of these languages has a rich and rapidly growing set of libraries, frameworks, and tutorials that make state-of-the-art techniques accessible to anyone with an internet connection and a computer, for the most part. Java is an important vehicle for this spread of tools and technology, especially in large-scale machine learning projects, owing to its maturity and stability in enterprise-level deployments and the portable JVM platform, not to mention the legions of professional programmers who have adopted it over the years. Consequently, mastery of the skills so lacking in the workforce today will put any aspiring professional with a desire to enter the field at a distinct advantage in the marketplace.

Perhaps you already apply machine learning techniques in your professional work, or maybe you simply have a hobbyist's interest in the subject. If you're reading this, it's likely you can already bend Java to your will, no problem, but now you feel you're ready to dig deeper and learn how to use the best of breed open source ML Java frameworks in your next data science project. If that is indeed you, how fortuitous is it that the chapters in this book are designed to do all that and more!

Mastery of a subject, especially one that has such obvious applicability as machine learning, requires more than an understanding of its core concepts and familiarity with its mathematical underpinnings. Unlike an introductory treatment of the subject, a book that purports to help you master the subject must be heavily focused on practical aspects in addition to introducing more advanced topics that would have stretched the scope of the introductory material. To warm up before we embark on sharpening our skills, we will devote this chapter to a quick review of what we already know. For the ambitious novice with little or no prior exposure to the subject (who is nevertheless determined to get the fullest benefit from this book), here's our advice: make sure you do not skip the rest of this chapter; instead, use it as a springboard to explore unfamiliar concepts in more depth. Seek out external resources as necessary. Wikipedia them. Then jump right back in.

For the rest of this chapter, we will review the following:

- History and definitions
- What is not machine learning?
- Concepts and terminology
- Important branches of machine learning
- Different data types in machine learning
- Applications of machine learning
- Issues faced in machine learning
- The meta-process used in most machine learning projects
- Information on some well-known tools, APIs, and resources that we will employ in this book

Machine learning – history and definition

It is difficult to give an exact history, but the definition of machine learning we use today finds its usage as early as the 1860s. In Rene Descartes' *Discourse on the Method*, he refers to *Automata* and says:

> *For we can easily understand a machine's being constituted so that it can utter words, and even emit some responses to action on it of a corporeal kind, which brings about a change in its organs; for instance, if touched in a particular part it may ask what we wish to say to it; if in another part it may exclaim that it is being hurt, and so on.*

```
http://www.earlymoderntexts.com/assets/pdfs/
descartes1637.pdf
https://www.marxists.org/reference/archive/
descartes/1635/discourse-method.htm
```

Alan Turing, in his famous publication *Computing Machinery and Intelligence* gives basic insights into the goals of machine learning by asking the question "Can machines think?".

```
http://csmt.uchicago.edu/annotations/turing.htm
http://www.csee.umbc.edu/courses/471/papers/turing.pdf
```

Arthur Samuel in 1959 wrote, "*Machine Learning is the field of study that gives computers the ability to learn without being explicitly programmed.*".

Tom Mitchell in recent times gave a more exact definition of machine learning: "*A computer program is said to learn from experience E with respect to some task T and some performance measure P, if its performance on T, as measured by P, improves with experience E.*"

Machine learning has a relationship with several areas:

- **Statistics**: It uses the elements of data sampling, estimation, hypothesis testing, learning theory, and statistical-based modeling, to name a few

- **Algorithms and computation**: It uses the basic concepts of search, traversal, parallelization, distributed computing, and so on from basic computer science

- **Database and knowledge discovery**: For its ability to store, retrieve, and access information in various formats

- **Pattern recognition**: For its ability to find interesting patterns from the data to explore, visualize, and predict

- **Artificial intelligence**: Though it is considered a branch of artificial intelligence, it also has relationships with other branches, such as heuristics, optimization, evolutionary computing, and so on

What is not machine learning?

It is important to recognize areas that share a connection with machine learning but cannot themselves be considered part of machine learning. Some disciplines may overlap to a smaller or larger extent, yet the principles underlying machine learning are quite distinct:

- **Business intelligence (BI) and reporting**: Reporting **key performance indicators (KPI's)**, querying OLAP for slicing, dicing, and drilling into the data, dashboards, and so on that form the central components of BI are not machine learning.

- **Storage and ETL**: Data storage and ETL are key elements in any machine learning process, but, by themselves, they don't qualify as machine learning.

- **Information retrieval, search, and queries**: The ability to retrieve data or documents based on search criteria or indexes, which form the basis of information retrieval, are not really machine learning. Many forms of machine learning, such as semi-supervised learning, can rely on the searching of similar data for modeling, but that doesn't qualify searching as machine learning.

- **Knowledge representation and reasoning**: Representing knowledge for performing complex tasks, such as ontology, expert systems, and semantic webs, does not qualify as machine learning.

Machine learning – concepts and terminology

In this section, we will describe the different concepts and terms normally used in machine learning:

- **Data or dataset**: The basics of machine learning rely on understanding the data. The data or dataset normally refers to content available in structured or unstructured format for use in machine learning. Structured datasets have specific formats, and an unstructured dataset is normally in the form of some free-flowing text. Data can be available in various storage types or formats. In structured data, every element known as an instance or an example or row follows a predefined structure. Data can also be categorized by size: small or medium data have a few hundreds to thousands of instances, whereas *big* data refers to a large volume, mostly in millions or billions, that cannot be stored or accessed using common devices or fit in the memory of such devices.

- **Features, attributes, variables, or dimensions**: In structured datasets, as mentioned before, there are predefined elements with their own semantics and data type, which are known variously as features, attributes, metrics, indicators, variables, or dimensions.

- **Data types**: The features defined earlier need some form of typing in many machine learning algorithms or techniques. The most commonly used data types are as follows:

    ○ **Categorical or nominal**: This indicates well-defined categories or values present in the dataset. For example, eye color—black, blue, brown, green, grey; document content type—text, image, video.

    ○ **Continuous or numeric**: This indicates a numeric nature of the data field. For example, a person's weight measured by a bathroom scale, the temperature reading from a sensor, or the monthly balance in dollars on a credit card account.

    ○ **Ordinal**: This denotes data that can be ordered in some way. For example, garment size—small, medium, large; boxing weight classes: heavyweight, light heavyweight, middleweight, lightweight, and bantamweight.

- **Target or label**: A feature or set of features in the dataset, which is used for learning from training data and predicting in an unseen dataset, is known as a target or a label. The term "ground truth" is also used in some domains. A label can have any form as specified before, that is, categorical, continuous, or ordinal.

- **Machine learning model**: Each machine learning algorithm, based on what it learned from the dataset, maintains the state of its learning for predicting or giving insights into future or unseen data. This is referred to as the machine learning model.

- **Sampling**: Data sampling is an essential step in machine learning. Sampling means choosing a subset of examples from a population with the intent of treating the behavior seen in the (smaller) sample as being representative of the behavior of the (larger) population. In order for the sample to be representative of the population, care must be taken in the way the sample is chosen. Generally, a population consists of every object sharing the properties of interest in the problem domain, for example, all people eligible to vote in the general election, or all potential automobile owners in the next four years. Since it is usually prohibitive (or impossible) to collect data for all the objects in a population, a well-chosen subset is selected for the purpose of analysis. A crucial consideration in the sampling process is that the sample is unbiased with respect to the population. The following are types of probability-based sampling:

  - **Uniform random sampling**: This refers to sampling that is done over a uniformly distributed population, that is, each object has an equal probability of being chosen.

  - **Stratified random sampling**: This refers to the sampling method used when the data can be categorized into multiple classes. In such cases, in order to ensure all categories are represented in the sample, the population is divided into distinct strata based on these classifications, and each stratum is sampled in proportion to the fraction of its class in the overall population. Stratified sampling is common when the population density varies across categories, and it is important to compare these categories with the same statistical power. Political polling often involves stratified sampling when it is known that different demographic groups vote in significantly different ways. Disproportional representation of each group in a random sample can lead to large errors in the outcomes of the polls. When we control for demographics, we can avoid oversampling the majority over the other groups.

- ○ **Cluster sampling**: Sometimes there are natural groups among the population being studied, and each group is representative of the whole population. An example is data that spans many geographical regions. In cluster sampling, you take a random subset of the groups followed by a random sample from within each of those groups to construct the full data sample. This kind of sampling can reduce the cost of data collection without compromising the fidelity of distribution in the population.

- ○ **Systematic sampling**: Systematic or interval sampling is used when there is a certain ordering present in the sampling frame (a finite set of objects treated as the population and taken to be the source of data for sampling, for example, the corpus of Wikipedia articles, arranged lexicographically by title). If the sample is then selected by starting at a random object and skipping a constant k number of objects before selecting the next one, that is called systematic sampling. The value of k is calculated as the ratio of the population to the sample size.

- **Model evaluation metrics**: Evaluating models for performance is generally based on different evaluation metrics for different types of learning. In classification, it is generally based on accuracy, **receiver operating characteristics (ROC)** curves, training speed, memory requirements, false positive ratio, and so on, to name a few (see *Chapter 2, Practical Approach to Real-World Supervised Learning*). In clustering, the number of clusters found, cohesion, separation, and so on form the general metrics (see *Chapter 3, Unsupervised Machine Learning Techniques*). In stream-based learning, apart from the standard metrics mentioned earlier, adaptability, speed of learning, and robustness to sudden changes are some of the conventional metrics for evaluating the performance of the learner (see *Chapter 5, Real-Time Stream Machine Learning*).

To illustrate these concepts, a concrete example in the form of a commonly used sample weather dataset is given. The data gives a set of weather conditions and a label that indicates whether the subject decided to play a game of tennis on the day or not:

```
@relation weather

@attribute outlook {sunny, overcast, rainy}
@attribute temperature numeric
@attribute humidity numeric
@attribute windy {TRUE, FALSE}
@attribute play {yes, no}

@data
sunny,85,85,FALSE,no
sunny,80,90,TRUE,no
overcast,83,86,FALSE,yes
rainy,70,96,FALSE,yes
rainy,68,80,FALSE,yes
rainy,65,70,TRUE,no
overcast,64,65,TRUE,yes
sunny,72,95,FALSE,no
sunny,69,70,FALSE,yes
rainy,75,80,FALSE,yes
sunny,75,70,TRUE,yes
overcast,72,90,TRUE,yes
overcast,81,75,FALSE,yes
rainy,71,91,TRUE,no
```

The dataset is in the format of an **ARFF (attribute-relation file format)** file. It consists of a header giving the information about features or attributes with their data types and actual comma-separated data following the data tag. The dataset has five features, namely outlook, temperature, humidity, windy, and play. The features outlook and windy are categorical features, while humidity and temperature are continuous. The feature play is the target and is categorical.

Machine learning – types and subtypes

We will now explore different subtypes or branches of machine learning. Though the following list is not comprehensive, it covers the most well-known types:

- **Supervised learning**: This is the most popular branch of machine learning, which is about learning from labeled data. If the data type of the label is categorical, it becomes a classification problem, and if numeric, it is known as a regression problem. For example, if the goal of using of the dataset is the detection of fraud, which has categorical values of either true or false, we are dealing with a classification problem. If, on the other hand, the target is to predict the best price to list the sale of a home, which is a numeric dollar value, the problem is one of regression. The following figure illustrates labeled data that warrants the use of classification techniques, such as logistic regression that is suitable for linearly separable data, that is, when there exists a line that can cleanly separate the two classes. For higher dimensional data that may be linearly separable, one speaks of a separating hyperplane:

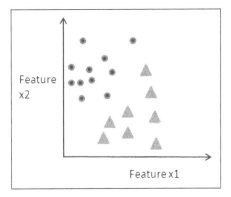

Linearly separable data

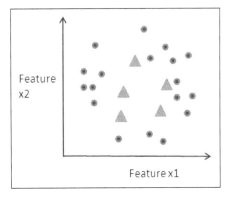

An example of a dataset that is not linearly separable.

This type of problem calls for classification techniques, such as support vector machines.

- **Unsupervised learning**: Understanding the data and exploring it for building machine learning models when the labels are not given is called unsupervised learning. Clustering, manifold learning, and outlier detection are techniques that are covered under this topic, which are dealt with in detail in *Chapter 3, Unsupervised Machine Learning Techniques*. Examples of problems that require unsupervised learning are many. Grouping customers according to their purchasing behavior is one example. In the case of biological data, tissues samples can be clustered based on similar gene expression values using unsupervised learning techniques.

The following figure represents data with inherent structure that can be revealed as distinct clusters using an unsupervised learning technique, such as k-means:

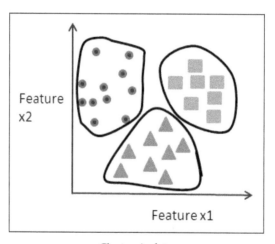

Clusters in data

Different techniques are used to detect global outliers – examples that are anomalous with respect to the entire dataset, and local outliers – examples that are misfits in their neighborhood. In the following figure, the notion of local and global outliers is illustrated for a two-feature dataset:

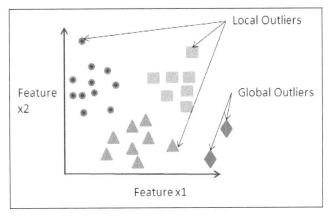

Local and global outliers

- **Semi-supervised learning**: When the dataset has only some labeled data and a large amount of data that is not labeled, learning from such a dataset is called **semi-supervised learning**. When dealing with financial data with the goal of detecting fraud, for example, there may be a large amount of unlabeled data and only a small number of known fraud and non-fraud transactions. In such cases, semi-supervised learning may be applied.

- **Graph mining**: Mining data represented as graph structures is known as **graph mining**. It is the basis of social network analysis and structure analysis in different bioinformatics, web mining, and community mining applications.

- **Probabilistic graph modeling and inferencing**: Learning and exploiting conditional dependence structures present between features expressed as a graph-based model comes under the branch of **probabilistic graph modeling**. Bayesian networks and Markov random fields are two classes of such models.

- **Time-series forecasting**: This refers to a form of learning where data has distinct temporal behavior and the relationship with time is modeled. A common example is in financial forecasting, where the performance of stocks in a certain sector may be the target of the predictive model.

- **Association analysis**: This is a form of learning where data is in the form of an item set or market basket, and association rules are modeled to explore and predict the relationships between the items. A common example in association analysis is to learn the relationships between the most common items bought by customers when they visit the grocery store.

- **Reinforcement learning**: This is a form of learning where machines learn to maximize performance based on feedback in the form of rewards or penalties received from the environment. A recent example that famously used reinforcement learning, among other techniques, was AlphaGo, the machine developed by Google that decisively beat the World Go Champion Lee Sedol in March 2016. Using a reward and penalty scheme, the model first trained on millions of board positions in the supervised learning stage, then played itself in the reinforcement learning stage to ultimately become good enough to triumph over the best human player.

>
> http://www.theatlantic.com/technology/
> archive/2016/03/the-invisible-opponent/475611/
> https://gogameguru.com/i/2016/03/deepmind-
> mastering-go.pdf

- **Stream learning or incremental learning**: Learning in a supervised, unsupervised, or semi-supervised manner from stream data in real time or pseudo-real time is called stream or incremental learning. Learning the behaviors of sensors from different types of industrial systems for categorizing into normal and abnormal is an application that needs real-time feeds and real-time detection.

Datasets used in machine learning

To learn from data, we must be able to understand and manage data in all forms. Data originates from many different sources, and consequently, datasets may differ widely in structure or have little or no structure at all. In this section, we present a high-level classification of datasets with commonly occurring examples.

Based on their structure, or the lack thereof, datasets may be classified as containing the following:

- **Structured data**: Datasets with structured data are more amenable to being used as input to most machine learning algorithms. The data is in the form of records or rows following a well-known format with features that are either columns in a table or fields delimited by separators or tokens. There is no explicit relationship between the records or instances. The dataset is available chiefly in flat files or relational databases. The records of financial transactions at a bank shown in the following figure are an example of structured data:

Account No	Card	Amount	Fraud	Mode	Zipcode	Time
A*122	xxxx2345	50.23	N	Device	20147	06/22/2003:10:46 AM
A*121	xxxx1245	12.43	F	Online	20123	06/22/2003:10:47 AM
A*122	xxxx2345	1000.00	F	ATM	20901	06/22/2003:10:47 AM

Financial card transactional data with labels of fraud

- **Transaction or market data**: This is a special form of structured data where each entry corresponds to a collection of items. Examples of market datasets are the lists of grocery items purchased by different customers or movies viewed by customers, as shown in the following table:

Customer Id	Items
1121	Bread, Milk, Soda, Juice
1127	Diaper, Beer, Milk
1189	Cookies, Beer, Soda

Market dataset for items bought from grocery store

- **Unstructured data**: Unstructured data is normally not available in well-known formats, unlike structured data. Text data, image, and video data are different formats of unstructured data. Usually, a transformation of some form is needed to extract features from these forms of data into a structured dataset so that traditional machine learning algorithms can be applied.

> 'Go until jurong point, crazy...... Cine there got amore wat...', ham
> 'Ok lar... Joking wif u oni...', ham
> 'Free entry in 2 a wkly comp to win FA Cup final tkts 21st, CONTACT 88122823 over 18s', spam
> 'U dun say so early hor... U c already then say...', ham
> 'Nah f, he lives around here though', ham

Sample text data, with no discernible structure, hence unstructured. Separating spam from normal messages (ham) is a binary classification problem. Here true positives (spam) and true negatives (ham) are distinguished by their labels, the second token in each instance of data. SMS Spam Collection Dataset (UCI Machine Learning Repository), source: Tiago A. Almeida from the Federal University of Sao Carlos.

- **Sequential data**: Sequential data have an explicit notion of "order" to them. The order can be some relationship between features and a time variable in time series data, or it can be symbols repeating in some form in genomic datasets. Two examples of sequential data are weather data and genomic sequence data. The following figure shows the relationship between time and the sensor level for weather:

'Go until jurong point, crazy...... Cine there got amore wat...', ham
'Ok lar... Joking wif u oni...', ham
'Free entry in 2 a wkly comp to win FA Cup final tkts 21st, CONTACT 88122823 over 18s', spam
'U dun say so early hor... U c already then say...', ham
'Nah f, he lives around here though', ham

Time series from sensor data

Three genomic sequences are taken into consideration to show the repetition of the sequences CGGGT and TTGAAAGTGGTG in all three genomic sequences:

Gene 1>
CGGGTGCGGATTGTTGGGAGGGGTTGAAAGTGGTGCCG
Gene 2>
CGGGTTGGAGGAGGTTGGAGGGGTTGAAAGTGGTGCG
Gene 3>
TTGAAAGTGGTGCCGGGTTGGAGGAGGTTGAGGGGCG

Genomic sequences of DNA as a sequence of symbols.

- **Graph data**: Graph data is characterized by the presence of relationships between entities in the data to form a graph structure. Graph datasets may be in a structured record format or an unstructured format. Typically, the graph relationship has to be mined from the dataset. Claims in the insurance domain can be considered structured records containing relevant claim details with claimants related through addresses, phone numbers, and so on. This can be viewed in a graph structure. Using the World Wide Web as an example, we have web pages available as unstructured data containing links, and graphs of relationships between web pages that can be built using web links, producing some of the most extensively mined graph datasets today:

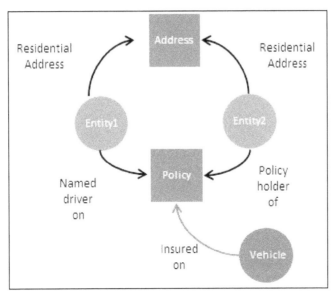

Insurance claim data, converted into a graph structure showing the relationship
between vehicles, drivers, policies, and addresses

Machine learning applications

Given the rapidly growing use of machine learning in diverse areas of human
endeavor, any attempt to list typical applications in the different industries
where some form of machine learning is in use must necessarily be incomplete.
Nevertheless, in this section, we list a broad set of machine learning applications by
domain and the type of learning employed:

Domain/Industry	Applications	Machine Learning Type
Financial	Credit risk scoring, fraud detection, and anti-money laundering	Supervised, unsupervised, graph models, time series, and stream learning
Web	Online campaigns, health monitoring, and ad targeting	Supervised, unsupervised, semi-supervised
Healthcare	Evidence-based medicine, epidemiological surveillance, drug events prediction, and claim fraud detection	Supervised, unsupervised, graph models, time series, and stream learning

Internet of things (IoT)	Cyber security, smart roads, and sensor health monitoring	Supervised, unsupervised, semi-supervised, and stream learning
Environment	Weather forecasting, pollution modeling, and water quality measurement	Time series, supervised, unsupervised, semi-supervised, and stream learning
Retail	Inventory, customer management and recommendations, layout, and forecasting	Time series, supervised, unsupervised, semi-supervised, and stream learning

Applications of machine learning

Practical issues in machine learning

It is necessary to appreciate the nature of the constraints and potentially sub-optimal conditions one may face when dealing with problems requiring machine learning. An understanding of the nature of these issues, the impact of their presence, and the methods to deal with them will be addressed throughout the discussions in the coming chapters. Here, we present a brief introduction to the practical issues that confront us:

- **Data quality and noise**: Missing values, duplicate values, incorrect values due to human or instrument recording error, and incorrect formatting are some of the important issues to be considered while building machine learning models. Not addressing data quality can result in incorrect or incomplete models. In the next chapter, we will highlight some of these issues and some strategies to overcome them through data cleansing.

- **Imbalanced datasets**: In many real-world datasets, there is an imbalance among labels in the training data. This imbalance in a dataset affects the choice of learning, the process of selecting algorithms, model evaluation and verification. If the right techniques are not employed, the models can suffer large biases, and the learning is not effective. Detailed in the next few chapters are various techniques that use meta-learning processes, such as cost-sensitive learning, ensemble learning, outlier detection, and so on, which can be employed in these situations.

- **Data volume, velocity, and scalability**: Often, a large volume of data exists in raw form or as real-time streaming data at high speed. Learning from the entire data becomes infeasible either due to constraints inherent to the algorithms or hardware limitations, or combinations thereof. In order to reduce the size of the dataset to fit the resources available, data sampling must be done. Sampling can be done in many ways, and each form of sampling introduces a bias. Validating the models against sample bias must be performed by employing various techniques, such as stratified sampling, varying sample sizes, and increasing the size of experiments on different sets. Using big data machine learning can also overcome the volume and sampling biases.

- **Overfitting**: One of the core problems in predictive models is that the model is not generalized enough and is made to fit the given training data *too well*. This results in poor performance of the model when applied to unseen data. There are various techniques described in later chapters to overcome these issues.

- **Curse of dimensionality**: When dealing with high-dimensional data, that is, datasets with a large number of features, scalability of machine learning algorithms becomes a serious concern. One of the issues with adding more features to the data is that it introduces sparsity, that is, there are now fewer data points on average per unit volume of feature space unless an increase in the number of features is accompanied by an exponential increase in the number of training examples. This can hamper performance in many methods, such as distance-based algorithms. Adding more features can also deteriorate the predictive power of learners, as illustrated in the following figure. In such cases, a more suitable algorithm is needed, or the dimensionality of the data must be reduced.

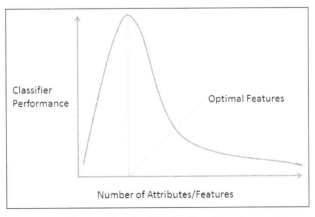

Curse of dimensionality illustrated in classification learning, where adding more features deteriorates classifier performance.

Machine learning – roles and process

Any effort to apply machine learning to a large-sized problem requires the collaborative effort of a number of roles, each abiding by a set of systematic processes designed for rigor, efficiency, and robustness. The following roles and processes ensure that the goals of the endeavor are clearly defined at the outset and the correct methodologies are employed in data analysis, data sampling, model selection, deployment, and performance evaluation—all as part of a comprehensive framework for conducting analytics consistently and with repeatability.

Roles

Participants play specific parts in each step. These responsibilities are captured in the following four roles:

- **Business domain expert**: A subject matter expert with knowledge of the problem domain
- **Data engineer**: Involved in the collecting, transformation, and cleaning of the data
- **Project manager**: Overseer of the smooth running of the process
- **Data scientist or machine learning expert**: Responsible for applying descriptive or predictive analytic techniques

Process

CRISP (Cross Industry Standard Process) is a well-known high-level process model for data mining that defines the analytics process. In this section, we have added some of our own extensions to the CRISP process that make it more comprehensive and better suited for analytics using machine learning. The entire iterative process is demonstrated in the following schematic figure. We will discuss each step of the process in detail in this section.

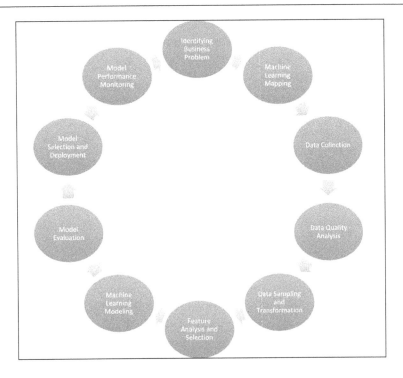

- **Identifying the business problem**: Understanding the objectives and the end goals of the project or process is the first step. This is normally carried out by a business domain expert in conjunction with the project manager and machine learning expert. What are the end goals in terms of data availability, formats, specification, collection, ROI, business value, deliverables? All these questions are discussed in this phase of the process. Identifying the goals clearly, and *in quantifiable terms* where possible, such as dollar amount saved, finding a pre-defined number of anomalies or clusters, or predicting no more than a certain number of false positives, and so on, is an important objective of this phase.

- **Machine learning mapping**: The next step is mapping the business problem to one or more machine learning types discussed in the preceding section. This step is generally carried out by the machine learning expert. In it, we determine whether we should use just one form of learning (for example, supervised, unsupervised, semi-supervised) or if a hybrid of forms is more suitable for the project.

- **Data collection**: Obtaining the raw data in the agreed format and specification for processing follows next. This step is normally carried out by data engineers and may require handling some basic ETL steps.

- **Data quality analysis**: In this step, we perform analysis on the data for missing values, duplicates, and so on, conduct basic statistical analysis on the categorical and continuous types, and similar tasks to evaluate the quality of data. Data engineers and data scientists can perform the tasks together.

- **Data sampling and transformation**: Determining whether data needs to be divided into samples and performing data sampling of various sizes for training, validation, or testing — these are the tasks performed in this step. It consists of employing different sampling techniques, such as oversampling and random sampling of the training datasets for effective learning by the algorithms, especially when the data is highly imbalanced in the labels. The data scientist is involved in this task.

- **Feature analysis and selection**: This is an iterative process combined with modeling in many tasks to make sure the features are analyzed for either their discriminating values or their effectiveness. It can involve finding new features, transforming existing features, handling the data quality issues mentioned earlier, selecting a subset of features, and so on ahead of the modeling process. The data scientist is normally assigned this task.

- **Machine learning modeling**: This is an iterative process working on different algorithms based on data characteristics and learning types. It involves different steps, such as generating hypotheses, selecting algorithms, tuning parameters, and getting results from evaluation to find models that meet the criteria. The data scientist carries out this task.

- **Model evaluation**: While this step is related to all the preceding steps to some degree, it is more closely linked to the business understanding phase and machine learning mapping phase. The evaluation criteria must map in some way to the business problem or the goal. Each problem/project has its own goal, whether that be improving true positives, reducing false positives, finding anomalous clusters or behaviors, or analyzing data for different clusters. Different techniques that implicitly or explicitly measure these targets are used based on learning techniques. Data scientists and business domain experts normally take part in this step.

- **Model selection and deployment**: Based on the evaluation criteria, one or more models—independent or as an ensemble—are selected. The deployment of models normally needs to address several issues: runtime scalability measures, execution specifications of the environment, and audit information, to name a few. Audit information that captures the key parameters based on learning is an essential part of the process. It ensures that model performance can be tracked and compared to check for the deterioration and aging of the models. Saving key information, such as training data volumes, dates, data quality analysis, and so on, is independent of learning types. Supervised learning might involve saving the confusion matrix, true positive ratios, false positive ratios, area under the ROC curve, precision, recall, error rates, and so on. Unsupervised learning might involve clustering or outlier evaluation results, cluster statistics, and so on. This is the domain of the data scientist, as well as the project manager.

- **Model performance monitoring**: This task involves periodically tracking the model performance in terms of the criteria it was evaluated against, such as the true positive rate, false positive rate, performance speed, memory allocation, and so on. It is imperative to measure the deviations in these metrics with respect to the metrics between successive evaluations of the trained model's performance. The deviations and tolerance in the deviation will give insights into repeating the process or retuning the models as time progresses. The data scientist is responsible for this stage.

As may be observed from the preceding diagram, the entire process is an iterative one. After a model or set of models has been deployed, business and environmental factors may change in ways that affect the performance of the solution, requiring a re-evaluation of business goals and success criteria. This takes us back through the cycle again.

Machine learning – tools and datasets

A sure way to master the techniques necessary to successfully complete a project of any size or complexity in machine learning is to familiarize yourself with the available tools and frameworks by performing experiments with widely-used datasets, as demonstrated in the chapters to follow. A short survey of the most popular Java frameworks is presented in the following list. Later chapters will include experiments that you will do using the following tools:

- **RapidMiner**: A leading analytics platform, RapidMiner has multiple offerings, including Studio, a visual design framework for processes, Server, a product to facilitate a collaborative environment by enabling sharing of data sources, processes, and practices, and Radoop, a system with translations to enable deployment and execution on the Hadoop ecosystem. RapidMiner Cloud provides a cloud-based repository and on-demand computing power.
    - ° **License**: GPL (Community Edition) and Commercial (Enterprise Edition)
    - ° **Website**: https://rapidminer.com/

- **Weka**: This is a comprehensive open source Java toolset for data mining and building machine learning applications with its own collection of publicly available datasets.
    - ° **License**: GPL
    - ° **Website**: http://www.cs.waikato.ac.nz/ml/weka/

- **Knime**: KNIME (we are urged to pronounce it with a silent k, as "naime") Analytics Platform is written in Java and offers an integrated toolset, a rich set of algorithms, and a visual workflow to do analytics without the need for standard programming languages, such as Java, Python, and R. However, one can write scripts in Java and other languages to implement functionality not available natively in KNIME.
    - ° **License**: GNU GPL v3
    - ° **Website**: https://www.knime.org/

- **Mallet**: This is a Java library for NLP. It offers document classification, sequence tagging, topic modeling, and other text-based applications of machine learning, as well as an API for task pipelines.
    - ° **License**: Common Public License version 1.0 (CPL-1)
    - ° **Website**: http://mallet.cs.umass.edu/

- **Elki**: This is a research-oriented Java software primarily focused on data mining with unsupervised algorithms. It achieves high performance and scalability using data index structures that improve access performance of multi-dimensional data.
    - ° **License**: AGPLv3
    - ° **Website**: `http://elki.dbs.ifi.lmu.de/`

- **JCLAL**: This is a Java Class Library for Active Learning, and is an open source framework for developing Active Learning methods, one of the areas that deal with learning predictive models from a mix of labeled and unlabeled data (semi-supervised learning is another).
    - ° **License**: GNU General Public License version 3.0 (GPLv3)
    - ° **Website**: `https://sourceforge.net/projects/jclal/`

- **KEEL**: This is an open source software written in Java for designing experiments primarily suited to the implementation of evolutionary learning and soft computing based techniques for data mining problems.
    - ° **License**: GPLv3
    - ° **Website**: `http://www.keel.es/`

- **DeepLearning4J**: This is a distributed deep learning library for Java and Scala. DeepLearning4J is integrated with Spark and Hadoop. Anomaly detection and recommender systems are use cases that lend themselves well to the models generated via deep learning techniques.
    - ° **License**: Apache License 2.0
    - ° **Website**: `http://deeplearning4j.org/`

- **Spark-MLlib**: (Included in Apache Spark distribution) MLlib is the machine learning library included in Spark mainly written in Scala and Java. Since the introduction of Data Frames in Spark, the `spark.ml` package, which is written on top of Data Frames, is recommended over the original `spark.mllib` package. MLlib includes support for all stages of the analytics process, including statistical methods, classification and regression algorithms, clustering, dimensionality reduction, feature extraction, model evaluation, and PMML support, among others. Another aspect of MLlib is the support for the use of pipelines or workflows. MLlib is accessible from R, Scala, and Python, in addition to Java.
    - ° **License**: Apache License v2.0
    - ° **Website**: `http://spark.apache.org/mllib/`

- **H2O**: H2O is a Java-based library with API support in R and Python, in addition to Java. H2O can also run on Spark as its own application called Sparkling Water. H2O Flow is a web-based interactive environment with executable cells and rich media in a single notebook-like document.
    - ○ **License**: Apache License v2.0
    - ○ **Website**: http://www.h2o.ai/

- **MOA/SAMOA**: Aimed at machine learning from data streams with a pluggable interface for stream processing platforms, SAMOA, at the time of writing, is an Apache Incubator project.
    - ○ **License**: Apache License v2.0
    - ○ **Website**: https://samoa.incubator.apache.org/

- **Neo4j**: Neo4j is an open source NoSQL graphical database implemented in Java and Scala. As we will see in later chapters, graph analytics has a variety of use cases, including matchmaking, routing, social networks, network management, and so on. Neo4j supports fully ACID transactions.
    - ○ **License**: Community Edition—GPLv3 and Enterprise Edition— multiple options, including Commercial and Educational (https://neo4j.com/licensing/)
    - ○ **Website**: https://neo4j.com/

- **GraphX**: This is included in the Apache Spark distribution. GraphX is the graph library accompanying Spark. The API has extensive support for viewing and manipulating graph structures, as well as some graph algorithms, such as PageRank, Connected Components, and Triangle Counting.
    - ○ **License**: Apache License v2.0
    - ○ **Website**: http://spark.apache.org/graphx/

- **OpenMarkov**: OpenMarkov is a tool for editing and evaluating **probabilistic graphical models (PGM)**. It includes a GUI for interactive learning.
    - ○ **License**: EUPLv1.1 (https://joinup.ec.europa.eu/community/eupl/og_page/eupl)
    - ○ **Website**: http://www.openmarkov.org/

- **Smile**: Smile is a machine learning platform for the JVM with an extensive library of algorithms. Its capabilities include NLP, manifold learning, association rules, genetic algorithms, and a versatile set of tools for visualization.

  ° **License**: Apache License 2.0

  ° **Website**: `http://haifengl.github.io/smile/`

Datasets

A number of publicly available datasets have aided research and learning in data science immensely. Several of those listed in the following section are well known and have been used by scores of researchers to benchmark their methods over the years. New datasets are constantly being made available to serve different communities of modelers and users. The majority are real-world datasets from different domains. The exercises in this volume will use several datasets from this list.

- **UC Irvine (UCI) database**: Maintained by the Center for Machine Learning and Intelligent Systems at UC Irvine, the UCI database is a catalog of some 350 datasets of varying sizes, from a dozen to more than forty million records and up to three million attributes, with a mix of multivariate text, time-series, and other data types. (`https://archive.ics.uci.edu/ml/index.html`)

- **Tunedit**: (`http://tunedit.org/`) This offers Tunedit Challenges and tools to conduct repeatable data mining experiments. It also offers a platform for hosting data competitions.

- **Mldata.org**: (`http://mldata.org/`) Supported by the PASCAL 2 organization that brings together researchers and students across Europe and the world, mldata.org is primarily a repository of user-contributed datasets that encourages data and solution sharing amongst groups of researchers to help with the goal of creating reproducible solutions.

- **KDD Challenge Datasets**: (`http://www.kdnuggets.com/datasets/index.html`) KDNuggets aggregates multiple dataset repositories across a wide variety of domains.

- **Kaggle**: Billed as the *Home of Data Science*, Kaggle is a leading platform for data science competitions and also a repository of datasets from past competitions and user-submitted datasets.

Summary

Machine learning has already demonstrated impressive successes despite being a relatively young field. With the ubiquity of Java resources, Java's platform independence, and the selection of ML frameworks in Java, superior skill in machine learning using Java is a highly desirable asset in the market today.

Machine learning has been around in some form — if only in the imagination of thinkers, in the beginning — for a long time. More recent developments, however, have had a radical impact in many spheres of our everyday lives. Machine learning has much in common with statistics, artificial intelligence, and several other related areas. Whereas some data management, business intelligence, and knowledge representation systems may also be related in the central role of data in each of them, they are not commonly associated with principles of learning from data as embodied in the field of machine learning.

Any discourse on machine learning would assume an understanding of what data is and what data types we are concerned with. Are they categorical, continuous, or ordinal? What are the data features? What is the target, and which ones are predictors? What kinds of sampling methods can be used — uniform random, stratified random, cluster, or systematic sampling? What is the model? We saw an example dataset for weather data that included categorical and continuous features in the ARFF format.

The types of machine learning include supervised learning, the most common when labeled data is available, unsupervised when it's not, and semi-supervised when we have a mix of both. The chapters that follow will go into detail on these, as well as graph mining, probabilistic graph modeling, deep learning, stream learning, and learning with Big Data.

Data comes in many forms: structured, unstructured, transactional, sequential, and graphs. We will use data of different structures in the exercises to follow later in this book.

The list of domains and the different kinds of machine learning applications keeps growing. This review presents the most active areas and applications.

Understanding and dealing effectively with practical issues, such as noisy data, skewed datasets, overfitting, data volumes, and the curse of dimensionality, is the key to successful projects — it's what makes each project unique in its challenges.

Analytics with machine learning is a collaborative endeavor with multiple roles and well-defined processes. For consistent and reproducible results, adopting the enhanced CRISP methodology outlined here is critical—from understanding the business problem to data quality analysis, modeling and model evaluation, and finally to model performance monitoring.

Practitioners of data science are blessed with a rich and growing catalog of datasets available to the public and an increasing set of ML frameworks and tools in Java as well as other languages. In the following chapters, you will be introduced to several datasets, APIs, and frameworks, along with advanced concepts and techniques to equip you with all you will need to attain mastery in machine learning.

Ready? Onward then!

2
Practical Approach to Real-World Supervised Learning

The ability to learn from observations accompanied by marked targets or labels, usually in order to make predictions about unseen data, is known as **supervised machine learning**. If the targets are categories, the problem is one of classification and if they are numeric values, it is called **regression**. In effect, what is being attempted is to infer the function that maps the data to the target. Supervised machine learning is used extensively in a wide variety of machine learning applications, whenever labeled data is available or the labels can be added manually.

The core assumption of supervised machine learning is that the patterns that are learned from the data used in training will manifest themselves in yet unseen data.

In this chapter, we will discuss the steps used to explore, analyze, and pre-process the data before proceeding to training models. We will then introduce different modeling techniques ranging from simple linear models to complex ensemble models. We will present different evaluation metrics and validation criteria that allow us to compare model performance. Some of the discussions are accompanied by brief mathematical explanations that should help express the concepts more precisely and whet the appetite of the more mathematically inclined readers. In this chapter, we will focus on classification as a method of supervised learning, but the principles apply to both classification and regression, the two broad applications of supervised learning.

Beginning with this chapter, we will introduce tools to help illustrate how the concepts presented in each chapter are used to solve machine learning problems. Nothing reinforces the understanding of newly learned material better than the opportunity to apply that material to a real-world problem directly. In the process, we often gain a clearer and more relatable understanding of the subject than what is possible with passive absorption of the theory alone. If the opportunity to learn new tools is part of the learning, so much the better! To meet this goal, we will introduce a classification dataset familiar to most data science practitioners and use it to solve a classification problem while highlighting the process and methodologies that guide the solution.

In this chapter, we will use RapidMiner and Weka for building the process by which we learn from a single well-known dataset. The workflows and code are available on the website for readers to download, execute, and modify.

RapidMiner is a GUI-based Java framework that makes it very easy to conduct a data science project, end-to-end, from within the tool. It has a simple drag-and-drop interface to build process workflows to ingest and clean data, explore and transform features, perform training using a wide selection of machine learning algorithms, do validation and model evaluation, apply your best models to test data, and more. It is an excellent tool to learn how to make the various parts of the process work together and produce rapid results. Weka is another GUI-based framework and it has a Java API that we will use to illustrate more of the coding required for performing analysis.

The major topics that we will cover in this chapter are:

- Data quality analysis
- Descriptive data analysis
- Visualization analysis
- Data transformation and preprocessing
- Data sampling
- Feature relevance analysis and dimensionality reduction
- Model building
- Model assessment, evaluation, and comparison
- Detailed case study — Horse Colic Classification

Formal description and notation

We would like to introduce some notation and formal definitions for the terms used in supervised learning. We will follow this notation through the rest of the book when not specified and extend it as appropriate when new concepts are encountered. The notation will provide a precise and consistent language to describe the terms of art and enable a more rapid and efficient comprehension of the subject.

- **Instance**: Every observation is a data instance. Normally the variable X is used to represent the input space. Each data instance has many variables (also called features) and is referred to as **x** (vector representation with bold) of dimension d where d denotes the number of variables or features or attributes in each instance. The features are represented as $\mathbf{x} = (x_1, x_2 \ldots x_d)^T$, where each value is a scalar when it is numeric corresponding to the feature value.

- **Label**: The label (also called target) is the dependent variable of interest, generally denoted by y. In **classification**, values of the label are well-defined categories in the problem domain; they need not be numeric or things that can be ordered. In **regression**, the label is real-valued.

- **Binary classification**, where the target takes only two values, it is mathematically represented as:

$$y \in \{1, -1\}$$

- **Regression**, where the target can take any value in the real number domain, is represented as:

$$y \in \mathbb{R}$$

- **Dataset**: Generally, the dataset is denoted by D and consists of individual data instances and their labels. The instances are normally represented as set $\{\mathbf{x}_1, \mathbf{x}_2 \ldots \mathbf{x}_n\}$. The labels for each instance are represented as the set $\mathbf{y} = \{y_1, y_2 \ldots y_n\}$. The entire labeled dataset is represented as paired elements in a set as given by $D = \{(\mathbf{x}_1, y_1), (\mathbf{x}_2, y_2) \ldots (\mathbf{x}_n, y_n)\}$ where $\mathbf{x}_i \in \mathbb{R}^d$ for real-valued features.

Data quality analysis

There are limitations to what can be learned from data that suffers from poor quality. Problems with quality can include, among other factors, noisy data, missing values, and errors in labeling. Therefore, the first step is to understand the data before us in order that we may determine how to address any data quality issues. Are the outliers merely noise or indicative of interesting anomalies in the population? Should missing data be handled the same way for all features? How should sparse features be treated? These and similar questions present themselves at the very outset.

If we're fortunate, we receive a cleansed, accurately labeled dataset accompanied by documentation describing the data elements, the data's pedigree, and what if any transformations were already done to the data. Such a dataset would be ready to be split into train, validation, and test samples, using methods described in the section on Data Sampling. However, if data is not cleansed and suitable to be partitioned for our purposes, we must first prepare the data in a principled way before sampling can begin. (The significance of partitioning the data is explained later in this chapter in a section dedicated to train, validation, and test sets).

In the following sections, we will discuss the data quality analysis and transformation steps that are needed before we can analyze the features.

Descriptive data analysis

The complete data sample (including train, validation, and test) should be analyzed and summarized for the following characteristics. In cases where the data is not already split into train, validate, and test, the task of data transformation needs to make sure that the samples have similar characteristics and statistics. This is of paramount importance to ensure that the trained model can generalize over unseen data, as we will learn in the section on data sampling.

Basic label analysis

The first step of analysis is understanding the distribution of labels in different sets as well as in the data as a whole. This helps to determine whether, for example, there is imbalance in the distribution of the target variable, and if so, whether it is consistent across all the samples. Thus, the very first step is usually to find out how many examples in the training and test sets belong to each class.

Basic feature analysis

The next step is to calculate the statistics for each feature, such as

- Number of unique values
- Number of missing values: May include counts grouped by different missing value surrogates (NA, null, ?, and so on).
- For categorical: This counts across feature categories, counts across feature categories by label category, most frequently occurring category (mode), mode by label category, and so on.
- For numeric: Minimum, maximum, median, standard deviation, variance, and so on.

Feature analysis gives basic insights that can be a useful indicator of missing values and noise that can affect the learning process or choice of the algorithms.

Visualization analysis

Visualization of the data is a broad topic and it is a continuously evolving area in the field of machine learning and data mining. We will only cover some of the important aspects of visualization that help us analyze the data in practice.

Univariate feature analysis

The goal here is to visualize one feature at a time, in relation to the label. The techniques used are as follows:

Categorical features

Stacked bar graphs are a simple way of showing the distribution of each feature category among the labels, when the problem is one of classification.

Continuous features

Histograms and box plots are two basic visualization techniques for continuous features.

Histograms have predefined bins whose widths are either fixed intervals or based on some calculation used to split the full range of values of the feature. The number of instances of data that falls within each bin is then counted and the height of the bin is adjusted based on this count. There are variations of histograms such as relative or frequency-based histograms, Pareto histograms, two-dimensional histograms, and so on; each is a slight variation of the concept and permits a different insight into the feature. For those interested in finding out more about these variants, the Wikipedia article on histograms is a great resource.

Box plots are a key visualization technique for numeric features as they show distributions in terms of percentiles and outliers.

Multivariate feature analysis

The idea of multivariate feature analysis is to visualize more than one feature to get insights into relationships between them. Some of the well-known plots are explained here.

- **Scatter plots**: An important technique for understanding the relationship between different features and between features and labels. Typically, two-dimensional scatter plots are used in practice where numeric features form the dimensions. Alignment of data points on some imaginary axis shows correlation while scattering of the data points shows no correlation. It can also be useful to identify clusters in lower dimensional space. A bubble chart is a variation of a scatter plot where two features form the dimensional axes and the third is proportional to the size of the data point, with the plot giving the appearance of a field of "bubbles". Density charts help visualize even more features together by introducing data point color, background color, and so on, to give additional insights.

- **ScatterPlot Matrix**: ScatterPlot Matrix is an extension of scatter plots where pair-wise scatter plots for each feature (and label) is visualized. It gives a way to compare and perform multivariate analysis of high dimensional data in an effective way.

- **Parallel Plots**: In this visualization, each feature is linearly arranged on the x-axis and the ranges of values for each feature form the y axis. So each data element is represented as a line with values for each feature on the parallel axis. Class labels, if available, are used to color the lines. Parallel plots offer a great understanding of features that are effective in separating the data. Deviation charts are variations of parallel plots, where instead of showing actual data points, mean and standard deviations are plotted. Andrews plots are another variation of parallel plots where data is transformed using Fourier series and the function values corresponding to each is projected.

Data transformation and preprocessing

In this section, we will cover the broad topic of data transformation. The main idea of data transformation is to take the input data and transform it in careful ways so as to clean it, extract the most relevant information from it, and to turn it into a usable form for further analysis and learning. During these transformations, we must only use methods that are designed while keeping in mind not to add any bias or artifacts that would affect the integrity of the data.

Feature construction

In the case of some datasets, we need to create more features from features we are already given. Typically, some form of aggregation is done using common aggregators such as average, sum, minimum, or maximum to create additional features. In financial fraud detection, for example, Card Fraud datasets usually contain transactional behaviors of accounts over various time periods during which the accounts were active. Performing behavioral synthesis such as by capturing the "Sum of Amounts whenever a Debit transaction occurred, for each Account, over One Day" is an example of feature construction that adds a new dimension to the dataset, built from existing features. In general, designing new features that enhance the predictive power of the data requires domain knowledge and experience with data, making it as much an art as a science.

Handling missing values

In real-world datasets, often, many features have missing values. In some cases, they are missing due to errors in measurement, lapses in recording, or because they are not available due to various circumstances; for example, individuals may choose not to disclose age or occupation. Why care about missing values at all? One extreme and not uncommon way to deal with it is to ignore the records that have any missing features, in other words, retain only examples that are "whole". This approach may severely reduce the size of the dataset when missing features are widespread in the data. As we shall see later, if the system we are dealing with is complex, dataset size can afford us precious advantage. Besides, there is often predictive value that can be exploited even in the "un-whole" records, despite the missing values, as long as we use appropriate measures to deal with the problem. On the other hand, one may unwittingly be throwing out key information when the omission of the data itself is significant, as in the case of deliberate misrepresentation or obfuscation on a loan application by withholding information that could be used to conclusively establish bone fides.

Suffice it to say, that an important step in the learning process is to adopt some systematic way to handle missing values and understand the consequences of the decision in each case. There are some algorithms such as Naïve Bayes that are less sensitive to missing values, but in general, it is good practice to handle these missing values as a pre-processing step before any form of analysis is done on the data. Here are some of the ways to handle missing values.

- **Replacing by means and modes**: When we replace the missing value of a continuous value feature with the mean value of that feature, the new mean clearly remains the same. But if the mean is heavily influenced by outliers, a better approach may be to use the mean after dropping the outliers from the calculation, or use the median or mode, instead. Likewise, when a feature is sparsely represented in the dataset, the mean value may not be meaningful. In the case of features with categorical values, replacing the missing value with the one that occurs with the highest frequency in the sample makes for a reasonable choice.

- **Replacing by imputation**: When we impute a missing value, we are in effect constructing a classification or regression model of the feature and making a prediction based on the other features in the record in order to classify or estimate the missing value.

- **Nearest Neighbor imputation**: For missing values of a categorical feature, we consider the feature in question to be the target and train a KNN model with k taken to be the known number of distinct categories. This model is then used to predict the missing values. (A KNN model is non-parametric and assigns a value to the "incoming" data instance based on a function of its neighbors—the algorithm is described later in this chapter when we talk about non-linear models).

- **Regression-based imputation**: In the case of continuous value variables, we use linear models like Linear Regression to estimate the missing data—the principle is the same as for categorical values.

- **User-defined imputation**: In many cases, the most suitable value for imputing missing values must come from the problem domain. For instance, a pH value of 7.0 is neutral, higher is basic, and lower is acidic. It may make most sense to impute a neutral value for pH than either mean or median, and this insight is an instance of a user-defined imputation. Likewise, in the case of substitution with normal body temperature or resting heart rate—all are examples from medicine.

Outliers

Handling outliers requires a lot of care and analysis. Outliers can be noise or errors in the data, or they can be anomalous behavior of particular interest. The latter case is treated in depth in *Chapter 3, Unsupervised Machine Learning Techniques*. Here we assume the former case, that the domain expert is satisfied that the values are indeed outliers in the first sense, that is, noise or erroneously acquired or recorded data that needs to be handled appropriately.

Following are different techniques in detecting outliers in the data

- **Interquartile Ranges (IQR)**: Interquartile ranges are a measure of variability in the data or, equivalently, the statistical dispersion. Each numeric feature is sorted based on its value in the dataset and the ordered set is then divided into quartiles. The median value is generally used to measure central tendency. IQR is measured as the difference between upper and lower quartiles, Q3-Q1. The outliers are generally considered to be data values above Q3 + 1.5 * IQR and below Q1 - 1.5 * IQR.

- **Distance-based Methods**: The most basic form of distance-based methods uses **k-Nearest Neighbors (k-NN)** and distance metrics to score the data points. The usual parameter is the value *k* in k-NN and a distance metric such as Euclidean distance. The data points at the farthest distance are considered outliers. There are many variants of these that use local neighborhoods, probabilities, or other factors, which will all be covered in *Chapter 3, Unsupervised Machine Learning Techniques*. Mixed datasets, which have both categorical and numeric features, can skew distance-based metrics.

- **Density-based methods**: Density-based methods calculate the proportion of data points within a given distance *D*, and if the proportion is less than the specified threshold p, it is considered an outlier. The parameter p and D are considered user-defined values; the challenge of selecting these values appropriately presents one of the main hurdles in using these methods in the preprocessing stage.

- **Mathematical transformation of feature**: With non-normal data, comparing the mean value is highly misleading, as in the case when outliers are present. Non-parametric statistics allow us to make meaningful observations about highly skewed data. Transformation of such values using the logarithm or square root function tends to normalize the data in many cases, or make them more amenable to statistical tests. These transformations alter the shape of the distribution of the feature drastically — the more extreme an outlier, the greater the effect of the log transformation, for example.

- **Handling outliers using robust statistical algorithms in machine learning models**: Many classification algorithms which we discuss in the next section on modeling, implicitly or explicitly handle outliers. Bagging and Boosting variants, which work as meta-learning frameworks, are generally resilient to outliers or noisy data points and may not need a preprocessing step to handle them.

- **Normalization**: Many algorithms—distance-based methods are a case in point—are very sensitive to the scale of the features. Preprocessing the numeric features makes sure that all of them are in a well-behaved range. The most well-known techniques of normalization of features are given here:

  ◦ **Min-Max Normalization**: In this technique, given the range *[L,U]*, which is typically *[0,1]*, each feature with value x is normalized in terms of the minimum and maximum values, x_{max} and x_{min}, respectively, using the formula:

  $$x' = \frac{\left(x - x_{min}\right)}{\left(x_{max} - x_{min}\right)} * \left(U - L\right) + L$$

  ◦ **Z-Score Normalization**: In this technique, also known as standardization, the feature values get auto-transformed so that the mean is 0 and standard deviation is 1. The technique to transform is as follows: for each feature f, the mean value $\mu(f)$ and standard deviation $\sigma(f)$ are computed and then the feature with value x is transformed as:

  $$x' = \frac{\left(x - \mu(f)\right)}{\sigma(f)}$$

Discretization

Many algorithms can only handle categorical values or nominal values to be effective, for example Bayesian Networks. In such cases, it becomes imperative to discretize the numeric features into categories using either supervised or unsupervised methods. Some of the techniques discussed are:

- **Discretization by binning**: This technique is also referred to as equal width discretization. The entire scale of data for each feature f, ranging from values x_{max} and x_{min} is divided into a predefined number, k, of equal intervals, each having the width $w = \frac{\left(x_{max} - x_{min}\right)}{k}$.

The "cut points" or discretization intervals are:

$$\left\{ x_{min} + w, \quad x_{min} + 2w, \quad \ldots, \quad x_{min} + (k-1)w \right\}$$

- **Discretization by frequency**: This technique is also referred to as equal frequency discretization. The feature is sorted and then the entire data is discretized into predefined k intervals, such that each interval contains the same proportion. Both the techniques, discretization by binning and discretization by frequency, suffer from loss of information due to the predefined value of k.

- **Discretization by entropy**: Given the labels, the entropy is calculated over the split points where the value changes in an iterative way, so that the bins of intervals are as pure or discriminating as possible. Refer to the *Feature evaluation techniques* section for entropy-based (information gain) theory and calculations.

Data sampling

The dataset one receives may often require judicious sampling in order to effectively learn from the data. The characteristics of the data as well as the goals of the modeling exercise determine whether sampling is needed, and if so, how to go about it. Before we begin to learn from this data it is crucially important to create train, validate, and test data samples, as explained in this section.

Is sampling needed?

When the dataset is large or noisy, or skewed towards one type, the question as to whether to sample or not to sample becomes important. The answer depends on various aspects such as the dataset itself, the objective and the evaluation criteria used for selecting the models, and potentially other practical considerations. In some situations, algorithms have scalability issues in memory and space, but work effectively on samples, as measured by model performance with respect to the regression or classification goals they are expected to achieve. For example, SVM scales as $O(n^2)$ and $O(n^3)$ in memory and training times, respectively. In other situations, the data is so imbalanced that many algorithms are not robust enough to handle the skew. In the literature, the step intended to re-balance the distribution of classes in the original data extract by creating new training samples is also called **resampling**.

Undersampling and oversampling

Datasets exhibiting a marked imbalance in the distribution of classes can be said to contain a distinct minority class. Often, this minority class is the set of instances that we are especially interested in precisely because its members occur in such rare cases. For example, in credit card fraud, less than 0.1% of the data belongs to fraud. This skewness is not conducive to learning; after all, when we seek to minimize the total error in classification, we give equal weight to all classes regardless of whether one class is underrepresented compared to another. In binary classification problems, we call the minority class the positive class and the majority class as the negative class, a convention that we will follow in the following discussion.

Undersampling of the majority class is a technique that is commonly used to address skewness in data. Taking credit-card fraud as an example, we can create different training samples from the original dataset such that each sample has all the fraud cases from the original dataset, whereas the non-fraud instances are distributed across all the training samples in some fixed ratios. Thus, in a given training set created by this method, the majority class is now underrepresented compared to the original skewed dataset, effectively balancing out the distribution of classes. Training samples with labeled positive and labeled negative instances in ratios of, say, 1:20 to 1:50 can be created in this way, but care must be taken that the sample of negative instances used should have similar characteristics to the data statistics and distributions of the main datasets. The reason for using multiple training samples, and in different proportions of positive and negative instances, is so that any sampling bias that may be present becomes evident.

Alternatively, we may choose to oversample the minority class. As before, we create multiple samples wherein instances from the minority class have been selected by either sampling with replacement or without replacement from the original dataset. When sampling without replacement, there are no replicated instances across samples. With replacement, some instances may be found in more than one sample. After this initial seeding of the samples, we can produce more balanced distributions of classes by random sampling with replacement from within the minority class in each sample until we have the desired ratios of positive to negative instances. Oversampling can be prone to over-fitting as classification decision boundaries tend to become more specific due to replicated values. **SMOTE (Synthetic Minority Oversampling Technique)** is a technique that alleviates this problem by creating synthetic data points in the interstices of the feature space by interpolating between neighboring instances of the positive class (*References* [20]).

Stratified sampling

Creating samples so that data with similar characteristics is drawn in the same proportion as they appear in the population is known as stratified sampling. In multi-class classification, if there are N classes each in a certain proportion, then samples are created such that they represent each class in the same proportion as in the original dataset. Generally, it is good practice to create multiple samples to train and test the models to validate against biases of sampling.

Training, validation, and test set

The Holy Grail of creating good classification models is to train on a set of good quality, representative, (training data), tune the parameters and find effective models (validation data), and finally, estimate the model's performance by its behavior on unseen data (test data).

The central idea behind the logical grouping is to make sure models are validated or tested on data that has not been seen during training. Otherwise, a simple "rote learner" can outperform the algorithm. The generalization capability of the learning algorithm must be evaluated on a dataset which is different from the training dataset, but comes from the same population (*References* [11]). The balance between removing too much data from training to increase the budget of validation and testing can result in models which suffer from "underfitting", that is, not having enough examples to build patterns that can help in generalization. On the other hand, the extreme choice of allocating all the labeled data for training and not performing any validation or testing can lead to "overfitting", that is, models that fit the examples too faithfully and do not generalize well enough.

Typically, in most machine learning challenges and real world customer problems, one is given a training set and testing set upfront for evaluating the performance of the models. In these engagements, the only question is how to validate and find the most effective parameters given the training set. In some engagements, only the labeled dataset is given and you need to consider the training, validation, and testing sets to make sure your models do not overfit or underfit the data.

Three logical processes are needed for modeling and hence three logical datasets are needed, namely, training, validation, and testing. The purpose of the training dataset is to give labeled data to the learning algorithm to build the models. The purpose of the validation set is to see the effect of the parameters of the training model being evaluated by training on the validation set. Finally, the best parameters or models are retrained on the combination of the training and validation sets to find an optimum model that is then tested on the blind test set.

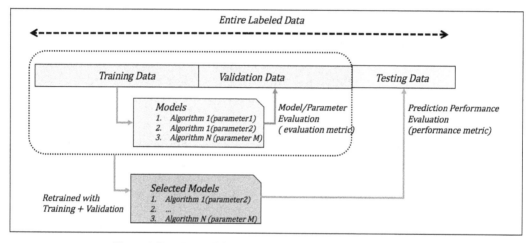

Figure 1: Training, Validation, and Test data and how to use them

Two things affect the learning or the generalization capability: the choice of the algorithm (and its parameters) and number of training data. This ability to generalize can be estimated by various metrics including the prediction errors. The overall estimate of unseen error or risk of the model is given by:

$$\mathbb{E}\left(Risk\right) = Noise + \mathbb{E}_X\left(Var\left(G,n\right)\right) + \mathbb{E}_X\left(Bias_X^2\left(G,n\right)\right)$$

Here, *Noise* is the stochastic noise, *Var (G,n)* is called the variance error and is a measure of how susceptible our hypothesis or the algorithm *(G)* is, if given different datasets. $Bias_X^2(G,n)$ is called the bias error and represents how far away the best algorithm in the model (average learner over all possible datasets) is from the optimal one.

Learning curves as shown in *Figure 2* and *Figure 3* — where training and testing errors are plotted keeping either the algorithm with its parameters constant or the training data size constant — give an indication of underfitting or overfitting.

When the training data size is fixed, different algorithms or the same algorithms with different parameter choices can exhibit different learning curves. The *Figure 2* shows two cases of algorithms on the same data size giving two different learning curves based on bias and variance.

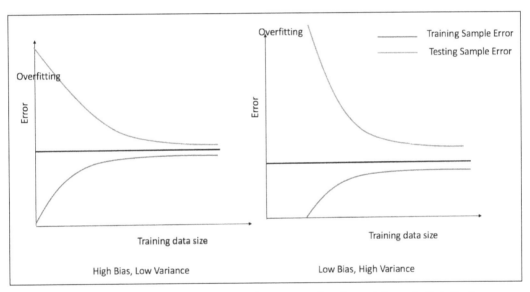

Figure 2: The training data relationship with error rate when the model complexity is fixed indicates different choices of models.

The algorithm or model choice also impacts model performance. A complex algorithm, with more parameters to tune, can result in overfitting, while a simple algorithm with less parameters might be underfitting. The classic figure to illustrate the model performance and complexity when the training data size is fixed is as follows:

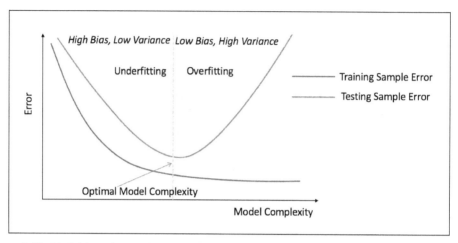

Figure 3: The Model Complexity relationship with Error rate, over the training and the testing data when training data size is fixed.

Validation allows for exploring the parameter space to find the model that generalizes best. Regularization (will be discussed in linear models) and validation are two mechanisms that should be used for preventing overfitting. Sometimes the "k-fold cross-validation" process is used for validation, which involves creating k samples of the data and using $(k - 1)$ to train on and the remaining one to test, repeated k times to give an average estimate. The following figure shows 5-fold cross-validation as an example:

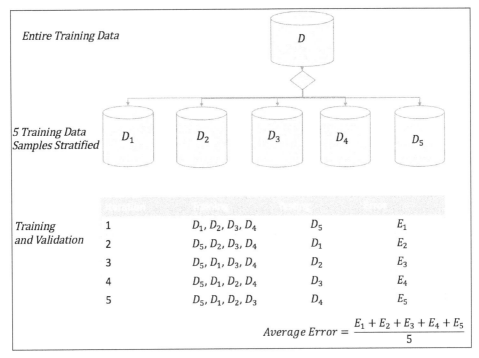

Figure 4: 5-fold cross-validation.

The following are some commonly used techniques to perform data sampling, validation, and learning:

- **Random split of training, validation, and testing**: 60, 20, 20. Train on 60%, use 20% for validation, and then combine the train and validation datasets to train a final model that is used to test on the remaining 20%. Split may be done randomly, based on time, based on region, and so on.

- **Training, cross-validation, and testing**: Split into Train and Test two to one, do validation using cross-validation on the train set, train on whole two-thirds and test on one-third. Split may be done randomly, based on time, based on region, and so on.

- **Training and cross-validation**: When the training set is small and only model selection can be done without much parameter tuning. Run cross-validation on the whole dataset and chose the best models with learning on the entire dataset.

Feature relevance analysis and dimensionality reduction

The goal of feature relevance and selection is to find the features that are discriminating with respect to the target variable and help reduce the dimensions of the data [1,2,3]. This improves the model performance mainly by ameliorating the effects of the curse of dimensionality and by removing noise due to irrelevant features. By carefully evaluating models on the validation set with and without features removed, we can see the impact of feature relevance. Since the exhaustive search for k features involves $2^k - 1$ sets (consider all combinations of k features where each feature is either retained or removed, disregarding the degenerate case where none is present) the corresponding number of models that have to be evaluated can become prohibitive, so some form of heuristic search techniques are needed. The most common of these techniques are described next.

Feature search techniques

Some of the very common search techniques employed to find feature sets are:

- **Forward or hill climbing**: In this search, one feature is added at a time until the evaluation module outputs no further change in performance.

- **Backward search**: Starting from the whole set, one feature at a time is removed until no performance improvement occurs. Some applications interleave both forward and backward techniques to search for features.

- **Evolutionary search**: Various evolutionary techniques such as genetic algorithms can be used as a search mechanism and the evaluation metrics from either filter- or wrapper-based methods can be used as fitness criterion to guide the process.

Feature evaluation techniques

At a high level, there are three basic methods to evaluate features.

Filter approach

This approach refers to the use of techniques without using machine learning algorithms for evaluation. The basic idea of the filter approach is to use a search technique to select a feature (or subset of features) and measure its importance using some statistical measure until a stopping criterion is reached.

Univariate feature selection

This search is as simple as ranking each feature based on the statistical measure employed.

Information theoretic approach

All information theoretic approaches use the concept of entropy mechanism at their core. The idea is that if the feature is randomly present in the dataset, there is maximum entropy, or, equivalently, the ability to compress or encode is low, and the feature may be irrelevant. On the other hand, if the distribution of the feature value is such some range of values are more prevalent in one class relative to the others, then the entropy is minimized and the feature is discriminating. Casting the problem in terms of entropy in this way requires some form of discretization to convert the numeric features into categories in order to compute the probabilities.

Consider a binary classification problem with training data D_X. If X_i is the ith feature with v distinct categorical values such that $D_{Xi} = \{D_1, D_2 \ldots D_v\}$, then information or the entropy in feature X_i is:

$$Info\left(D_{X_i}\right) = \sum_{j=1}^{v} \frac{\left|D_j\right|}{\left|D\right|} Info\left(D_j\right)$$

Here, *Info(D_j)* is the entropy of the partition and is calculated as:

$$Info\left(D\right) = -p_+\left(D\right)\log_2 p_+\left(D\right) - p_-\left(D\right)\log_2 p_-\left(D\right)$$

Here, $p_+(D)$ is the probability that the data in set D is in the positive class and $p_-(D)$ is the probability that it is in the negative class, in that sample. Information gain for the feature is calculated in terms of the overall information and information of the feature as

$$InfoGain(X_i) = Info(D) - Info(D_{Xi})$$

For numeric features, the values are sorted in ascending order and split points between neighboring values are considered as distinct values.

The greater the decrease in entropy, the higher the relevance of the feature. Information gain has problems when the feature has a large number of values; that is when Gain Ratio comes in handy. Gain Ratio corrects the information gain over large splits by introducing Split Information. Split Information for feature X_i and *GainRatio* is given by:

$$SplitInfo(D_{X_i}) = \sum_{j=1}^{v} \frac{|D_j|}{|D|} \log_2 \left(\frac{|D_j|}{|D|} \right)$$

$$GainRatio(X_i) = \frac{InfoGain(X_i)}{SplitInfo(D_{X_i})}$$

There are other impurity measures such as Gini Impurity Index (as described in the section on the *Decision Tree* algorithm) and Uncertainty-based measures to compute feature relevance.

Statistical approach

Chi-Squared feature selection is one of the most common feature selection methods that has statistical hypothesis testing as its base. The null hypothesis is that the feature and the class variable are independent of each other. The numeric features are discretized so that all features have categorical values. The contingency table is calculated as follows:

Feature Values	Class=P	Class=N	Sum over classes $niP + niN$
X_1	$(n_{1P} \mid \mu_{1P})$	$(n_{1N} \mid \mu_{1N})$	n_1
....	...	....	...
X_m	$(n_{mP} \mid \mu_{mP})$	$(n_{mN} \mid \mu_{mN})$	n_m
	n_{*P}	n_{*P}	n

Contingency Table 1: Showing feature values and class distribution for binary class.

In the preceding table, n_{ij} is a count of the number of features with value — after discretization — equal to x_i and class value of j.

The value summations are:

$$n_{*p} = \sum_1^m n_{ij}$$

$$n_{i*} = n_{iP} + n_{iN}$$

$$n = n_{*P} + n_{*N}$$

$$\mu_{ij} = \frac{\left(n_{*j} * n_{i*} \right)}{n}$$

Here n is number of data instances, j = P, N is the class value and i =1,2, ... m indexes the different discretized values of the feature and the table has $m - 1$ degrees of freedom.

The Chi-Square Statistic is given by:

$$\chi^2 = \sum_{i=1}^{m} \left(\left(\frac{\left(n_{iP} - \mu_{iP} \right)^2}{\mu_{iP}} \right) + \left(\frac{\left(n_{iN} - \mu_{iN} \right)^2}{\mu_{iN}} \right) \right)$$

The Chi-Square value is compared to confidence level thresholds for testing significance. For example, for i = 2, the Chi-Squared value at threshold of 5% is 3.84; if our value is smaller than the table value of 3.83, then we know that the feature is interesting and the null hypothesis is rejected.

Multivariate feature selection

Most multivariate methods of feature selection have two goals:

- Reduce the redundancy between the feature and other selected features
- Maximize the relevance or correlation of the feature with the class label

The task of finding such subsets of features cannot be exhaustive as the process can have a large search space. Heuristic search methods such as backward search, forward search, hill-climbing, and genetic algorithms are typically used to find a subset of features. Two very well-known evaluation techniques for meeting the preceding goals are presented next.

Minimal redundancy maximal relevance (mRMR)

In this technique, numeric features are often discretized—as done in univariate pre-processing—to get distinct categories of values.

For each subset S, the redundancy between two features X_i and X_j can be measured as:

$$W_I(S) = \frac{1}{|S|^2} \sum_{X_i, X_j \in S} MI(X_i, X_j)$$

Here, $MI(X_i, X_j)$ = measure of mutual information between two features X_i and X_j. Relevance between feature X_i and class C can be measured as:

$$V_I(S) = \frac{1}{|S|} \sum_{X_i \in S} MI(X_i, C)$$

Also, the two goals can be combined to find the best feature subset using:

$$S^2 = \underset{S \subseteq U}{argmax} \left(V_I(S) - W_I(S) \right)$$

Correlation-based feature selection (CFS)

The basic idea is similar to the previous example; the overall merit of subset S is measured as:

$$Merit(S) = \frac{k\overline{r_{cf}}}{\sqrt{k + (k-1)\overline{r_{ff}}}}$$

Here, k is the total number of features, $\overline{r_{cf}}$ is the average feature class correlation and $\overline{r_{ff}}$ is the average feature-feature inter correlation. The numerator gives the relevance factor while the denominator gives the redundancy factor and hence the goal of the search is to maximize the overall ratio or the *Merit (S)*.

There are other techniques such as Fast-Correlation-based feature selection that is based on the same principles, but with variations in computing the metrics. Readers can experiment with this and other techniques in Weka.

The advantage of the Filter approach is that its methods are independent of learning algorithms and hence one is freed from choosing the algorithms and parameters. They are also faster than wrapper-based approaches.

Wrapper approach

The search technique remains the same as discussed in the feature search approach; only the evaluation method changes. In the wrapper approach, a machine learning algorithm is used to evaluate the subset of features that are found to be discriminating based on various metrics. The machine learning algorithm used as the wrapper approach may be the same or different from the one used for modeling.

Most commonly, cross-validation is used in the learning algorithm. Performance metrics such as area under curve or F-score, obtained as an average on cross-validation, guide the search process. Since the cost of training and evaluating models is very high, we choose algorithms that have fast training speed, such as Linear Regression, linear SVM, or ones that are Decision Tree-based.

Some wrapper approaches have been very successful using specific algorithms such as Random Forest to measure feature relevance.

Embedded approach

This approach does not require feature search techniques. Instead of performing feature selection as preprocessing, it is done in the machine learning algorithm itself. Rule Induction, Decision Trees, Random Forest, and so on, perform feature selection as part of the training algorithm. Some algorithms such as regression or SVM-based methods, known as **shrinking methods**, can add a regularization term in the model to overcome the impact of noisy features in the dataset. Ridge and lasso-based regularization are well-known techniques available in regressions to provide feature selection implicitly.

There are other techniques using unsupervised algorithms that will be discussed in *Chapter 3, Unsupervised Machine Learning Techniques*, that can be used effectively in a supervised setting too, for example, **Principal Component Analysis (PCA)**.

Model building

In real-world problems, there are many constraints on learning and many ways to assess model performance on unseen data. Each modeling algorithm has its strengths and weaknesses when applied to a given problem or to a class of problems in a particular domain. This is articulated in the famous **No Free Lunch Theorem (NFLT)**, which says — for the case of supervised learning — that averaged over all distributions of data, every classification algorithm performs about as well as any other, including one that always picks the same class! Application of NFLT to supervised learning and search and optimization can be found at http://www.no-free-lunch.org/.

In this section, we will discuss the most commonly used practical algorithms, giving the necessary details to answer questions such as what are the algorithm's inputs and outputs? How does it work? What are the advantages and limitations to consider while choosing the algorithm? For each model, we will include sample code and outputs obtained from testing the model on the chosen dataset. This should provide the reader with insights into the process. Some algorithms such as neural networks and deep learning, Bayesian networks, stream-based earning, and so on, will be covered separately in their own chapters.

Linear models

Linear models work well when the data is linearly separable. This should always be the first thing to establish.

Linear Regression

Linear Regression can be used for both classification and estimation problems. It is one of the most widely used methods in practice. It consists of finding the best-fitting hyperplane through the data points.

Algorithm input and output

Features must be numeric. Categorical features are transformed using various pre-processing techniques, as when a categorical value becomes a feature with 1 and 0 values. Linear Regression models output a categorical class in classification or numeric values in regression. Many implementations also give confidence values.

How does it work?

The model tries to learn a "hyperplane" in the input space that minimizes the error between the data points of each class (*References* [4]).

A hyperplane in d-dimensional inputs that linear model learns is given by:

$$G(\mathbf{x}) = w_0 + \sum_{j=1}^{d} w_j x_j$$

The two regions (binary classification) the model divides the input space into are $w_0 + \sum_{j=1}^{d} w_j x_j > 0$ and $w_0 + \sum_{j=1}^{d} w_j x_j < 0$. Associating a value of 1 to the coordinate of feature 0, that is, $x_0=1$, the vector representation of hypothesis space or the model is:

$$G(\mathbf{x}) = sign(\mathbf{w}^T \mathbf{x})$$

The weight matrix can be derived using various methods such as ordinary least squares or iterative methods using matrix notation as follows:

$$\hat{\mathbf{W}} = \mathbf{X}(\mathbf{X}^T \mathbf{X})^{-1} \mathbf{X}^T \mathbf{y}$$

Here $\mathbf{X}$ is the input matrix and $\mathbf{y}$ is the label. If the matrix $\mathbf{X}^T\mathbf{X}$ in the least squares problem is not of full rank or if encountering various numerical stability issues, the solution is modified as:

$$\widehat{\mathbf{W}} = \mathbf{X}(\mathbf{X}^T \mathbf{X} + \lambda \mathbf{I}_n)^{-1} \mathbf{X}^T \mathbf{y}$$

Here, $\lambda \in \mathbb{R}$ is added to the diagonal of an identity matrix $\mathbf{I}_n$ of size $(n + 1, n + 1)$ with the rest of the values being set to 0. This solution is called **ridge regression** and parameter λ theoretically controls the trade-off between the square loss and low norm of the solution. The constant λ is also known as regularization constant and helps in preventing "overfitting".

Advantages and limitations

- It is an appropriate method to try and get insights when there are less than 100 features and a few thousand data points.

- Interpretable to some level as the weights give insights on the impact of each feature.

- Assumes linear relationship, additive and uncorrelated features, hence it doesn't model complex non-linear real-world data. Some implementations of Linear Regression allow removing collinear features to overcome this issue.

- Very susceptible to outliers in the data, if there are huge outliers, they have to be treated prior to performing Linear Regression.

- Heteroskedasticity, that is, unequal training point variances, can affect the simple least square regression models. Techniques such as weighted least squares are employed to overcome this situation.

Naïve Bayes

Based on the Bayes rule, the Naïve Bayes classifier assumes the features of the data are independent of each other (*References* [9]). It is especially suited for large datasets and frequently performs better than other, more elaborate techniques, despite its naïve assumption of feature independence.

Algorithm input and output

The Naïve Bayes model can take features that are both categorical and continuous. Generally, the performance of Naïve Bayes models improves if the continuous features are discretized in the right format. Naïve Bayes outputs the class and the probability score for all class values, making it a good classifier for scoring models.

How does it work?

It is a probability-based modeling algorithm. The basic idea is using Bayes' rule and measuring the probabilities of different terms, as given here. Measuring probabilities can be done either using pre-processing such as discretization, assuming a certain distribution, or, given enough data, mapping the distribution for numeric features.

Bayes' rule is applied to get the posterior probability as predictions and k represents k^{th} class.:

$$P\left(y = y^k \mid \mathbf{x}\right) = \frac{P\left(y = y^k\right) * \prod_{j=1}^{d} P\left(x_j \mid y = y^k\right)}{P(\mathbf{x})}$$

$$P\left(y = y^k \mid \mathbf{x}\right) \propto P\left(y = y^k\right) * \prod_{j=1}^{d} P\left(x_j \mid y = y^k\right)$$

Advantages and limitations

- It is robust against isolated noisy data points because such points are averaged when estimating the probabilities of input data.

- Probabilistic scores as confidence values from Bayes classification can be used as scoring models.

- Can handle missing values very well as they are not used in estimating probabilities.
- Also, it is robust against irrelevant attributes. If the features are not useful the probability distribution for the classes will be uniform and will cancel itself out.
- Very good in training speed and memory, it can be parallelized as each computation of probability in the equation is independent of the other.
- Correlated features can be a big issue when using Naïve Bayes because the conditional independence assumption is no longer valid.
- Normal distribution of errors is an assumption in most optimization algorithms.

Logistic Regression

If we employ Linear Regression model using, say, the least squares regression method, the outputs have to be converted to classes, say 0 and 1. Many Linear Regression algorithms output class and confidence as probability. As a rule of thumb, if we see that the probabilities of Linear Regression are mostly beyond the ranges of 0.2 to 0.8, then logistic regression algorithm may be a better choice.

Algorithm input and output

Similar to Linear Regression, all features must be numeric. Categorical features have to be transformed to numeric. Like in Naïve Bayes, this algorithm outputs class and probability for each class and can be used as a scoring model.

How does it work?

Logistic regression models the posterior probabilities of classes using linear functions in the input features.

The logistic regression model for a binary classification is given as:

$$\log \frac{P(y=0|\mathbf{x})}{P(y=1|\mathbf{x})} = w_0 + \sum_{j=1}^{d} w_j x_j$$

The model is a log-odds or logit transformation of linear models (*References* [6]). The weight vector is generally computed using various optimization methods such as **iterative reweighted least squares** (**IRLS**) or the **Broyden–Fletcher–Goldfarb–Shanno** (**BFGS**) method, or variants of these methods.

Advantages and limitations

- Overcomes the issue of heteroskedasticity and some non-linearity between inputs and outputs.

- No need of normal distribution assumptions in the error estimates.

- It is interpretable, but less so than Linear Regression models as some understanding of statistics is required. It gives information such as odds ratio, p values, and so on, which are useful in understanding the effects of features on the classes as well as doing implicit feature relevance based on significance of p values.

- L1 or L2 regularization has to be employed in practice to overcome overfitting in the logistic regression models.

- Many optimization algorithms are available for improving speed of training and robustness.

Non-linear models

Next, we will discuss some of the well-known, practical, and most commonly used non-linear models.

Decision Trees

Decision Trees are also known as **Classification and Regression Trees (CART)** (*References* [5]). Their representation is a binary tree constructed by evaluating an inequality in terms of a single attribute at each internal node, with each leaf-node corresponding to the output value or class resulting from the decisions in the path leading to it. When a new input is provided, the output is predicted by traversing the tree starting at the root.

Algorithm inputs and outputs

Features can be both categorical and numeric. It generates class as an output and most implementations give a score or probability using frequency-based estimation. Decision Trees probabilities are not smooth functions like Naïve Bayes and Logistic Regression, though there are extensions that are.

How does it work?

Generally, a single tree is created, starting with single features at the root with decisions split into branches based on the values of the features while at the leaf there is either a class or more features. There are many choices to be made, such as how many trees, how to choose features at the root level or at subsequent leaf level, and how to split the feature values when not categorical. This has resulted in many different algorithms or modifications to the basic Decision Tree. Many techniques to split the feature values are similar to what was discussed in the section on discretization. Generally, some form of pruning is applied to reduce the size of the tree, which helps in addressing overfitting.

Gini index is another popular technique used to split the features. Gini index of data in set S of all the data points is $G(S) = 1 - \sum_{j=1}^{k} p_j^2$ where $p_1, p_2 \dots p_k$ are probability distribution for each class.

If p is the fraction or probability of data in set S of all the data points belonging to say class positive, then $1 - p$ is the fraction for the other class or the error rate in binary classification. If the dataset S is split in r ways $S_1, S_2 \dots S_r$ then the error rate of each set can be quantified as $|S_i|$. Gini index for an r way split is as follows:

$$GiniSplit\left(S \Rightarrow S_1, S_2 \dots S_r\right) = \sum_{i=1}^{r} \frac{|S_i|}{|S|} G(S_i)$$

The split with the lowest Gini index is used for selection. The CART algorithm, a popular Decision Tree algorithm, uses Gini index for split criteria.

The entropy of the set of data points S can similarly be computed as:

$$E(S) = \sum_{j=1}^{k} p_j \log_2 p_j$$

Similarly, entropy-based split is computed as:

$$EntropySplit\left(S \Rightarrow S_1, S_2 \dots S_r\right) = \sum_{i=1}^{r} \frac{|S_i|}{|S|} E(S_i)$$

The lower the value of the entropy split, the better the feature, and this is used in ID3 and C4.5 Decision Tree algorithms (*References* [12]).

The stopping criteria and pruning criteria are related. The idea behind stopping the growth of the tree early or pruning is to reduce the "overfitting" and it works similar to regularization in linear and logistic models. Normally, the training set is divided into tree growing sets and pruning sets so that pruning uses different data to overcome any biases from the growing set. **Minimum Description Length (MDL)**, which penalizes the complexity of the tree based on number of nodes is a popular methodology used in many Decision Tree algorithms.

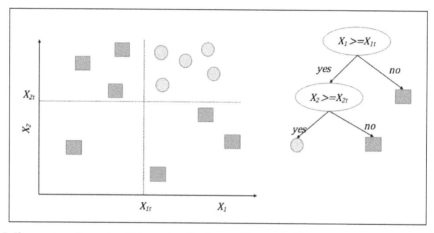

Figure 5: Shows a two-dimensional binary classification problem and a Decision Tree induced using splits at thresholds X_{1t} and X_{1t}, respectively

Advantages and limitations

- The main advantages of Decision Trees are they are quite easily interpretable. They can be understood in layman's terms and are especially suited for business domain experts to easily understand the exact model.

- If there are a large number of features, then building Decision Tree can take lots of training time as the complexity of the algorithm increases.

- Decision Trees have an inherent problem with overfitting. Many tree algorithms have pruning options to reduce the effect. Using pruning and validation techniques can alleviate the problem to a large extent.

- Decision Trees work well when there is correlation between the features.

- Decision Trees build axis-parallel boundaries across classes, the bias of which can introduce errors, especially in a complex, smooth, non-linear boundary.

K-Nearest Neighbors (KNN)

K-Nearest Neighbors falls under the branch of non-parametric and lazy algorithms. K-Nearest neighbors doesn't make any assumptions on the underlying data and doesn't build and generalize models from training data (*References* [10]).

Algorithm inputs and outputs

Though KNN's can work with categorical and numeric features, the distance computation, which is the core of finding the neighbors, works better with numeric features. Normalization of numeric features to be in the same ranges is one of the mandatory steps required. KNN's outputs are generally the classes based on the neighbors' distance calculation.

How does it work?

KNN uses the entire training data to make predictions on unseen test data. When unseen test data is presented KNN finds the K "nearest neighbors" using some distance computation and based on the neighbors and the metric of deciding the category it classifies the new point. If we consider two vectors represented by $\mathbf{x}_1$ and $\mathbf{x}_2$ corresponding to two data points the distance is calculated as:

- Euclidean Distance:

$$d_{EUC}\left(\mathbf{x}_1,\mathbf{x}_2\right) = \left[\left(\mathbf{x}_1-\mathbf{x}_2\right)\left(\mathbf{x}_1-\mathbf{x}_2\right)\right]^{\frac{1}{2}}$$

- Cosine Distance or similarity:

$$S_{cos}\left(\mathbf{x}_1,\mathbf{x}_2\right) = \frac{\mathbf{x}_1\cdot\mathbf{x}_2}{\left\|\mathbf{x}_1\right\|\left\|\mathbf{x}_2\right\|}$$

The metric used to classify an unseen may simply be the majority class among the K neighbors.

The training time is small as all it has to do is build data structures to hold the data in such a way that the computation of the nearest neighbor is minimized when unseen data is presented. The algorithm relies on choices of how the data is stored from training data points for efficiency of searching the neighbors, which distance computation is used to find the nearest neighbor, and which metrics are used to categorize based on classes of all neighbors. Choosing the value of "K" in KNN by using validation techniques is critical.

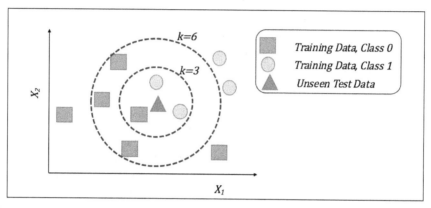

Figure 6: K-Nearest Neighbor illustrated using two-dimensional data with different choices of k.

Advantages and limitations

- No assumption on underlying data distribution and minimal training time makes it a very attractive method for learning.

- KNN uses local information for computing the distances and in certain domains can yield highly adaptive behaviors.

- It is robust to noisy training data when K is effectively chosen.

- Holding the entire training data for classification can be problematic depending on the number of data points and hardware constraints

- Number of features and the curse of dimensionality affects this algorithm more hence some form of dimensionality reduction or feature selection has to be done prior to modeling in KNN.

Support vector machines (SVM)

SVMs, in simple terms, can be viewed as linear classifiers that maximize the margin between the separating hyperplane and the data by solving a constrained optimization problem. SVMs can even deal with data that is not linearly separable by invoking transformation to a higher dimensional space using kernels described later.

Algorithm inputs and outputs

SVM is effective with numeric features only, though most implementations can handle categorical features with transformation to numeric or binary. Normalization is often a choice as it helps the optimization part of the training. Outputs of SVM are class predictions. There are implementations that give probability estimates as confidences, but this requires considerable training time as they use k-fold cross-validation to build the estimates.

How does it work?

In its linear form, SVM works similar to Linear Regression classifier, where a linear decision boundary is drawn between the two classes. The difference between the two is that with SVM, the boundary is drawn in such a way that the "margin" or the distance between the points near the boundary is maximized. The points on the boundaries are known as "support vectors" (*References* [13 and 8]).

Thus, SVM tries to find the weight vector in linear models similar to Linear Regression model as given by the following:

$$G(\mathbf{x}) = b + \sum_{j=1}^{d} w_j x_j$$

The weight w_0 is represented by b here. SVM for a binary class y $\in \{1,-1\}$ tries to find a hyperplane:

$$b + \sum_{j=1}^{d} w_j x_j = 0$$

The hyperplane tries to separate the data points such that all points with the class lie on the side of the hyperplane as:

$$b + \sum_{j=1}^{d} w_j x_j \geq 0 \, \forall i : y = 1$$

$$b + \sum_{j=1}^{d} w_j x_j \leq 0 \, \forall i : y = -1$$

The models are subjected to maximize the margin using constraint-based optimization with a penalty function denoted by C for overcoming the errors denoted by ξ_i :

$$\min\left(\frac{1}{2}\|\mathbf{w}\|^2\right) + C\sum_i \xi_i$$

Such that $y_i\left(\mathbf{w}.\mathbf{x}_i + b\right) \geq 1 - \xi_i \forall \mathbf{x}_i$ and $\xi_i \geq 0$.

They are also known as large margin classifiers for the preceding reason. The kernel-based SVM transforms the input data into a hypothetical feature space where SV machinery works in a linear way and the boundaries are drawn in the feature spaces.

A kernel function on the transformed representation is given by:

$$k\left(\mathbf{x}_i, \mathbf{x}_j\right) = \Phi\left(\mathbf{x}_i\right) \cdot \Phi\left(\mathbf{x}_j\right)$$

Here Φ is a transformation on the input space. It can be seen that the entire optimization and solution of SVM remains the same with the only exception that the dot-product $\mathbf{x}_i \cdot \mathbf{x}_j$ is replaced by the kernel function $k(\mathbf{x}_i, \mathbf{x}_j)$, which is a function involving the two vectors in a different space without actually transforming to that space. This is known as the **kernel trick**.

The most well-known kernels that are normally used are:

- **Gaussian Radial Basis Kernel**:

$$k\left(\mathbf{x}_i, \mathbf{x}_j\right) = e^{\frac{-\left\|\mathbf{x}_i - \mathbf{x}_j\right\|^2}{2\sigma^2}}$$

- **Polynomial Kernel**:

$$k\left(\mathbf{x}_i, \mathbf{x}_j\right) = \left(\mathbf{x}_i \cdot \mathbf{x}_j + c\right)^d$$

- **Sigmoid Kernel**:

$$k\left(\mathbf{x}_i, \mathbf{x}_j\right) = \tan h\left(\mathbf{x}_i \cdot \mathbf{x}_j - d\right)$$

SVM's performance is very sensitive to some of the parameters of optimization and the kernel parameters and the core SV parameter such as the cost function C. Search techniques such as grid search or evolutionary search combined with validation techniques such as cross-validation are generally used to find the best parameter values.

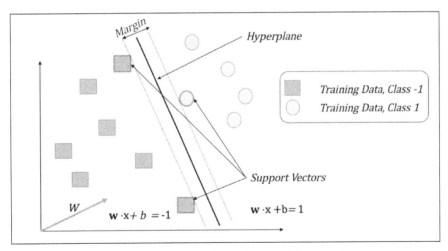

Figure 7: SVM Linear Hyperplane learned from training data that creates a maximum margin separation between two classes.

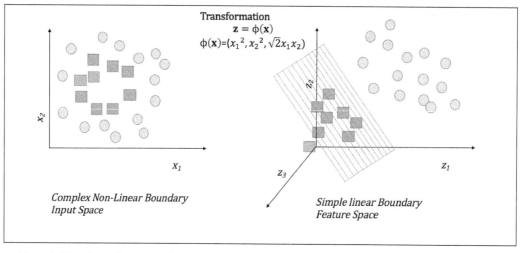

Figure 8: Kernel transformation illustrating how two-dimensional input space can be transformed using a polynomial transformation into a three-dimensional feature space where data is linearly separable.

Advantages and limitations

- SVMs are among the best in generalization, low overfitting, and have a good theoretical foundation for complex non-linear data if the parameters are chosen judiciously.

- SVMs work well even with a large number of features and less training data.

- SVMs are less sensitive to noisy training data.

- The biggest disadvantage of SVMs is that they are not interpretable.

- Another big issue with SVM is its training time and memory requirements. They are $O(n^2)$ and $O(n^3)$ and can result in major scalability issues when the data is large or there are hardware constraints. There are some modifications that help in reducing both.

- SVM generally works well for binary classification problems, but for multiclass classification problems, though there are techniques such as one versus many and one versus all, it is not as robust as some other classifiers such as Decision Trees.

Ensemble learning and meta learners

Combining multiple algorithms or models to classify instead of relying on just one is known as ensemble learning. It helps to combine various models as each model can be considered — at a high level — as an expert in detecting specific patterns in the whole dataset. Each base learner can be made to learn on slightly different datasets too. Finally, the results from all models are combined to perform prediction. Based on how similar the algorithms used in combination are, how the training dataset is presented to each algorithm, and how the algorithms combine the results to finally classify the unseen dataset, there are many branches of ensemble learning:

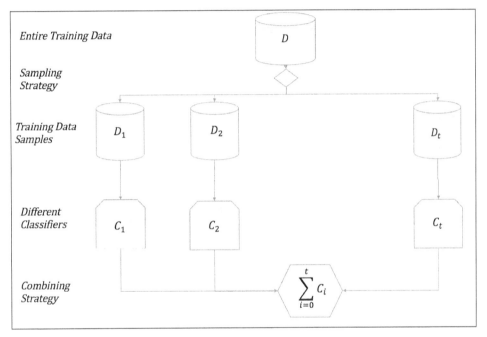

Figure 9: Illustration of ensemble learning strategies

Some common types of ensemble learning are:

- Different learning algorithms
- Same learning algorithms, but with different parameter choices
- Different learning algorithms on different feature sets
- Different learning algorithms with different training data

Bootstrap aggregating or bagging

It is one of the most commonly used ensemble methods for dividing the data in different samples and building classifiers on each sample.

Algorithm inputs and outputs

The input is constrained by the choice of the base learner used – if using Decision Trees there are basically no restrictions. The method outputs class membership along with the probability distribution for classes.

How does it work?

The core idea of bagging is to apply the bootstrapping estimation to different learners that have high variance, such as Decision Trees. Bootstrapping is any statistical measure that depends on random sampling with replacement. The entire data is split into different samples using bootstrapping and for each sample, a model is built using the base learner. Finally, while predicting, the average prediction is arrived at using a majority vote – this is one technique to combine over all the learners.

Random Forest

Random Forest is an improvement over basic bagged Decision Trees. Even with bagging, the basic Decision Tree has a choice of all the features at every split point in creating a tree. Because of this, even with different samples, many trees can form highly correlated submodels, which causes the performance of bagging to deteriorate. By giving random features to different models in addition to a random dataset, the correlation between the submodels reduces and Random Forest shows much better performance compared to basic bagged trees. Each tree in Random Forest grows its structure on the random features, thereby minimizing the bias; combining many such trees on decision reduces the variance (*References* [15]). Random Forest is also used to measure feature relevance by averaging the impurity decrease in the trees and ranking them across all the features to give the relative importance of each.

Advantages and limitations

- Better generalization than the single base learner. Overcomes the issue of overfitting of base learners.

- Interpretability of bagging is very low as it works as meta learner combining even the interpretable learners.

- Like most other ensemble learners, Bagging is resilient to noise and outliers.

- Random Forest generally does not tend to overfit given the training data is iid.

Boosting

Boosting is another popular form of ensemble learning, which is based on using a weak learner and iteratively learning the points that are "misclassified" or difficult to learn. Thus, the idea is to "boost" the difficult to learn instances and making the base learners learn the decision boundaries more effectively. There are various flavors of boosting such as AdaBoost, LogitBoost, ConfidenceBoost, Gradient Boosting, and so on. We present a very basic form of AdaBoost here (*References* [14]).

Algorithm inputs and outputs

The input is constrained by the choice of the base learner used – if using Decision Trees there are basically no restrictions. Outputs class membership along with probability distribution for classes.

How does it work?

The basic idea behind boosting is iterative reweighting of input samples to create new distribution of the data for learning a model from a simple base learner in every iteration.

Initially, all the instances are uniformly weighted with weights $D_0 = \dfrac{1}{n}$ and at every iteration t, the population is resampled or reweighted as

$$D_{t+1} = \frac{D_t(i)}{z_t}\left(\exp\left(-a_t h_t y_i\left(x_i\right)\right)\right) \text{ where } \alpha_t = \frac{1}{2}\ln\frac{\left(1 - errD_t\left(h_t\right)\right)}{errD_t\left(h_t\right)} \text{ and } Z_t \text{ is the}$$

normalization constant.

The final model works as a linear combination of all the models learned in the iteration:

$$G(\mathbf{x}) = sign\left(\sum_{t=1}^{T} a_t h_t(\mathbf{x})\right)$$

The reweighting or resampling of the data in each iteration is based on "errors"; the data points that result in errors are sampled more or have larger weights.

Advantages and limitations

- Better generalization than the base learner and overcomes the issue of overfitting very effectively.

- Some boosting algorithms such as AdaBoost can be susceptible to uniform noise. There are variants of boosting such as "GentleBoost" and "BrownBoost" that decrease the effect of outliers.

- Boosting has a theoretical bounds and guarantee on the error estimation making it a statistically robust algorithm.

Model assessment, evaluation, and comparisons

The key ideas discussed here are:

- How to assess or estimate the performance of the classifier on unseen datasets that it will be predicting on future unseen datasets.

- What are the metrics that we should use to assess the performance of the model?

- How do we compare algorithms if we have to choose between them?

Model assessment

In order to train the model(s), tune the model parameters, select the models, and finally estimate the predictive behavior of models on unseen data, we need many datasets. We cannot train the model on one set of data and estimate its behavior on the same set of data, as it will have a clear optimistic bias and estimations will be unlikely to match the behavior in the unseen data. So at a minimum, there is a need to partition data available into training sets and testing sets. Also, we need to tune the parameters of the model and test the effect of the tuning on a separate dataset before we perform testing on the test set. The same argument of optimistic bias and wrong estimation applies if we use the same dataset for training, parameter tuning, and testing. Thus there is a theoretical and practical need to have three datasets, that is, training, validation, and testing.

The models are trained on the training set, the effect of different parameters on the training set are validated on the validation set, and the finalized model with the selected parameters is run on the test set to gauge the performance of the model on future unseen data. When the dataset is not large enough, or is large but the imbalance between classes is wide, that is, one class is present only in a small fraction of the total population, we cannot create too many samples. Recall that one of the steps described in our methodology is to create different data samples and datasets. If the total training data is large and has a good proportion of data and class ratios, then creating these three sets using random stratified partitioning is the most common option employed. In certain datasets that show seasonality and time-dependent behaviors, creating datasets based on time bounds is a common practice. In many cases, when the dataset is not large enough, only two physical partitions, that is, training and testing may be created. The training dataset ranges roughly from 66% to 80% while the rest is used for testing. The validation set is then created from the training dataset using the k-fold cross-validation technique. The training dataset is split k times, each time producing $k-1/k$ random training $1/k$ testing data samples, and the average metrics of performance needed is generated. This way the limited training data is partitioned k times and average performance across different split of training/testing is used for gauging the effect of the parameters. Using 10-fold cross-validation is the most common practice employed in cross-validation.

Model evaluation metrics

The next important decision when tuning parameters or selecting models is to base your decision on certain performance metrics. In classification learning, there are different metrics available on which you can base your decision, depending on the business requirement. For example, in certain domains, not missing a single true positive is the most important concern, while in other domains where humans are involved in adjudicating results of models, having too many false positives is the greater concern. In certain cases, having overall good accuracy is considered more vital. In highly imbalanced datasets such as fraud or cyber attacks, there are just a handful of instances of one class and millions of the other classes. In such cases accuracy gives a wrong indication of model performance and some other metrics such as precision, true positive ratio, or area under the curve are used as metrics.

We will now discuss the most commonly employed metrics in classification algorithms evaluation (*References* [16, 17, and 19]).

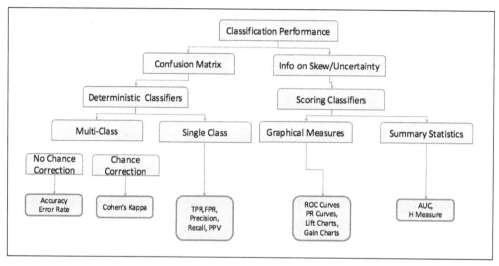

Figure 10: Model evaluation metrics for classification models

Confusion matrix and related metrics

Actual		Predicted			
		Class Positive	Class Negative		
	Class Positive	True Positive	False Negative *Type II Error*	TPR, Sensitivity, Recall $\dfrac{\sum True\ Positive}{\sum Actual\ Class\ Positive}$	FNR $\dfrac{\sum False\ Negative}{\sum Actual\ Class\ Positive}$
	Class Negative	False Positive *Type I Error*	True Negative	FPR, Fall out $\dfrac{\sum False\ Positive}{\sum Actual\ Class\ Negative}$	TNR, Specificity $\dfrac{\sum True\ Negative}{\sum Actual\ Class\ Negative}$
		PPV, Precision $\dfrac{\sum True\ Positive}{\sum Predicted\ Class\ Positive}$	False Omission Rate $\dfrac{\sum False\ Negative}{\sum Predicted\ Class\ Negative}$	ACCURACY	
		False Discovery Rate $\dfrac{\sum False\ Positive}{\sum Predicted\ Class\ Positive}$	NPV $\dfrac{\sum True\ Negative}{\sum Predicted\ Class\ Negative}$	$\dfrac{\sum True\ Positive + \sum True\ Negative}{\sum Total\ Data}$	

Figure 11: Confusion Matrix

The confusion matrix is central to the definition of a number of model performance metrics. The proliferation of metrics and synonymous terms is a result of the utility of different quantities derived from the elements of the matrix in various disciplines, each emphasizing a different aspect of the model's behavior.

The four elements of the matrix are raw counts of the number of False Positives, False Negatives, True Positives, and True Negatives. Often more interesting are the different ratios of these quantities, the True Positive Rate (or Sensitivity, or Recall), and the False Positive Rate (FPR, or $1-$Specificity, or Fallout). Accuracy reflects the percentage of correct predictions, whether Class 1 or Class 0. For skewed datasets, accuracy is not particularly useful, as even a constant prediction can appear to perform well.

ROC and PRC curves

The previously mentioned metrics such as accuracy, precision, recall, sensitivity, and specificity are aggregates, that is, they describe the behavior of the entire dataset. In many complex problems it is often valuable to see the trade-off between metrics such as TPs and say FPs.

Many classifiers, mostly probability-based classifiers, give confidence or probability of the prediction, in addition to giving classification. The process to obtain the ROC or PRC curves is to run the unseen validation or test set on the learned models, and then obtain the prediction and the probability of prediction. Sort the predictions based on the confidences in decreasing order. For every probability or confidence calculate two metrics, the fraction of FP (FP rate) and the fraction of TP (TP rate).

Plotting the TP rate on the y axis and FP rate on the x axis gives the ROC curves. ROC curves of random classifiers lie close to the diagonal while the ROC curves of good classifiers tend towards the upper left of the plot. The **area under the curve (AUC)** is the area measured under the ROC curve by using the trapezoidal area from 0 to 1 of ROC curves. While running cross-validation for instance there can be many ROC curves. There are two ways to get "average" ROC curves: first, using vertical averaging, that is, TPR average is plotted at different FP rate or second, using horizontal averaging, that is, FPR average is plotted at different TP rate. The classifiers that have area under curves greater than 0.8, as a rule-of-thumb are considered good for prediction for unseen data.

Precision Recall curves or PRC curves are similar to ROC curves, but instead of TPR versus FPR, metrics Precision and Recall are plotted on the y and x axis, respectively. When the data is highly imbalanced, that is, ROC curves don't really show the impact while PRC curves are more reliable in judging performance.

Gain charts and lift curves

Lift and Gain charts are more biased towards sensitivity or true positives. The whole purpose of these two charts is to show how instead of random selection, the models prediction and confidence can detect better quality or true positives in the sample of unseen data.

This is usually very appealing for detection engines that are used in detecting fraud in financial crime or threats in cyber security. The gain charts and lift curves give exact estimates of real true positives that will be detected at different quartiles or intervals of total data. This will give insight to the business decision makers on how many investigators would be needed or how many hours would be spent towards detecting fraudulent actions or cyber attacks and thus can give real ROI of the models.

The process for generating gain charts or lift curves has a similar process of running unseen validation or test data through the models and getting the predictions along with the confidences or probabilities. It involves ranking the probabilities in decreasing order and keeping count of TPs per quartile of the dataset. Finally, the histogram of counts per quartile give the lift curve, while the cumulative count of TPs added over quartile gives the gains chart. In many tools such as RapidMiner, instead of coarse intervals such as quartiles, fixed larger intervals using binning is employed for obtaining the counts and cumulative counts.

Model comparisons

When it comes to choosing between algorithms, or the right parameters for a given algorithm, we make the comparison either on different datasets, or, as in the case of cross-validation, on different splits of the same dataset. Measures of statistical testing are employed in decisions involved in these comparisons. The basic idea of using hypothesis testing from classical statistics is to compare the two metrics from the algorithms. The null hypothesis is that there is no difference between the algorithms based on the measured metrics and so the test is done to validate or reject the null hypothesis based on the measured metrics (*References* [16]). The main question answered by statistical tests is- are the results or metrics obtained by the algorithm its real characteristics, or is it by chance?

In this section, we will discuss the most common methods for comparing classification algorithms used in practical scenarios.

Comparing two algorithms

The general process is to train the algorithms on the same training set and run the models on either multiple validation sets, different test sets, or cross-validation, gauge the metrics of interest discussed previously, such as error rate or area under curve, and then get the statistics of the metrics for each of the algorithms to decide which worked better. Each method has its advantages and disadvantages.

McNemar's Test

This is a non-parametric test and thus it makes no assumptions on data and distribution. McNemar's test builds a contingency table of a performance metric such as "misclassification or errors" with:

Count of misclassification by both algorithms (c_{00})

- Count of misclassification by algorithm $G1$, but correctly classified by algorithm $G2(c_{01})$
- Count of misclassification by algorithm $G2$, but correctly classified by algorithm $G1$ (c_{10})
- Count of correctly classified by both $G1$ and $G2(c_{11})$

$$\chi^2 = \frac{\left(\left(c_{01} - c_{10}\right) - 1\right)^2}{c_{01} + c_{10}}$$

If χ^2 exceeds $\chi^2_{1,1-\alpha}$ statistic then we can reject the null hypothesis that the two performance metrics on algorithms $G1$ and $G2$ were equal under the confidence value of $1 - \alpha$.

Paired-t test

This is a parametric test and an assumption of normally distributed computed metrics becomes valid. Normally it is coupled with cross-validation processes and results of metrics such as area under curve or precision or error rate is computed for each and then the mean and standard deviations are measured. Apart from normal distribution assumption, the additional assumption that two metrics come from a population of equal variance can be a big disadvantage for this method.

$$\overline{d} = \overline{pm(G1)} - \overline{pm(G2)}$$

$\bar{d}$ is difference of means in performance metrics of two algorithms *G1* and *G2*.

$$\sigma_d = \sqrt{\frac{\sum_{i=1}^{n}(d_i - \bar{d})^2}{n-1}}$$

Here, d_i is the difference between the performance metrics of two algorithms *G1* and *G2* in the trial and there are n trials.

The *t*-statistic is computed using the mean differences and the standard errors from the standard deviation as follows and is compared to the table for the right alpha value to check for significance:

$$t = \frac{\bar{d}}{\sigma_d / \sqrt{n}}$$

Wilcoxon signed-rank test

The most popular non-parametric method of testing two metrics over datasets is to use the Wilcoxon signed-rank test. The algorithms are trained on the same training data and metrics such as error rate or area under accuracy are calculated over different validation or test sets. Let d_i be the difference between the performance metrics of two classifiers in the ith trial for N datasets. Differences are then ranked according to their absolute values, and mean ranks associated for ties. Let R^+ be the sum of ranks where the second algorithm outperformed the first and R⁻ be the sum of ranks where the first outperformed the second:

$$R^+ = \sum_{d_i > 0} rank(d_i) + \frac{1}{2}\sum_{d_i=0} rank(d_i)$$

$$R^- = \sum_{d_i < 0} rank(d_i) + \frac{1}{2}\sum_{d_i=0} rank(d_i)$$

The statistic $T_{wilcoxon} = \min\left(R^+, R^-\right)$ is then compared to threshold value at an alpha, $T_{wilcoxon} \leq V_\alpha$ to reject the hypothesis.

Comparing multiple algorithms

We will now discuss the two most common techniques used when there are more than two algorithms involved and we need to perform comparison across many algorithms for evaluation metrics.

ANOVA test

These are parametric tests that assume normal distribution of the samples, that is, metrics we are calculating for evaluations. ANOVA test follows the same process as others, that is, train the models/algorithms on similar training sets and run it on different validation or test sets. The main quantities computed in ANOVA are the metric means for each algorithm performance and then compute the overall metric means across all algorithms.

Let p_{ij} be the performance metric for $i = 1,2\ldots k$ and $j = 1,2\ldots l$ for k trials and l classifiers. The mean performance of classifier j on all trials and overall mean performance is:

$$m_j = \frac{\sum_{i=1}^{k} p_{ij}}{k} \qquad m = \frac{\sum_{j=1}^{l} m_j}{l}$$

Two types of variation are evaluated. The first is within-group variation, that is, total deviation of each algorithm from the overall metric mean, and the second is between-group variation, that is, deviation of each algorithm metric mean. Within-group variation and between-group variation are used to compute the respective within- and between- sum of squares as:

$$SS_b = k \sum_j \left(m_j - m\right)^2, SS_w = \sum_j \sum_i \left(X_{ij} - m_j\right)^2$$

Using the two sum of squares and a computation such as F-statistic, which is the ratio of the two, the significance test can be done at alpha values to accept or reject the null hypothesis:

$$f = \frac{SS_b\big/(l-1)}{SS_w\big/k(l-1)}$$

ANOVA tests have the same limitations as paired-t tests on the lines of assumptions of normal distribution of metrics and assuming the variances being equal.

Friedman's test

Friedman's test is a non-parametric test for multiple algorithm comparisons and it has no assumption on the data distribution or variances of metrics that ANOVA does. It uses ranks instead of the performance metrics directly for its computation. On each dataset or trials, the algorithms are sorted and the best one is ranked 1 and so on for all classifiers. The average rank of an algorithm over n datasets is computed, say R_j. The Friedman's statistic over l classifiers is computed as follows and compared to alpha values to accept or reject the null hypothesis:

$$\chi^2 = \left[\frac{12}{n \times l \times (l+1)} \times \sum_{j=1}^{l} R_j^2 \right] - 3 \times n \times (l+1)$$

Case Study – Horse Colic Classification

To illustrate the different steps and methodologies described in *Chapter 1, Machine Learning Review,* from data analysis to model evaluation, a representative dataset that has real-world characteristics is essential.

We have chosen "Horse Colic Dataset" from the UCI Repository available at the following link: https://archive.ics.uci.edu/ml/datasets/Horse+Colic

The dataset has 23 features and has a good mix of categorical and continuous features. It has a large number of features and instances with missing values, hence understanding how to replace these missing values and using it in modeling is made more practical in this treatment. The large number of missing data (30%) is in fact a notable feature of this dataset. The data consists of attributes that are continuous, as well as nominal in type. Also, the presence of self-predictors makes working with this dataset instructive from a practical standpoint.

The goal of the exercise is to apply the techniques of supervised learning that we have assimilated so far. We will do this using a real dataset and by working with two open source toolkits—WEKA and RapidMiner. With the help of these tools, we will construct the pipeline that will allow us to start with the ingestion of the data file through data cleansing, the learning process, and model evaluation.

Weka is a Java framework for machine learning—we will see how to use this framework to solve a classification problem from beginning to end in a few lines of code. In addition to a Java API, Weka also has a GUI.

RapidMiner is a graphical environment with drag and drop capability and a large suite of algorithms and visualization tools that makes it extremely easy to quickly run experiments with data and different modeling techniques.

Business problem

The business problem is to determine given values for the well-known variables of the dataset—if the lesion of the horse was surgical. We will use the test set as the unseen data that must be classified.

Machine learning mapping

Based on the data and labels, this is a binary classification problem. The data is already split into training and testing data. This makes the evaluation technique simpler as all methodologies from feature selection to models can be evaluated on the same test data.

The dataset contains 300 training and 68 test examples. There are 28 attributes and the target corresponds to whether or not a lesion is surgical.

Data analysis

After looking at the distribution of the label categories over the training and test samples, we combine the 300 training samples and the 68 test samples prior to feature analyzes.

Label analysis

The ratio of the No Class to Yes Class is 109/191 = 0.57 in the Training set and 0.66 in the Test set:

Training dataset		
Surgical Lesion?	1 (Yes)	2 (No)
Number of examples	191	109
Testing dataset		
Surgical Lesion?	1 (Yes)	2 (No)
Number of examples	41	27

Table 2: Label analysis

Features analysis

The following is a screenshot of top features with characteristics of types, missing values, basic statistics of minimum, maximum, modes, and standard deviations sorted by missing values. Observations are as follows:

- There are no categorical or continuous features with non-missing values; the least is the feature "pulse" with 74 out of 368 missing, that is, 20% values missing, which is higher than general noise threshold!

- Most numeric features have missing values, for example, "nasogastric reflux PH" has 247 out of 368 values missing, that is, 67% values are missing!

- Many categorical features have missing values, for example, "abidominocentesis appearance" have 165 out of 368 missing, that is, 45% values are missing!

- Missing values have to be handled in some way to overcome the noise created by such large numbers!

'nasogastric reflux PH'	Numeric	247	Min 1	Max 7.500	Average 4.708
'abdomcentesis total protein'	Numeric	198	Min 0.100	Max 10.100	Average 3.020
'abdominocentesis appearance'	Nominal	165	Least 1 (41)	Most 2 (48)	Values 2 (48), 3 (46), ...[1 more]
abdomen	Nominal	118	Least 3 (13)	Most 5 (79)	Values 5 (79), 4 (43), ...[3 more]
'nasogastric reflux'	Nominal	106	Least 2 (35)	Most 1 (120)	Values 1 (120), 3 (39), ...[1 more]
'nasogastric tube'	Nominal	104	Least 3 (23)	Most 2 (102)	Values 2 (102), 1 (71), ...[1 more]
'rectal examination'	Nominal	102	Least 2 (13)	Most 4 (79)	Values 4 (79), 1 (57), ...[2 more]
'peripheral pulse'	Nominal	69	Least 2 (5)	Most 1 (115)	Values 1 (115), 3 (103), ...[2 more]
'rectal temperature'	Numeric	60	Min 35.400	Max 40.800	Average 38.168
'respiratory rate'	Numeric	58	Min 8	Max 96	Average 30.417
'temperature of extremities'	Nominal	56	Least 4 (27)	Most 3 (109)	Values 3 (109), 1 (78), ...[2 more]
'abdominal distension'	Nominal	56	Least 4 (38)	Most 1 (76)	Values 1 (76), 2 (65), ...[2 more]
pain	Nominal	55	Least 1 (38)	Most 3 (67)	Values 3 (67), 2 (59), ...[3 more]
'mucous membranes'	Nominal	47	Least 6 (20)	Most 1 (79)	Values 1 (79), 3 (58), ...[4 more]
peristalsis	Nominal	44	Least 2 (16)	Most 3 (128)	Values 3 (128), 4 (73), ...[2 more]
'total protein'	Numeric	33	Min 3.300	Max 89	Average 24.457
'capillary refill time'	Nominal	32	Least 3 (2)	Most 1 (188)	Values 1 (188), 2 (78), ...[1 more]
'packed cell volume'	Numeric	29	Min 23	Max 75	Average 46.295
pulse	Numeric	24	Min 30	Max 184	Average 71.913

Figure 12: Basic statistics of features from datasets.

Supervised learning experiments

In this section, we will cover supervised learning experiments using two different tools—highlighting coding and analysis in one tool and the GUI framework in the other. This gives the developers the opportunity to explore whichever route they are most comfortable with.

Weka experiments

In this section, we have given the entire code and will walk through the process from loading data, transforming the data, selecting features, building sample models, evaluating them on test data, and even comparing the algorithms for statistical significance.

Sample end-to-end process in Java

In each algorithm, the same training/testing data is used and evaluation is performed for all the metrics as follows. The training and testing file is loaded in memory as follows:

```
DataSource source = new DataSource(trainingFile);
Instances data = source.getDataSet();
if (data.classIndex() == -1)
  data.setClassIndex(data.numAttributes() - 1);
```

The generic code, using WEKA, is shown here, where each classifier is wrapped by a filtered classifier for replacing missing values:

```
//replacing the nominal and numeric with modes and means
Filter missingValuesFilter= new ReplaceMissingValues();
//create a filtered classifier to use filter and classifier
FilteredClassifier filteredClassifier = new FilteredClassifier();
filteredClassifier.setFilter(f);
// create a bayesian classifier
NaiveBayes naiveBayes = new NaiveBayes();
// use supervised discretization
naiveBayes.setUseSupervisedDiscretization(true);
//set the base classifier e.g naïvebayes, linear //regression etc.
fc.setClassifier(filteredClassifier)
```

When the classifier needs to perform Feature Selection, in Weka, `AttributeSelectedClassifier` further wraps the `FilteredClassifier` as shown in the following listing:

```
AttributeSelectedClassifier attributeSelectionClassifier = new
AttributeSelectedClassifier();
//wrap the classifier
```

```
attributeSelectionClassifier.setClassifier(filteredClassifier);
//univariate information gain based feature evaluation
    InfoGainAttributeEval evaluator = new InfoGainAttributeEval();
//rank the features
Ranker ranker = new Ranker();
//set the threshold to be 0, less than that is rejected
ranker.setThreshold(0.0);
attributeSelectionClassifier.setEvaluator(evaluator);
attributeSelectionClassifier.setSearch(ranker);
//build on training data
attributeSelectionClassifier.buildClassifier(trainingData);
// evaluate classifier giving same training data
Evaluation eval = new Evaluation(trainingData);
//evaluate the model on test data
eval.evaluateModel(attributeSelectionClassifier,testingData);
```

The sample output of evaluation is given here:

```
=== Summary ===

Correctly Classified Instances        53           77.9412 %
Incorrectly Classified Instances      15           22.0588 %
Kappa statistic                   0.5115
Mean absolute error               0.3422
Root mean squared error            0.413
Relative absolute error           72.4875 %
Root relative squared error        84.2167 %
Total Number of Instances           68


=== Detailed Accuracy By Class ===


       TP Rate FP Rate Precision Recall F-Measure MCC    ROC Area PRC
Area Class
       0.927  0.444  0.760   0.927  0.835    0.535  0.823  0.875  1
       0.556  0.073  0.833   0.556  0.667    0.535  0.823  0.714  2
Weighted Avg.  0.779  0.297  0.789   0.779  0.768    0.535  0.823  0.812


=== Confusion Matrix ===

 a b <-- classified as
38 3 | a = 1
12 15 | b = 2
```

Weka experimenter and model selection

As explained in the *Model evaluation metrics* section, to select models, we need to validate which one will work well on unseen datasets. Cross-validation must be done on the training set and the performance metric of choice needs to be analyzed using standard statistical testing metrics. Here we show an example using the same training data, 10-fold cross validation, performing 30 experiments on two models, and comparison of results using paired-t tests.

One uses Naïve Bayes with preprocessing that includes replacing missing values and performing feature selection by removing any features with a score below 0.0.

Another uses the same preprocessing and AdaBoostM1 with Naïve Bayes.

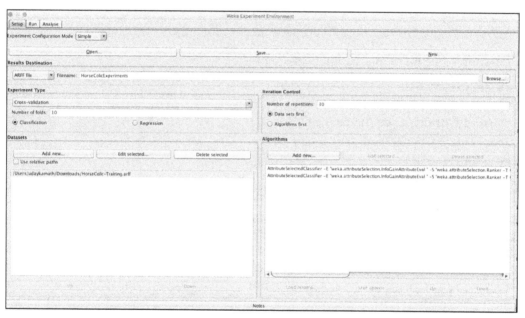

Figure 13: WEKA experimenter showing the process of using cross-validation runs with 30 repetitions with two algorithms.

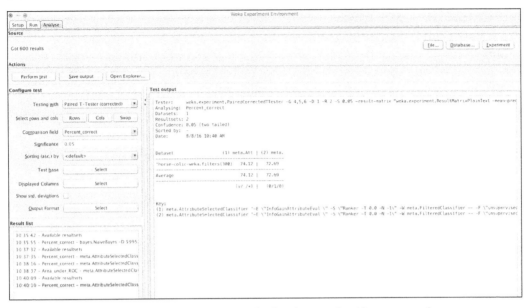

Figure 14: WEKA Experimenter results showing two algorithms compared on
metric of percent correct or accuracy using paired-t test.

RapidMiner experiments

Let's now run some experiments using the Horse-colic dataset in RapidMiner. We
will again follow the methodology presented in the first part of the chapter.

This section is not intended as a tutorial on the RapidMiner tool.
The experimenter is expected to read the excellent documentation
and user guide to familiarize themselves with the use of the tool.
There is a tutorial dedicated to every operator in the software—we
recommend you make use of these tutorials whenever you want to
learn how a particular operator is to be used.

Once we have imported the test and training data files using the data access tools,
we will want to visually explore the dataset to familiarize ourselves with the lay of
the land. Of particular importance is to recognize whether each of the 28 attributes
are continuous (numeric, integer, or real in RapidMiner) or categorical (nominal,
binominal, or polynominal in RapidMiner).

Visualization analysis

From the **Results** panel of the tool, we perform univariate, bivariate, and multivariate analyses of the data. The Statistics tool gives a short summary for each feature—min, max, mean, and standard deviation for continuous types and least, most, and frequency by category for nominal types.

Interesting characteristics of the data begin to show themselves as we get into bivariate analysis. In the Quartile Color Matrix, the color represents the two possible target values. As seen in the box plots, we immediately notice some attributes discriminate between the two target values more clearly than others. Let's examine a few:

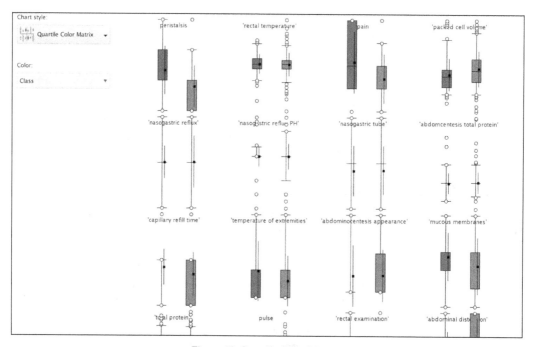

Figure 15: Quartile Color Matrix

Peristalsis: This feature shows a marked difference in distribution when separated by target value. There is almost no overlap in the inter-quartile regions between the two. This points to the discriminating power of this feature with respect to the target.

The plot for Rectal Temperature, on the other hand, shows no perceptible difference in the distributions. This suggests that this feature has low correlation with the target. A similar inference may be drawn from the feature Pulse. We expect these features to rank fairly low when we evaluate the features for their discriminating power with respect to the target.

Lastly, the plot for Pain has a very different characteristic. It is also discriminating of the target, but in a very different way than Peristalsis. In the case of Pain, the variance in data for Class 2 is much larger than Class 1. Abdominal Distension also has markedly dissimilar variance across the classes, except with the larger variance in Class 2 compared to Class 1.

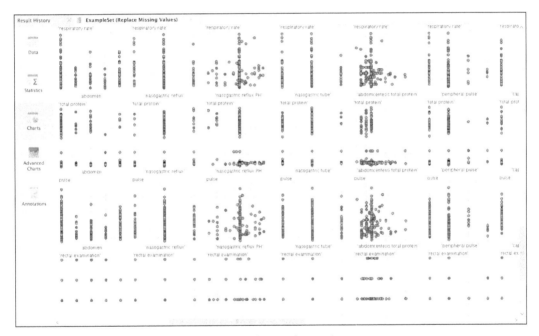

Figure 16: Scatter plot matrix

An important part of exploring the data is understanding how different attributes correlate with each other and with the target. Here we consider pairs of features and see if the occurrence of values *in combination* tells us something about the target. In these plots, the color of the data points is the target.

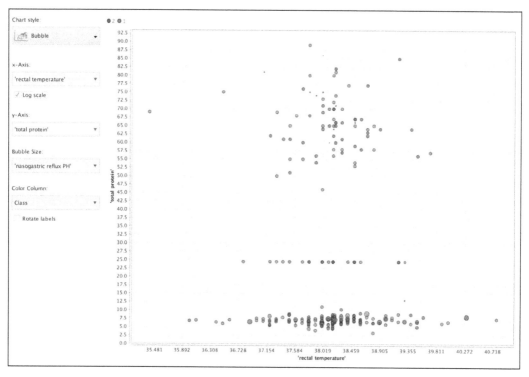

Figure 17: Bubble chart

In the bubble chart we can visualize four features at once by using the graphing tools to specify the *x* and *y* axes as well as a third dimension expressed as the size of bubble representing the feature. The target class is denoted by the color.

At the low end of total protein, we see higher pH values in the mid-range of rectal temperature values. In this cluster, high pH values appear to show a stronger correlation to lesions that were surgical. Another cluster with wider variance in total protein is also found for values of total protein greater than 50. The variance in pH is also low in this cluster.

Feature selection

Having gained some insight into the data, we are ready to use some of the techniques presented in the theory that evaluate feature relevance.

Here we use two techniques: one that calculates the weights for features based on Chi-squared statistics with respect to the target attribute and the other based on the Gini Impurity Index. The results are shown in the table. Note that as we inferred while doing analysis of the features via visualization, both Pulse and Rectal Temperature prove to have low relevance as shown by both techniques.

Chi-squared		Gini index	
Attribute	**Weight**	**Attribute**	**Weight**
Pain	54.20626	Pain	0.083594
Abdomen	53.93882	Abdomen	0.083182
Peristalsis	38.73474	Peristalsis	0.059735
AbdominalDistension	35.11441	AbdominalDistension	0.054152
PeripheralPulse	23.65301	PeripheralPulse	0.036476
AbdominocentesisAppearance	20.00392	AbdominocentesisAppearance	0.030849
TemperatureOfExtremeties	17.07852	TemperatureOfExtremeties	0.026338
MucousMembranes	15.0938	MucousMembranes	0.023277
NasogastricReflux	14.95926	NasogastricReflux	0.023069
PackedCellVolume	13.5733	PackedCellVolume	0.020932
RectalExamination-Feces	11.88078	RectalExamination-Feces	0.018322
CapillaryRefillTime	8.078319	CapillaryRefillTime	0.012458
RespiratoryRate	7.616813	RespiratoryRate	0.011746
TotalProtein	5.616841	TotalProtein	0.008662
NasogastricRefluxPH	2.047565	NasogastricRefluxPH	0.003158
Pulse	1.931511	Pulse	0.002979
Age	0.579216	Age	8.93E-04
NasogastricTube	0.237519		
AbdomcentecisTotalProtein	0.181868		
RectalTemperature	0.139387		

Table 3: Relevant features determined by two different techniques, Chi-squared and Gini index.

Model process flow

In RapidMiner you can define a pipeline of computations using operators with inputs and outputs that can be chained together. The following process represents the flow used to perform the entire set of operations starting with loading the training and test data, handling missing values, weighting features by relevance, filtering out low scoring features, training an ensemble model that uses Bagging with Random Forest as the algorithm, and finally applying the learned model to the test data and outputting the performance metrics. Note that all the preprocessing steps that are applied to the training dataset must also be applied, in the same order, to the test set by means of the Group Models operator:

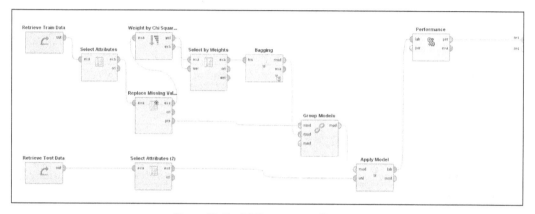

Figure 18: RapidMiner process diagram

Following the top of the process, the training set is ingested in the left-most operator, followed by the exclusion of non-predictors (Hospital Number, CP data) and self-predictors (Lesion 1). This is followed by the operator that replaces missing values with the mean and mode for continuous and categorical attributes, respectively. Next, the Feature Weights operator evaluates weights for each feature based on the Chi-squared statistic, which is followed by a filter that ignores low-weighted features. This pre-processed dataset is then used to train a model using Bagging with a Random Forest classifier.

The preprocessing steps used on the training data are grouped together in the appropriate order via the Group Models operator and applied to the test data in the penultimate step. Finally, the predictions of the target variable on the test examples accompanied by the confusion matrix and other performance metrics are made evaluated and presented in the last step.

Model evaluation metrics

We are now ready to compare the results from the various models. If you have followed along you may find that your results vary from what's presented here—that may be due to the stochastic nature of some learning algorithms, or differences in the values of some hyper-parameters used in the models.

We have considered three different training datasets:

- Original training data with missing values
- Training data transformed with missing values handled
- Training data transformed with missing values handled and with feature selection (Chi-Square) applied to select features that are highly discriminatory.

We have considered three different sets of algorithms on each of the datasets:

- Linear algorithms (Naïve Bayes and Logistic Regression)
- Non-linear algorithms (Decision Tree and KNN)
- Ensemble algorithms (Bagging, Ada Boost, and Random Forest).

Evaluation on Confusion Metrics

Models	TPR	FPR	Precision	Specificity	Accuracy	AUC
Naïve Bayes	68.29%	14.81%	87.50%	85.19%	75.00%	0.836
Logistic Regression	78.05%	14.81%	88.89%	85.19%	80.88%	0.856
Decision Tree	68.29%	33.33%	75.68%	66.67%	67.65%	0.696
k-NN	90.24%	85.19%	61.67%	14.81%	60.29%	0.556
Bagging (GBT)	90.24%	74.07%	64.91%	25.93%	64.71%	0.737
Ada Boost (Naïve Bayes)	63.41%	48.15%	66.67%	51.85%	58.82%	0.613

Table 4: Results on unseen (Test) data for models trained on Horse-colic data with missing values

Models	TPR	FPR	Precision	Specificity	Accuracy	AUC
Naïve Bayes	68.29%	66.67%	60.87%	33.33%	54.41%	0.559
Logistic Regression	78.05%	62.96%	65.31%	37.04%	61.76%	0.689
Decision Tree	97.56%	96.30%	60.61%	3.70%	60.29%	0.812
k-NN	75.61%	48.15%	70.45%	51.85%	66.18%	0.648
Bagging (Random Forest)	97.56%	74.07%	66.67%	25.93%	69.12%	0.892
Bagging (GBT)	82.93%	18.52%	87.18%	81.48%	82.35%	0.870
Ada Boost (Naïve Bayes)	68.29%	7.41%	93.33%	92.59%	77.94%	0.895

Table 5: Results on unseen (Test) data for models trained on Horse-colic data with missing values replaced

Models	TPR	FPR	Precision	Specificity	Accuracy	AUC
Naïve Bayes	75.61%	77.78%	59.62%	29.63%	54.41%	0.551
Logistic Regression	82.93%	62.96%	66.67%	37.04%	64.71%	0.692
Decision Tree	95.12%	92.59%	60.94%	7.41%	60.29%	0.824
k-NN	75.61%	48.15%	70.45%	51.85%	66.18%	0.669
Bagging (Random Forest)	92.68%	33.33%	80.85%	66.67%	82.35%	0.915
Bagging (GBT)	78.05%	22.22%	84.21%	77.78%	77.94%	0.872
Ada Boost (Naïve Bayes)	68.29%	18.52%	84.85%	81.48%	73.53%	0.848

Table 6: Results on unseen (Test) data for models trained on Horse-colic data using features selected by Chi-squared statistic technique

ROC Curves, Lift Curves, and Gain Charts

The performance plots enable us to visually assess the models used in two of the three experiments—without any replacement of missing data, and with using features from Chi-squared weighting after replacing missing data—and to compare them against each other. Pairs of plots display the performance curves of each Linear (Logistic Regression), Non-linear (Decision Tree), and Ensemble (Bagging, using Gradient Boosted Tree) technique we learned about earlier in the chapter, drawn from results of the two experiments.

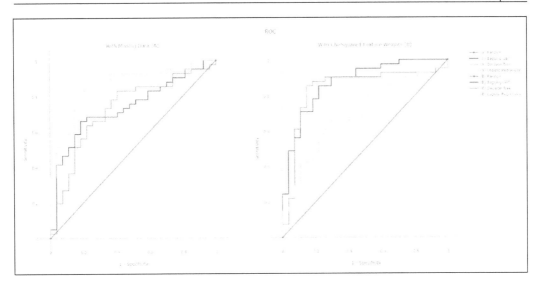

Figure 19: ROC Performance curves for experiment using Missing Data

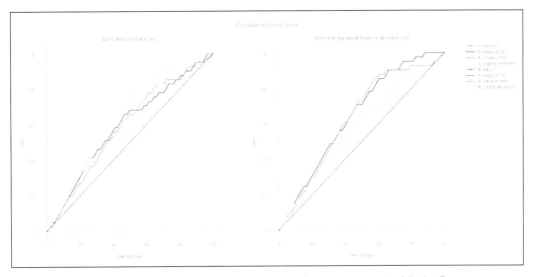

Figure 20: Cumulative Gains performance curves for experiment using Missing Data

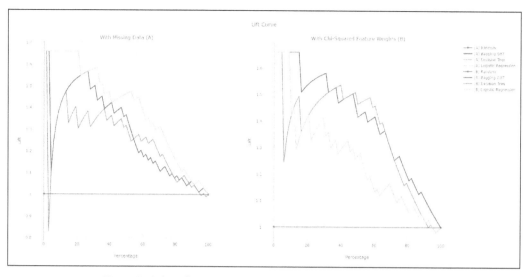

Figure 21: Lift performance curves for experiment using Missing Data

Results, observations, and analysis

The impact of handling missing values is significant. Of the seven classifiers, with the exception of Naïve Bayes and Logistic Regression, all show remarkable improvement when missing values are handled as indicated by various metrics, including AUC, precision, accuracy, and specificity. This tells us that handling missing values that can be "noisy" is an important aspect of data transformation. Naive Bayes has its own internal way of managing missing values and the results from our experiments show that it does a better job of null-handling than our external transformations. But in general, the idea of transforming missing values seems beneficial when you consider all of the classifiers.

As discussed in the section on modeling, some of the algorithms require the right handling of missing values and feature selection to get optimum performance. From the results, we can see that the performance of Decision Trees, for example, improved incrementally from 0.696 with missing data, 0.812 with managed missing data, and for the best performance of 0.824 with missing data handled together with feature selection. Six out of seven classifiers improve the performance in AUC (and in others metrics) when both the steps are performed; comparing *Table 5* and *Table 6* for AUC gives us these quick insights. This demonstrates the importance of doing preprocessing such as missing value handling along with feature selection before performing modeling.

A major conclusion from the results is that the problem is highly non-linear and therefore most non-linear classifiers from the simplest Decision Trees to ensemble Random Forest perform very well. The best performance comes from the meta-learning algorithm Random Forest, with missing values properly handled and the most relevant features used in training. The best linear model performance measured by AUC was 0.856 for Logistic Regression with data as-is (that is, with missing values), whereas Random Forest achieved AUC performance of 0.915 with proper handling of missing data accompanied by feature selection. Generally, as evident from *Table 3*, the non-linear classifiers or meta-learners performed better than linear classifiers by most performance measures.

Handling missing values, which can be thought as "noise", in the appropriate manner improves the performance of AdaBoost by a significant amount. The AUC improves from 0.613 to 0.895 and FPR reduces from 48.15 to 7.41%. This indeed conforms to the expected theoretical behavior for this technique.

Meta-learning techniques, which use concepts of boosting and bagging, are relatively more effective when dealing with real-world data, when compared to other common techniques. This seems to be justified by the results since AdaBoost with Naïve Bayes as base learner trained on data that has undergone proper handling of noise outperforms Naive Bayes in most of the metrics, as shown in *Table 5* and *Table 6*. Random Forest and GBTs also show the best performance along with AdaBoost as compared to base classifiers in *Table 6*, again confirming that the right process and ensemble learning can produce the most optimum results in real-world noisy datasets.

All data, models, and results for both WEKA and RapidMiner process files from this chapter are available at: `https://github.com/mjmlbook/mastering-java-machine-learning/tree/master/Chapter2.`

Summary

Supervised learning is the predominant technique used in machine learning applications. The methodology consists of a series of steps beginning with data exploration, data transformation, and data sampling, through feature reduction, model building, and ultimately, model assessment and comparison. Each step of the process involves some decision making which must answer key questions: How should we impute missing values? What data sampling strategy should we use? What is the most appropriate algorithm given the amount of noise in the dataset and the prescribed goal of interpretability? This chapter demonstrated the application of these processes and techniques to a real-world problem—the classification problem using the UCI Horse Colic dataset.

Whether the problem is one of classification, when the target is a categorical value, or Regression, when it is a real-valued continuous variable, the methodology used for supervised learning is similar. In this chapter, we have used classification for illustration.

The first step is data quality analysis, which includes descriptive statistics of the features, visualization analysis using univariate, and multivariate feature analysis. With the help of various plot types, we can uncover different trends in the data and examine how certain features may or may not correlate with the label values and with each other. Data analysis is followed by data pre-processing, where the techniques include ways to address noise, as in the case of missing data, and outliers, as well as preparing the data for modeling techniques through normalization and discretization.

Following pre-processing, we must suitably split the data into train, validation, and test samples. Different sampling strategies may be used depending on the characteristics of the data and the problem at hand, for example, when the data is skewed or when we have a multi-class classification problem. Depending on data size, cross-validation is a common alternative to creating a separate validation set.

The next step is the culling of irrelevant features. In the filter approach, techniques that use univariate analysis are either entropy-based (Information Gain, Gains Ratio) or based on statistical hypothesis testing (Chi-Squared). With the main multivariate methods, the aim is reduction of redundant features when considered together, or using the ones that correlate most closely with the target label. In the wrapper approach, we use machine learning algorithms to tell us about the more discriminating features. Finally, some learning techniques have feature selection embedded in the algorithm in the form of a regularization term, typically using ridge or lasso techniques. These represent the embedded approach.

Modeling techniques are broadly classified into linear, non-linear, and ensemble methods. Among linear algorithms, the type of features can determine the algorithms to use – Linear Regression (numeric features only), Naïve Bayes (numeric or categorical), and logistic regression (numeric features only, or categorical transformed to numeric) are the work-horses. The outlined advantages and disadvantages of each method must be understood when choosing between them or interpreting the results of learning using these models.

Decision Tree, k-NN, and SVM are non-linear techniques, each with their own strengths and limitations. For example, interpretability is the main advantage of Decision Tree. k-NN is robust in the face of noisy data, but it does poorly with high-dimensional data. SVM suffers from poor interpretability, but shines even when the dataset is limited, and the number of features is large.

With a number of different models collaborating, ensemble methods can leverage the best of all. Bagging and boosting both are techniques that generalize better in the ensemble compared to the base learner they use and are popular in many applications.

Finally, what are the strategies and methods that can be used in evaluating model performance and comparing models to each other? The role of validation sets or cross-validation is essential to the ability to generalize over unseen data. Performance evaluation metrics derived from the confusion matrix are used universally to evaluate classifiers; some are used more commonly in certain domains and disciplines than others. ROC, Gain, and Lift curves are great visual representations of the range of model performance as the classification threshold is varied. When comparing models in pairs, several metrics based on statistical hypothesis testing are used. Wilcoxon and McNemar's are two non-parametric tests; Paired-t test is an example of a parametric method. Likewise, when comparing multiple algorithms, a common non-parametric test that does not make assumptions about the data distribution is Friedman's test. ANOVA, which are parametric tests, assume normal distribution of the metrics and equal variances.

The final sections of the chapter present the process undertaken using the RapidMiner tool to develop and evaluate models generated to classify test data from the UCI Horse-colic dataset. Three experiments are designed to compare and contrast the performance of models under different data pre-processing conditions, namely, without handling missing data, with replacement of missing data using standard techniques, and finally, with feature selection following null replacement. In each experiment we choose multiple linear, non-linear, and ensemble methods. As part of the overall process, we illustrate how the modeling environment is used. We can draw revealing conclusions from the results, which give us insights into the data as well as demonstrating the relative strengths and weakness of the various classes of techniques in different situations. We conclude that the data is highly non-linear and that ensemble learning demonstrates clear advantages over other techniques.

References

1. D. Bell and H. Wang (2000). *A Formalism for Relevance and its Application in Feature Subset Selection. Machine Learning*, 41(2):175–195.

2. J. Doak (1992). *An Evaluation of Feature Selection Methods and their Application to Computer Security.* Technical Report CSE–92–18, Davis, CA: University of California, Department of Computer Science.

3. M. Ben-Bassat (1982). *Use of Distance Measures, Information Measures and Error Bounds in Feature Evaluation.* In P. R. Krishnaiah and L. N. Kanal, editors, Handbook of Statistics, volume 2, pages 773–791, North Holland.

4. Littlestone N, Warmuth M (1994) *The weighted majority algorithm.* Information Computing 108(2):212–261

5. Breiman L., Friedman J.H., Olshen R.A., Stone C.J. (1984) *Classification and Regression Trees*, Wadsforth International Group.

6. B. Ripley(1996), *Pattern recognition and neural networks.* Cambridge University Press, Cambridge.

7. Breiman, L., (1996). *Bagging Predictors, Machine Learning*, 24 123-140.

8. Burges, C. (1998). *A tutorial on support vector machines for pattern recognition. Data Mining and Knowledge Discovery.* 2(2):1-47.

9. Bouckaert, R. (2004), *Naive Bayes Classifiers That Perform Well with Continuous Variables, Lecture Notes in Computer Science*, Volume 3339, Pages 1089 – 1094.

10. Aha D (1997). *Lazy learning*, Kluwer Academic Publishers, Dordrecht

11. Nadeau, C. and Bengio, Y. (2003), *Inference for the generalization error.* In Machine Learning 52:239– 281.

12. Quinlan, J.R. (1993). C4.5: *Programs for machine learning*, Morgan Kaufmann, San Francisco.

13. Vapnik, V. (1995), *The Nature of Statistical Learning Theory.* Springer Verlag.

14. Schapire RE, Singer Y, Singhal A (1998). *Boosting and Rocchio applied to text filtering.* In SIGIR '98: Proceedings of the 21st Annual International Conference on Research and Development in Information Retrieval, pp 215–223

15. Breiman L.(2001). *Random Forests.* Machine Learning, 45 (1), pp 5-32.

16. Nathalie Japkowicz and Mohak Shah (2011). *Evaluating Learning Algorithms: A Classification Perspective.* Cambridge University Press.

17. Hanley, J. & McNeil, B. (1982). *The meaning and use of the area under a receiver operating characteristic (ROC) curve.* Radiology 143, 29–36.

18. Tjen-Sien, L., Wei-Yin, L., Yu-Shan, S. (2000). *A Comparison of Prediction Accuracy, Complexity, and Training Time of Thirty-Three Old and New Classification Algorithms.* Machine Learning 40: 203–228.

19. A. W. Moore and M. S. Lee (1994). *Efficient Algorithms for Minimizing Cross Validation Error.* In Proc. of the 11th Int. Conf. on Machine Learning, pages 190–198, New Brunswick, NJ. Morgan Kaufmann.

20. Nitesh V. Chawla et. al. (2002). *Synthetic Minority Over-sampling Technique.* Journal of Artificial Intelligence Research. 16:321-357.

3
Unsupervised Machine Learning Techniques

In the last chapter, we focused on supervised learning, that is, learning from a training dataset that was labeled. In the real world, obtaining data with labels is often difficult. In many domains, it is virtually impossible to label data either due to the cost of labeling or difficulty in labeling due to the sheer volume or velocity at which data is generated. In those situations, unsupervised learning, in its various forms, offers the right approaches to explore, visualize, and perform descriptive and predictive modeling. In many applications, unsupervised learning is often coupled with supervised learning as a first step to isolate interesting data elements for labeling.

In this chapter, we will focus on various methodologies, techniques, and algorithms that are practical and well-suited for unsupervised learning. We begin by noting the issues that are common between supervised and unsupervised learning when it comes to handling data and transformations. We will then briefly introduce the particular challenges faced in unsupervised learning owing to the lack of "ground truth" and the nature of learning under those conditions.

We will then discuss the techniques of feature analysis and dimensionality reduction applied to unlabeled datasets. This is followed by an introduction to the broad spectrum of clustering methods and discussions on the various algorithms in practical use, just as we did with supervised learning in *Chapter 2, Practical Approach to Real-World Supervised Learning*, showing how each algorithm works, when to use it, and its advantages and limitations. We will conclude the section on clustering by presenting the different cluster evaluation techniques.

Following the treatment of clustering, we will approach the subject of outlier detection. We will contrast various techniques and algorithms that illustrate what makes some objects outliers — also called anomalies — within a given dataset.

The chapter will conclude with clustering and outlier detection experiments, conducted with a real-world dataset and an analysis of the results obtained. In this case study, we will be using ELKI and SMILE Java libraries for the machine learning tasks and will present code and results from the experiments. We hope that this will provide the reader with a sense of the power and ease of use of these tools.

Issues in common with supervised learning

Many of the issues that we discussed related to supervised learning are also common with unsupervised learning. Some of them are listed here:

- **Types of features handled by the algorithm**: Most clustering and outlier algorithms need numeric representation to work effectively. Transforming categorical or ordinal data has to be done carefully

- **Curse of dimensionality**: Having a large number of features results in sparse spaces and affects the performance of clustering algorithms. Some option must be chosen to suitably reduce dimensionality — either feature selection where only a subset of the most relevant features are retained, or feature extraction, which transforms the feature space into a new set of principal variables of a lower dimensional space

- **Scalability in memory and training time**: Many unsupervised learning algorithms cannot scale up to more than a few thousands of instances either due to memory or training time constraints

- **Outliers and noise in data**: Many algorithms are affected by noise in the features, the presence of anomalous data, or missing values. They need to be transformed and handled appropriately

Issues specific to unsupervised learning

The following are some issues that pertain to unsupervised learning techniques:

- **Parameter setting**: Deciding on number of features, usefulness of features, number of clusters, shapes of clusters, and so on, pose enormous challenges to certain unsupervised methods

- **Evaluation methods**: Since unsupervised learning methods are ill-posed due to lack of ground-truth, evaluation of algorithms becomes very subjective.

- **Hard or soft labeling**: Many unsupervised learning problems require giving labels to the data in an exclusive or probabilistic manner. This poses a problem for many algorithms

- **Interpretability of results and models**: Unlike supervised learning, the lack of ground truth and the nature of some algorithms make interpreting the results from both model and labeling even more difficult

Feature analysis and dimensionality reduction

Among the first tools to master are the different feature analysis and dimensionality reduction techniques. As in supervised learning, the need for reducing dimensionality arises from numerous reasons similar to those discussed earlier for feature selection and reduction.

A smaller number of discriminating dimensions makes visualization of data and clusters much easier. In many applications, unsupervised dimensionality reduction techniques are used for compression, which can then be used for transmission or storage of data. This is particularly useful when the larger data has an overhead. Moreover, applying dimensionality reduction techniques can improve the scalability in terms of memory and computation speeds of many algorithms.

Notation

We will use similar notation to what was used in the chapter on supervised learning. The examples are in d dimensions and are represented as vector:

$$\mathbf{x} = (x_1, x_2, \ldots x_d)^T$$

The entire dataset containing n examples can be represented as an observation matrix:

$$\mathbf{X} = \left\{ x_{ij} : 1 \le i \le d, 1 \le j \le n \right\}$$

The idea of dimensionality reduction is to find k $\le d$ features either by transformation of the input features, projecting or combining them such that the lower dimension k captures or preserves interesting properties of the original dataset.

Linear methods

Linear dimensionality methods are some of the oldest statistical techniques to reduce features or transform the data into lower dimensions, preserving interesting discriminating properties.

Mathematically, with linear methods we are performing a transformation, such that a new data element is created using a linear transformation of the original data element:

$$s_i = w_{i,1} x_1 + w_{i2} x_2 + \cdots w_{id} x_d \; for \; i = 1, 2, ..k$$

$$s = \mathbf{W}x$$

Here, $\mathbf{W}_{k \times d}$ is the linear transformation matrix. The variables **s** are also referred to as latent or hidden variables.

In this topic, we will discuss the two most practical and often-used methodologies. We will list some variants of these techniques so that the reader can use the tools to experiment with them. The main assumption here — which often forms the limitation — is the linear relationships between the transformations.

Principal component analysis (PCA)

PCA is a widely-used technique for dimensionality reduction (*References* [1]). The original coordinate system is rotated to a new coordinate system that exploits the directions of maximum variance in the data, resulting in uncorrelated variables in a lower-dimensional subspace that were correlated in the original feature space. PCA is sensitive to the scaling of the features.

Inputs and outputs

PCA is generally effective on numeric datasets. Many tools provide the categorical-to-continuous transformations for the nominal features, but this affects the performance. The number of principal components, or k, is also an input provided by the user.

How does it work?

PCA, in its most basic form, tries to find projections of data onto new axes, which are known as **principal components**. Principal components are projections that capture maximum variance directions from the original space. In simple words, PCA finds the first principal component through rotation of the original axes of the data in the direction of maximum variance. The technique finds the next principal component by again determining the next best axis, orthogonal to the first axis, by seeking the second highest variance and so on until most variances are captured. Generally, most tools give either a choice of number of principal components or the option to keep finding components until some percentage, for example, 99%, of variance in the original dataset is captured.

Mathematically, the objective of finding maximum variance can be written as

$$= \max_{\|w\|=1} \left\| \mathbf{W}^\mathbf{T} \mathbf{X} \right\|^2$$

$$= \text{largest eigenvalue of } \mathbf{X}^\mathbf{T} \mathbf{X} \left(\text{covariance matrix} \right)$$

$$\lambda \mathbf{v} = \mathbf{C} \mathbf{v} \text{ is the eigendecomposition}$$

This is equivalent to:

$$\mathbf{X}_{\mathbf{d \times n}} = \mathbf{W}_{\mathbf{d \times d}} \times \mathbf{S}_{\mathbf{d \times n}}$$

Here, **W** is the principal components and **S** is the new transformation of the input data. Generally, eigenvalue decomposition or singular value decomposition is used in the computation part.

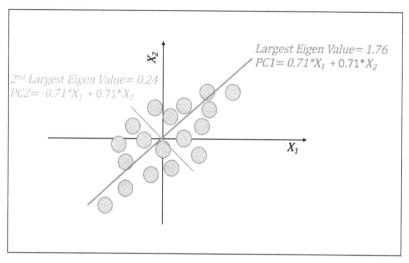

Figure 1: Principal Component Analysis

Advantages and limitations

- One of the advantages of PCA is that it is optimal in that it minimizes the reconstruction error of the data.

- PCA assumes normal distribution.

- The computation of variance-covariance matrix can become intensive for large datasets with high-dimensions. Alternatively, **Singular Value Decomposition (SVD)** can be used as it works iteratively and there is no need for an explicit covariance matrix.

- PCA has issues when there is noise in the data.

- PCA fails when the data lies in the complex manifold, a topic that we will discuss in the non-linear dimensionality reduction section.

- PCA assumes a correlation between the features and in the absence of those correlations, it is unable to do any transformations; instead, it simply ranks them.

- By transforming the original feature space into a new set of variables, PCA causes a loss in interpretability of the data.

- There are many other variants of PCA that are popular and overcome some of the biases and assumptions of PCA.

Independent Component Analysis (ICA) assumes that there are mixtures of non-Gaussians from the source and, using the generative technique, tries to find the decompositions of original data in the smaller mixtures or components (*References* [2]). The key difference between PCA and ICA is that PCA creates components that are uncorrelated, while ICA creates components that are independent.

Mathematically, it assumes $X \in \mathbb{R}^{d \times n}$ as a mixture of independent sources $\in \mathbb{R}^{k \times n}$, such that each data element $y = [y^1, y^2, \dots, y^k]^T$ and independence is implied by $p(y) \approx \prod_{j=1}^{k} p(y^j)$:

Probabilistic Principal Component Analysis (PPCA) is based on finding the components using mixture models and maximum likelihood formulations using **Expectation Maximization (EM)** (*References* [3]). It overcomes the issues of missing data and outlier impacts that PCA faces.

Random projections (RP)

When data is separable by a large margin—even if it is high-dimensional data—one can randomly project the data down to a low-dimensional space without impacting separability and achieve good generalization with a relatively small amount of data. Random Projections use this technique and the details are described here (*References* [4]).

Inputs and outputs

Random projections work with both numeric and categorical features, but categorical features are transformed into binary. Outputs are lower dimensional representations of the input data elements. The number of dimensions to project, k, is part of user-defined input.

How does it work?

This technique uses random projection matrices to project the input data into a lower dimensional space. The original data $\mathbf{X} \in R^d$ is transformed to the lower dimension space $\mathbf{S} \in \mathcal{R}^k$ where $k << p$ using:

$$\mathbf{S} = \mathbf{RX}$$

Here columns in the $k \times d$ matrix $\mathbf{R}$ are i.i.d zero mean normal variables and are scaled to unit length. There are variants of how the random matrix $\mathbf{R}$ is constructed using probabilistic sampling. Computational complexity of RP is $O(knd)$, which scales much better than PCA. In many practical datasets, it has been shown that RP gives results comparable to PCA and can scale to large dimensions and datasets.

Advantages and limitations

- It scales to very large values of dataset size and dimensionalities. In text and image learning problems, with large dimensions, this technique has been successfully used as the preprocessing technique.

- Sometimes a large information loss can occur while using RP.

Multidimensional Scaling (MDS)

There are many forms of MDS—classical, metric, and non-metric. The main idea of MDS is to preserve the pairwise similarity/distance values. It generally involves transforming the high dimensional data into two or three dimensions (*References* [5]).

Inputs and outputs

MDS can work with both numeric and categorical data based on the user-selected distance function. The number of dimensions to transform to, k, is a user-defined input.

How does it work?

Given n data elements, an $n \times n$ affinity or distance matrix is computed. There are choices of using distances such as Euclidean, Mahalanobis, or similarity concepts such as cosine similarity, Jaccard coefficients, and so on. MDS in its very basic form tries to find a mapping of the distance matrix in a lower dimensional space where the Euclidean distance between the transformed points is similar to the affinity matrix.

Mathematically:

$$\min_{Y} \sum_{i=1}^{n} \sum_{j=1}^{n} \left(d_{ij}^{X} - d_{ij}^{Y} \right)^2$$

Here $d_{ij}^{X} = \left\| x_i - x_j \right\|$ input space and $d_{ij}^{Y} = \left\| y_i - y_j \right\|$ mapped space.

If the input affinity space is transformed using kernels then the MDS becomes a non-linear method for dimensionality reduction. Classical MDS is equivalent to PCA when the distances between the points in input space is Euclidean distance.

Advantages and limitations

- The key disadvantage is the subjective choice of the lower dimension needed to interpret the high dimensional data, normally restricted to two or three for humans. Some data may not map effectively in this lower dimensional space.

- The advantage is you can perform linear and non-linear mapping to the lowest dimensions using the framework.

Nonlinear methods

In general, nonlinear dimensionality reduction involves either performing nonlinear transformations to the computations in linear methods such as KPCA or finding nonlinear relationships in the lower dimension as in manifold learning. In some domains and datasets, the structure of the data in lower dimensions is nonlinear – and that is where techniques such as KPCA are effective – while in some domains the data does not unfold in lower dimensions and you need manifold learning.

Kernel Principal Component Analysis (KPCA)

Kernel PCA uses the Kernel trick described in *Chapter 2, Practical Approach to Real-World Supervised Learning*, with the PCA algorithm for transforming the data in a high-dimensional space to find effective mapping (*References* [6]).

Inputs and outputs

Similar to PCA with addition of choice of kernel and kernel parameters. For example, if **Radial Basis Function** (**RBF**) or Gaussian Kernel is chosen, then the kernel, along with the gamma parameter, becomes user-selected values.

How does it work?

In the same way as **Support Vector Machines** (**SVM**) was discussed in the previous chapter, KPCA transforms the input space to high dimensional feature space using the "kernel trick". The entire PCA machinery of finding maximum variance is then carried out in the transformed space.

As in PCA:

$$= \text{largest eigenvalue of } \mathbf{X}^T\mathbf{X} \left(\text{covariance matrix}\right)$$

$$C = \frac{1}{n}\sum_{i=1}^{n} x_i x_i^{T}$$

Instead of linear covariance matrix, a nonlinear transformation is applied to the input space using kernel methods by constructing the $N \times N$ matrix, in place of doing the actual transformations using $\phi(x)$.

$$k(x,y) = ((\phi(x),\phi(y)) = \phi(x)^T \phi(y)$$

Since the kernel transformation doesn't actually transform the features into explicit feature space, the principal components found can be interpreted as projections of data onto the components. In the following figure, a binary nonlinear dataset, generated using the scikit-learn example on circles (*References* [27]), demonstrates the linear separation after KPCA using the RBF kernel and returning to almost similar input space by the inverse transform:

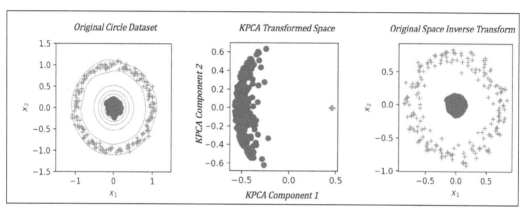

Figure 2: KPCA on Circle Dataset and Inverse Transform.

Advantages and limitations

- KPCA overcomes the nonlinear mapping presented by PCA.

- KPCA has similar issues with outlier, noisy, and missing values to standard PCA. There are robust methods and variations to overcome this.

- KPCA has scalability issues in space due to an increase in the kernel matrix, which can become a bottleneck in large datasets with high dimensions. SVD can be used in these situations, as an alternative.

Manifold learning

When high dimensional data is embedded in lower dimensions that are nonlinear, but have complex structure, manifold learning is very effective.

Inputs and outputs

Manifold learning algorithms require two user-provided parameters: k, representing the number of neighbors for the initial search, and n, the number of manifold coordinates.

How does it work?

As seen in the following figure, the three-dimensional S-Curve, plotted using the scikit-learn utility (*References* [27]), is represented in 2D PCA and in 2D manifold using LLE. It is interesting to observe how the blue, green, and red dots are mixed up in the PCA representation while the manifold learning representation using LLE cleanly separates the colors. It can also be observed that the rank ordering of Euclidean distances is not maintained in the manifold representation:

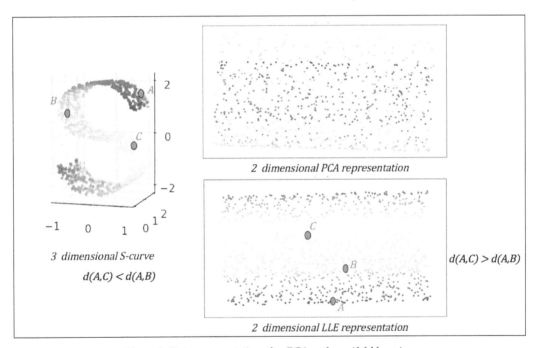

Figure 3: Data representation after PCA and manifold learning

To preserve the structure, the geodesic distance is preserved instead of the Euclidean distance. The general approach is to build a graph structure such as an adjacency matrix, and then compute geodesic distance using different assumptions. In the Isomap Algorithm, the global pairwise distances are preserved (*References* [7]). In the **Local Linear Embedding (LLE)** Algorithm, the mapping is done to take care of local neighborhood, that is, nearby points map to nearby points in the transformation (*References* [9]). Laplacian Eigenmaps is similar to LLE, except it tries to maintain the "locality" instead of "local linearity" in LLE by using graph Laplacian (*References* [8]).

Advantages and limitations

- Isomap is non-parametric; it preserves the global structure, and has no local optimum, but is hampered by speed.

- LLE and Laplacian Eigenmaps are non-parametric, have no local optima, are fast, but don't preserve global structure.

Clustering

Clustering algorithms can be categorized in different ways based on the techniques, the outputs, the process, and other considerations. In this topic, we will present some of the most widely used clustering algorithms.

Clustering algorithms

There is a rich set of clustering techniques in use today for a wide variety of applications. This section presents some of them, explaining how they work, what kind of data they can be used with, and what their advantages and drawbacks are. These include algorithms that are prototype-based, density-based, probabilistic partition-based, hierarchy-based, graph-theory-based, and those based on neural networks.

k-Means

k-means is a centroid- or prototype-based iterative algorithm that employs partitioning and relocation methods (*References* [10]). k-means finds clusters of spherical shape depending on the distance metric used, as in the case of Euclidean distance.

Inputs and outputs

k-means can handle mostly numeric features. Many tools provide categorical to numeric transformations, but having a large number of categoricals in the computation can lead to non-optimal clusters. User-defined k, the number of clusters to be found, and the distance metric to use for computing closeness are two basic inputs. k-means generates clusters, association of data to each cluster, and centroids of clusters as the output.

How does it work?

The most common variant known as Lloyd's algorithm initializes *k* centroids for the given dataset by picking data elements randomly from the set. It assigns each data element to the centroid it is closest to, using some distance metric such as Euclidean distance. It then computes the mean of the data points for each cluster to form the new centroid and the process is repeated until either the maximum number of iterations is reached or there is no change in the centroids.

Mathematically, each step of the clustering can be seen as an optimization step where the equation to optimize is given by:

$$arg_c min \sum_{i=1}^{k} \sum_{x \in c_i} (x - \mu_i) = arg_c min \sum_{i=1}^{k} \sum_{x \in c_i} \|x - \mu_i\|_2^2$$

Here, c_i is all points belong to cluster *i*. The problem of minimizing is classified as NP-hard and hence k-Means has a tendency to get stuck in local optimum.

Advantages and limitations

*   The choice of the number of clusters, *k*, is difficult to pick, but normally search techniques such as varying *k* for different values and measuring metrics such as sum of square errors can be used to find a good threshold. For smaller datasets, hierarchical k-Means can be tried.

*   k-means can converge faster than most algorithms for smaller values of *k* and can find effective global clusters.

*   k-means convergence can be affected by initialization of the centroids and hence there are many variants to perform random restarts with different seeds and so on.

*   k-means can perform badly when there are outliers and noisy data points. Using robust techniques such as medians instead of means, k-Medoids, overcomes this to a certain extent.

*   k-means does not find effective clusters when they are of arbitrary shapes or have different densities.

DBSCAN

Density-based spatial clustering of applications with noise (DBSCAN) is a density-based partitioning algorithm. It separates dense region in the space from sparse regions (*References* [14]).

Inputs and outputs

Only numeric features are used in DBSCAN. The user-defined parameters are *MinPts* and the neighborhood factor given by ϵ.

How does it work?

The algorithm first finds the ϵ-neighborhood of every point p, given by $N_\epsilon : \{q \mid d(p,q) \leq \epsilon\}$. A *high density* region is identified as a region where the number of points in a ϵ-neighborhood is greater than or equal to the given *MinPts*; the point such a ϵ-neighborhood is defined around is called a *core points*. Points within the ϵ-neighborhood of a *core point* are said to be *directly reachable*. All *core points* that can in effect be reached by hopping from one directly reachable core point to another point *directly reachable* from the second point, and so on, are considered to be in the same cluster. Further, any point that has fewer than *MinPts* in its ϵ-neighborhood, but is directly reachable from a core point, belongs to the same cluster as the core point. These points at the edge of a cluster are called *border points*. A *noise point* is any point that is neither a core point nor a border point.

Advantages and limitations

- The DBSCAN algorithm does not require the number of clusters to be specified and can find it automatically from the data.
- DBSCAN can find clusters of various shapes and sizes.
- DBSCAN has in-built robustness to noise and can find outliers from the datasets.
- DBSCAN is not completely deterministic in its identification of the points and its categorization into border or core depends on the order of data processed.
- Distance metrics selected such as Euclidean distance can often affect performance due to the curse of dimensionality.
- When there are clusters with large variations in the densities, the static choice of *{MinPts, ϵ}* can pose a big limitation.

Mean shift

Mean shift is a very effective clustering algorithm in many image, video, and motion detection based datasets (*References* [11]).

Inputs and outputs

Only numeric features are accepted as data input in the mean shift algorithm. The choice of kernel and the bandwidth of the kernel are user-driven choices that affect the performance. Mean shift generates modes of data points and clusters data around the modes.

How does it work?

Mean shift is based on the statistical concept of **kernel density estimation (KDE)**, which is a probabilistic method to estimate the underlying data distribution from the sample.

A kernel density estimate for kernel $K(\mathbf{x})$ of given bandwidth h is given by:

$$f(\mathbf{x}) = \frac{1}{nh^d} \sum_{i=1}^{n} K\left(\frac{\mathbf{x} - \mathbf{x}_i}{h}\right)$$

For n points with dimensionality d. The mean shift algorithm works by moving each data point in the direction of local increasing density. To estimate this direction, gradient is applied to the KDE and the gradient takes the form of:

$$\nabla f(\mathbf{x}) = \frac{2}{nh^{d+2}} \left(\sum_{i=1}^{n} g\left(\left\|\frac{\mathbf{x} - \mathbf{x}_1}{h}\right\|\right)\right) m(\mathbf{x})$$

$$m(\mathbf{x}) = \left[\frac{\sum_{i=1}^{n} \mathbf{x}_i g\left(\left\|\frac{\mathbf{x} - \mathbf{x}_1}{h}\right\|\right)}{\sum_{i=1}^{n} g\left(\left\|\frac{\mathbf{x} - \mathbf{x}_1}{h}\right\|\right)} \right]$$

Here g(**x**)= –K'(**x**) is the derivative of the kernel. The vector, m(**x**), is called the mean shift vector and it is used to move the points in the direction

$$\mathbf{x}^{(t+1)} = \mathbf{x}^t + m(\mathbf{x})$$

Also, it is guaranteed to converge when the gradient of the density function is zero. Points that end up in a similar location are marked as clusters belonging to the same region.

Advantages and limitations

- Mean shift is non-parametric and makes no underlying assumption on the data distribution.

- It can find non-complex clusters of varying shapes and sizes.

- There is no need to explicitly give the number of clusters; the choice of the bandwidth parameter, which is used in estimation, implicitly controls the clusters.

- Mean shift has no local optima for a given bandwidth parameter and hence it is deterministic.

- Mean shift is robust to outliers and noisy points because of KDE.

- The mean shift algorithm is computationally slow and does not scale well with large datasets.

- Bandwidth selection should be done judiciously; otherwise it can result in merged modes, or the appearance of extra, shallow modes.

Expectation maximization (EM) or Gaussian mixture modeling (GMM)

GMM or EM is a probabilistic partition-based method that partitions data into k clusters using probability distribution-based techniques (*References* [13]).

Input and output

Only numeric features are allowed in EM/GMM. The model parameter is the number of mixture components, given by k.

How does it work?

GMM is a generative method that assumes that there are k Gaussian components, each Gaussian component has a mean μ_i and covariance Σ_i. The following expression represents the probability of the dataset given the k Gaussian components:

$$= p\left(data \big| \mu_1, \mu_2, \dots \mu_k, \right)$$

$$= \prod_{i=1}^{n} p\left(\mathbf{x}_i \big| \mu_1, \mu_2, \dots \mu_k, \right)$$

$$= \prod_{i=1}^{n} \sum_{j=1}^{k} p\left(\mathbf{x}_i \left| \mathbf{\mu}_1, \mathbf{\mu}_2, \ldots \mathbf{\mu}_k \right.\right) P\left(w_j\right)$$

The two-step task of finding the means {μ_1, μ_2, ...μ_k} for each of the k Gaussian components such that the data points assigned to each maximizes the probability of that component is done using the **Expectation Maximization (EM)** process.

The iterative process can be defined into an E-step, that computes the *expected* cluster for all data points for the cluster, in an iteration i:

$$P\left(w_i \mid x_k, \lambda_t\right) = \frac{p\left(x_k \mid w_i, \lambda_t\right) P\left(w_i \mid \lambda_t\right)}{p\left(x_k \mid \lambda_t\right)}$$

The M-step maximizes to compute μ_{t+1} given the data points belonging to the cluster:

$$\mu_{t+1} = \frac{\sum_k P\left(w_i \mid x_k, \lambda_t\right) x_k}{\sum_k P\left(w_i \mid x_k, \lambda_t\right)}$$

The EM process can result in GMM convergence into local optimum.

Advantages and limitations

- Works very well with any features; for categorical data, discrete probability is calculated, while for numeric a continuous probability function is estimated.
- It has computational scalability problems. It can result in local optimum.
- The value of k Gaussians has to be given *apriori*, similar to k-Means.

Hierarchical clustering

Hierarchical clustering is a connectivity-based method of clustering that is widely used to analyze and explore the data more than it is used as a clustering technique (*References* [12]). The idea is to iteratively build binary trees either from top or bottom, such that similar points are grouped together. Each level of the tree provides interesting summarization of the data.

Input and output

Hierarchical clustering generally works on similarity-based transformations and so both categorical and continuous data are accepted. Hierarchical clustering only needs the similarity or distance metric to compute similarity and does not need the number of clusters like in k-means or GMM.

How does it work?

There are many variants of hierarchical clustering, but we will discuss agglomerative clustering. Agglomerative clustering works by first putting all the data elements in their own groups. It then iteratively merges the groups based on the similarity metric used until there is a single group. Each level of the tree or groupings provides unique segmentation of the data and it is up to the analyst to choose the right level that fits the problem domain. Agglomerative clustering is normally visualized using a dendrogram plot, which shows merging of data points at similarity. The popular choices of similarity methods used are:

- **Single linkage**: Similarity is the minimum distance between the groups of points:

$$d_{SL}(A,B) = \min_{i \in A, j \in B} d_{ij}$$

- **Complete linkage**: Similarity is the maximum distance between the groups of points:

$$d_{CL}(A,B) = \max_{i \in A, j \in B} d_{ij}$$

- **Average linkage**: Average similarity between the groups of points:

$$d_{AL}(A,B) = \frac{1}{N_A N_B} \sum_{i \in A} \sum_{i \in B} d_{ij}$$

Advantages and limitations

- Hierarchical clustering imposes a hierarchical structure on the data even when there may not be such a structure present.
- The choice of similarity metrics can result in a vastly different set of merges and dendrogram plots, so it has a large dependency on user input.
- Hierarchical clustering suffers from scalability with increased data points. Based on the distance metrics used, it can be sensitive to noise and outliers.

Self-organizing maps (SOM)

SOM is a neural network based method that can be viewed as dimensionality reduction, manifold learning, or clustering technique (*References* [17]). Neurobiological studies show that our brains map different functions to different areas, known as topographic maps, which form the basis of this technique.

Inputs and outputs

Only numeric features are used in SOM. Model parameters consists of distance function, (generally Euclidean distance is used) and the lattice parameters in terms of width and height or number of cells in the lattice.

How does it work?

SOM, also known as Kohonen networks, can be thought of as a two-layer neural network where each output layer is a two-dimensional lattice, arranged in rows and columns and each neuron is fully connected to the input layer.

Like neural networks, the weights are initially generated using random values. The process has three distinct training phases:

- **Competitive phase**: Neurons in this phase compete based on the discriminant values, generally based on distance between neuron weight and input vector; such that the minimal distance between the two decides which neuron the input gets assigned to. Using Euclidean distance, the distance between an input x_i and neuron in the lattice position (j, i) is given by w_{ji}:

$$d_j(\mathbf{x}) = \sum_{i=1}^{d} \left(x_i - w_{ji} \right)^2$$

- **Cooperation phase**: In this phase, the winning neurons find the best spatial location in the topological neighborhood. The topological neighborhood for the winning neuron $I(\mathbf{x})$ for a given neuron (j, i), at a distance S_{ij}, neighborhood of size σ, is defined by:

$$T_{j,l(x)} = \exp\left({-S_{ij}^{2}} \Big/ {2\sigma(t)^2} \right)$$

The neighborhood size is defined in the way that it decreases with time using some well-known decay functions such as an exponential, function defined as follows:

$$\sigma(t) = \sigma_0 \exp\left(-t/\tau_0\right)$$

- **Adaptive phase**: In this phase, the weights of the winning neuron and its neighborhood neurons are updated. The update to weights is generally done using:

$$\Delta w_{ji} = \eta(t) \cdot T_{j,l(x)}(t) \cdot (x_i - w_{ji})$$

Here, the learning rate *n(t)* is again defined as exponential decay like the neighborhood size.

SOM Visualization using Unified Distance Matrix (U-Matrix) creates a single metric of average distance between the weights of the neuron and its neighbors, which then can be visualized in different color intensities. This helps to identify *similar* neurons in the neighborhood.

Advantages and limitations

- The biggest advantage of SOM is that it is easy to understand and clustering of the data in two dimensions with U-matrix visualization enables understanding the patterns very effectively.

- Choice of similarity/distance function makes vast difference in clusters and must be carefully chosen by the user.

- SOM's computational complexity makes it impossible to use on datasets greater than few thousands in size.

Spectral clustering

Spectral clustering is a partition-based clustering technique using graph theory as its basis (*References* [15]). It converts the dataset into a connected graph and does graph partitioning to find the clusters. This is a popular method in image processing, motion detection, and some unstructured data-based domains.

Inputs and outputs

Only numeric features are used in spectral clustering. Model parameters such as the choice of kernel, the kernel parameters, the number of eigenvalues to select, and partitioning algorithms such as k-Means must be correctly defined for optimum performance.

How does it work?

The following steps describe how the technique is used in practice:

1. Given the data points, an affinity (or adjacency) matrix is computed using a smooth kernel function such as the Gaussian kernel:

$$A_{ij} \approx \exp\left(-\alpha \left\| \mathbf{x}_i - \mathbf{x}_j \right\|^2 \right)$$

   For the points that are closer, $A_{ij} \to 0$ and for points further away, $A_{ij} \to 1$

2. The next step is to compute the graph Laplacian matrix using various methods of normalizations. All Laplacian matrix methods use the diagonal degree matrix D, which measures degree at each node in the graph:

$$D_{ij} = \sum_{j}^{n} a_{ij}$$

   A simple Laplacian matrix is $L = D$ *(degree matrix)* $- A$ *(affinity matrix)*.

3. Compute the first k eigenvalues from the eigenvalue problem or the generalized eigenvalue problem.

4. Use a partition algorithm such as k-Means to further separate clusters in the k-dimensional subspace.

Advantages and limitations

- Spectral clustering works very well when the cluster shape or size is irregular and non-convex. Spectral clustering has too many parameter choices and tuning to get good results is quite an involved task.

- Spectral clustering has been shown, theoretically, to be more stable in the presence of noisy data. Spectral clustering has good performance when the clusters are not well separated.

Affinity propagation

Affinity propagation can be viewed as an extension of K-medoids method for its similarity with picking exemplars from the data (*References* [16]). Affinity propagation uses graphs with distance or the similarity matrix and picks all examples in the training data as exemplars. Iterative message passing as *affinities* between data points automatically detects clusters, the exemplars, and even the number of clusters.

Inputs and outputs

Typically, other than maximum number of iterations, which is common to most algorithms, no input parameters are required.

How does it work?

Two kinds of messages are exchanged between the data points that we will explain first:

- Responsibility *r(i,k)*: This is a message from the data point to the candidate exemplar. This gives a metric of how well the exemplar is suited for that data point compared to other exemplars. The rules for updating the responsibility are as follows:

$$r(i,k) \leftarrow s(i,k) - \max_{k \neq k'}\left(a(i,k') + s(i,k')\right) \text{ where}$$

s(i, k) = similarity between two data points *i* and *k*.

a(i, k) = availability of exemplar *k* for *i*.

- Availability *a(i,k)*: This is a message from the candidate exemplar to a data point. This gives a metric indicating how good of a support the exemplar can be to the data point, considering other data points in the calculations. This can be viewed as soft cluster assignment. The rule for updating the availability is as follows:

$$a(i,k) \leftarrow \min\left\{0, r(k,k) + \sum_{i' \notin \{i,k\}} \max\left(0, r(i',k)\right)\right\}$$

$$a(i,k) \leftarrow \sum_{i' \notin k} \max\left(0, r(i',k)\right)$$

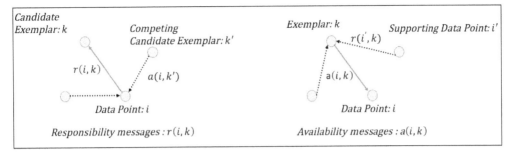

Figure 4: Message types used in Affinity Propagation

The algorithm can be summed up as follows:

1. Initialize $r(i,j) = 0, a(i,j) = 0 \, \forall i, j$
2. For all increments i to n:

    1. $r(i,k) \leftarrow s(i,k) - \max_{k \neq k}\left(a(i,k') + s(i,k')\right)$
    2. $a(i,k) \leftarrow \min\left\{0, r(k,k) + \sum_{i' \notin \{i,k\}} \max\left(0, r(i',k)\right)\right\}$
    3. $(i,k) \leftarrow \sum_{i' \notin k} \max\left(0, r(i',k)\right)$

3. End.
4. For all $\mathbf{x}_i$ such that $(r(i,i) + a(i,i) > 0)$

    1. $\mathbf{x}_i$ is exemplar.
    2. All non-exemplars $\mathbf{x}_j$ are assigned to the closest exemplar using the similarity measure $s(i, j)$.

5. End.

Advantages and limitations

*   Affinity propagation is a deterministic algorithm. Both k-means or K-medoids are sensitive to the selection of initial points, which is overcome by considering every point as an exemplar.
*   The number of clusters doesn't have to be specified and is automatically determined through the process.
*   It works in non-metric spaces and doesn't require distances/similarity to even have constraining properties such as triangle inequality or symmetry. This makes the algorithm usable on a wide variety of datasets with categorical and text data and so on:
*   The algorithm can be parallelized easily due to its update methods and it has fast training time.

Clustering validation and evaluation

Clustering validation and evaluation is one of the most important mechanisms to determine the usefulness of the algorithms (*References* [18]). These topics can be broadly classified into two categories:

- **Internal evaluation measures**: In this the measures uses some form of clustering quality from the data themselves, without any access to the ground truth.

- **External evaluation measures**: In this the measures use some external information such as known ground truth or class labels.

Internal evaluation measures

Internal evaluation uses only the clusters and data information to gather metrics about how good the clustering results are. The applications may have some influence over the choice of the measures. Some algorithms are biased towards particular evaluation metrics. So care must be taken in choosing the right metrics, algorithms, and parameters based on these considerations. Internal evaluation measures are based on different qualities, as mentioned here:

- **Compactness**: Variance in the clusters measured using different strategies is used to give compactness values; the lower the variance, the more compact the cluster.

- **Separation**: How well are the clusters separated from each other?

Notation

Here's a compact explanation of the notation used in what follows: dataset with all data elements $=D$, number of data elements $=n$, dimensions or features of each data element $=d$, center of entire data $D = c$, number of clusters $= NC$, i^{th} cluster $= C_i$, number of data in the ith cluster $=n_i$, center of ith cluster $= c_i$, variance in the ith cluster $= \sigma(C_i)$, distance between two points x and $y = d\,(x,y)$.

R-Squared

The goal is to measure the degree of difference between clusters using the ratio of the sum of squares between clusters to the total sum of squares on the whole data. The formula is given as follows:

$$\frac{\sum_{x \in D}\left(\|x - c\|^2 - \sum_i \sum_{x \in C_i}\|x - c_i\|^2\right)}{\sum_{x \in D}\|x - c\|^2}$$

Dunn's Indices

The goal is to identify dense and well-separated clusters. The measure is given by maximal values obtained from the following formula:

$$\min_i \left\{ \min_j \left(\frac{\min\limits_{x \in C_i, y \in C_j} d(x, y)}{\max\limits_k \left\{ \max\limits_{x, y \in C_k} d(x, y) \right\}} \right) \right\}$$

Davies-Bouldin index

The goal is to identify clusters with low intra-cluster distances and high inter-cluster distances:

$$\frac{1}{NC} \cdot \sum_i \max_{j, j \neq i} \left\{ \frac{\left[\left(\frac{1}{n_i}\sum_{x \in c_i} d(x, c_i) + \frac{1}{n_j}\sum_{x \in c_j} d(x, c_j)\right)\right]}{d(c_i, c_j)} \right\}$$

Silhouette's index

The goal is to measure the pairwise difference of between-cluster and within-cluster distances. It is also used to find optimal cluster number by maximizing the index. The formula is given by:

$$\frac{1}{NC} \cdot \sum_i \left\{ \frac{1}{n_i} \sum_{x \in C_i} \frac{b(x) - a(x)}{\max\left[b(x) - a(x)\right]} \right\}$$

Here $a(x) = \dfrac{1}{n_i - 1} \sum_{y \in c_i, y \neq x} d(x, y)$ and $b(x) = \min_{j, j \neq i} \left[\dfrac{1}{n_i} \sum_{y \in C_j} d(x, y) \right]$.

External evaluation measures

The external evaluation measures of clustering have similarity to classification metrics using elements from the confusion matrix or using information theoretic metrics from the data and labels. Some of the most commonly used measures are as follows.

Rand index

Rand index measures the correct decisions made by the clustering algorithm using the following formula:

$$= \frac{TP + TN}{TP + FP + FN + TN}$$

F-Measure

F-Measure combines the precision and recall measures applied to clustering as given in the following formula:

$$Precision(i, j) = \frac{n_{ij}}{n_j} \qquad Recall(i, j) = \frac{n_{ij}}{n_i}$$

$$F\text{-}Measure = \frac{2 \cdot Precision(i, j) \, Recall(i, j)}{Precision(i, j) + Recall(i, j)}$$

Here, n_{ij} is the number of data elements of class i in the cluster j, n_j is the number of data in the cluster j and n_i is the number of data in the class i. The higher the F-Measure, the better the clustering quality.

Normalized mutual information index

NMI is one of the many entropy-based measures applied to clustering. The entropy associated with a clustering C is a measure of the uncertainty about a cluster picking a data element randomly.

$\mathcal{H}(C) = -\sum_{i=1}^{k} P(i) \cdot \log_2 P(i)$ where $P(i) = \frac{|c_i|}{n}$ is the probability of the element getting picked in cluster C_i.

Mutual information between two clusters is given by:

$$I(C,C') = \sum_{i=1}^{k}\sum_{j=1}^{i} P(i,j) \cdot \log_2 \frac{P(i,j)}{P(i) \cdot P(j)}$$

Here $P(i,j) = \frac{|c_i \cap c_j|}{n}$, which is the probability of the element being picked by both clusters C and C''.

Normalized mutual information (NMI) has many forms; one is given by:

$$NMI = \frac{I(C,C')}{\sqrt{\mathcal{H}(C)\mathcal{H}(C')}}$$

Outlier or anomaly detection

Grubbs, in 1969, offers the definition, "An outlying observation, or outlier, is one that appears to deviate markedly from other members of the sample in which it occurs".

Hawkins, in 1980, defined outliers or anomaly as "an observation which deviates so much from other observations as to arouse suspicions that it was generated by a different mechanism".

Barnett and Lewis, 1994, defined it as "an observation (or subset of observations) which appears to be inconsistent with the remainder of that set of data".

Outlier algorithms

Outlier detection techniques are classified based on different approaches to what it means to be an outlier. Each approach defines outliers in terms of some property that sets apart some objects from others in the dataset:

- **Statistical-based**: This is improbable according to a chosen distribution
- **Distance-based**: This is isolated from neighbors according to chosen distance measure and fraction of neighbors within threshold distance

- **Density-based**: This is more isolated from its neighbors than they are in turn from their neighbors
- **Clustering-based**: This is in isolated clusters relative to other clusters or is not a member of any cluster
- **High-dimension-based**: This is an outlier by usual techniques after data is projected to lower dimensions, or by choosing an appropriate metric for high dimensions

Statistical-based

Statistical-based techniques that use parametric methods for outlier detection assume some knowledge of the distribution of the data (*References* [19]). From the observations, the model parameters are estimated. Data points that have probabilities lower than a threshold value in the model are considered outliers. When the distribution is not known or none is suitable to assume, non-parametric methods are used.

Inputs and outputs

Statistical methods for outlier detection work with real-valued datasets. The choice of distance metric may be a user-selected input in the case of parametric methods assuming multivariate distributions. In the case of non-parametric methods using frequency-based histograms, a user-defined threshold frequency is used. Selection of kernel method and bandwidth are also user-determined in Kernel Density Estimation techniques. The output from statistical-based methods is a score indicating outlierness.

How does it work?

Most of the statistical-based outlier detections either assume a distribution or fit a distribution to the data to detect probabilistically the least likely data generated from the distribution. These methods have two distinct steps:

1. **Training step**: Here, an estimate of the model to fit the data is performed
2. **Testing step**: On each instance a goodness of fit is performed based on the model and the particular instance, yielding a score and the outlierness

Parametric-based methods assume a distribution model such as multivariate Gaussians and the training normally involves estimating the means and variance using techniques such as **Maximum Likelihood Estimates** (MLE). The testing typically includes techniques such as mean-variance or box-plot tests, accompanied by assumptions such as "if outside three standard deviations, then outlier".

A normal multivariate distribution can be estimated as:

$$N(\mathbf{x}) = \frac{1}{(2\pi)^{d/2}|\Sigma|^{1/2}} e^{\frac{-1}{2}(\mathbf{x}-\mu)\Sigma^{-1}(\mathbf{x}-\mu)}$$

with the mean μ and covariance Σ.

The Mahalanobis distance can be the estimate of the data point from the distribution given by the equation $(\mathbf{x}-\mu)\Sigma^{-1}(\mathbf{x}-\mu)$. Some variants such as **Minimum Covariant Determinant** (**MCD**) are also used when Mahalanobis distance is affected by outliers.

A non-parametric method involves techniques such as constructing histograms for every feature using frequency or width-based methods. When the ratio of the data in a bin to that of the average over the histogram is below a user defined threshold, such a bin is termed sparse. A lower probability of feature results in a higher outlier score. The total outlier score can be computed as:

$$OutlierScore = \sum_{f \in F} w_f \frac{(1 - p_f)}{|F|}$$

Here, w_f is the weight given to feature f, p_f is the probability of the value of the feature in the test data point, and F is the sum of weights of the feature set. Kernel Density Estimations are also used in non-parametric methods using user-defined kernels and bandwidth.

Advantages and limitations

- When the model fits or distribution of the data is known, these methods are very efficient as you don't have to store entire data, just the key statistics for doing tests.

- Assumptions of distribution, however, can pose a big issue in parametric methods. Most non-parametric methods using kernel density estimates don't scale well with large datasets.

Distance-based methods

Distance-based algorithms work under the general assumption that normal data has other data points closer to it while anomalous data is well isolated from its neighbors (*References* [20]).

Inputs and outputs

Distance-based techniques require natively numeric or categorical features to be transformed to numeric values. Inputs to distance-based methods are the distance metric used, the distance threshold ϵ, and π, the threshold fraction, which together determine if a point is an outlier. For KNN methods, the choice k is an input.

How does it work?

There are many variants of distance-based outliers and we will discuss how each of them works at a high level:

- DB (ϵ, π) Algorithms: Given a radius of ϵ and threshold of π, a data point is considered as an outlier if π percentage of points have distance to the point less than ϵ. There are further variants using nested loop structures, grid-based structures, and index-based structures on how the computation is done.

- *KNN*-based methods are also very common where the outlier score is computed either by taking the *KNN* distance to the point or the average distance to point from *{1NN,2NN,3NN...KNN}*.

Advantages and limitations

- The main advantage of distance-based algorithms is that they are non-parametric and make no assumptions on distributions and how to fit models.

- The distance calculations are straightforward and computed in parallel, helping the algorithms to scale on large datasets.

- The major issues with distance-based methods is the curse of dimensionality discussed in the first chapter; for large dimensional data, sparsity can lead to noisy outlierness.

Density-based methods

Density-based methods extend the distance-based methods by not only measuring the local density of the given point, but also the local densities of its neighborhood points. Thus, the relative factor added gives it the edge in finding more complex outliers that are local or global in nature, but at the added cost of computation.

Inputs and outputs

Density-based algorithm must be supplied the minimum number of points *MinPts* in a neighborhood of input radius ϵ centered on an object that determines it is a core object in a cluster.

How does it work?

We will first discuss the **Local Outlier Factor** (**LOF**) method and then discuss some variants of LOF [21].

Given the *MinPts* as the parameter, LOF of a data point is:

$$LOF_{MinPts}(p) = \frac{\sum_{o \in MinPts(p)} \frac{lrd_{MinPts}(o)}{lrd_{MinPts}(p)}}{\left| N_{MinPts}(p) \right|}$$

Here $|N_{MinPts}(p)|$ is the number of data points in the neighborhood of point p, and lrd_{MinPts} is the local reachability density of the point and is defined as:

$$lrd_{MinPts}(p) = \frac{1}{\sum_{o \in MinPts(p)} reachDist_{MinPts}(o,p) \Big/ \left| N_{MinPts}(p) \right|}$$

Here $reachDist_{MinPts}(o,p)$ is the reachability of the point and is defined as:

$$reachDist_{MinPts}(o,p) = \max\left(MinPtsDistance(o,p), distance(o,p) \right)$$

One of the disadvantages of LOF is that it may miss outliers whose neighborhood density is close to that of its neighborhood. **Connectivity-based outliers** (**COF**) using set-based nearest path and set-based nearest trail originating from the data point are used to improve on LOF. COF treats the low-density region differently to the isolated region and overcomes the disadvantage of LOF:

$$COF(p)_k = \frac{\left| N(p)_k \right| \cdot averageChainDist_{N(p)_k}(p)}{\sum_{o \in N(p)_k} averageChainDist_{N(p)_k}(p)}$$

Another disadvantage of LOF is that when clusters are in varying densities and not separated, LOF will generate counter-intuitive scores. One way to overcome this is to use the **influence space (IS)** of the points using KNNs and its reverse KNNs or RNNs. RNNs have the given point as one of their K nearest neighbors. Outlierness of the point is known as Influenced Outliers or INFLO and is given by:

$$INFLO(p)_k = \frac{den_{avg}IS_k(p)}{den(p)}$$

Here, *den(p)* is the local density of *p*:

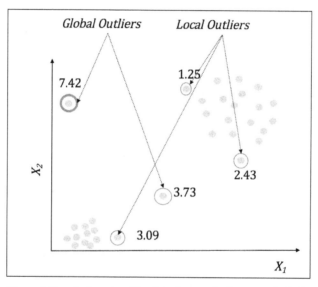

Figure 5: Density-based outlier detection methods are particularly suited for finding local as well as global outliers

Advantages and limitations

- It has been shown that density-based methods are more effective than distance-based methods.

- Density-based outlier detection has high computational cost and, often, poor interpretability.

Clustering-based methods

Some believe that clustering techniques, where the goal is to find groups of data points located together, are in some sense antithetical to the problem of anomaly or outlier detection. However, as an advanced unsupervised learning technique, clustering analysis offers several methods to find interesting groups of clusters that are either located far off from other clusters or do not lie in any clusters at all.

Inputs and outputs

As seen before, clustering techniques work well with real-valued data, although some categorical values translated to numeric values are tolerated. In the case of k-Means and k-Medoids, input values include the number of clusters k and the distance metric. Variants may require a threshold score to identify outlier groups. For Gaussian Mixture Models using EM, the number of mixture components must be supplied by the user. When using CBLOF, two user-defined parameters are expected: the size of small clusters and the size of large clusters. Depending on the algorithm used, individual or groups of objects are output as outliers.

How does it work?

As we discussed in the section on clustering, there are various types of clustering methods and we will give a few examples of how clustering algorithms have been extended for outlier detection.

k-Means or k-Medoids and their variants generally cluster data elements together and are affected by outliers or noise. Instead of preprocessing these data points by removal or transformation, such points that weaken the "tightness" of the clusters are considered outliers. Typically, outliers are revealed by a two-step process of first running clustering algorithms and then evaluating some form of outlier score that measures distance from point to centroid. Also, many variants treat clusters of size smaller than a threshold as an outlier group.

Gaussian mixture modeling (GMM) using **Expectation maximization (EM)** is another well-known clustering-based outlier detection technique, where a data point that has low probability of belonging to a cluster becomes an outlier and the outlier score becomes the inverse of the EM probabilistic output score.

Cluster-based Local Outlier Factor (CBLOF) uses a two-stage process to find outliers. First, a clustering algorithm performs partitioning of data into clusters of various sizes. Using two user-defined parameters, size of large clusters, and size of small clusters, two sets of clusters are formed:

$$LC = Set\ of\ Large\ Clusters\ \{C_1, C_2, ...C_i\}$$

$$SC = Set\ of\ Small\ Clusters\ \{C_{i+1}, C_{i+2}, ...C_n\}$$

$$CBLOF(p) = \begin{cases} |C_i|.\min\left(p, d\left(p, C_j\right)if\ p \in C_i, C_i \in SC, C_j \in LC\right) \\ |C_i|.d\left(p, C_i\right)if\ p \in C_i, C_i \in LC \end{cases}$$

Advantages and limitations

- Given that clustering-based techniques are well-understood, results are more interpretable and there are more tools available for these techniques.

- Many clustering algorithms only detect clusters, and are less effective in unsupervised techniques compared to outlier algorithms that give scores or ranks or otherwise identify outliers.

High-dimensional-based methods

One of the key issues with distance-, density-, or even clustering-based methods, is the curse of dimensionality. As dimensions increase, the contrast between distances diminishes and the concept of neighborhood becomes less meaningful. The normal points in this case look like outliers and false positives increase by large volume. We will discuss some of the latest approaches taken in addressing this problem.

Inputs and outputs

Algorithms that project data to lower-dimensional subspaces can handle missing data well. In these techniques, such as SOD, ϕ, the number of ranges in each dimension becomes an input (*References* [25]). When using an evolutionary algorithm, the number of cells with the lowest sparsity coefficients is another input parameter to the algorithm.

How does it work?

The broad idea to solve the high dimensional outlier issue is to:

- Either have a robust distance metric coupled with all of the previous techniques, so that outliers can be identified in full dimensions

- Or project data on to smaller subspaces and find outliers in the smaller subspaces

The **Angle-based Outlier Degree (ABOD)** method uses the basic assumption that if a data point in high dimension is an outlier, all the vectors originating from it towards data points nearest to it will be in more or less the same direction.

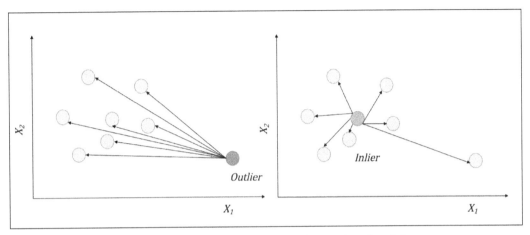

Figure 6: The ABOD method of distinguishing outliers from inliers

Given a point p, and any two points x and y, the angle between the two points and p is given by:

$$\left(\overrightarrow{px}, \overrightarrow{py} \right)$$

Measure of variance used as the ABOD score is given by:

$$ABOD(p) = VAR_{x,y} \left[\frac{\left(\overrightarrow{px}, \overrightarrow{py} \right)}{\left\| \overrightarrow{px} \right\|^2 \left\| \overrightarrow{py} \right\|^2} \right]$$

The smaller the ABOD value, the smaller the measure of variance in the angle spectrum, and the larger the chance of the point being the outlier.

Another method that has been very useful in high dimensional data is using the **Subspace Outlier Detection (SOD)** approach (*References* [23]). The idea is to partition the high dimensional space such that there are an equal number of ranges, say ϕ, in each of the d dimensions. Then the Sparsity Coefficient for a cell C formed by picking a range in each of the d dimensions is measured as follows:

$$\text{Sparsity}\left(C\right) = \frac{N\left(C\right) - n * \left(\frac{1}{\phi}\right)^{d}}{\sqrt{n * \left(\frac{1}{\phi}\right)^{d} * \left(1 - n * \left(\frac{1}{\phi}\right)^{d}\right)}}$$

Here, n is the total number of data points and $N(C)$ is the number of data points in cell C. Generally, the data points lying in cells with negative sparsity coefficient are considered outliers.

Advantages and limitations

- The ABOD method is $O(n^3)$ with the number of data points and becomes impractical with larger datasets.

- The sparsity coefficient method in subspaces requires efficient search in lower dimension and the problem becomes NP-Hard and some form of evolutionary or heuristic based search is employed.

- The sparsity coefficient methods being NP-Hard can result in local optima.

One-class SVM

In many domains there is a particular class or category of interest and the "rest" do not matter. Finding a boundary around this class of interest is the basic idea behind one-class SVM (*References* [26]). The basic assumption is that all the points of the positive class (class of interest) cluster together while the other class elements are spread around and we can find a tight hyper-sphere around the clustered instances. SVM, which has great theoretical foundations and applications in binary classifications is reformulated to solve one-class SVM. The following figure illustrates how a nonlinear boundary is simplified by using one-class SVM with slack so as to not overfit complex functions:

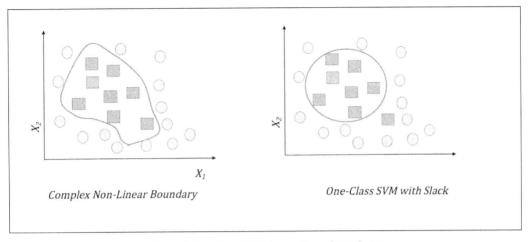

Complex Non-Linear Boundary

One-Class SVM with Slack

Figure 7: One-Class SVM for nonlinear boundaries

Inputs and outputs

Data inputs are generally numeric features. Many SVMs can take nominal features and apply binary transformations to them. Also needed are: marking the class of interest, SVM hyper-parameters such as kernel choice, kernel parameters and cost parameter, among others. Output is a SVM model that can predict whether instances belong to the class of interest or not. This is different from scoring models, which we have seen previously.

How does it work?

The input is training instances $\{\mathbf{x}_1, \mathbf{x}_2 \ldots \mathbf{x}_n\}$ with certain instances marked to be in class +1 and rest in -1.

The input to SVM also needs a kernel that does the transformation ϕ from input space to features space as $x \to \mathcal{H}$ using:

$$k(\mathbf{x}, \mathbf{x}') = (\phi(\mathbf{x}), \phi(\mathbf{x}'))_{\mathcal{H}}$$

Create a hyper-sphere that bounds the classes using SVM reformulated equation as:

$$\min_{R, \xi, c} R^2 + \frac{1}{vn} \sum_i \xi_i$$

Such that $\|\phi(\mathbf{x}_i)-\mathbf{c}\|^2 \le R^2+\xi_i\,,\ \xi_i \ge 0 \forall i \in [\mathrm{n}]$

R is the radius of the hyper-sphere with center $\mathbf{c}$ and $\nu \in (0,1]$ represents an upper bound on the fraction of the data that are outliers.

As in normal SVM, we perform optimization using quadratic programming is done to obtain the solution as the decision boundary.

Advantages and limitations

- The key advantage to using one-class SVM — as is true of binary SVM — is the many theoretical guarantees in error and generalization bounds.

- High-dimensional data can be easily mapped in one-class SVM.

- Non-linear SVM with kernels can even find non-spherical shapes to bound the clusters of data.

- The training cost in space and memory increases as the size of the data increases.

- Parameter tuning, especially the kernel parameters and the cost parameter tuning with unlabeled data is a big challenge.

Outlier evaluation techniques

Measuring outliers in terms of labels, ranks, and scores is an area of active research. When the labels or the ground truth is known, the idea of evaluation becomes much easier as the outlier class is known and standard metrics can be employed. But when the ground truth is not known, the evaluation and validation methods are very subjective and there is no well-defined, rigorous statistical process.

Supervised evaluation

In cases where the ground truth is known, the evaluation of outlier algorithms is basically the task of finding the best thresholds for outlier scores (scoring-based outliers).

The balance between reducing the false positives and improving true positives is the key concept and Precision-Recall curves (described in *Chapter 2, Practical Approach to Real-World Supervised Learning*) are used to find the best optimum threshold. Confidence score, predictions, and actual labels are used in supervised learning to plot PRCurves, and instead of confidence scores, outlier scores are ranked and used here. ROC curves and area under curves are also used in many applications to evaluate thresholds. Comparing two or more algorithms and selection of the best can also be done using area under curve metrics when the ground truth is known.

Unsupervised evaluation

In most real-world cases, knowing the ground truth is very difficult, at least during the modeling task. Hawkins describes the evaluation method in this case at a very high level as "a sample containing outliers would show up such characteristics as large gaps between 'outlying' and 'inlying' observations and the deviation between outliers and the group of inliers, as measured on some suitably standardized scale".

The general technique used in evaluating outliers when the ground truth is not known is:

- **Histogram of outlier scores**: A visualization-based method, where outlier scores are grouped into predefined bins and users can select thresholds based on outlier counts, scores, and thresholds.

- **Score normalization and distance functions**: In this technique, some form of normalization is done to make sure all outlier algorithms that produce scores have the same ranges. Some form of distance or similarity or correlation based method is used to find commonality of outliers across different algorithms. The general intuition here is: the more the algorithms that weigh the data point as outlier, the higher the probability of that point actually being an outlier.

Real-world case study

Here we present a case study that illustrates how to apply clustering and outlier techniques described in this chapter in the real world, using open-source Java frameworks and a well-known image dataset.

Tools and software

We will now introduce two new tools that were used in the experiments for this chapter: SMILE and Elki. SMILE features a Java API that was used to illustrate feature reduction using PCA, Random Projection, and IsoMap. Subsequently, the graphical interface of Elki was used to perform unsupervised learning—specifically, clustering and outlier detection. Elki comes with a rich set of algorithms for cluster analysis and outlier detection including a large number of model evaluators to choose from.

 Find out more about SMILE at: `http://haifengl.github.io/smile/` and to learn more about Elki, visit `http://elki.dbs.ifi.lmu.de/`.

Business problem

Character-recognition is a problem that occurs in many business areas, for example, the translation of medical reports and hospital charts, postal code recognition in the postal service, check deposit service in retail banking, and others. Human handwriting can vary widely among individuals. Here, we are looking exclusively at handwritten digits, 0 to 9. The problem is made interesting due to the verisimilitude within certain sets of digits, such as 1/2/7 and 6/9/0. In our experiments in this chapter we use clustering and outlier analysis using several different algorithms to illustrate the relative strengths and weaknesses of the methods. Given the widespread use of these techniques in data mining applications, our main focus is to gain insights into the data and the algorithms and evaluation measures; we do not apply the models for prediction on test data.

Machine learning mapping

As suggested by the title of the chapter, our experiments aim to demonstrate Unsupervised Learning by ignoring the labels identifying the digits in the dataset. Having learned from the dataset, clustering and outlier analyses can yield invaluable information for describing patterns in the data, and are often used to explore these patterns and inter-relationships in the data, and not just to predict the class of unseen data. In the experiments described here, we are concerned with description and exploration rather than prediction. Labels are used when available by external evaluation measures, as they are in these experiments as well.

Data collection

This is already done for us. For details on how the data was collected, see: The MNIST database: `http://yann.lecun.com/exdb/mnist/`.

Data quality analysis

Each feature in a data point is the greyscale value of one of 784 pixels. Consequently, the type of all features is numeric; there are no categorical types except for the class attribute, which is a numeral in the range 0-9. Moreover, there are no missing data elements in the dataset. Here is a table with some basic statistics for a few pixels. The images are pre-centred in the 28 x 28 box so in most examples, the data along the borders of the box are zeros:

Feature	Average	Std Dev	Min	Max
pixel300	94.25883	109.117	0	255

Feature	Average	Std Dev	Min	Max
pixel301	72.778	103.0266	0	255
pixel302	49.06167	90.68359	0	255
pixel303	28.0685	70.38963	0	255
pixel304	12.84683	49.01016	0	255
pixel305	4.0885	27.21033	0	255
pixel306	1.147	14.44462	0	254
pixel307	0.201667	6.225763	0	254
pixel308	0	0	0	0
pixel309	0.009167	0.710047	0	55
pixel310	0.102667	4.060198	0	237

Table 1: Summary of features from the original dataset before pre-processing

The **Mixed National Institute of Standards and Technology (MNIST)** dataset is a widely used dataset for evaluating unsupervised learning methods. The MNIST dataset is mainly chosen because the clusters in high dimensional data are not well separated.

The original MNIST dataset had black and white images from NIST. They were normalized to fit in a 20 x 20 pixel box while maintaining the aspect ratio. The images were centered in a 28 x 28 image by computing the center of mass and translating it to position it at the center of the 28 x 28 dimension grid.

Each pixel is in a range from 0 to 255 based on the intensity. The 784 pixel values are flattened out and become a high dimensional feature set for each image. The following figure depicts a sample digit 3 from the data, with mapping to the grid where each pixel has an integer value from 0 to 255.

The experiments described in this section are intended to show the application of unsupervised learning techniques to a well-known dataset. As was done in *Chapter 2, Practical Approach to Real-World Supervised Learning* with supervised learning techniques, multiple experiments were carried out using several clustering and outlier methods. Results from experiments with and without feature reduction are presented for each of the selected methods followed by an analysis of the results.

Data sampling and transformation

Since our focus is on exploring the dataset using various unsupervised techniques and not on the predictive aspect, we are not concerned with train, validation, and test samples here. Instead, we use the entire dataset to train the models to perform clustering analysis.

In the case of outlier detection, we create a reduced sample of only two classes of data, namely, 1 and 7. The choice of a dataset with two similarly shaped digits was made in order to set up a problem space in which the discriminating power of the various anomaly detection techniques would stand out in greater relief.

Feature analysis and dimensionality reduction

We demonstrate different feature analysis and dimensionality reduction methods — PCA, Random Projection, and IsoMap — using the Java API of the SMILE machine learning toolkit.

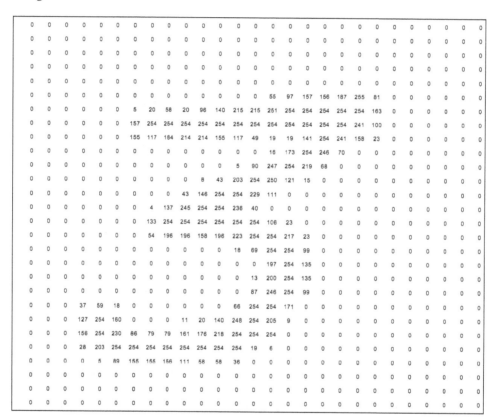

Figure 8: Showing digit 3 with pixel values distributed in a 28 by 28 matrix ranging from 0 to 254.

The code for loading the dataset and reading the values is given here along with inline comments:

```
//parser to parse the tab delimited file
DelimitedTextParser parser = new DelimitedTextParser();parser.
setDelimiter("[\t]+");
//parse the file from the location
```

```
parser.parse("mnistData", new File(fileLocation);
//the header data file has column names to map
parser.setColumnNames(true);
//the class attribute or the response variable index
AttributeDataSet dataset = parser.setResponseIndex(new
NominalAttribute("class"), 784);

//convert the data into two-dimensional array for using various
techniques
double[][] data = dataset.toArray(new double[dataset.size()][]);
```

PCA

The following snippet illustrates dimensionality reduction achieved using the API
for PCA support:

```
//perform PCA with double data and using covariance //matrix
PCA pca = new PCA(data, true);
//set the projection dimension as two (for plotting here)
pca.setProjection(2);
//get the new projected data in the dimension
double[][] y = pca.project(data);
```

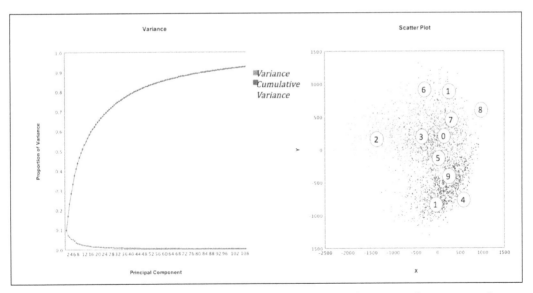

Figure 9: PCA on MNIST – On the left, we see that over 90 percent of variance in data is accounted
for by fewer than half the original number of features; on the right, a representation of the data using
the first two principal components.

The PCA computation reduces the number of features to 274. In the following table you can see basic statistics for a randomly selected set of features. Feature data has been normalized as part of the PCA:

Features	Average	Std Dev	Min	Max
1	0	2.982922	-35.0821	19.73339
2	0	2.415088	-32.6218	31.63361
3	0	2.165878	-21.4073	16.50271
4	0	1.78834	-27.537	31.52653
5	0	1.652688	-21.4661	22.62837
6	0	1.231167	-15.157	10.19708
7	0	0.861705	-6.04737	7.220233
8	0	0.631403	-6.80167	3.633182
9	0	0.606252	-5.46206	4.118598
10	0	0.578355	-4.21456	3.621186
11	0	0.528816	-3.48564	3.896156

Table 2: Summary of set of 11 random features after PCA

Random projections

Here, we illustrate the straightforward usage of the API for performing data transformation using random projection:

```
//random projection done on the data with projection in //2 dimension
RandomProjection rp = new RandomProjection(data.length, 2, false);
//get the transformed data for plotting
double[][] projectedData = rp.project(data);
```

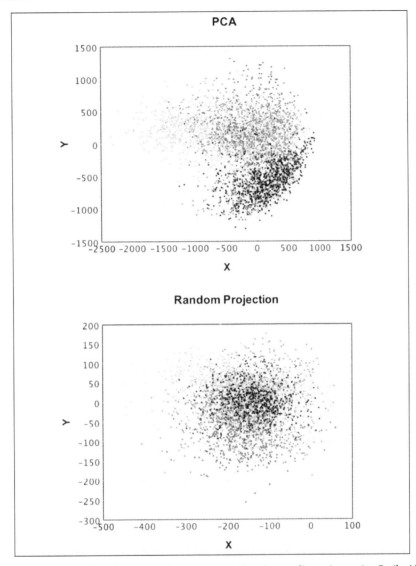

Figure 10: PCA and Random projection - representations in two dimensions using Smile API

ISOMAP

This code snippet illustrates use of the API for Isomap transformation:

```
//perform isomap transformation of data, here in 2 //dimensions with
k=10
IsoMap isomap = new IsoMap(data, 2, 10);
//get the transformed data back
double[][] y = isomap.getCoordinates();
```

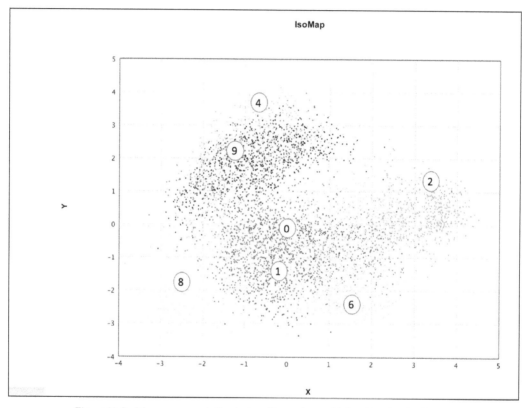

Figure 11: IsoMap – representation in two dimensions with k = 10 using Smile API

Observations on feature analysis and dimensionality reduction

We can make the following observations from the results shown in the plots:

- The PCA variance and number of dimensions plot clearly shows that around 100 linearly combined features have a similar representation or variance in the data (> 95%) as that of the 784 original features. This is the key first step in any unsupervised feature reduction analysis.

- Even PCA with two dimensions and not 100 as described previously shows some really good insights in the scatterplot visualization. Clearly, digits 2, 8, and 4 are very well separated from each other and that makes sense as they are written quite distinctly from each other. Digits such as {1,7}, {3,0,5}, and {1,9} in the low dimensional space are either overlapping or tightly clustered. This shows that with just two features it is not possible to discriminate effectively. It also shows that there is overlap in the characteristics or features amongst these classes.

- The next plot comparing PCA with Random Projections, both done in lower dimension of 2, shows that there is much in common between the outputs. Both have similar separation for distinct classes as described in PCA previously. It is interesting to note that PCA does much better in separating digits {8,9,4}, for example, than Random Projections.

- Isomap, the next plot, shows good discrimination, similar to PCA. Subjectively, it seems to be separating the data better than Random Projections. Visually, for instance, {3,0,5} is better separated out in Isomap than PCA.

Clustering models, results, and evaluation

Two sets of experiments were conducted using the MNIST-6000 dataset. The dataset consists of 6,000 examples, each of which represents a hand-written digit as greyscale values of a 28 x 28 square of pixels.

First, we run some clustering techniques to identify the 10 clusters of digits. For the experiments in this part of the case study, we use the software Elki.

In the first set of experiments, there is no feature-reduction involved. All 28x28 pixels are used. Clustering techniques including k-Means, EM (Diagonal Gaussian Model Factory), DBSCAN, Hierarchical (HDBSCAN Hierarchy Extraction), as well as Affinity Propagation were used. In each case, we use metrics from two internal evaluators: Davies Bouldin and Silhouette, and several external evaluators: Precision, Recall, F1 measure, and Rand Index.

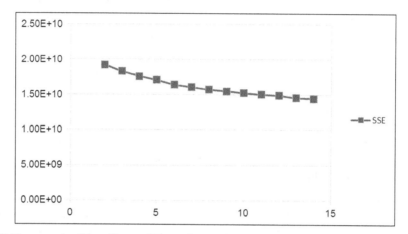

Figure 12: K-Means – using Sum of Squared Errors (SSE) to find optimal *k*, the number of clusters. An elbow in the curve, which is typically used to pick the optimal k value, is not particularly detectable in the plot.

In the case of k-Means, we did several runs using a range of k values. The plot shows that the Sum of Squared Errors (SSE) metric decreases with k.

The table shows results for *k=10* and ranks for each are in parentheses:

Algorithm	Silhouette	Davies-Bouldin Index	Precision	Recall	F1	Rand
K-Means Lloyd	+-0.09 0.0737 (1)	2.8489 (3)	0.4463 (3)	0.47843 (3)	0.4618 (1)	0.8881 (3)
EM (Diagonal Gaussian Model Factory)	NaN	0 (1)	0.1002 (6)	1 (1)	0.1822 (4)	0.1003 (5)
DBSCAN	0 (4)	0 (1)	0.1003 (5)	1 (1)	0.1823 (3)	0.1003 (5)
Hierarchical (HDBSCAN Hierarchy Extraction)	+-0.05 0.0435 (3)	2.7294	0.1632 (4)	0.9151 (2)	0.2770 (2)	0.5211 (4)
Hierarchical (Simplified Hierarchy Extraction)	NaN	0 (1)	1 (1)	0.0017 (5)	0.0033 (6)	0.8999 (2)
Affinity Propagation	+-0.07 0.04690 (2)	1.7872 (2)	0.8279 (2)	0.0281 (4)	0.0543 (5)	0.9019 (1)

Table 3. Evaluation of clustering algorithms for MNIST data

In the second clustering experiment, the dataset was first pre-processed using PCA, and the resulting data with 273 features per example was used with the same algorithms as in the first experiment. The results are shown in the table:

Algorithm	Silhouette	Davies-Bouldin Index	Precision	Recall	F1	Rand
K-Means Lloyd	+-0.14 0.0119	3.1830	0.3456	0.4418	0.3878 (1)	0.8601
EM (Diagonal Gaussian Model Factory)	+-0.16 -0.0402	3.5429	0.1808	0.3670	0.2422	0.7697
DBSCAN	+-0.13 -0.0351	1.3236	0.1078	0.9395 (1)	0.1934	0.2143
Hierarchical (HDBSCAN Hierarchy Extraction)	+-0.05 0.7920 (1)	0.0968	0.1003	0.9996	0.1823	0.1005
Affinity Propagation	+-0.09 0.0575	1.6296	0.6130 (1)	0.0311	0.0592	0.9009 (1)
Subspace (DOC)	+-0.00 0.0	0 (1)	0.1003	1	0.1823	0.1003

Table 4. Evaluation of clustering algorithms for MNIST data after PCA

Observations and clustering analysis

As shown in tables 2.1 and 2.2, different algorithms discussed in the sections on clustering are compared using different evaluation measures.

Generally, comparing different internal and external measures based on technical, domain and business requirements is very important. When labels or outcomes are available in the dataset, using external measures becomes an easier choice. When labeled data is not available, the norm is to use internal measures with some ranking for each and looking at comparative ranking across all measures. The important and often interesting observations are made at this stage:

- Evaluating the performance of k-Means with varying k, (shown in the figure) using a measure such as Sum of Squared Errors, is the basic step to see "optimality" of number of clusters. The figure clearly shows that as k increases the score improves as cluster separation improves.

- When we analyze Table 2.1 where all 784 features were used and all evaluation measures for the different algorithms are shown, some key things stand out:

    ◦ k-Means and Affinity Propagation both show a large overlap in the Silhouette index in terms of standard deviation and average, respectively (k-Means +-0.09 0.0737; Affinity Propagation +-0.07 0.04690). Hence it is difficult to analyze them on this metric.

- In the measures such as DB Index (minimal is good), Rand Index (closer to 1 is good), we see that Affinity Propagation and Hierarchical Clustering show very good results.

- In the measures where the labels are taken into account, Hierarchical Clustering, DBSCAN, and EM has either high Precision or high Recall and consequently, the F1 measure is low. k-Means gives the highest F1 measure when precision and recall are taken into consideration.

- In Table 2.2 where the dataset with 273 features — reduced using PCA with 95% variance retained — is run through the same algorithms and evaluated by the same measures, we make the following interesting observations:

By reducing the features there is a negative impact on every measure for certain algorithms; for example, all the measures of k-Means degrade. An algorithm such as Affinity Propagation has a very low impact and in some cases even a positive impact when using reduced features. When compared to the results where all the features were used, AP shows similar Rand Index and F1, better Recall, DB Index and Silhouette measures, and small changes in Precision, demonstrating clear robustness.

Hierarchical Clustering shows similar results as before in terms of better DB index and Rand Index, and scores close to AP in Rand Index.

Outlier models, results, and evaluation

For the outlier detection techniques, we used a subset of the original dataset containing all examples of digit 1 and an under-sampled subset of digit 7 examples. The idea is that the similarity in shape of the two digits would cause the digit 7 examples to be found to be outliers.

The models used were selected from Angular, Distance-based, clustering, LOF, and One-Class SVM.

The outlier metrics used in the evaluation were ROC AUC, Average Precision, R-Precision, and Maximum F1 measure.

The following table shows the results obtained, with ranks in parentheses:

Algorithm	ROC AUC	Avg. Precision	R-Precision	Maximum F1
Angular (ABOD)	0.9515 (3)	0.1908 (4)	0.24 (4)	0.3298 (4)
Distance-based (KNN Outlier)	0.9863 (1)	0.4312 (3)	0.4533 (3)	0.4545 (3)
Distance Based (Local Isolation Coefficient)	0.9863 (1)	0.4312 (3)	0.4533 (3)	0.4545 (3)

Algorithm	ROC AUC	Avg. Precision	R-Precision	Maximum F1
Clustering (EM Outlier)	0.5 (5)	0.97823827 (1)	0.989 (1)	0.9945 (1)
LOF	0.4577 (6)	0.0499 (6)	0.08 (6)	0.0934 (6)
LOF (ALOKI)	0.5 (5)	0.0110 (7)	0.0110 (7)	0.0218 (7)
LOF (COF)	0.4577 (6)	0.0499 (6)	0.08 (6)	0.0934 (6)
One-Class SVM (RBF)	0.9820 (2)	0.5637 (2)	0.5333 (2)	0.5697 (2)
One-Class SVM (Linear)	0.8298 (4)	0.1137 (5)	0.16 (5)	0.1770 (5)

Table 5 Evaluation measures of Outlier analysis algorithms

Observations and analysis

In the same way as we evaluated different clustering methods, we used several observations to compare a number of outlier algorithms. Once again, the right methodology is to judge an algorithm based on ranking across all the metrics and then getting a sense of how it does across the board as compared to other algorithms. The outlier metrics used here are all standard external measures used to compare outlier algorithms:

- It is interesting to see with the right parameters, that is, $k=2$, EM can find the right distribution and find outliers more efficiently than most. It ranks very high and is first among the important metrics that include Maximum F1, R-Precision, and Avg. Precision.

- 1-Class SVM with non-linear RBF Kernel does consistently well across most measures, that is, ranks second best in ROC area, R-Precision and Avg. Precision, and Maximum F1. The difference between Linear SVM, which ranks about fifth in most rankings and 1-Class SVM, which ranks second shows that the problem is indeed nonlinear in nature. Generally, when the dimensions are high (784), and outliers are nonlinear and rare, 1-Class SVM with kernels do really well.

- Local outlier-based techniques (LOF and its variants) are consistently ranked lower in almost all the measures. This gives the insight that the outlier problem may not be local, but rather global. Distance-based algorithms (KNN and Local Isolation) perform the best in ROC area under the curve and better than local outlier-based, even though using distance-based metrics gives the insight that the problem is indeed global and suited for distance-based measures.

Summary

Both supervised and unsupervised learning methods share common concerns with respect to noisy data, high dimensionality, and demands on memory and time as the size of data grows. Other issues peculiar to unsupervised learning, due to the lack of ground truth, are questions relating to subjectivity in the evaluation of models and their interpretability, effect of cluster boundaries, and so on.

Feature reduction is an important preprocessing step that mitigates the scalability problem, in addition to presenting other advantages. Linear methods such as PCA, Random Projection, and MDS, each have specific benefits and limitations, and we must be aware of the assumptions inherent in each. Nonlinear feature reduction methods include KPCA and Manifold learning.

Among clustering algorithms, k-Means is a centroid-based technique initialized by selecting the number of clusters and it is sensitive to the initial choice of centroids. DBSCAN is one of the density-based algorithms that does not need initializing with number of clusters and is robust against noise and outliers. Among the probabilistic-based techniques are Mean Shift, which is deterministic and robust to noise, and EM/GMM, which performs well with all types of features. Both Mean Shift and EM/GMM tend to have scalability problems.

Hierarchical clustering is a powerful method involving building binary trees that iteratively groups data points until a similarity threshold is reached. Tolerance to noise depends on the similarity metric used. SOM is a two-layer neural network, allowing visualization of clusters in a 2-D grid. Spectral clustering treats the dataset as a connected graph and identifies clusters by graph partitioning. Affinity propagation, another graph-based technique, uses message passing between data points as affinities to detect clusters.

The validity and usefulness of clustering algorithms is demonstrated using various validation and evaluation measures. Internal measures have no access to ground truth; when labels are available, external measures can be used. Examples of internal measures are Silhouette index and Davies-Bouldin index. Rand index and F-measure are external evaluation measures.

Outlier and anomaly detection is an important area of unsupervised learning. Techniques are categorized as Statistical-based, Distance-based, Density-based, Clustering-based, High-dimensional-based, and One Class SVM. Outlier evaluation techniques include supervised evaluation, where ground truth is known, and unsupervised evaluation, when ground truth is not known.

Experiments using the SMILE Java API and Elki toolkit illustrate the use of the various clustering and outlier detection techniques on the MNIST6000 handwritten digits dataset. Results from different evaluation techniques are presented and compared.

References

1. K. Pearson (1901). *On lines and planes of closest fit to systems of points in space.* Philosophical Magazine, 2:559–572.

2. A. D. Back (1997). "*A first application of independent component analysis to extracting structure from stock returns,*" Neural Systems, vol. 8, no. 4, pp. 473–484.

3. Tipping ME, Bishop CM (1999). *Probabilistic principal component analysis.* Journal of the Royal Statistical Society, Series B, 61(3):611–622. 10.1111/1467-9868.00196

4. Sanjoy Dasgupta (2000). *Experiments with random projection.* In Proceedings of the Sixteenth conference on Uncertainty in artificial intelligence (UAI'00), Craig Boutilier and Moisés Goldszmidt (Eds.). Morgan Kaufmann Publishers Inc., San Francisco, CA, USA, 143-151.

5. T. Cox and M. Cox (2001). *Multidimensional Scaling.* Chapman Hall, Boca Raton, 2nd edition.

6. Bernhard Schoelkopf, Alexander J. Smola, and Klaus-Robert Mueller (1999). *Kernel principal component analysis.* In Advances in kernel methods, MIT Press, Cambridge, MA, USA 327-352.

7. Tenenbaum, J.B.; De Silva, V.; & Langford, J.C (2000).*A global geometric framework for nonlinear dimensionality reduction.* Science. Vol. 290, Issue 5500, pp. 2319-2323

8. M. Belkin and P. Niyogi (2003). *Laplacian eigenmaps for dimensionality reduction and data representation.* Neural Computation, 15(6):1373–1396.

9. S. Roweis and L. Saul (2000). *Nonlinear dimensionality reduction by locally linear embedding.* Science, 290:2323–2326.

10. Hartigan, J. and Wong, M (1979). *Algorithm AS136: A k-means clustering algorithm.* Applied Statistics, 28, 100-108.

11. Dorin Comaniciu and Peter Meer (2002). *Mean Shift: A robust approach toward feature space analysis.* IEEE Transactions on Pattern Analysis and Machine Intelligence pp. 603-619.

12. Hierarchical Clustering Jain, A. and Dubes, R (1988). *Algorithms for Clustering Data.* Prentice-Hall, Englewood Cliffs, NJ.

13. Mclachlan, G. and Basford, K (1988). *Mixture Models: Inference and Applications to Clustering.* Marcel Dekker, New York, NY

14. Ester, M., Kriegel, H-P., Sander, J. and Xu, X (1996). *A density-based algorithm for discovering clusters in large spatial databases with noise.* In Proceedings of the 2nd ACM SIGKDD, 226-231, Portland, Oregon.

15. Y. Ng, M. I. Jordan, and Y. Weiss (2001). *On spectral clustering: Analysis and an algorithm,* in Advances in Neural Information Processing Systems. MIT Press, pp. 849–856.

16. Delbert Dueck and Brendan J. Frey (2007). *Non-metric affinity propagation for unsupervised image categorization.* In IEEE Int. Conf. Computer Vision (ICCV), pages 1–8.

17. Teuvo Kohonen (2001). *Self-Organizing Map.* Springer, Berlin, Heidelberg. 1995.Third, Extended Edition.

18. M. Halkidi, Y. Batistakis, and M. Vazirgiannis (2001). *On clustering validation techniques,* J. Intell. Inf. Syst., vol. 17, pp. 107–145.

19. M. Markou, S. Singh (2003). *Novelty detection: a review – part 1: statistical approaches,* Signal Process. 83 (12) 2481–2497

20. Byers, S. D. AND Raftery, A. E (1998). *Nearest neighbor clutter removal for estimating features in spatial point processes.* J. Amer. Statis. Assoc. 93, 577–584.

21. Breunig, M. M., Kriegel, H.-P., Ng, R. T., AND Sander, J (1999). *Optics-of: Identifying local outliers.* In Proceedings of the 3rd European Conference on Principles of Data Mining and Knowledge Discovery. Springer-Verlag, 262–270.

22. Brito, M. R., Chavez, E. L., Quiroz, A. J., AND yukich, J. E (1997). *Connectivity of the mutual k-nearest neighbor graph in clustering and outlier detection.* Statis. Prob. Lett. 35, 1, 33–42.

23. Aggarwal C and Yu P S (2000). *Outlier detection for high dimensional data.* In Proc ACM SIGMOD International Conference on Management of Data (SIGMOD), Dallas, TX.

24. Ghoting, A., Parthasarathy, S., and Otey, M (2006). *Fast mining of distance-based outliers in high dimensional spaces* In Proceedings SIAM Int Conf on Data Mining (SDM) Bethesda ML dimensional spaces. In Proc. SIAM Int. Conf. on Data Mining (SDM), Bethesda, ML.

25. Kriegel, H.-P., Schubert, M., and Zimek, A (2008). *Angle-based outlier detection,* In Proceedings ACM SIGKDD Int. Conf on Knowledge Discovery and Data Mining (SIGKDD) Las Vegas NV Conf. on Knowledge Discovery and Data Mining (SIGKDD), Las Vegas, NV.

26. Schoelkopf, B., Platt, J. C., Shawe-Taylor, J. C., Smola, A. J., AND Williamson, R. C (2001). *Estimating the support of a high-dimensional distribution*. Neural Comput. 13, 7, 1443–1471.

27. F Pedregosa, et al. *Scikit-learn: Machine learning in Python*. Journal of Machine Learning Research, 2825-2830.

4
Semi-Supervised and Active Learning

In *Chapter 2, Practical Approach to Real-World Supervised Learning* and *Chapter 3, Unsupervised Machine Learning Techniques*, we discussed two major groups of machine learning techniques which apply to opposite situations when it comes to the availability of labeled data—one where all target values are known and the other where none are. In contrast, the techniques in this chapter address the situation when we must analyze and learn from data that is a mix of a small portion with labels and a large number of unlabeled instances.

In speech and image recognition, a vast quantity of data is available, and in various forms. However, the cost of labeling or classifying all that data is costly and therefore, in practice, the proportion of speech or images that are classified to those that are not classified is very small. Similarly, in web text or document classification, there are an enormous number of documents on the World Wide Web but classifying them based on either topics or contexts requires domain experts—this makes the process complex and expensive. In this chapter, we will discuss two broad topics that cover the area of "learning from unlabeled data", namely **Semi-Supervised Learning** (**SSL**) and Active Learning. We will introduce each of the topics and discuss the taxonomy and algorithms associated with each as we did in previous chapters. Since the book emphasizes the practical approach, we will discuss tools and libraries available for each type of learning. We will then consider real-world case studies and demonstrate the techniques that are useful when applying the tools in practical situations.

Here is the list of topics that are covered in this chapter:

- Semi-Supervised Learning:
  - Representation, notation, and assumptions
  - Semi-Supervised Learning techniques:
    - Self-training SSL
    - Co-training SSL
    - Cluster and label SSL
    - Transductive graph label propagation
    - Transductive SVM
  - Case study in Semi-Supervised Learning

- Active Learning:
  - Representation and notation
  - Active Learning scenarios
  - Active Learning approaches:
    - Uncertainty sampling
      - Least confident sampling
      - Smallest margin sampling
      - Label entropy sampling
    - Version space sampling:
      - Query by disagreement
      - Query by committee
    - Data distribution sampling:
      - Expected model change
      - Expected error reduction
      - Variance reduction
      - Density weighted methods
  - Case study in Active Learning

Semi-supervised learning

The idea behind semi-supervised learning is to learn from labeled and unlabeled data to improve the predictive power of the models. The notion is explained with a simple illustration, *Figure 1*, which shows that when a large amount of unlabeled data is available, for example, HTML documents on the web, the expert can classify a few of them into known categories such as sports, news, entertainment, and so on. This small set of labeled data together with the large unlabeled dataset can then be used by semi-supervised learning techniques to learn models. Thus, using the knowledge of both labeled and unlabeled data, the model can classify unseen documents in the future. In contrast, supervised learning uses labeled data only:

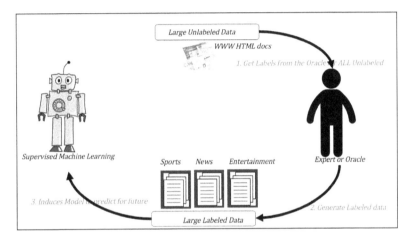

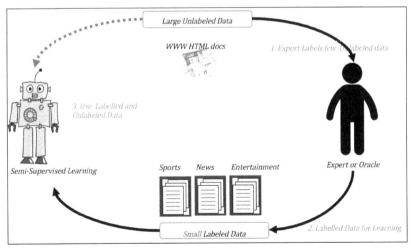

Figure 1. Semi-Supervised Learning process (bottom) contrasted with Supervised Learning (top) using classification of web documents as an example. The main difference is the amount of labeled data available for learning, highlighted by the qualifier "small" in the semi-supervised case.

Representation, notation, and assumptions

As before, we will introduce the notation we use in this chapter. The dataset D consists of individual data instances represented as $\mathbf{x}$, which is also represented as a set $\{\mathbf{x}_1, \mathbf{x}_2, \ldots \mathbf{x}_n\}$, the set of data instances without labels. The labels associated with these data instances are $\{y_1, y_2, \ldots y_n\}$. The entire labeled dataset can be represented as paired elements in a set, as given by $D = \{(\mathbf{x}_1, y_1), (\mathbf{x}_2, y_2), \ldots (\mathbf{x}_n, y_n)\}$ where $\mathbf{x}_i \in R^d$. In semi-supervised learning, we divide the dataset D further into two sets U and L for unlabeled and labeled data respectively.

The labeled data $\mathcal{L} = \left\{\mathbf{x}_i, y_i\right\}_{i=1}^{l}$ consists of all labeled data with known outcomes $\{y_1, y_2, \ldots y_l\}$. The unlabeled data $\mathcal{U} = \left\{\mathbf{x}_i, y_i\right\}_{i=l+1}^{n}$ is the dataset where the outcomes are not known. $|U| > |L|$.

Inductive semi-supervised learning consists of a set of techniques, which, given the training set D with labeled data $\mathcal{L} = \left\{\mathbf{x}_i, y_i\right\}_{i=1}^{l}$ and unlabeled data $\mathcal{U} = \left\{\mathbf{x}_i, y_i\right\}_{i=l+1}^{n}$, learns a model represented as $f : \mathbf{x} \rightarrow y$ so that the model f can be a good predictor on unseen data beyond the training unlabeled data U. It "induces" a model that can be used just like supervised learning algorithms to predict on unseen instances.

Transductive semi-supervised learning consists of a set of techniques, which, given the training set D, learns a model $f : x_{l+1}^{n} \rightarrow y_{l+1}^{n}$ that makes predictions on unlabeled data alone. It is not required to perform on unseen future instances and hence is a simpler form of SSL than inductive based learning.

Some of the assumptions made in the semi-supervised learning algorithms that should hold true for these types of learning to be successful are noted in the following list. For SSL to work, one or more of these assumptions must be true:

- **Semi-supervised smoothness**: In simple terms, if two points are "close" in terms of density or distance, then their labels agree. Conversely, if two points are separated and in different density regions, then their labels need not agree.

- **Cluster togetherness**: If the data instances of classes tend to form a cluster, then the unlabeled data can aid the clustering algorithm to find better clusters.

- **Manifold togetherness**: In many real-world datasets, the high-dimensional data lies in a low-dimensional manifold, enabling learning algorithms to overcome the curse of dimensionality. If this is true in the given dataset, the unlabeled data also maps to the manifold and can improve the learning.

Semi-supervised learning techniques

In this section, we will describe different SSL techniques, and some accompanying algorithms. We will use the same structure as in previous chapters and describe each method in three subsections: *Inputs and outputs, How does it work?*, and *Advantages and limitations*.

Self-training SSL

Self-training is the simplest form of SSL, where we perform a simple iterative process of imputing the data from the unlabeled set by applying the model learned from the labeled set (*References* [1]):

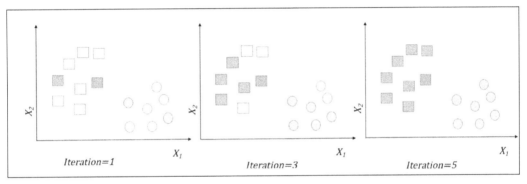

Figure 2. Self-training SSL in binary classification with some labeled data shown with blue rectangles and yellow circles. After various iterations, the unlabeled data gets mapped to the respective classes.

Inputs and outputs

The input is training data with a small amount of labeled and a large amount of unlabeled data. A base classifier, either linear or non-linear, such as Naïve Bayes, KNN, Decision Tree, or other, is provided along with the hyper-parameters needed for each of the algorithms. The constraints on data types will be similar to the base learner. Stopping conditions such as *maximum iterations reached* or *unlabeled data exhausted* are choices that must be made as well. Often, we use base learners which give probabilities or ranks to the outputs. As output, this technique generates models that can be used for performing predictions on unseen datasets other than the unlabeled data provided.

How does it work?

The entire algorithm can be summarized as follows:

1. While stopping criteria not reached:
    1. Train the classifier model $f : \mathbf{x} \rightarrow y$ with labeled data L
    2. Apply the classifier model f on unlabeled data U
    3. Choose k most confident predictions from U as set L_u
    4. Augment the labeled data with the k data points $L = L \cup L_u$

2. Repeat all the steps under 2.

In the abstract, self-training can be seen as an expectation maximization process applied to a semi-supervised setting. The process of training the classifier model is finding the parameter θ using MLE or MAP. Computing the labels using the learned model is similar to the *EXPECTATION* step where $\mathbb{E}[y_i]$ is estimating the label from U given the parameter θ. The iterative next step of learning the model with augmented labels is akin to the *MAXIMIZATION* step where the new parameter is tuned to θ'.

Advantages and limitations

The advantages and limitations are as follows:

- Simple, works with most supervised learning techniques.
- Outliers and noise can cause mistakes in predictions to be reinforced and the technique to degrade.

Co-training SSL or multi-view SSL

Co-training based SSL involves learning from two different "views" of the same data. It is a special case of multi-view SSL (References [2]). Each view can be considered as a feature set of the point capturing some domain knowledge and is orthogonal to the other view. For example, a web documents dataset can be considered to have two views: one view is features representing the text and the other view is features representing hyperlinks to other documents. The assumption is that there is enough data for each view and learning from each view improves the overall labeling process. In datasets where such partitions of features are not possible, splitting features randomly into disjoint sets forms the views.

Inputs and outputs

Input is training data with a few labeled and a large number of unlabeled data. In addition to providing the data points, there are feature sets corresponding to each view and the assumption is that these feature sets are not overlapping and solve different classification problems. A base classifier, linear or non-linear, such as Naïve Bayes, KNN, Decision Tree, or any other, is selected along with the hyper-parameters needed for each of the algorithms. As output, this method generates models that can be used for performing predictions on unseen datasets other than the unlabeled data provided.

How does it work?

We will demonstrate the algorithm using two views of the data:

1. Initialize the data as $\mathcal{L} = \{\mathbf{x}_i, y_i\}_{i=1}^{l}$ labeled and $\mathcal{U} = \{\mathbf{x}_i, y_i\}_{i=l+1}^{n}$ unlabeled. Each data point has two views $\mathbf{x} = [\mathbf{x}^1, \mathbf{x}^2]$ and $L = [L^1, L^2]$.

2. While stopping criteria not reached:

   1. Train the classifier models $f^1 : \mathbf{x} \rightarrow y$ and $f^2 : \mathbf{x} \rightarrow y$ with labeled data L^1 and L^2 respectively.

   2. Apply the classifier models f^1 and f^2 on unlabeled data U using their own features.

   3. Choose k the most confident predictions from U, applying f^1 and f^2 as set L_u^1 and L_u^2 respectively.

   4. Augment the labeled data with the k data points $L^1 = L^1 \cup L_u^1$ and $L^2 = L^2 \cup L_u^2$

3. Repeat all the steps under 2.

Advantages and limitations

The advantages and limitations are:

- When the features have different aspects or a mix of different domains, co-training becomes more beneficial than simple self-training

- The necessary and sufficient condition of having orthogonal views and ability to learn from them poses challenges for the generality of the technique

Cluster and label SSL

This technique, like self-training, is quiet generic and applicable to domains and datasets where the clustering supposition mentioned in the assumptions section holds true (References [3]).

Inputs and outputs

Input is training data with a few labeled and a large number of unlabeled instances. A clustering algorithm and its parameters along with a classification algorithm with its parameters constitute additional inputs. The technique generates a classification model that can help predict the classes of unseen data.

How does it work?

The abstract algorithm can be given as:

1. Initialize data as $\mathcal{L} = \{\mathbf{x}_i, y_i\}_{i=1}^{l}$ labeled and $\mathcal{U} = \{\mathbf{x}_i, y_i\}_{i=l+1}^{n}$ unlabeled.
2. Cluster the entire data, both labeled and unlabeled using the clustering algorithm.
3. For each cluster let S be the set of labeled instances drawn from set L.

    1. Learn a supervised model from $S, f_s = L_s$.
    2. Apply the model f_s and classify unlabeled instances for each cluster using the preceding model.

4. Since all the unlabeled instances $\mathcal{U} = \{\mathbf{x}_i, y_i\}_{i=l+1}^{n}$ get assigned a label by the preceding process, a supervised classification model is run on the entire set.

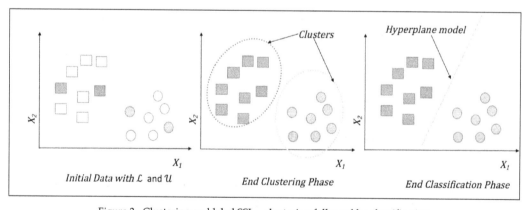

Figure 3. Clustering and label SSL – clustering followed by classification

Advantages and limitations

The advantages and limitations are:

- Works very well when the cluster assumption holds true and the choice of clustering algorithm and parameters are correct

- Large number of parameters and choices make this an unwieldy technique in many real-world problems

Transductive graph label propagation

The key idea behind graph-based methods is to represent every instance in the dataset, labeled and unlabeled, as a node and compute the edges as some form of "similarity" between them. Known labels are used to propagate labels in the unlabeled data using the basic concepts of label smoothness as discussed in the assumptions section, that is, similar data points will lie "close" to each other graphically (*References* [4]).

Figure 4 shows how the similarity indicated by the thickness of the arrow from the first data point to the last varies when the handwritten digit pattern changes. Knowing the first label, the label propagation can effectively label the next three digits due to the similarity in features while the last digit, though labeled the same, has a lower similarity as compared to the first three.

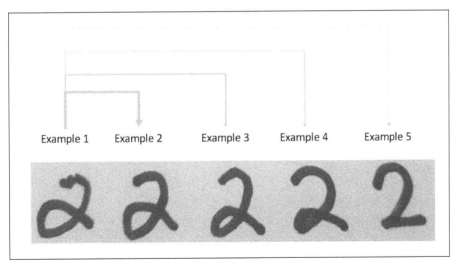

Figure 4. Transductive graph label propagation – classification of hand-written digits. Leftmost and rightmost images are labeled, others are unlabeled. Arrow thickness is a visual measure of similarity to labeled digit "2" on the left.

Inputs and outputs

Input is training data with a few labeled and a large number of unlabeled data. The graph weighting or similarity computing method, such as k-nearest weighting, Gaussian decaying distance, or ε-radius method is chosen. Output is the labeled set for the entire data; it generally doesn't build inductive models like the algorithms seen previously.

How does it work?

The general label propagation method follows:

1. Build a graph $g = (V,E)$ where:
   - Vertices $V = \{1, 2...n\}$ correspond to data belonging to both labeled set L and unlabeled set U.
   - Edges E are weight matrices $\mathbf{W}$, such that $\mathbf{W}_{i,j}$ represents similarity in some form between two data points $\mathbf{x}_i, \mathbf{x}_j$.

2. Compute the diagonal degree matrix $\mathbf{D}$ by $\mathbf{D}_{i,i} \leftarrow \sum_j \mathbf{W}_{i,j}$.

3. Assume the labeled set is binary and has $y_i \in \{1,-1\}$. Initialize the labels of all unlabeled data to be 0. $\hat{y}^{(0)} = \{y_1, y_2, \ldots y_l, 0, 0 \ldots .0\}$

4. Iterate at $t = 0$:

   1. $\hat{y}^{(t+1)} \leftarrow \mathbf{D}^{-1}\mathbf{W}\hat{y}^{(t)}$

   2. $\hat{Y}_l^{(t+1)} \leftarrow Y_l$ (reset the labels of labeled instances back to the original)

   3. Go back to step 4, until convergence $\hat{Y}^{(\infty)}$

5. Label the unlabeled points $\mathcal{U} = \{\mathbf{x}_i, y_i\}_{i=l+1}^n$ using the convergence labels $\hat{Y}^{(\infty)}$.

There are many variations based on similarity, optimization selected in iterations, and so on.

Advantages and limitations

The advantages and limitations are:

- The graph-based semi-supervised learning methods are costly in terms of computations — generally O(n^3) where n is the number of instances. Though speeding and caching techniques help, the computational cost over large data makes it infeasible in many real-world data situations.

- The transductive nature makes it difficult for practical purposes where models need to be induced for unseen data. There are extensions such as Harmonic Mixtures, and so on, which address these concerns.

Transductive SVM (TSVM)

Transductive SVM is one of the oldest and most popular transductive semi-supervised learning methods, introduced by Vapnik (*References* [5]). The key principle is that unlabeled data along with labeled data can help find the decision boundary using concepts of large margins. The underlying principle is that the decision boundaries normally don't lie in high density regions!

Inputs and outputs

Input is training data with few labeled and a large number of unlabeled data. Input has to be numeric features for TSVM computations. The choice of kernels, kernel parameters, and cost factors, which are all SVM-based parameters, are also input variables. The output is labels for the unlabeled dataset.

How does it work?

Generally, SVM works as an optimization problem in the labeled hard boundary SVM formulated in terms of weight vector **w** and the bias b $\min\left(f\left(\mathbf{w},b\right)\right)=\frac{1}{2}\mathbf{w}\cdot\mathbf{w}$ subject to $\forall_{i=1}^{n}:y_i\left|\mathbf{w}_i\mathbf{x}_i+b\right|\geq 1$

1. Initialize the data as $\mathcal{L}=\left\{\mathbf{x}_i,y_i\right\}_{i=1}^{l}$ labeled and $\mathcal{U}=\left\{\mathbf{x}_i,y_i\right\}_{i=l+1}^{n}$ unlabeled.
2. In TSVM, the equation is modified as follows:

$$\min\left(f\left(y_{l+1},y_{l+2}\cdots y_n,\mathbf{w},b\right)\right)=\frac{1}{2}\mathbf{w}\cdot\mathbf{w}$$

This is subject to the following condition:

$$\forall_{i=1}^{l} : y_{l_i} \left| \mathbf{w}_i \mathbf{x}_{li} + b \right| \geq 1$$

$$\forall_{j=1}^{u} : y_{u_j} \left| \mathbf{w}_i \mathbf{x}_{u_j} + b \right| \geq 1$$

$$\forall_{j=1}^{u} : y_{u_i} \in \left(+1, -1 \right)$$

This is exactly like inductive SVM but using only labeled data. When we constrain the unlabeled data to conform to the side of the hyperplane of labeled data in order to maximize the margin, it results in unlabeled data being labeled with maximum margin separation! By adding the penalty factor to the constraints or replacing the dot product in the input space with kernels as in inductive SVM, complex non-linear noisy datasets can be labeled from unlabeled data.

Figure 5 illustrates the concept of TSVM in comparison with inductive SVM run on labeled data only and why TSVM can find better decision boundaries using the unlabeled datasets. The unlabeled datasets on either side of hyperplane are closer to their respective classes, thus helping find better margin separators.

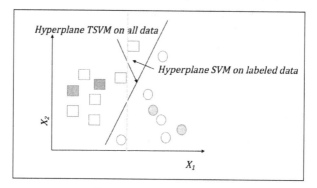

Figure 5. Transductive SVM

Advantages and limitations

The advantages and limitations:

- TSVMs can work very well in linear or non-linear datasets given noiseless labeled data.

- TSVMs have the same issues in finding hyper-parameters and tuning them to get the best results as inductive SVMs.

Case study in semi-supervised learning

For this case study, we use another well-studied dataset from the UCI Repository, the Wisconsin Breast Cancer dataset. In the first part of the experiment, we demonstrate how to apply the Transductive SVM technique of semi-supervised learning using the open-source library called `JKernelMachines`. We choose the SVMLight algorithm and a Gaussian kernel for this technique.

In the second part, we use KEEL, a GUI-based framework and compare results from several evolutionary learning based algorithms using the UCI Breast Cancer dataset. The tools, methodology, and evaluation measures are described in the following subsections.

Tools and software

The two open source Java tools used in the semi-supervised learning case study are `JKernelMachines`, a Transductive SVM, and KEEL, a GUI-based tool that uses evolutionary algorithms for learning.

JKernelMachines (Transductive SVM)

`JKernelMachines` is a pure Java library that provides an efficient framework for using and rapidly developing specialized kernels. Kernels are similarity functions used in SVMs. `JKernelMachines` provides kernel implementations defined on structured data in addition to standard kernels on vector data such as Linear and Gaussian. In particular, it offers a combination of kernels, kernels defined over lists, and kernels with various caching strategies. The library also contains SVM optimization algorithm implementations including LaSVM and One-Class SVM using SMO. The creators of the library report that the results of JKernelMachines on some common UCI repository datasets are comparable to or better than the Weka library.

The example of loading data and running Transductive SVM using `JKernelMachines` is given here:

```
try {
//load the labeled training data
List<TrainingSample<double[]>> labeledTraining = ArffImporter.
importFromFile("resources/breast-labeled.arff");
//load the unlabeled data
List<TrainingSample<double[]>> unlabeledData =ArffImporter.
importFromFile("resources/breast-unlabeled.arff");
//create a kernel with Gaussian and gamma set to 1.0
DoubleGaussL2 k = new DoubleGaussL2(1.0);
```

```
//create transductive SVM with SVM light
S3VMLight<double[]> svm = new S3VMLight<double[]>(k);
//send the training labeled and unlabeled data
svm.train(labeledTraining, unlabeledData);
} catch (IOException e) {
    e.printStackTrace();
}
```

In the second approach, we use KEEL with the same dataset.

KEEL

KEEL (Knowledge Extraction based on Evolutionary Learning) is a non-commercial (GPLv3) Java tool with GUI which enables users to analyze the behavior of evolutionary learning for a variety of data mining problems, including regression, classification, and unsupervised learning. It relieves users from the burden of programming sophisticated evolutionary algorithms and allows them to focus on new learning models created using the toolkit. KEEL is intended to meet the needs of researchers as well as students.

KEEL contains algorithms for data preprocessing and post-processing as well as statistical libraries, and a Knowledge Extraction Algorithms Library which incorporates multiple evolutionary learning algorithms with classical learning techniques.

The GUI wizard included in the tool offers different functional components for each stage of the pipeline, including:

- Data management: Import, export of data, data transformation, visualization, and so on
- Experiment design: Selection of classifier, estimator, unsupervised techniques, validation method, and so on
- SSL experiments: Transductive and inductive classification (see image of off-line method for SSL experiment design in this section)
- Statistical analysis: This provides tests for pair-wise and multiple comparisons, parametric, and non-parametric procedures.

For more info, visit http://sci2s.ugr.es/keel/ and http://sci2s.ugr.es/keel/pdf/keel/articulo/Alcalaetal-SoftComputing-Keel1.0.pdf.

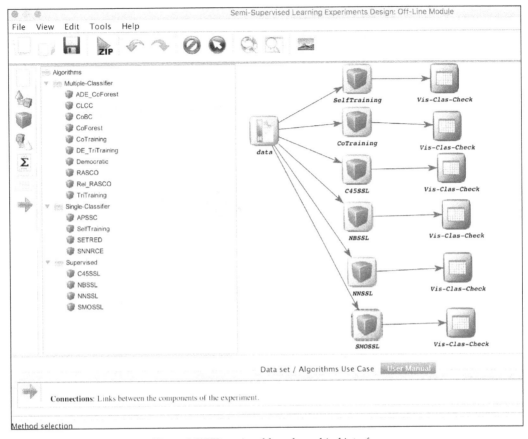

Figure 6: KEEL – wizard-based graphical interface

Business problem

Breast cancer is the top cancer in women worldwide and is increasing particularly in developing countries where the majority of cases are diagnosed in late stages. Examination of tumor mass using a non-surgical procedure is an inexpensive and preventative measure for early detection of the disease.

In this case-study, a marked dataset from such a procedure is used and the goal is to classify the breast cancer data into Malignant and Benign using multiple SSL techniques.

Machine learning mapping

To illustrate the techniques learned in this chapter so far, we will use SSL to classify. Whereas the dataset contains labels for all the examples, in order to treat this as a problem where we can apply SSL, we will consider a fraction of the data to be unlabeled. In fact, we run multiple experiments using different fractions of unlabeled data for comparison. The different base learners used are classification algorithms familiar to us from previous chapters.

Data collection

This dataset was collected by the University of Wisconsin Hospitals, Madison. The dataset is available in Weka AARF format. The data is not partitioned into training, validation and test.

Data quality analysis

The examples in the data contain no unique identifier. There are 16 examples for which the Bare Nuclei attribute has missing values. The target Class is the only categorical attribute and has two values. All other attributes are continuous and in the range [1, 10].

Data sampling and transformation

In the experiments, we present results for 10-fold cross-validation. For comparison, four runs were performed each using a different fraction of labeled data – 10%, 20%, 30%, and 40%.

A numeric sample code number was added to each example as a unique identifier. The categorical values Malignant and Benign, for the class attribute, were replaced by the numeric values 4 and 2 respectively.

Datasets and analysis

The Breast Cancer Dataset Wisconsin (Original) is available from the UCI Machine Learning Repository at: `https://archive.ics.uci.edu/ml/datasets/Breast+Ca ncer+Wisconsin+(Original)`.

This database was originally obtained from the University of Wisconsin Hospitals, Madison from Dr. William H. Wolberg. The dataset was created by Dr. Wolberg for the diagnosis and prognosis of breast tumors. The data is based exclusively on measurements involving the **Fine Needle Aspirate (FNA)** test. In this test, fluid from a breast mass is extracted using a small-gauge needle and then visually examined under a microscope.

A total of 699 instances with nine numeric attributes and a binary class (malignant/benign) constitute the dataset. The percentage of missing values is 0.2%. There are 65.5% malignant and 34.5% benign cases in the dataset. The feature names and range of valid values are listed in the following table:

Num.	Feature Name	Domain
1	Sample code number	id number
2	Clump Thickness	1 - 10
3	Uniformity of Cell Size	1 - 10
4	Uniformity of Cell Shape	1 - 10
5	Marginal Adhesion	1 - 10
6	Single Epithelial Cell Size	1 - 10
7	Bare Nuclei	1 - 10
8	Bland Chromatin	1 - 10
9	Normal Nucleoli	1 - 10
10	Mitoses	1 - 10
11	Class	2 for benign, 4 for malignant

Feature analysis results

Summary statistics by feature appear in Table 1.

	Clump Thickness	Cell Size Uniformity	Cell Shape Uniformity	Marginal Adhesion	Single Epi Cell Size	Bare Nuclei	Bland Chromatin	Normal Nucleoli	Mitoses
mean	4.418	3.134	3.207	2.807	3.216	3.545	3.438	2.867	1.589
std	2.816	3.051	2.972	2.855	2.214	3.644	2.438	3.054	1.715
min	1	1	1	1	1	1	1	1	1
25%	2	1	1	1	2		2	1	1
50%	4	1	1	1	2		3	1	1
75%	6	5	5	4	4		5	4	1
max	10	10	10	10	10	10	10	10	10

Table 1. Features summary

Experiments and results

Two SSL algorithms were selected for the experiments — self-training and co-training. In addition, four classification methods were chosen as base learners — Naïve Bayes, C4.5, K-NN, and SMO. Further, each experiment was run using four different partitions of labeled and unlabeled data (10%, 20%, 30%, and 40% labeled).

The hyper-parameters for the algorithms and base classifiers are given in Table 2. You can see the accuracy across the different runs corresponding to four partitions of labeled and unlabeled data for the two SSL algorithms.

Finally, we give the performance results for each experiment for the case of 40% labeled. Performance metrics provided are Accuracy and the Kappa statistic with standard deviations.

Method	Parameters
Self-Training	MAX_ITER = 40
Co-Training	MAX_ITER = 40, Initial Unlabeled Pool=75
KNN	K = 3, Euclidean distance
C4.5	pruned tree, confidence = 0.25, 2 examples per leaf
NB	No parameters specified
SMO	C = 1.0, Tolerance Parameter = 0.001, Epsilon= 1.0E-12, Kernel Type = Polynomial, Polynomial degree = 1, Fit logistic models = true

Table 2. Base classifier hyper-parameters for self-training and co-training

SSL Algorithm	10%	20%	30%	40%
Self-Training C 4.5	0.9	0.93	0.94	0.947
Co-Training SMO	0.959	0.949	0.962	0.959

Table 3. Model accuracy for samples with varying fraction of labeled examples

Algorithm	Accuracy (no unlabeled)
C4.5 10-fold CV	0.947
SMO 10 fold CV	0.967

		10 fold CV Wisconsin 40% Labeled Data		
Self-Training (kNN)	Accuracy	0.9623 (1)	Kappa	0.9170 (2)
	Std Dev	0.0329	Std Dev	0.0714
Self-Training (C45)	Accuracy	0.9606 (3)	Kappa	0.9144
	Std Dev	0.0241	Std Dev	0.0511
Self-Training (NB)	Accuracy	0.9547	Kappa	0.9036
	Std Dev	0.0252	Std Dev	0.0533
Self-Training (SMO)	Accuracy	0.9547	Kappa	0.9035
	Std Dev	0.0208	Std Dev	0.0435
Co-Training (NN)	Accuracy	0.9492	Kappa	0.8869
	Std Dev	0.0403	Std Dev	0.0893
Co-Training (C45)	Accuracy	0.9417	Kappa	0.8733
	Std Dev	0.0230	Std Dev	0.0480
Co-Training (NB)	Accuracy	0.9622 (2)	Kappa	0.9193 (1)
	Std Dev	0.0290	Std Dev	0.0614
Co-Training (SMO)	Accuracy	0.9592	Kappa	0.9128 (3)
	Std Dev	0.0274	Std Dev	0.0580

Table 4. Model performance comparison using 40% labeled examples. The top ranking performers in each category are shown in parentheses.

Analysis of semi-supervised learning

With 40% of labeled data, semi-supervised self-training with C4.5 achieves the same result as 100% of labeled data with just C4.5. This shows the strength of semi-supervised learning when the data is sparsely labeled.

SMO with polynomial kernel, with 30-40% data comes close to the 100% data but not as good as C4.5.

Self-training and co-training with four classifiers on 40% labeled training data shows

- KNN as base classifier and self-training has the highest accuracy (0.9623) which indicates the non-linear boundary of the data. Co-training with Naïve Bayes comes very close.

- Self-training with classifiers such as linear Naïve Bayes, non-linear C4.5 and highly non-linear KNN shows steady improvements in accuracy: 0.9547, 0.9606, 0.9623, which again shows that using self-training but choosing the right underlying classifier for the problem is very important.

- Co-training with Naive Bayes has highest Kappa statistic (0.9193) and almost similar accuracy as KNN with self-training. The independence relationship between features — hence breaking the feature sets into orthogonal feature sets and using them for classifiers — improves the learning.

Active learning

Although active learning has many similarities with semi-supervised learning, it has its own distinctive approach to modeling with datasets containing labeled and unlabeled data. It has roots in the basic human psychology that asking more questions often tends to solve problems.

The main idea behind active learning is that if the learner gets to pick the instances to learn from rather than being handed labeled data, it can learn more effectively with less data (*References* [6]). With very small amount of labeled data, it can carefully pick instances from unlabeled data to get label information and use that to iteratively improve learning. This basic approach of querying for unlabeled data to get labels from a so-called oracle — an expert in the domain — distinguishes active learning from semi-supervised or passive learning. The following figure illustrates the difference and the iterative process involved:

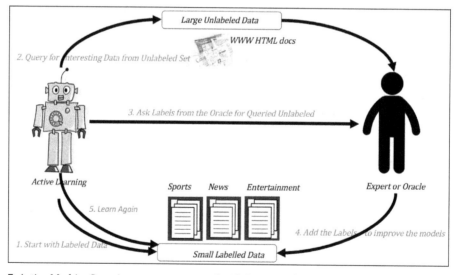

Figure 7. Active Machine Learning process contrasted with Supervised and Semi-Supervised Learning process.

Representation and notation

The dataset D, which represents all the data instances and their labels, is given by $D = \{(\mathbf{x}_1, y_2), (\mathbf{x}_2, y_2), \dots (\mathbf{x}_n, y_n)\}$ where $\mathbf{x}_i \in \mathbb{R}^d$ are the individual instances of data and $\{y_1, y_2, \dots y_n\}$ is the set of associated labels. D is composed of two sets U, labeled data and L, unlabeled data. $\mathbf{x}$ is the set $\{\mathbf{x}_1, \mathbf{x}_2, \dots \mathbf{x}_n\}$ of data instances without labels.

The dataset $\mathcal{L} = \left\{ \mathbf{x}_i, y_i \right\}_{i=1}^{l}$ consists of all labeled data with known outcomes $\{y_1, y_2, \dots y_l\}$ whereas $\mathcal{U} = \left\{ \mathbf{x}_i, y_i \right\}_{i=l+1}^{n}$ is the dataset where the outcomes are not known. As before, $|U| \gg |L|$.

Active learning scenarios

Active learning scenarios can be broadly classified as:

- **Stream-based active learning**: In this approach, an instance or example is picked only from the unlabeled dataset and a decision is made whether to ignore the data or pass it on to the oracle to get its label (*References* [10,11]).

- **Pool-based active learning**: In this approach, the instances are queried from the unlabeled dataset and then ranked on the basis of informativeness and a set from these is sent to the Oracle to get the labels (*References* [12]).

- **Query synthesis**: In this method, the learner has only information about input space (features) and synthesizes queries from the unlabeled set for the membership. This is not used in practical applications, as most often it doesn't consider the data generating distribution and hence often the queries are arbitrary or meaningless.

Active learning approaches

Regardless of the scenario involved, every active learning approach includes selecting a query strategy or sampling method which establishes the mechanism for picking the queries in each iteration. Each method reveals a distinct way of seeking out unlabeled examples with the best information content for improving the learning process. In the following subsections, we describe the major query strategy frameworks, how they work, their merits and limitations, and the different strategies within each framework.

Uncertainty sampling

The key idea behind this form of sampling is to select instances from the unlabeled pool that the current model is most uncertain about. The learner can then avoid the instances the model is more certain or confident in classifying (*References* [8]).

Probabilistic based models (Naïve Bayes, Logistic Regression, and so on) are the most natural choices for such methods as they give confidence measures on the given model, say θ for the data $\mathbf{x}$, for a class y_i i ϵ classes, and the probability $P_\theta(\hat{y}|x)$ as the posterior probability.

How does it work?

The general process for all uncertainty-based algorithms is outlined as follows:

1. Initialize the data as labeled, $\mathcal{L} = \{\mathbf{x}_i, y_i\}_{i=1}^{l}$ and unlabeled, $\mathcal{U} = \{\mathbf{x}_i, y_i\}_{i=l+1}^{n}$.
2. While there is still unlabeled data:
    1. Train the classifier model $f : \mathbf{x} \rightarrow y$ with the labeled data L.
    2. Apply the classifier model f on the unlabeled data U to assess informativeness J using one of the sampling mechanisms (see next section)
    3. Choose k most informative data from U as set L_u to get labels from the oracle.
    4. Augment the labeled data with the k new labeled data points obtained in the previous step: $L = L \cup L_u$.
3. Repeat all the steps under 2.

Some of the most common query synthesis algorithms to sample the informative instances from the data are given next.

Least confident sampling

In this technique, the data instances are sorted based on their confidence in reverse, and the instances most likely to be queried or selected are the ones the model is least confident about. The idea behind this is the least confident ones are the ones near the margin or separating hyperplane and getting their labels will be the best way to learn the boundaries effectively.

This can be formulated as $Q\{\mathbf{x}_u\} = argmin\, P_\theta(\hat{y}|\mathbf{x})$.

The disadvantage of this method is that it effectively considers information of the best; information on the rest of the posterior distribution is not used.

Smallest margin sampling

This is margin-based sampling, where the instances with smaller margins have more ambiguity than instances with larger margins.

This can be formulated as $Q\{\mathbf{x}_u\} = argmin\left[P_\theta\left(\hat{y}_1 | \mathbf{x}\right) - P_\theta\left(\hat{y}_2 | \mathbf{x}\right)\right]$ where $\hat{y}_1$ and $\hat{y}_2$ are two labels for the instance $\mathbf{x}$.

Label entropy sampling

Entropy, which is the measure of average information content in the data and is the impurity measure, can be used to sample the instances. This can be formulated as:

$$Q\{\mathbf{x}_u\} = argmax_x - \sum_{y \in classes} P_\theta\left(y | \mathbf{x}\right) log\left(P_\theta\left(y | \mathbf{x}\right)\right)$$

Advantages and limitations

The advantages and limitations are:

- Label entropy sampling is the simplest approach and can work with any probabilistic classifiers—this is the biggest advantage
- Presence of outliers or wrong feedback can go unnoticed and models can degrade

Version space sampling

Hypothesis H is the set of all the particular models that generalize or explain the training data; for example, all possible sets of weights that separate two linearly separable classes. Version spaces V are subsets of hypothesis H, which are consistent with the training data as defined by Tom Mitchell (*References* [15]) such that $V \subseteq H$.

The idea behind this sampling is to query instances from the unlabeled dataset that reduce the size of the version space or minimize $|V|$.

Query by disagreement (QBD)

QBD is one of the earliest algorithms which works on maintaining a version space V—when two hypotheses disagree on the label of new incoming data, that instance is selected for getting labels from the oracle or expert.

How does it work?

The entire algorithm can be summarized as follows:

1. Initialize $V \subseteq \mathcal{H}$ as the set of all legal hypotheses.
2. Initialize the data as $\mathcal{L} = \{\mathbf{x}_i, y_i\}_{i=1}^{l}$ labeled and $\mathcal{U} = \{\mathbf{x}_i, y_i\}_{i=l+1}^{n}$ unlabeled.
3. While data $\mathbf{x}'$ is in U:
    1. If $h_1(\mathbf{x}') \neq h_2(\mathbf{x}')$ for any $h_2 \in V$:
        1. Query the label of $\mathbf{x}'$ and get y'.
        2. $V = \{h: h(\mathbf{x}') = y'$ for all points.
    2. Otherwise:
        1. Ignore $\mathbf{x}'$.

Query by Committee (QBC)

Query by Committee overcomes the limitation of Query by Disagreement related to maintaining all possible version spaces by creating a committee of classifiers and using their votes as the mechanism to capture the disagreement (*References* [7]).

How does it work?

For this algorithm:

1. Initialize the data as $\mathcal{L} = \{\mathbf{x}_i, y_i\}_{i=1}^{l}$ labeled and $\mathcal{U} = \{\mathbf{x}_i, y_i\}_{i=l+1}^{n}$ unlabeled.
2. Train the committee of models $C = \{\theta^1, \theta^2, ... \theta^c\}$ on the labeled data w (see the following).
3. For all data $\mathbf{x}'$ in the U:
    1. Vote for predictions on $\mathbf{x}'$ as $\{y_\theta^1, y_\theta^2 ....y_\theta^c\}$.
    2. Rank the instances based on maximum disagreement (see the following).
    3. Choose k most informative data from U as set L_u to get labels from the oracle.
    4. Augment the labeled data with the k new labeled data points $L = L \cup L_u$.
    5. Retrain the models $\{\theta^1, \theta^2, ... \theta^c\}$ with new L.

With the two tasks of training the committee of learners and choosing the disagreement methods, each has various choices.

Training different models can be either done using different samples from L or they can be trained using ensemble methods such as boosting and bagging.

Vote entropy is one of the methods chosen as the disagreement metric to rank. The mathematical way of representing it is:

$$Q\{\mathbf{x}_u\} = argmax_x \sum_i \frac{V(y_i)}{|C|} \log \frac{V(y_i)}{|C|}$$

Here, $V(y_i)$ is number of votes given to the label y_i from all possible labels and $|C|$ is size of the committee.

Kullback-Leibler (KL) divergence is an information theoretic measure of divergence between two probability distributions. The disagreement is quantified as the average divergence of each committee's prediction from that of the consensus in the committee C:

$$Q\{\mathbf{x}_u\} = argmax_x \frac{1}{|C|} \sum_{\theta \in C} KL\left(P_\theta\left(y|\mathbf{x}\right) \| P_C\left(y|\mathbf{x}\right)\right)$$

Advantages and limitations

The advantages and limitations are the following:

- Simplicity and the fact that it can work with any supervised algorithm gives it a great advantage.
- There are theoretical guarantees of minimizing errors and generalizing in some conditions.
- Query by Disagreement suffers from maintaining a large number of valid hypotheses.
- These methods still suffer from the issue of wrong feedback going unnoticed and models potentially degrading.

Data distribution sampling

The previous methods selected the best instances from the unlabeled set based either on the uncertainty posed by the samples on the models or by reducing the hypothesis space size. Neither of these methods worked on what is best for the model itself. The idea behind data distribution sampling is that adding samples that help reduce the errors to the model serves to improve predictions on unseen instances using expected values (*References* [13 and 14]).

How does it work?

There are different ways to find what is the best sample for the given model and here we will describe each one in some detail.

Expected model change

The idea behind this is to select examples from the unlabeled set that that will bring maximum change in the model:

$$Q\{\mathbf{x}_u\} = argmin_x \sum_y P_\theta\left(y\,|\,\mathbf{x}\right) \sum_{x' \in u} H_{\theta+}\left(y\,|\,\mathbf{x}'\right)$$

Here, $P_\theta\left(y\,|\,\mathbf{x}\right)$ = expectation over labels of $\mathbf{x}$, $\sum_{x' \in u} H_{\theta+}\left(y\,|\,\mathbf{x}'\right)$ is the sum over unlabeled instances of the entropy of including $\mathbf{x}'$ after retraining with $\mathbf{x}$.

Expected error reduction

Here, the approach is to select examples from the unlabeled set that reduce the model's generalized error the most. The generalized error is measured using the unlabeled set with expected labels:

$$Q\{\mathbf{x}_u\} = argmin_x \sum_y P_\theta\left(y\,|\,\mathbf{x}\right) \sum_{x' \in u} 1 - p_\theta + \left(y\,|\,\mathbf{x}'\right)$$

Here, $P_\theta\left(y\,|\,\mathbf{x}\right)$ = expectation over labels of $\mathbf{x}$, $\sum_{x' \in u} H_{\theta+}\left(y\,|\,\mathbf{x}'\right)$ is the sum over unlabeled instances of the entropy of including $\mathbf{x}'$ after retraining with $\mathbf{x}$.

Variance reduction

The general equation of estimation on an out-of-sample error in terms of noise-bias-variance is given by the following:

$$E\left(\left(G(\mathbf{x}) - y\right)\right)^2\big|\,\mathbf{x}) = \textit{noise} + \textit{bias} + \textit{variance}$$

Here, $\mathbf{G}(\mathbf{x})$ is the model's prediction given the label y. In variance reduction, we select examples from the unlabeled set that most reduce the variance in the model:

$$Q\{\mathbf{x}_u\} = argmin_x \sum_{x' \in u} VAR_\theta + (y'|\mathbf{x}')$$

Here, $\theta +$ represents the model after it has been retrained with the new point $\mathbf{x}'$ and its label y'.

Density weighted methods

In this approach, we select examples from the unlabeled set that have average similarity to the labeled set.

This can be represented as follows:

$$Q\{\mathbf{x}_u\} = argmax_x \sum_{x \in u} sim(\mathbf{x}|\mathbf{x}') \times H_\theta(y|\mathbf{x})$$

Here, $sim(\mathbf{x}, \mathbf{x}')$ is the density term or the similarity term where $H_\theta(y|\mathbf{x})$ is the base utility measure.

Advantages and limitations

The advantages and limitations are as follows:

- The biggest advantage is that they work directly on the model as an optimization objective rather than implicit or indirect methods described before
- These methods can work on pool- or stream-based scenarios
- These methods have some theoretical guarantees on the bounds and generalizations
- The biggest disadvantage of these methods is computational cost and difficulty in implementation

Case study in active learning

This case study uses another well-known publicly available dataset to demonstrate active learning techniques using open source Java libraries. As before, we begin with defining the business problem, what tools and frameworks are used, how the principles of machine learning are realized in the solution, and what the data analysis steps reveal. Next, we describe the experiments that were conducted, evaluate the performance of the various models, and provide an analysis of the results.

Tools and software

For the experiments in Active Learning, JCLAL was the tool used. JCLAL is a Java framework for Active Learning, supporting single-label and multi-label learning.

 JCLAL is open source and is distributed under the GNU general public license: `https://sourceforge.net/p/jclal/git/ci/master/tree/`.

Business problem

The abalone dataset, which is used in these experiments, contains data on various physical and anatomical characteristics of abalone—commonly known as sea snails. The goal is to predict the number of rings in the shell, which is indicative of the age of the specimen.

Machine learning mapping

As we have seen, active learning is characterized by starting with a small set of labeled data accompanied by techniques of querying the unlabeled data such that we incrementally add instances to the labeled set. This is performed over multiple iterations, a batch at a time. The number of iterations and batch size are hyper-parameters for these techniques. The querying strategy and the choice of supervised learning method used to train on the growing number of labeled instances are additional inputs.

Data Collection

As before, we will use an existing dataset available from the UCI repository (`https://archive.ics.uci.edu/ml/datasets/Abalone`). The original owners of the database are the Department of Primary Industry and Fisheries in Tasmania, Australia.

The data types and descriptions of the attributes accompany the data and are reproduced in *Table 5*. The class attribute, Rings, has 29 distinct classes:

Name	Data type	Measurement units	Description
Sex	nominal	M, F, and I (infant)	sex of specimen
Length	continuous	mm	longest shell measurement
Diameter	continuous	mm	perpendicular to length
Height	continuous	mm	with meat in shell
Whole weight	continuous	grams	whole abalone
Shucked weight	continuous	grams	weight of meat
Viscera weight	continuous	grams	gut weight (after bleeding)
Shell weight	continuous	grams	after being dried
Rings	integer	count	+1.5 gives the age in years

Table 5. Abalone dataset features

Data sampling and transformation

For this experiment, we treated a randomly selected 4,155 records as unlabeled and kept the remaining 17 as labeled. There is no transformation of the data.

Feature analysis and dimensionality reduction

With only eight features, there is no need for dimensionality reduction. The dataset comes with some statistics on the features, reproduced in *Table 6*:

	Length	Diameter	Height	Whole	Shucked	Viscera	Shell	Rings
Min	0.075	0.055	0	0.002	0.001	0.001	0.002	1
Max	0.815	0.65	1.13	2.826	1.488	0.76	1.005	29
Mean	0.524	0.408	0.14	0.829	0.359	0.181	0.239	9.934
SD	0.12	0.099	0.042	0.49	0.222	0.11	0.139	3.224
Correl	0.557	0.575	0.557	0.54	0.421	0.504	0.628	1

Table 6. Summary statistics by feature

Models, results, and evaluation

We conducted two sets of experiments. The first used pool-based scenarios and the second, stream-based. In each set, we used entropy sampling, least confident sampling, margin sampling, and vote entropy sampling. The classifiers used were Naïve Bayes, Logistic Regression, and J48 (implementation of C4.5). For every experiment, 100 iterations were run, with batch sizes of 1 and 10. In *Table 7*, we present a subset of these results, specifically, pool-based and stream-based scenarios for each sampling method using Naïve Bayes, Simple Logistic, and C4.5 classifiers with a batch size of 10.

 The full set of results can be seen at `https://github.com/mjmlbook/` `mastering-java-machine-learning/tree/master/Chapter4`.

The JCLAL library requires an XML configuration file to specify which scenario to use, the query strategy selected, batch size, max iterations, and base classifier. The following is an example configuration:

```xml
<?xml version="1.0" encoding="UTF-8" standalone="no"?>
<experiment>
    <process evaluation-method-
    type="net.sf.jclal.evaluation.method.RealScenario">
        <file-labeled>datasets/abalone-labeled.arff</file-labeled>
        <file-unlabeled>datasets/abalone-unlabeled.arff</file-
        unlabeled>
        <algorithm type="net.sf.jclal.activelearning.algorithm
        .ClassicalALAlgorithm">
        <stop-criterion
        type="net.sf.jclal.activelearning.stopcriteria
        .MaxIteration">
                <max-iteration>10</max-iteration>
        </stop-criterion>
        <stop-criterion
        type="net.sf.jclal.activelearning.stopcriteria
        .UnlabeledSetEmpty"/>
            <listener
            type="net.sf.jclal.listener.RealScenarioListener">
                <informative-instances>reports/real-scenario-
                informative-data.txt</informative-instances>
            </listener>
            <scenario type="net.sf.jclal.activelearning.scenario
            .PoolBasedSamplingScenario">
                <batch-mode
                type="net.sf.jclal.activelearning.batchmode
                .QBestBatchMode">
                    <batch-size>1</batch-size>
```

```
            </batch-mode>
            <oracle type="net.sf.jclal.activelearning.oracle
            .ConsoleHumanOracle"/>
          <query-strategy
          type="net.sf.jclal.activelearning.singlelabel
          .querystrategy.EntropySamplingQueryStrategy">
              <wrapper-classifier
              type="net.sf.jclal.classifier.WekaClassifier">
                 <classifier
                 type="weka.classifiers.bayes.NaiveBayes"/>
              </wrapper-classifier>
          </query-strategy>
       </scenario>
     </algorithm>
   </process>
 </experiment>
```

The tools itself is invoked via the following:

```
java -jar jclal-<version>.jar -cfg <config-file>
```

Pool-based scenarios

In the following three tables, we compare results using pool-based scenarios when using Naïve Bayes, Simple Logistic, and C4.5 classifiers.

Naïve Bayes:

Experiment	Area Under ROC	F Measure	False Positive Rate	Precision	Recall
PoolBased-EntropySampling-NaiveBayes-b10	0.6021	0.1032	0.0556(1)	0.1805	0.1304
PoolBased-KLDivergence-NaiveBayes-b10	0.6639(1)	0.1441(1)	0.0563	0.1765	0.1504
PoolBased-LeastConfidentSampling-NaiveBayes-b10	0.6406	0.1300	0.0827	0.1835(1)	0.1810(1)
PoolBased-VoteEntropy-NaiveBayes-b10	0.6639(1)	0.1441(1)	0.0563	0.1765	0.1504

Table 7. Performance of pool-based scenario using Naïve Bayes classifier

Logistic Regression:

Experiment	Area Under ROC	F Measure	False Positive Rate	Precision	Recall
PoolBased-EntropySampling-SimpleLogistic-b10	0.6831	0.1571	0.1157	0.1651	0.2185(1)
PoolBased-KLDivergence-SimpleLogistic-b10	0.7175(1)	0.1616	0.1049	0.2117(1)	0.2065
PoolBased-LeastConfidentSampling-SimpleLogistic-b10	0.6629	0.1392	0.1181(1)	0.1751	0.1961
PoolBased-VoteEntropy-SimpleLogistic-b10	0.6959	0.1634(1)	0.0895	0.2307	0.1880

Table 8. Performance of pool-based scenario using Logistic Regression classifier

C4.5:

Experiment	Area Under ROC	F Measure	False Positive Rate	Precision	Recall
PoolBased-EntropySampling-J48-b10	0.6730(1)	0.3286(1)	0.0737	0.3432(1)	0.32780(1)
PoolBased-KLDivergence-J48-b10	0.6686	0.2979	0.0705(1)	0.3153	0.2955
PoolBased-LeastConfidentSampling-J48-b10	0.6591	0.3094	0.0843	0.3124	0.3227
PoolBased-VoteEntropy-J48-b10	0.6686	0.2979	0.0706	0.3153	0.2955

Table 9. Performance of pool-based scenario using C4.5 classifier

Stream-based scenarios

In the following three tables, we have results for experiments on stream-based scenarios using Naïve Bayes, Logistic Regression, and C4.5 classifiers with four different sampling methods.

Naïve Bayes:

Experiment	Area Under ROC	F Measure	False Positive Rate	Precision	Recall
StreamBased-EntropySampling-NaiveBayes-b10	0.6673(1)	0.1432(1)	0.0563	0.1842(1)	0.1480
StreamBased-LeastConfidentSampling-NaiveBayes-b10	0.5585	0.0923	0.1415	0.1610	0.1807(1)
StreamBased-MarginSampling-NaiveBayes-b10	0.6736(1)	0.1282	0.0548(1)	0.1806	0.1475
StreamBased-VoteEntropyQuery-NaiveBayes-b10	0.5585	0.0923	0.1415	0.1610	0.1807(1)

Table 10. Performance of stream-based scenario using Naïve Bayes classifier

Logistic Regression:

Experiment	Area Under ROC	F Measure	False Positive Rate	Precision	Recall
StreamBased-EntropySampling-SimpleLogistic-b10	0.7343(1)	0.1994(1)	0.0871	0.2154	0.2185(1)
StreamBased-LeastConfidentSampling-SimpleLogistic-b10	0.7068	0.1750	0.0906	0.2324(1)	0.2019
StreamBased-MarginSampling-SimpleLogistic-b10	0.7311	0.1994(1)	0.0861	0.2177	0.214
StreamBased-VoteEntropy-SimpleLogistic-b10	0.5506	0.0963	0.0667(1)	0.1093	0.1117

Table 11. Performance of stream-based scenario using Logistic Regression classifier

C4.5:

Experiment	Area Under ROC	F Measure	False Positive Rate	Precision	Recall
StreamBased-EntropySampling-J48-b10	0.6648	0.3053	0.0756	0.3189(1)	0.3032
StreamBased-LeastConfidentSampling-J48-b10	0.6748(1)	0.3064(1)	0.0832	0.3128	0.3189(1)
StreamBased-MarginSampling-J48-b10	0.6660	0.2998	0.0728(1)	0.3163	0.2967
StreamBased-VoteEntropy-J48-b10	0.4966	0.0627	0.0742	0.1096	0.0758

Table 12. Performance of stream-based scenario using C4.5 classifier

Analysis of active learning results

It is quite interesting to see that pool-based, Query By Committee — an ensemble method — using KL-Divergence sampling does really well across most classifiers. As discussed in the section, these methods have been proven to have a theoretical guarantee on reducing the errors by keeping a large hypothesis space, and this experimental result supports that empirically.

Pool-based, entropy-based sampling using C4.5 as a classifier has the highest Precision, Recall, FPR and F-Measure. Also with stream-based, entropy sampling with C4.5, the metrics are similarly high. With different sampling techniques and C4.5 using pool-based as in KL-Divergence, LeastConfident or vote entropy, the metrics are significantly higher. Thus, this can be attributed more strongly to the underlying classifier C4.5 in finding non-linear patterns.

The Logistic Regression algorithm performs very well in both stream-based and pool-based when considering AUC. This may be completely due to the fact that LR has a good probabilistic approach in confidence mapping, which is an important factor for giving good AUC scores.

Summary

After a tour of supervised and unsupervised machine learning techniques and their application to real-world datasets in the previous chapters, this chapter introduces the concepts, techniques, and tools of **Semi-Supervised Learning (SSL)** and **Active Learning (AL)**.

In SSL, we are given a few labeled examples and many unlabeled ones — the goal is either to simply train on the labeled ones in order to classify the unlabeled ones (transductive SSL), or use the unlabeled and labeled examples to train models to correctly classify new, unseen data (inductive SSL). All techniques in SSL are based on one or more of the assumptions related to semi-supervised smoothness, cluster togetherness, and manifold togetherness.

Different SSL techniques are applicable to different situations. The simple self-training SSL is straightforward and works with most supervised learning algorithms; when the data is from more than just one domain, the co-training SSL is a suitable method. When the cluster togetherness assumption holds, the cluster and label SSL technique can be used; a "closeness" measure is exploited by transductive graph label propagation, which can be computationally expensive. Transductive SVM performs well with linear or non-linear data and we see an example of training a TSVM with a Gaussian kernel on the UCI Breast Cancer dataset using the JKernelMachines library. We present experiments comparing SSL models using the graphical Java tool KEEL in the concluding part of the SSL portion of the chapter.

We introduced active learning (AL) in the second half of the chapter. In this type of learning, various strategies are used to query the unlabeled portion of the dataset in order to present the expert with examples that will prove most effective in learning from the entire dataset. As the expert, or oracle, provides the labels to the selected instances, the learner steadily improves its ability to generalize. The techniques of AL are characterized by the choice of classifier, or committee of classifiers, and importantly, on the querying strategy chosen. These strategies include uncertainty sampling, where the instances with the least confidence are queries, version sampling, where a subset of the hypotheses that explain the training data are selected, and data distribution sampling, which involves improving the model by selections that would decrease the generalization error. We presented a case study using the UCI abalone dataset to demonstrate active learning in practice. The tool used here is the JCLAL Java framework for active learning.

References

1. Yarowsky, D (1995). *Unsupervised word sense disambiguation rivaling supervised methods*. Proceedings of the 33rd Annual Meeting of the Association for Computational Linguistics (pp. 189–196)

2. Blum, A., and Mitchell, T (1998). *Combining labeled and unlabeled data with co-training*. COLT: Proceedings of the Workshop on Computational Learning Theory.

3. Demiriz, A., Bennett, K., and Embrechts, M (1999). *Semi-supervised clustering using genetic algorithms*. Proceedings of Artificial Neural Networks in Engineering.

4. Yoshua Bengio, Olivier Delalleau, Nicolas Le Roux (2006). *Label Propagation and Quadratic Criterion*. In Semi-Supervised Learning, pp. 193-216

5. T. Joachims (1998). *Transductive Inference for Text Classification using Support Vector Machines*, ICML.

6. B. Settles (2008). *Curious Machines: Active Learning with Structured Instances*. PhD thesis, University of Wisconsin–Madison.

7. D. Angluin (1988). *Queries and concept learning*. Machine Learning, 2:319–342.

8. D. Lewis and W. Gale (1994). *A sequential algorithm for training text classifiers*. In Proceedings of the ACM SIGIR Conference on Research and Development in Information Retrieval, pages 3–12. ACM/Springer.

9. H.S. Seung, M. Opper, and H. Sompolinsky (1992). *Query by committee*. In Proceedings of the ACM Workshop on Computational Learning Theory, pages 287–294.

10. D. Cohn, L. Atlas, R. Ladner, M. El-Sharkawi, R. Marks II, M. Aggoune, and D. Park (1992). *Training connectionist networks with queries and selective sampling*. In Advances in Neural Information Processing Systems (NIPS). Morgan Kaufmann.

11. D. Cohn, L. Atlas, and R. Ladner (1994). *Improving generalization with active learning*. Machine Learning, 15(2):201–221.

12. D. Lewis and J. Catlett (1994). *Heterogeneous uncertainty sampling for supervised learning*. In Proceedings of the International Conference on Machine Learning (ICML), pages 148–156. Morgan Kaufmann.

13. S. Dasgupta, A. Kalai, and C. Monteleoni (2005). *Analysis of perceptron-based active learning*. In Proceedings of the Conference on Learning Theory (COLT), pages 249–263. Springer.

14. S. Dasgupta, D. Hsu, and C. Monteleoni (2008). *A general agnostic active learning algorithm*. In Advances in Neural Information Processing Systems (NIPS), volume 20, pages 353–360. MIT Press.

15. T. Mitchell (1982). *Generalization as search*. Artificial Intelligence, 18:203–226.

5
Real-Time Stream Machine Learning

In *Chapter 2, Practical Approach to Real-World Supervised Learning, Chapter 3, Unsupervised Machine Learning Techniques,* and *Chapter 4, Semi-Supervised and Active Learning,* we discussed various techniques of classification, clustering, outlier detection, semi-supervised, and active learning. The form of learning done from existing or historic data is traditionally known as batch learning.

All of these algorithms or techniques assume three things, namely:

- Finite training data is available to build different models.
- The learned model will be static; that is, patterns won't change.
- The data distribution also will remain the same.

In many real-world data scenarios, there is either no training data available a priori or the data is dynamic in nature; that is, changes continuously with respect to time. Many real-world applications may also have data which has a transient nature to it and comes in high velocity or volume such as IoT sensor information, network monitoring, and Twitter feeds. The requirement here is to learn from the instance immediately and then update the learning.

The nature of dynamic data and potentially changing distribution renders existing batch-based algorithms and techniques generally unsuitable for such tasks. This gave rise to adaptable or updatable or incremental learning algorithms in machine learning. These techniques can be applied to continuously learn from the data streams. In many cases, the disadvantage of learning from Big Data due to size and the need to fit the entire data into memory can also be overcome by converting the Big Data learning problem into an incremental learning problem and inspecting one example at a time.

In this chapter, we will discuss the assumptions and discuss different techniques in supervised and unsupervised learning that facilitate real-time or stream machine learning. We will use the open source library **Massive Online Analysis (MOA)** for performing a real-world case study.

The major sections of this chapter are:

- Assumptions and mathematical notation.

- Basic stream processing and computational techniques. A discussion of stream computations, sliding windows including the ADWIN algorithm, and sampling.

- Concept drift and drift detection: Introduces learning evolving systems and data management, detection methods, and implicit and explicit adaptation.

- Incremental supervised learning: A discussion of learning from labeled stream data, modeling techniques including linear, non-linear, and ensemble algorithms. This is followed by validation, evaluation, and model comparison methods.

- Incremental unsupervised learning: Clustering techniques similar to those discussed in *Chapter 3, Unsupervised Machine Learning Techniques*, including validation and evaluation techniques.

- Unsupervised learning using outlier detection: Partition-based and distance-based, and the validation and evaluation techniques used.

- Case study for stream-based learning: Introduces the MOA framework, presents the business problem, feature analysis, mapping to machine learning blueprint; describes the experiments, and concludes with the presentation and analysis of the results.

Assumptions and mathematical notations

There are some key assumptions made by many stream machine learning techniques and we will state them explicitly here:

- The number of features in the data is fixed.

- Data has small to medium dimensions, or number of features, typically in the hundreds.

- The number of examples or training data can be infinite or very large, typically in the millions or billions.

- The number of class labels in supervised learning or clusters are small and finite, typically less than 10.

- Normally, there is an upper bound on memory; that is, we cannot fit all the data in memory, so learning from data must take this into account, especially lazy learners such as K-Nearest-Neighbors.

- Normally, there is an upper bound on the time taken to process the event or the data, typically a few milliseconds.

- The patterns or the distributions in the data can be evolving over time.

- Learning algorithms must converge to a solution in finite time.

Let $D_t = \{\mathbf{x}_i, y_i : y = f(x)\}$ be the given data available at time $t \in \{1, 2, \dots i\}$.

An incremental learning algorithm produces sequences of models/hypotheses $\{.., G_{j-1}, G_j, G_{j+1}..\}$ for the sequence of data $\{.., D_{j-1}, D_j, D_{j+1}..\}$ and model/hypothesis G_i depends only on the previous hypothesis G_{i-1} and current data D_i.

Basic stream processing and computational techniques

We will now describe some basic computations that can be performed on the stream of data. If we must run summary operations such as aggregations or histograms with limits on memory and speed, we can be sure that some kind of trade-off will be needed. Two well-known types of approximations in these situations are:

- ϵ Approximation: The computation is close to the exact value within the fraction ϵ of error.

- (ϵ, δ) Approximation: The computation is close to the exact value within $1 \pm \epsilon$ with probability within $1 - \delta$.

Stream computations

We will illustrate some basic computations and aggregations to highlight the difference between batch and stream-based calculations when we must compute basic operations with constraints on memory and yet consider the entire data:

- **Frequency count or point queries**: The generic technique of Count-Min Sketch has been successfully applied to perform various summarizations on the data streams. The primary technique is creating a window of size $w \times d$. Then, given a desired probability (δ) and admissible error (ϵ), the size of data in memory can be created using $w = 2/\epsilon$ and $d = \left\lceil \log\left(\frac{1}{\delta}\right) \right\rceil$.

  Associated with each row is a hash function: $h(.)$. This uniformly transforms a value x to a value in the interval $[1, 2 \dots w]$. This method of lookup and updates can be used for performing point queries of values or dot products or frequency counts.

- **Distinct count**: The generic technique of Hash-Sketch can be used to perform "distinct values" queries or counts. Given the domain of incoming stream values $x \in [0,1,2\dots N-1]$, the hash function $h(x)$ maps the values uniformly across $[0,1,\dots 2^L-1]$, where $L=O(\log N)$.

- **Mean**: Computing the mean without the need for storing all the values is very useful and is normally employed using a recursive method where only the number of observations (n) and sum of values seen so far $(\sum x_n)$ is needed:

$$\overline{x_n} = \frac{x_n + (n-1) \times \overline{x_{n-1}}}{n}$$

- **Standard deviation**: Like the mean, standard deviation can be computed using the memoryless option with only the number of observations (n), sum of values seen so far $(\sum x_n)$, and sum of squares of the values $(\sum x_n^2)$:

$$\sigma_n = \sqrt{\frac{\left(\sum x_n^2 - \frac{\left(\sum x_n^2 \right)}{n} \right)}{n-1}}$$

- **Correlation coefficient**: Given a stream of two different values, many algorithms need to compute the correlation coefficient between the two which can be done by maintaining the running sum of each stream ($\sum x_n$ and $\sum y_n$), the sum of squared values ($\sum x_n^2$ and $\sum y_n^2$), and the cross-product ($\sum x_n \times y_n$). The correlation is given by:

$$corr(x,y) = \frac{\sum x_n \times y_n - \dfrac{\sum x_n \times y_n}{n}}{\sqrt{\sum x_n^2 - \dfrac{\left(\sum x_n^2\right)}{n}}\sqrt{\sum y_n^2 - \dfrac{\left(\sum y_n^2\right)}{n}}}$$

Sliding windows

Often, you don't need the entire data for computing statistics or summarizations but only the "recent past". In such cases, sliding window techniques are used to calculate summary statistics by keeping the window size either fixed or adaptable and moving it over the recent past.

ADaptable sliding WINdow (**ADWIN**) is one well-known technique used to detect change as well as estimating values needed in the computation. The idea behind ADWIN is to keep a variable-length window of last seen values with the characteristic that the window has a maximum length statistically consistent with the fact that there has been no change in the average value within the window. In other words, the older values are dropped if and only if a new incoming value would change the average. This has the two-fold advantage of recording change and maintaining the dynamic value, such as aggregate, over the recent streams. The determination of the subjective notion "large enough" for dropping items can be determined using the well-known Hoeffding bound as:

$$\varepsilon_{cut} = \sqrt{\left(\frac{1}{2m}\ln\frac{4|W|}{\delta}\right)}$$

Here $m = \dfrac{2}{\left(\frac{1}{|W_0|} + \frac{1}{|W_1|}\right)}$ is the harmonic mean between two windows W_0 and W_1 of size $|W_0|$ and $|W_1|$ respectively, with W_1 containing the more recent elements.

Further, let $\hat{\mu}W_0$ and $\hat{\mu}W_1$ be the respective calculated averages.

The algorithm can be generalized as:

1. ADWIN (*x: inputstream, δ: confidence*)
2. init (*W*) //Initialize Window *W*
3. while (*x*){

   $W \leftarrow W \cup \{x_t\}$ //add new instance x_t to the head of Window *W*

4. repeat

   $W \leftarrow W - x_{old}$ //drop elements from tail of the window

5. until $|\hat{\mu}W_0 - \hat{\mu}W_1| < \varepsilon_{cut}$ holds for every split of *W*
6. output $\hat{\mu}V$
7. }

ADWIN has also shown that it provides theoretical bounds on false positives and false negatives, which makes it a very promising technique to use.

Sampling

In many stream-based algorithms, there is a need to reduce the data or select a subset of data for analysis. The normal methodology of sampling on the whole data must be augmented for stream-based data.

The key concerns in sampling that must be addressed are how unbiased the samples are and how representative they are of the population from which streams are being generated. In a non-streaming environment, this depends completely on the sample size and the sampling method. Uniform random sampling (*Chapter 2, Practical Approach to Real-World Supervised Learning*) is one of the most well-known techniques employed to reduce the data in the batch data world. The reservoir sampling technique is considered to be a very effective way of reducing the data given the memory constraints.

The basic idea of reservoir sampling is to keep a reservoir or sample of fixed size, say *k*, and every element that enters the stream has a probability *k/n* of replacing an older element in the reservoir. The detailed algorithm is shown here:

```
ReservoirSampling(x:inputstream, k:sizeOfReservoir)
//add first k elements to reservoir
for(i = 0; i < k; i++)
  addToReservoir(x)
  while (x) {
    for(i = 0; i < k; i++)
```

```
//flip a coin to get random integer
r = randomInteger[1..n]
if(r ≤ k){
    //move it inside the reservoir
    addToReservoir(x)
    //delete an instance randomly from reservoir
    position = randomInteger[1..k]
    removeInstance(position)
}
}
```

There are extensions to these such as the Min-wise Sampling and Load Shedding that overcome some issues associated with the base method.

Concept drift and drift detection

As discussed in the introduction of the chapter, the dynamic nature of infinite streams stands in direct opposition to the basic principles of stationary learning; that is, that the distribution of the data or patterns remain constant. Although there can be changes that are *swift* or *abrupt*, the discussion here is around slow, gradual changes. These slow, gradual changes are fairly hard to detect and separating the changes from the noise becomes tougher still:

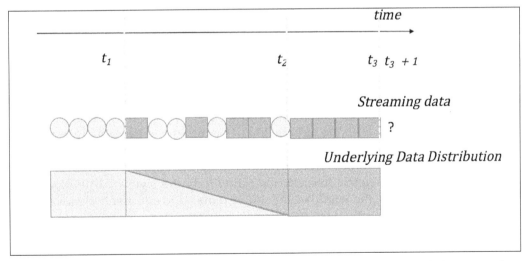

Figure 1 Concept drift illustrated by the gradual change in color from yellow to blue in the bottom panel. Sampled data reflects underlying change in data distribution, which must be detected and a new model learned.

There have been several techniques described in various studies in the last two decades that can be categorized as shown in the following figure:

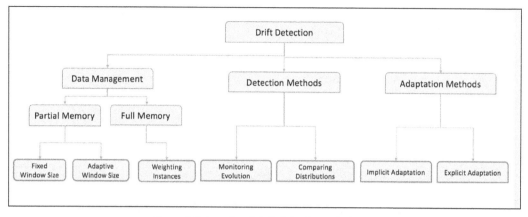

Figure 2 Categories of drift detection techniques

Data management

The main idea is to manage a model in memory that is consistent with the dynamic nature of the data.

Partial memory

These techniques use the most recently used data in a memory buffer to learn or derive summary information. The key question as discussed previously is: what is the right window size to be effective in detecting the change and learning effectively? In Fixed Window Size based techniques, we use the idea of a queue where a new instance with a recent timestamp comes in and the one with the oldest is evicted. The window thus contains all the recent enough examples and the size is generally chosen based on physical availability of memory and size of data elements in the queue. In Adaptive Window Size, the queue is used in conjunction with a detection algorithm. When the detection algorithm indicates signs of drifts based on performance evaluation, the window size can be reduced to effectively remove old examples which no longer help the model.

Full memory

The idea is to store sufficient statistics over all the examples or data seen. One way to do this is to put weights on the data and weights decay over time. Exponential weighting using the rate factor given by λ can be very effective:

$$w_\lambda(x) = exp(-\lambda * i)$$

Detection methods

Given the probability $P(X)$ that the given data is observed, the probability of patterns/class $P(C)$, and the probability of data given class $P(X|C)$—which is the model—the detection method can be divided into two categories, at a high level:

- Monitoring evolution or performance of the model, classifier, or $P(C|X)$
- Monitoring distributions from the environment or observing $P(X)$, $P(C)$, and $P(X|C)$

Monitoring model evolution

Although this method is based on the assumption that all the learning of models is stationary and data is coming from **independent, identical distributions (i.i.d.)**, which doesn't hold true in many applications, it has nevertheless been shown to be effective. Some of the well-known techniques are described next.

Widmer and Kubat

This is one of the earliest methods which observed the error rates or misclassification rates and the changes to the model such as tree structures due to new branches, for instance. Using these and known thresholds, the learning window size is increased or decreased.

Drift Detection Method or DDM

This method assumes that the parameter being observed, such as the classifier labeling things correctly or incorrectly, is a binary random variable which follows a binomial distribution. It assumes probability of misclassification at probability pi with standard deviation of $s_i = \sqrt{p_i(1-p_i)/i}$ where the values are computed at the ith point in the sequence. The method then uses two levels:

- Warning level: When $p_i + s_i \geq p_{min} + 2 * s_{min}$
- Detection level: When $p_i + s_i \geq p_{min} + 3 * s_{min}$

All the examples between the "warning" and "detection" levels are used to train a new classifier that will replace the "non-performing" classifier when the "detection" level is reached.

Early Drift Detection Method or EDDM

EDDM uses the same technique as DDM but with a slight modification. It uses classification rate (that is, recall) rather than error rate (1 – accuracy) and uses the distance between the number of right predictions and two wrong predictions to change the levels.

EDDM computes the mean distance between the two errors p_i' and standard deviation between the two s_i'. The levels are then:

- Warning level: $(p_i' + 2 * s_i') / (p'_{max} + 2 * s'_{max}) < a$
- Detection level: $(p_i' + 2 * s_i') / (p'_{max} + 2 * s'_{max}) < \beta$

The parameters a and β are normally tuned by the user to something around 90% and 95% respectively.

Monitoring distribution changes

When there are no models or classifiers to detect changes, we apply techniques that use some form of statistical tests for monitoring distribution changes. These tests are used to identify the distribution changes. Owing to assumptions, whether parametric or non-parametric, and different biases, it is difficult to say concretely which works best. Here we provide some of the well-known statistical tests.

Welch's t test

This is an adaptation of the Student t test with two samples. The test is adapted to take two windows of size N_1 and N_2 with means $\bar{X}_1$ and $\bar{X}_2$ and variances s_1^2 and s_2^2 to compute the p value and use that to reject or accept the null hypothesis:

$$pvalue = \left(\bar{X}_1 - \bar{X}_2\right) / \left(\sqrt{s_1^2/N + s_2^2/N_2}\right)$$

Kolmogorov-Smirnov's test

This statistical test is normally used to compare distances between two distributions and validate if they are below certain thresholds or not. This can be adapted for change detection by using windows of two different sample sizes, N_1 and N_2, with different cumulative distribution functions, $F_1(x)$ and $F_2(x)$, KS distance:

$$ksDistance = \max_x \left| F_1(x) - F_2(x) \right|$$

The null hypothesis, which assumes the two distributions are similar, is rejected with confidence of a if and only if $ksDistance * \sqrt{N_1 N_2 / (N_1 + N_2)} > K_\alpha$, which is obtained by a lookup in the Kolmogorov-Smirnov's table.

CUSUM and Page-Hinckley test

The **cumulative sum** (**CUSUM**) is designed to indicate when the mean of the input is significantly different from zero:

$g_0 = 0$, $g_t = max(0, g_{t-1}) + \epsilon_t - v)$

We raise change detection when $g_t > h$, where (h, v) are user-defined parameters. Note that the CUSUM test is memoryless and is one-sided or asymmetric, detecting only the increase.

The Page Hinckley test is similar to CUSUM with a small variation as shown here:

$g_0 = 0$, $g_t = g_{t-1} + \epsilon_t - v)$

For increasing and decreasing the values, we use $G_t = min(g_t, G_{t-1})$ or $G_t = max(g_t, G_{t-1})$, and $Gt - gt > h$ for change detection.

Adaptation methods

Explicit and implicit adaptation are the two well-known techniques for adapting to environment changes when a change is detected.

Explicit adaptation

In explicit adaptation, an additional technique from among the following is used:

- Retrain the model from scratch with new data so the previous model or data does not impact the new model

- Update the model with the changes or new data such that the transition is smooth—assumes changes are gradual and not drastic

- Create a sequence or ensemble of models that are learned over time—when a collaborative approach is better than any single model

Implicit adaptation

In implicit adaptation, we generally use ensemble algorithms/models to adapt to the concept change. This can mean using different combinations ranging from a single classifier, to predicting in the ensemble, to using ADWIN for adaptive window-based with the classifier—all fall within the choices for implicit adaptation.

Incremental supervised learning

This section introduces several techniques used to learn from stream data when the true label for each instance is available. In particular, we present linear, non-linear, and ensemble-based algorithms adapted to incremental learning, as well as methods required in the evaluation and validation of these models, keeping in mind that learning is constrained by limits on memory and CPU time.

Modeling techniques

The modeling techniques are divided into linear algorithms, non-linear algorithms, and ensemble methods.

Linear algorithms

The linear methods described here require little to no adaptation to handle stream data.

Online linear models with loss functions

Different loss functions such as hinge, logistic, and squared error can be used in this algorithm.

Inputs and outputs

Only numeric features are used in these methods. The choice of loss function l and learning rate λ at which to apply the weight updates are taken as input parameters. The output is typically updatable models that give predictions accompanied by confidence values.

How does it work?

The basic algorithm assumes linear weight combinations similar to linear/logistic regression explained in *Chapter 2, Practical Approach to Real-World Supervised Learning.* The stream or online learning algorithm can be summed up as:

1. for(t=1,2,...T) do
   1. $\mathbf{x}_t = receive()$; // receive the data
   2. $\hat{y}_t = \text{sgn}\left(f\left(\mathbf{x}_t, \mathbf{w}_t\right)\right)$; //predict the label
   3. $y_t = obtainTrueLabel()$; // get the true label
   4. $loss = l(\mathbf{w}_t, (\mathbf{x}_t, \mathbf{w}_t))$; // calculate the loss
   5. if($l(\mathbf{w}_t,(\mathbf{x}_t, \mathbf{w}_t)) > 0$ then
   6. $\mathbf{w}_{t+1} = \mathbf{w}_t + \lambda * \Delta\left(\mathbf{w}_t,(\mathbf{x}_t,\mathbf{w}_t)\right)$; //update the weights
   7. end

2. end

Different loss functions can be plugged in based on types of problems; some of the well-known types are shown here:

- Classification:
  - Hinge loss: $l(\mathbf{w}_t, (\mathbf{x}_t, \mathbf{w}_t)) = \max(0, 1 - yf(\mathbf{x}_t, \mathbf{w}_t))$
  - Logistic loss: $\ell\left(\mathbf{w}_t,(\mathbf{x}_t,\mathbf{w}_t)\right) = \frac{1}{\ln 2}\ln\left(1 + e^{-yf(\mathbf{x}_t,\mathbf{w}_t)}\right)$
- Regression:
  - Squared loss: $\ell\left(\mathbf{w}_t,(\mathbf{x}_t,\mathbf{w}_t)\right) = \left(1 - yf\left(\mathbf{x}_t,\mathbf{w}_t\right)\right)^2$

Stochastic Gradient Descent (SGD) can be thought of as changing the weights to minimize the squared loss as in the preceding loss functions but going in the direction of the gradient with each example. The update of weights can be described as:

$$\mathbf{w}_{t+1} = \mathbf{w}_t - \lambda * \Delta J * \mathbf{x}_t$$

$$\Delta J = -\left(y_t - \hat{y}_t \right) \hat{y}_t \left(1 - \hat{y}_t \right)$$

Advantages and limitations

Online linear models have similar advantages and disadvantages as the linear models described in *Chapter 2, Practical Approach to Real-World Supervised Learning*:

- Interpretable to some level as the weights of each features give insights on the impact of each feature

- Assumes linear relationship, additive and uncorrelated features, and hence doesn't model complex non-linear real-world data

- Very susceptible to outliers in the data

- Very fast and normally one of the first algorithms to try or baseline

Online Naïve Bayes

Bayes theorem is applied to get predictions as the posterior probability, given for an *m* dimensional input:

$$P\left(y \mid \mathbf{x} \right) = \frac{P(y) * \prod_{j=1}^{m} P\left(X_j \mid Y \right)}{P\left(\mathbf{x} \right)}$$

Inputs and outputs

Online Naïve Bayes can accept both categorical and continuous inputs. The categorical features are easier, as the algorithm must maintain counts for each class while computing the $P(X_j \mid Y)$ probability for each feature given the class. For continuous features, we must either assume a distribution, such as Gaussian, or to compute online Kernel Density estimates in an incremental way or discretize the numeric features incrementally. The outputs are updatable models and can predict the class accompanied by confidence value. Being probabilistic models, they have better confidence scores distributed between 0 and 1.

How does it work?

1. for(t = 1,2,...T) do
    1. x_t = *receive()*; // receive the data
    2. incrementCounters(x_t); //update the $P(X_j | Y)$
    3. $< \hat{y}_t, confidence > = applyBayesRule(x_t)$ //posterior probability
2. end

Advantages and limitations

- This is the fastest algorithm and has a low memory footprint as well as computation cost. It is very popular among online or fast learners.

- Assumes distribution or some biases on the numeric features that can impact the predictive quality.

Non-linear algorithms

One of the most popular non-linear stream learning classifiers in use is the Hoeffding Tree. In the following subsections, the notion of the Hoeffding bound is introduced, followed by the algorithm itself.

Hoeffding trees or very fast decision trees (VFDT)

The key idea behind **Hoeffding Trees (HT)** is the concept of the Hoeffding bound. Given a real-valued random variable **x** whose range of values has size **R**, suppose we have **n** independent observations of **x** and compute the mean as $\overline{x}$.

The Hoeffding bound states that, with a probability of 1 – δ, the actual mean of the variable **x** is at least $\overline{x} - \varepsilon$ where $\varepsilon = \sqrt{\dfrac{R^2 \ln 1/\delta}{2n}}$

The Hoeffding bound is independent of the probability distribution generating the samples and gives a good approximation with just **n** examples.

The idea of the Hoeffding bound is used in the leaf expansion. If x_1 is the most informative feature and x_2 ranks second, then split using a user-defined split function G(.) in a way such that:

$$G(x_1) - G(x_2) > \varepsilon = \sqrt{\frac{R^2 \ln 1/\delta}{2n}}$$

Inputs and outputs

Both categorical and continuous data can be part of the data input. Continuous features are discretized in many implementations. The desired probability parameter $1 - \delta$ and the split function common to Decision Trees $G(.)$ becomes part of the input. The output is the interpretable Decision Tree model and can predict/learn with class and confidence values.

How does it work?

HoeffdingTree(x:inputstream,G(.):splitFunction,δ:probabilityBound)

1. Let HT be a tree with single leaf(root)
2. InitCounts(n_{ijk}, root)
3. for(t=1,2,...T) do //all data from stream
    1. $xt = receive()$; //receive the data
    2. $y_t = obtainTrueLabel()$; //get the true label
    3. HTGrow((x_t, y_t), **HT**, δ)
    4. end

HTGrow((x_t, y_t), HT, $G(.)$, δ)

1. $l = sort((x_t, y_t), \textbf{HT})$; //sort the data to leaf l using HT
2. *updateCounts(n_{ijk}, l)*; // update the counts at leaf l
3. *if(examplesSoFarNotOfSameClass())*;// check if there are multiple classes
4. *computeForEachFeature(,G(.))*
    1. *if(G(x_1) – G(x_2)>* $\varepsilon = \sqrt{\dfrac{R^2 \ln 1/\delta}{2n}}$; //difference between two features
       splitLeaf(x_1)
       for each branch
       createNewLeaf
       initializeCounts();

Hoeffding Trees have interesting properties, such as:

- They are a robust low variance model
- They exhibit lower overfitting
- Theoretical guarantees with high probability on the error rate exist due to Hoeffding bounds

There are variations to Hoeffding Trees that can adapt concept drift, known as Concept-Adapting VFDT. They use the sliding window concept on the stream. Each node in the decision tree keeps sufficient statistics; based on the Hoeffding test, an alternate subtree is grown and swapped in when the accuracy is better.

Advantages and limitations

The advantages and limitations are as follows:

- The basic HT has issues with attributes being close to the chosen ϵ and breaks the ties. Deciding the number of attributes at any node is again an issue. Some of it is resolved in VFDT.

- Memory constraints on expansion of the trees as well as time spent on an instance becomes an issue as the tree changes.

- VFDT has issues with changes in patterns and CVFDT tries to overcome these as discussed previously. It is one of the most elegant, fast, interpretable algorithms for real-time and big data.

Ensemble algorithms

The idea behind ensemble learning is similar to batch supervised learning where multiple algorithms are trained and combined in some form to predict unseen data. The same benefits accrue even in the online setting from different approaches to ensembles; for example, using multiple algorithms of different types, using models of similar type but with different parameters or sampled data, all so that different search spaces or patterns are found and the total error is reduced.

Weighted majority algorithm

The **weighted majority algorithm (WMA)** trains a set of base classifiers and combines their votes, weighted in some way, and makes predictions based on the majority.

Inputs and outputs

The constraint on types of inputs (categorical only, continuous only, or mixed) depends on the chosen base classifiers. The interpretability of the model depends on the base model(s) selected but it is difficult to interpret the outputs of a combination of models. The weights for each model get updated by a factor (β) per example/instance when the prediction is incorrect. The combination of weights and models can give some idea of interpretability.

How does it work?

WeightedMajorityAlgorithm(x: inputstream, hm: m learner models)

1. *initializeWeights(w$_i$)*
2. for(t=1, 2,...T) do
    1. $x_t = receive();$
    2. *foreach model hk $\in$ h*
    3. $y_i \leftarrow h_k(\mathbf{x}_t);$

3. *if* $\sum_{i:y_1=1:} w_i \geq \sum_{i:y_1=0} w_i$ *then*

    $\hat{y} \leftarrow 1$

4. else

    $\hat{y} \leftarrow 0$

5. if y is known then
    1. for $i = 1$ to m do
    2. if $y_i \neq y$ then
    3. $wi \leftarrow w_i * \beta$
        end if
        end for

6. end

Advantages and limitations

The advantages and limitations are as follows:

- WMA has simple implementation and theoretic bounds on ensemble errors
- The difficulty is to choose the right base algorithm as the model and the number of models in the pool

Online Bagging algorithm

As we saw in the chapter on supervised learning, the bagging algorithm, which creates different samples from the training sets and uses multiple algorithms to learn and predict, reduces the variance and is very effective in learning.

Inputs and outputs

The constraint on the types of inputs (categorical only, continuous only, or mixed) depends on the chosen base classifiers. The base classifier algorithm with parameter choices corresponding to the algorithm are also the inputs. The output is the learned model that can predict the class/confidence based on the classifier chosen.

How does it work?

The basic batch bagging algorithm requires the entire data to be available to create different samples and provide these samples to different classifiers. Oza's Online Bagging algorithm changes this constraint and makes it possible to learn from unbounded data streams. Based on sampling, each training instance in the original algorithm gets replicated many times and each base model is trained with k copies of the original instances where:

$$P(k) = exp(-1)/k!$$

This is equivalent to taking one training example and choosing for each classifier $k{\sim}Poisson(1)$ and updating the base classifier k times. Thus, the dependency on the number of examples is removed and the algorithm can run on an infinite stream:

OnlineBagging(x: inputstream, h_m: m learner models)

1. initialize base models h_m for all $m \in \{1,2,..M\}$
2. for(t=1,2,...T) do
    1. x_t=receive();
    2. foreach model $m = \{1,2,..M\}$
       $w = Poisson(1)$
       updateModel(h_m, w, x_t)
    3. end
3. return
4. $\boldsymbol{h}_{final} = \boldsymbol{argmax}_{y \in Y} \sum_{t=1}^{T} \boldsymbol{I}\left(\boldsymbol{h}(\mathbf{x})_t = y\right)$

Advantages and limitations

The advantages and limitaions are as follows:

- It has been empirically shown to be one of the most successful online or stream algorithms.
- The weight must be given to the data instance without looking at the other instances; this reduces the choices of different weighting schemes which are available in batch and are good in model performance.

The performance is entirely determined by the choice of the M learners—the type of learner used for the problem domain. We can only decide on this choice by adopting different validation techniques described in the section on model validation techniques.

Online Boosting algorithm

The supervised boosting algorithm takes many *weak learners* whose accuracy is slightly greater than random and combines them to produce a strong learner by iteratively sampling the misclassified examples. The concept is identical in Oza's Online Boosting algorithm with modification done for a continuous data stream.

Inputs and outputs

The constraint on types of inputs (categorical only, continuous only, or mixed) depends on the chosen base classifiers. The base classifier algorithms and their respective parameters are inputs. The output is the learned model that can predict the class/confidence based on the classifier chosen.

How does it work?

The modification of batch boosting to online boosting is done as follows:

1. Keep two sets of weights for M base models, λ^c is a vector of dimension M which carries the sum of weights of correctly classified instances, and λ^w is a vector of dimension M, which carries the sum of weights of incorrectly classified instances.

2. The weights are initialized to 1.

3. Given a new instance $(\mathbf{x}_t, y_t)$, the algorithm goes through the iterations of updating the base models.

4. For each base model, the following steps are repeated:

   1. For the first iteration, $k = Poisson(\lambda)$ is set and the learning classifier updates the algorithm (denoted here by h_1) k times using $(\mathbf{x}_t, y_t)$:

   2. If h_1 incorrectly classifies the instance, the λ^{w1} is incremented, ϵ_1, the weighted fraction, incorrectly classified by h_1, is computed and the weight of the example is multiplied by $1/2 \, \epsilon_1$.

Advantages and limitations

The advantages and limitations are as follows:

- Again, the performance is determined by the choice of the multiple learners, their types and the particular domain of the problem. The different methods described in the section on model validation techniques help us in choosing the learners.
- Oza's Online Boosting has been shown theoretically and empirically not to be "lossless"; that is, the model is different compared to its batch version. Thus, it suffers from performance issues and different extensions have been studied in recent years to improve performance.

Validation, evaluation, and comparisons in online setting

In contrast to the modes of machine learning we saw in the previous chapters, stream learning presents unique challenges to performing the core steps of validation and evaluation. The fact that we are no longer dealing with batch data means the standard techniques for validation evaluation and model comparison must be adapted for incremental learning.

Model validation techniques

In the off-line or the batch setting, we discussed various methods of tuning the parameters of the algorithm or testing the generalization capability of the algorithms as a counter-measure against overfitting. Some of the techniques in the batch labeled data, such as cross-validation, are not directly applicable in the online or stream settings. The most common techniques used in online or stream settings are given next.

Prequential evaluation

The prequential evaluation method is a method where instances are provided to the algorithm and the output prediction of the algorithm is then measured in comparison with the actual label using a loss function. Thus, the algorithm is always tested on the unseen data and needs no "holdout" data to estimate the generalization. The prequential error is computed based on the sum of the accumulated loss function between actual values and predicted values, given by:

$$P = \sum_{i=1}^{N} l\left(y_i, \hat{y}_l\right)$$

Three variations of basic prequential evaluation are done for better estimation on changing data, which are:

- Using Landmark Window (basic)
- Using Sliding Window
- Using forgetting mechanism

The last two methods are extensions of previously described techniques where you put weights or fading factors on the predictions that reduce over time.

Holdout evaluation

This is the extension of the holdout mechanism or "independent test set" methodology of the batch learning. Here the total labeled set or stream data is separated into training and testing sets, either based on some fixed intervals or the number of examples/instances the algorithm has seen. Imagine a continuous stream of data and we place well-known intervals at $t = t_{start+trainingIntervalEnd}$ and $t = t_{trainingIntervalEnd+testingIntervalEnd}$ to compare the evaluation metrics, as discussed in next section, for performance.

Controlled permutations

The issue with the aforementioned mechanisms is that they provide "average" behavior over time and can mask some basic issues such as the algorithm doing well at the start and very poorly at the end due to drift, for example. The advantage of the preceding methods is that they can be applied to real incoming streams to get estimates. One way to overcome the disadvantage is to create different random sets of the data where the order is shuffled a bit while maintaining the proximity in time and the evaluation is done over a number of these random sets.

Evaluation criteria

Most of the evaluation criteria are the same as described in the chapter on supervised learning and should be chosen based on the business problem, the mapping of the business problem to the machine learning techniques, and on the benefits derived. In this section, the most commonly used online supervised learning evaluation criteria are summarized for the reader:

- **Accuracy**: A measure of getting the true positives and true negatives correctly classified by the learning algorithm:

$$Accuracy = \frac{\sum True\ Positive + \sum True\ Negative}{\sum Total\ Data}$$

- **Balanced accuracy**: When the classes are imbalanced, balanced accuracy is often used as a measure. Balanced accuracy is an arithmetic mean of specificity and sensitivity. It can be also thought of as accuracy when positive and negative instances are drawn from the same probability in a binary classification problem.

- **Area under the ROC curve (AUC)**: Area under the ROC curve gives a good measure of generalization of the algorithm. Closer to 1.0 means the algorithm has good generalization capability while close to 0.5 means it is closer to a random guess.

- **Kappa statistic (K)**: The Kappa statistic is used to measure the observed accuracy with the expected accuracy of random guessing in the classification. In online learning, the Kappa statistic is used by computing the prequential accuracy (p_o) and the random classifier accuracy (p_c) and is given by:

$$K = \frac{\left(p_o - p_c\right)}{\left(1 - p_c\right)}$$

- **Kappa Plus statistic**: The Kappa Plus statistic is a modification to the Kappa statistic obtained by replacing the random classifier by the persistent classifier. The persistent classifier is a classifier which predicts the next instance based on the label or outcome of the previous instance.

When considering "drift" or change in the concept as discussed earlier, in addition to these standard measures, some well-known measures given are used to give a quantitative measure:

- **Probability of true change detection**: Usually, measured with synthetic data or data where the changes are known. It gives the ability of the learning algorithm to detect the change.

- **Probability of false alarm**: Instead of using the False Positive Rate in the off-line setting, the online setting uses the inverse of *time to detection or the average run* length which is computed using the expected time between false positive detections.

- **Delay of detection**: This is measured as the time required, terms of instances, to identify the drift.

Comparing algorithms and metrics

When comparing two classifiers or learners in online settings, the usual mechanism is the method of taking a performance metric, such as the error rate, and using a statistical test adapted to online learning. Two widely used methods are described next:

- **McNemar test**: McNemar's test is a non-parametric statistical test normally employed to compare two classifiers' evaluation metrics, such as "error rate", by storing simple statistics about the two classifiers. By computing statistic a, the number of correctly classified points by one algorithm that are incorrectly classified by the other, and statistic b, which is the inverse, we obtain the McNemar's Test as:

$$\chi^2$$

  The test follows a χ2 distribution and the p-value can be used to check for statistical significance.

- **Nemenyi test**: When there are multiple algorithms and multiple datasets, we use the Nemenyi test for statistical significance, which is based on average ranks across all. Two algorithms are considered to be performing differently in a statistically significant way if the ranks differ by a critical difference given by:

$$CriticalDifference = q_\alpha \sqrt{k(k+1)/6N}$$

  Here, K=number of algorithms, N=number of datasets.

The critical difference values are assumed to follow a Student-T distribution.

Incremental unsupervised learning using clustering

The concept behind clustering in a data stream remains the same as in batch or offline modes; that is, finding interesting clusters or patterns which group together in the data while keeping the limits on finite memory and time required to process as constraints. Doing single-pass modifications to existing algorithms or keeping a small memory buffer to do mini-batch versions of existing algorithms, constitute the basic changes done in all the algorithms to make them suitable for stream or real-time unsupervised learning.

Modeling techniques

The clustering modeling techniques for online learning are divided into partition-based, hierarchical-based, density-based, and grid-based, similar to the case of batch-based clustering.

Partition based

The concept of partition-based algorithms is similar to batch-based clustering where **k** clusters are formed to optimize certain objective functions such as minimizing the inter-cluster distance, maximizing the intra-cluster distance, and so on.

Online k-Means

k-Means is the most popular clustering algorithm, which partitions the data into user-specified k clusters, mostly to minimize the squared error or distance between centroids and cluster assigned points. We will illustrate a very basic online adaptation of k-Means, of which several variants exist.

Inputs and outputs

Mainly, numeric features are considered as inputs; a few tools take categorical features and convert them into some form of numeric representation. The algorithm itself takes the parameters' number of clusters k and number of max iterations n as inputs.

How does it work?

1. The input data stream is considered to be infinite but of constant block size.
2. A memory buffer of the block size is kept reserved to store the data or a compressed representation of the data.
3. Initially, the first stream of data of block size is used to find the k centroids of the clusters, the centroid information is stored and the buffer is cleared.
4. For the next data after it reaches the block size:
    1. For either max number of iterations or until there is no change in the centroids:
    2. Execute k-Means with buffer data and the present centroids.
    3. Minimize the squared sum error between centroids and data assigned to the cluster.
    4. After the iterations, the buffer is cleared and new centroids are obtained.
5. Repeat step 4 until the data is no longer available.

Advantages and limitations

The advantages and limitations are as follows:

- Similar to batch-based, the shape of the detected cluster depends on the distance measure and is not appropriate in problem domains with irregular shapes.
- The choice of parameter **k**, as in batch-based, can limit the performance in datasets with many distinct patterns or clusters.
- Outliers and missing data can pose lots of irregularities in clustering behavior of online k-Means.
- If the selected buffer size or the block size of the stream on which iterative k-Means runs is small, it will not find the right clusters. If the chosen block size is large, it can result in slowdown or missed changes in the data. Extensions such as **Very Fast k-Means Algorithm (VFKM)**, which uses the Hoeffding bound to determine the buffer size, overcome this limitation to a large extent.

Hierarchical based and micro clustering

Hierarchical methods are normally based on **Clustering Features (CF)** and **Clustering Trees (CT)**. We will describe the basics and elements of hierarchical clustering and the BIRCH algorithm, the extension of which the CluStream algorithm is based on.

The Clustering Feature is a way to compute and preserve a summarization statistic about the cluster in a compressed way rather than holding on to the whole data belonging to the cluster. In a **d** dimensional dataset, with **N** points in the cluster, two aggregates in the form of total sum **LS** for each dimensions and total squared sum of data **SS** again for each dimension, are computed and the vector representing this triplet form the Clustering Feature:

$$CF_j = < N, LS_j, SS_j >$$

These statistics are useful in summarizing the entire cluster information. The centroid of the cluster can be easily computed using:

$$centroid_j = LS_j/N$$

The radius of the cluster can be estimated using:

$$radius_j = \sqrt{\left(\frac{SS_j}{N} - \left(\frac{LS_j}{N} \right)^2 \right)}$$

The diameter of the cluster can be estimated using:

$$diameter_j = \sqrt{\frac{2N * SS_j - 2LS_j^2}{N(N-1)}}$$

CF vectors have great incremental and additive properties which becomes useful in stream or incremental updates.

For an incremental update, when we must update the CF vector, the following holds true:

$$LS_j \leftarrow LS_j + x^j$$

$$SS_j \leftarrow SS_j + \left(x^j\right)^2$$

$$N \leftarrow N + 1$$

When two CFs have to be merged, the following holds true:

$$N_3 \leftarrow N_1 + N_2$$

$$LS_3^j \leftarrow LS_1^j + LS_2^j$$

$$SS_3^j \leftarrow SS_1^j + SS_2^j$$

The **Clustering Feature Tree (CF Tree)** represents an hierarchical tree structure. The construction of the CF tree requires two user defined parameters:

- Branching factor **b** which is the maximum number of sub-clusters or non-leaf nodes any node can have
- Maximum diameter (or radius) **T**, the number of examples that can be absorbed by the leaf node for a CF parent node

CF Tree operations such as insertion are done by recursively traversing the CF Tree and using the CF vector for finding the closest node based on distance metrics. If a leaf node has already absorbed the maximum elements given by parameter T, the node is split. At the end of the operation, the CF vector is appropriately updated for its statistic:

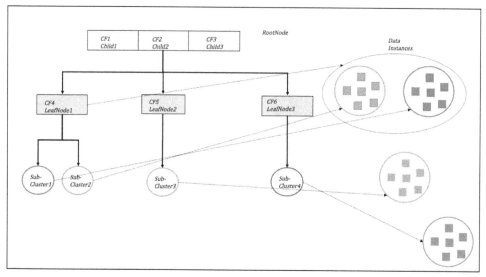

Figure 3 An example Clustering Feature Tree illustrating hierarchical structure.

We will discuss **BIRCH (Balanced Iterative Reducing and Clustering Hierarchies)** following this concept.

Inputs and outputs

BIRCH only accepts numeric features. CF and CF tree parameters, such as branching factor b and maximum diameter (or radius) T for leaf are user-defined inputs.

How does it work?

BIRCH, designed for very large databases, was meant to be a *two-pass* algorithm; that is, scan the entire data once and re-scan it again, thus being an $O(N)$ algorithm. It can be modified easily enough for online as a single pass algorithm preserving the same properties:

1. In the first phase or scan, it goes over the data and creates an in-memory CF Tree structure by sequentially visiting the points and carrying out CF Tree operations as discussed previously.

2. In the second phase, an optional phase, we remove outliers and merge sub-clusters.

3. Phase three is to overcome the issue of order of data in phase one. We use agglomerative hierarchical clustering to refactor the CF Tree.
4. Phase four is the last phase which is an optional phase to compute statistics such as centroids, assign data to closest centroids, and so on, for more effectiveness.

Advantages and limitations

The advantages and limitations are as follows:

- It is one of the most popular algorithms that scales linearly on a large database or stream of data.
- It has compact memory representation in the form of the CF and CF Tree for statistics and operations on incoming data.
- It handles outliers better than most algorithms.
- One of the major limitations is that it has been shown not to perform well when the shape of the clusters is not spherical.
- The concepts of CF vector and clustering in BIRCH were extended for efficient stream mining requirements by Aggarwal *et al* and named *micro-cluster and CluStream*.

Inputs and outputs

CluStream only accepts numeric features. Among the user-defined parameters are the number of micro-clusters in memory (q) and the threshold (δ) in time after which they can be deleted. Additionally, included in the input are time-sensitive parameters for storing the micro-clusters information, given by a and l.

How does it work?

1. The micro-cluster extends the CF vector and keeps two additional measures. They are the sum of the timestamps and sum of the squares of timestamps:

$$microCluster_j = \; < N, LS_j, SS_j, ST, SST>$$

2. The algorithm stores q micro-clusters in memory and each micro-cluster has a *maximum boundary* that can be computed based on means and standard deviations between centroid and cluster instance distances. The measures are multiplied by a factor which decreases exponentially with time.
3. For each new instance, we select the closest micro-cluster based on Euclidean distance and decide whether it should be absorbed:
   1. If the distance between the new instance and the centroid of the closest micro-cluster falls within the maximum boundary, it is absorbed and the micro-cluster statistics are updated.

2. If none of the micro-clusters can absorb, a new micro-cluster is created with the instance and based on the timestamp and threshold (δ), the oldest micro-cluster is deleted.

3. Assuming normal distribution of timestamps, if the relevance time — the time of arrival of instance found by CluStream — is below the user-specified threshold, it is considered an outlier and removed. Otherwise, the two closest micro-clusters are merged.

4. The micro-cluster information is stored in secondary storage from time to time by using a pyramidal time window concept. Each micro-cluster has time intervals decrease exponentially using a^l to create snapshots. These help in efficient search in both time and space.

Advantages and limitations

The advantages and limitations are as follows:

*   CluStream has been shown to be very effective in finding clusters in real time
*   The CluStream algorithm, through effective storage using a pyramidal timestamp, has efficient time and space usage. CluStream, like BIRCH, can find only spherical shaped clusters

Density based

Similar to batch clustering, density-based techniques overcome the "shape" issue faced by distance-based algorithms. Here we will present a well-known density-based algorithm, DenStream, which is based on the concepts of CF and CF Trees discussed previously.

Inputs and outputs

The extent of the neighborhood of a core micro-cluster is the user-defined radius ϵ. A second input value is the minimum total weight μ of the micro-cluster which is the sum over the weighted function of the arrival time of each instance in the object, where the weight decays with a time constant proportional to another user-defined parameter, λ. Finally, an input factor $\beta \in (0,1)$ is used to distinguish potential core micro-clusters from outlier micro-clusters.

How does it work?

1. Based on the micro-cluster concepts of CluStream, DenStream holds two data structures: *p-micro-cluster* for potential clusters and *o-micro-clusters* for outlier detection.

2. Each *p-micro-cluster* structure has:

   1. A weight associated with it which decreases exponentially with the timestamps it has been updated with. If there are j objects in the micro-cluster:

   $$w = \sum_{j \in p-microCluster} f\left(T - t^j\right) \text{ where } f(t) = 2^{-\lambda t}$$

   2. **Weighted linear sum (WLS)** and **weighted linear sum of squares (WSS)** are stored in micro-clusters similar to linear sum and sum of squares:

   $$WLS = \sum_{j \in p-microCluster} f\left(T - t^j\right) x^j$$

   $$WSS = w = \sum_{j \in p-microCluster} f\left(T - t^j\right)\left(x^j\right)^2$$

   3. The mean, radius, and diameter of the clusters are then computed using the weighted measures defined previously, exactly like in CF. For example, the radius can be given as:

   $$weightedRadius_j = \sqrt{\left(\frac{WSS_j}{w} - \left(\frac{WLS_j}{w}\right)^2\right)}$$

3. Each *o-micro-cluster* has the same structure as *p-micro-cluster* and timestamps associated with it.

4. When a new instance arrives:

   1. A closest *p-micro-cluster* is found and the instance is inserted if the new radius is within the user-defined boundary ϵ. If inserted, the *p-micro-cluster* statistics are updated accordingly.

   2. Otherwise, an *o-micro-cluster* is found and the instance is inserted if the new radius is again within the boundary. The boundary is defined by $\beta \times \mu$, the product of the user-defined parameters, and if the radius grows beyond this value, the *o-micro-cluster* is moved to the *p-micro-cluster*.

   3. If the instance cannot be absorbed by an *o-micro-cluster*, then a new micro-cluster is added to the *o-micro-clusters*.

5. At the time interval t based on weights, the *o-micro-cluster* can become the *p-micro-cluster* or vice versa. The time interval is defined in terms of λ, β, and μ as:

$$T = \frac{1}{\lambda} \log \frac{\beta\mu}{\beta\mu - 1}$$

Advantages and limitations

The advantages and limitations are as follows:

- Based on the parameters, DenStream can find effective clusters and outliers for real-time data.

- It has the advantage of finding clusters and outliers of any shape or size.

- The house keeping job of updating the *o-micro-cluster* and *p-micro-cluster* can be computationally expensive if not selected properly.

Grid based

This technique is based on discretizing the multi-dimensional continuous space into a multi-dimensional discretized version with grids. The mapping of the incoming instance to grid online and maintaining the grid offline results in an efficient and effective way of finding clusters in real-time.

Here we present D-Stream, which is a grid-based online stream clustering algorithm.

Inputs and outputs

As in density-based algorithms, the idea of decaying weight of instances is used in D-Stream. Additionally, as described next, cells in the grid formed from the input space may be deemed sparse, dense, or sporadic, distinctions that are central to the computational and space efficiency of the algorithm. The inputs to the grid-based algorithm, then, are:

- λ: The decay factor

- $0 < C_l < 1$ and $C_m > 1$: Parameters that control the boundary between dense and sparse cells in the grid

- $\beta > 0$: A constant that controls one of the conditions when a sparse cell is to be considered sporadic.

How does it work?

1. Each instance arriving at time *t* has a density coefficient that decreases exponentially over time:

$$D\left(x^{j},t\right)=\lambda^{t-t^{j}}$$

2. Density of the grid cell *g* at any given time *t* is given by *D(g, t)* and is the sum of the adjusted density of all instances given by *E(g, t)* that are mapped to grid cell *g*:

$$D\left(g,t\right)=\sum_{x\in E\left(g,t\right)}D\left(x,t\right)$$

3. Each cell in the grid captures the statistics as a characterization vector given by:

   ○ $CV(g) = <t_{g}, t_{m}, D, label, status>$ where:
   ○ t_{g} = last time grid cell was updated
   ○ t_{m} = last time grid cell was removed due to sparseness
   ○ *D* = density of the grid cell when last updated
   ○ *label* = class label of the grid cell
   ○ *status* = {NORMAL or SPORADIC}

4. When the new instance arrives, it gets mapped to a cell *g* and the characteristic vector is updated. If *g* is not available, it is created and the list of grids is updated.

5. Grid cells with empty instances are removed. Also, cells that have not been updated over a long time can become sparse, and conversely, when many instances are mapped, they become dense.

6. At a regular time interval known as a gap, the grid cells are inspected for status and the cells with fewer instances than a number—determined by a density threshold function—are treated as outliers and removed.

Advantages and limitations

The advantages and limitations are as follows:

- D-Streams have theoretically and empirically been shown to find sporadic and normal clusters with very high efficiency in space and time.
- It can find clusters of any shape or size effectively.

Validation and evaluation techniques

Many of the static clustering evaluation measures discussed in *Chapter 3, Unsupervised Machine Learning Techniques,* have an assumption of static and non-evolving patterns. Some of these internal and external measures are used even in streaming based cluster detection. Our goal in this section is to first highlight problems inherent to cluster evaluation in stream learning, then describe different internal and external measures that address these, and finally, present some existing measures — both internal and external — that are still valid.

Key issues in stream cluster evaluation

It is important to understand some of the important issues that are specific to streaming and clustering, as the measures need to address them:

- **Aging**: The property of points being not relevant to the clustering measure after a given time.

- **Missed points**: The property of a point not only being missed as belonging to the cluster but the amount by which it was missed being in the cluster.

- **Misplaced points**: Changes in clusters caused by evolving new clusters. Merging existing or deleting clusters results in ever-misplaced points with time. The impact of these changes with respect to time must be taken into account.

- **Cluster noise**: Choosing data that should not belong to the cluster or forming clusters around noise and its impact over time must be taken into account.

Evaluation measures

Evaluation measures for clustering in the context of streaming data must provide a useful index of the quality of clustering, taking into consideration the effect of evolving and noisy data streams, overlapping and merging clusters, and so on. Here we present some external measures used in stream clustering. Many internal measures encountered in *Chapter 3, Unsupervised Machine Learning Techniques,* such as the Silhouette coefficient, Dunn's Index, and R-Squared, are also used and are not repeated here.

Cluster Mapping Measures (CMM)

The idea behind CMM is to quantify the connectivity of the points to clusters given the ground truth. It works in three phases:

Mapping phase: In this phase, clusters assigned by the stream learning algorithm are mapped to the ground truth clusters. Based on these, various statistics of distance and point connectivity are measured using the concepts of k-Nearest Neighbors.

The average distance of point p to its closest k neighbors in a cluster C_i is given by:

$$KnnhDistance(p, C_i) = \frac{1}{k} \sum_{o \in knnh(p, C_i)} dist(o, p)$$

The average distance for a cluster C_i is given by:

$$knnhDistance(C_i) = \frac{1}{|C_i|} \sum_{p \in, C_i} KnnhDistance(p, C_i)$$

The point connectivity of a point p in a cluster C_i is given by:

$$conn(p, C_i) = \begin{cases} 1 \text{ if } KnnhDistance(p, C_i) < knnhDistance(C_i) \\ 0 \text{ if } C_i = 0 \\ \dfrac{knnhDistance(C_i)}{KnnhDistance(p, C_i)} \text{ otherwise} \end{cases}$$

Class frequencies are counted for each cluster and the mapping of the cluster to the ground truth is performed by calculating the histograms and similarity in the clustering.

Specifically, a cluster C_i is mapped to the ground truth class, and Cl_j is mapped to a ground truth cluster Cl_j^o, which covers the majority of class frequencies of C_i. The surplus is defined as the number of instances from class Cl_i not covered by the ground truth cluster Cl_j^o and total surplus for instances in classes $Cl_1, Cl_2, Cl_3 \dots Cl_l$ in cluster C_i compared to Cl_j^o is given by:

$$\Delta(C_i, Cl_j^o) = \sum_{a=1}^{l} \max\{0, \rho(C_i)_a - \rho(Cl_j^o)_a\}$$

Cluster C_i is mapped using:

$$map(C_i) = \begin{cases} \arg\min \left\{ \Delta\left(C_i, Cl_j^o\right) \right\} \text{ if } \forall Cl_j, \Delta\left(C_i, Cl_j^o\right) > 0 \\ 0 \text{ if } C_i = C_0 \\ \arg\max \left\{ \left\| C_i \cap Cl_j^o \right\| \right\} \end{cases}$$

Penalty phase: The penalty for every instance that is mapped incorrectly is calculated in this step using computations of fault objects; that is, objects which are not noise and yet incorrectly placed, using:

$$pen(o, C_i) = con\left(o, Cl(o)\right) * \left(1 - con\left(o, map\left(C_i\right)\right)\right)$$

The overall penalty of point o with respect to all clusters found is given by:

$$pen(o, C) = \max \left\{ pen\left(o, C_i\right) \right\}$$

CMM calculation: Using all the penalties weighted over the lifespan is given by:

$$CMM(C, Cl) = 1 - \frac{\sum_{o \in F} w(o) * pen(o, C)}{\sum_{o \in F} w(o) * conn\left(o, Cl(o)\right)}$$

Here, C is found clusters, Cl is ground truth clusters, F is the fault objects and $w(o)$ is the weight of instance.

V-Measure

Validity or V-Measure is an external measure which is computed based on two properties that are of interest in stream clustering, namely, **Homogeneity** and **Completeness**. If there are n classes as set $C = \{c_1, c_2 ..., c_n\}$ and k clusters $K = \{k_1, k_2..k_m\}$, contingency tables are created such that $A = \{a_{ij}\}$ corresponds to the count of instances in class c_i and cluster k_j.

Homogeneity: Homogeneity is defined as a property of a cluster that reflects the extent to which all the data in the cluster belongs to the same class.

Conditional entropy and class entropy:

$$H(C \mid K) = -\sum_{k=1}^{|K|} \sum_{c=1}^{|C|} \frac{a_{ck}}{N} \log \frac{a_{ck}}{\sum_{c=1}^{|C|} a_{ck}}$$

$$H(C) = -\sum_{c=1}^{|C|} \frac{\sum_{k=1}^{|K|} a_{ck}}{n} \log \frac{\sum_{k=1}^{|K|} a_{ck}}{n}$$

Homogeneity is defined as:

$$h = \begin{cases} 1 & if\ H(C \mid K) = 0 \\ 1 - \dfrac{H(C \mid K)}{H(C)} & otherwise \end{cases}$$

A higher value of homogeneity is more desirable.

Completeness: Completeness is defined as the mirror property of Homogeneity, that is, having all instances of a single class belong to the same cluster.

Similar to Homogeneity, conditional entropies and cluster entropy are defined as:

$$H(K \mid C) = -\sum_{c=1}^{|C|} \sum_{k=1}^{|K|} \frac{a_{ck}}{N} \log \frac{a_{ck}}{\sum_{k=1}^{|K|} a_{ck}}$$

$$H(K) = -\sum_{k=1}^{|K|} \frac{\sum_{c=1}^{|C|} a_{ck}}{n} \log \frac{\sum_{c=1}^{|C|} a_{ck}}{n}$$

Completeness is defined as:

$$c = \begin{cases} 1 & if\ H(K \mid C) = 0 \\ 1 - \dfrac{H(K \mid C)}{H(K)} & otherwise \end{cases}$$

V-Measure is defined as the harmonic mean of homogeneity and completeness using a weight factor β:

$$v_\beta = \frac{(1+\beta)h * c}{\beta * h + c}$$

A higher value of completeness or V-measure is better.

Other external measures

Some external measures which are quite popular in comparing the clustering algorithms or measuring the effectiveness of clustering when the classes are known are given next:

Purity and **Entropy**: They are similar to homogeneity and completeness defined previously.

Purity is defined as:

$$purity = \sum_{r=1}^{k} \frac{1}{n} \max_{i} n_r^i$$

Entropy is defined as:

$$entropy = \sum_{r=1}^{k} \frac{n_r}{n} \left(-\frac{1}{\log q} \sum_{i=1}^{q} \frac{n_r^i}{n_r} \log \frac{n_r^i}{n_r} \right)$$

Here, q = number of classes, k = number of clusters, n_r = size of cluster r and n_r^i = *number of data in cluster r belonging to class i* ·

Precision, Recall, and **F-Measure**: Information retrieval measures modified for clustering algorithms are as follows:

Given, N = *data points*, C = *set of classes*, K = *set of Clusters* and n_{ij} = *number of data points in class i belonging to cluster j* .

Precision is defined as:

$$P(c_i, k_j) = \frac{n_{ij}}{|k_j|}$$

Recall is defined as:

$$R\left(c_i, k_j\right) = \frac{n_{ij}}{|c_i|}$$

F-measures is defined as:

$$F - Measures\left(c_i, k_j\right) = \frac{2 * P\left(c_i, k_j\right) * R\left(c_i, k_j\right)}{P\left(c_i, k_j\right) + R\left(c_i, k_j\right)}$$

Unsupervised learning using outlier detection

The subject of finding outliers or anomalies in the data streams is one of the emerging fields in machine learning. This area has not been explored by researchers as much as classification and clustering-based problems have. However, there have been some very interesting ideas extending the concepts of clustering to find outliers from data streams. We will provide some of the research that has been proved to be very effective in stream outlier detection.

Partition-based clustering for outlier detection

The central idea here is to use an online partition-based clustering algorithm and based on either cluster size ranking or inter-cluster distance ranking, label the clusters as outliers.

Here we present one such algorithm proposed by Koupaie *et al.*, using incremental k-Means.

Inputs and outputs

Only numeric features are used, as in most k-Means algorithms. The number of clusters k and the number of windows of outliers n, on which offline clustering happens, are input parameters. The output is constant outliers (local and global) and an updatable model that detects these.

How does it work?

1. This algorithm works by having the k-Means algorithm in two modes, an offline mode and an online mode, both working in parallel.

2. For the online mode:

   1. Apply k-Means on the given window w and find clusters and partitions of the data with clusters.

   2. Rank the clusters based on the cluster distances and cluster size. The clusters which are farthest apart and small in size are considered outliers.

   3. Store the outliers in memory for the window as a set $O_w = \{x_1, x_2..x_n\}$ and regard them as local outliers.

   4. The window is cleared and the process is repeated.

3. For the offline mode:

   1. Get outliers from n, previous windows, and create a set:
      $$S = \{O_w^1, O_w^2 ... O_w^n\}$$

   2. Cluster this window with set S using k-Means and find clusters which are farthest away and small in size.

   3. These clusters are global outliers.

   4. The window is cleared and the process is repeated.

Advantages and limitations

The advantages and limitations are as follows:

- It is very sensitive to the two parameters k and n and can generate lots of noise.

- Only spherical clusters/outliers are found and outliers with different shapes get missed.

Distance-based clustering for outlier detection

Distance-based outlier detection is the most studied, researched, and implemented method in the area of stream learning. There are many variants of the distance-based methods, based on sliding windows, the number of nearest neighbors, radius and thresholds, and other measures for considering outliers in the data. We will try to give a sampling of the most important algorithms in this section.

Inputs and outputs

Most algorithms take the following parameters as inputs:

- Window size w, corresponding to the fixed size on which the algorithm looks for outlier patterns
- Sliding size s, corresponds to the number of new instances that will be added to the window, and old ones removed
- The count threshold k of instances when using nearest neighbor computation
- The distance threshold R used to define the outlier threshold in distances

Outliers as labels or scores (based on neighbors and distance) are outputs.

How does it work?

We present different variants of distance-based stream outlier algorithms, giving insights into what they do differently or uniquely. The unique elements in each algorithm define what happens when the slide expires, how a new slide is processed, and how outliers are reported.

Exact Storm

Exact Storm stores the data in the current window w in a well-known index structure, so that the range query search or query to find neighbors within the distance R for a given point is done efficiently. It also stores k preceding and succeeding neighbors of all data points:

- **Expired Slide**: Instances in expired slides are removed from the index structure that affects range queries but are preserved in the preceding list of neighbors.
- **New Slide**: For each data point in the new slide, range query R is executed, results are used to update the preceding and succeeding list for the instance, and the instance is stored in the index structure.
- **Outlier Reporting**: In any window, after the processing of expired and new slide elements is complete, any instance with at least k elements from the succeeding list and non-expired preceding list is reported as an outlier.

Abstract-C

Abstract-C keeps the index structure similar to Exact Storm but instead of preceding and succeeding lists for every object it just maintains a list of counts of neighbors for the windows the instance is participating in:

- **Expired Slide**: Instances in expired slides are removed from the index structure that affects range queries and the first element from the list of counts is removed corresponding to the last window.

- **New Slide**: For each data point in the new slide, range query R is executed and results are used to update the list count. For existing instances, the count gets updated with new neighbors and instances are added to the index structure.

- **Outlier Reporting**: In any window, after the processing of expired and new slide elements is complete, all instances with a neighbors count less than k in the current window are considered outliers.

Direct Update of Events (DUE)

DUE keeps the index structure for efficient range queries exactly like the other algorithms but has a different assumption, that when an expired slide occurs, not every instance is affected in the same way. It maintains two priority queues: the unsafe inlier queue and the outlier list. The unsafe inlier queue has sorted instances based on the increasing order of smallest expiration time of their preceding neighbors. The outlier list has all the outliers in the current window:

- **Expired Slide**: Instances in expired slides are removed from the index structure that affects range queries and the unsafe inlier queue is updated for expired neighbors. Those unsafe inliers which become outliers are removed from the priority queue and moved to the outlier list.

- **New Slide**: For each data point in the new slide, range query R is executed, results are used to update the succeeding neighbors of the point, and only the most recent preceding points are updated for the instance. Based on the updates, the point is added to the unsafe inlier priority queue or removed from the queue and added to the outlier list.

- **Outlier Reporting**: In any window, after the processing of expired and new slide elements is complete, all instances in the outlier list are reported as outliers.

Micro Clustering based Algorithm (MCOD)

Micro-clustering based outlier detection overcomes the computational issues of performing range queries for every data point. The micro-cluster data structure is used instead of range queries in these algorithms. A micro-cluster is centered around an instance and has a radius of R. All the points belonging to the micro-clusters become inliers. The points that are outside can be outliers or inliers and stored in a separate list. It also has a data structure similar to DUE to keep a priority queue of unsafe inliers:

- **Expired Slide**: Instances in expired slides are removed from both micro-clusters and the data structure with outliers and inliers. The unsafe inlier queue is updated for expired neighbors as in the DUE algorithm. Micro-clusters are also updated for non-expired data points.

- **New Slide**: For each data point in the new slide, the instance either becomes a center of a micro-cluster, or part of a micro-cluster or added to the event queue and the data structure of the outliers. If the point is within the distance R, it gets assigned to an existing micro-cluster; otherwise, if there are k points within R, it becomes the center of the new micro cluster; if not, it goes into the two structures of the event queue and possible outliers.

- **Outlier Reporting**: In any window, after the processing of expired and new slide elements is complete, any instance in the outlier structure with less than k neighboring instances is reported as an outlier.

Approx Storm

Approx Storm, as the name suggests, is an approximation of Exact Storm. The two approximations are:

- Reducing the number of data points in the window by adding a factor ρ and changing the window to ρW.

- Storing the number instead of the data structure of preceding neighbors by using the fraction of the number of neighbors which are safe inliers in the preceding list to the number in the current window.

The processing of expired and new slides and how outliers are determined based on these steps follows:

1. **Expired Slide**: Same as Exact Storm — instances in expired slides are removed from the index structure that affects range queries but preserved in the preceding list of neighbors.

2. **New Slide**: For each data point in the new slide, range query R is executed, results are used to compute the fraction discussed previously, and the index structure is updated. The number of safe inliers are constrained to ρW by removing random inliers if the size exceeds that value. The assumption is that most of the points in safe inliers are safe.

3. **Outlier Reporting**: In any window, after the processing of expired and new slide elements has been completed, when an approximation (see *References* [17]) of the number of neighbors of an instance based on the fraction, window size, and preceding list is a value less than k, it is considered as an outlier.

Advantages and limitations

The advantages and limitations are as follows:

*   Exact Storm is demanding in storage and CPU for storing lists and retrieving neighbors. Also, it introduces delays; even though they are implemented in efficient data structures, range queries can be slow.

*   Abstract-C has a small advantage over Exact Storm, as no time is spent on finding active neighbors for each instance in the window. The storage and time spent is still very much dependent on the window and slide chosen.

*   DUE has some advantage over Exact Storm and Abstract-C as it can efficiently re-evaluate the "inlierness" of points (that is, whether unsafe inliers remain inliers or become outliers) but sorting the structure impacts both CPU and memory.

*   MCOD has distinct advantages in memory and CPU owing to the use of the micro-cluster structure and removing the pair-wise distance computation. Storing the neighborhood information in micro-clusters helps memory too.

*   Approx Storm has an advantage of time over the others as it doesn't process the expired data points over the previous window.

Validation and evaluation techniques

Validation and evaluation of stream-based outliers is still an open research area. In many research comparisons, we see various metrics being used, such as:

- Time to evaluate in terms of CPU times per object

- Number of outliers detected in the streams

- Number of outliers that correlate to existing labels, TP/Precision/Recall/ Area under PRC curve, and so on

By varying parameters such as window-size, neighbors within radius, and so on, we determine the sensitivity to the performance metrics mentioned previously and determine the robustness.

Case study in stream learning

The case study in this chapter consists of several experiments that illustrate different methods of stream-based machine learning. A well-studied dataset was chosen as the stream data source and supervised tree based methods such as Naïve Bayes, Hoeffding Tree, as well as ensemble methods, were used. Among unsupervised methods, clustering algorithms used include k-Means, DBSCAN, CluStream, and CluTree. Outlier detection techniques include MCOD and SimpleCOD, among others. We also show results from classification experiments that demonstrate handling concept drift. The ADWIN algorithm for calculating statistics in a sliding window, as described earlier in this chapter, is employed in several algorithms used in the classification experiments.

Tools and software

One of the most popular and arguably the most comprehensive Java-based frameworks for data stream mining is the open source **Massive Online Analysis (MOA)** software created by the University of Waikato. The framework is a collection of stream classification, clustering, and outlier detection algorithms and has support for change detection and concept drift. It also includes data generators and several evaluation tools. The framework can be extended with new stream data generators, algorithms, and evaluators. In this case study, we employ several stream data learning methods using a file-based data stream.

Product homepage: `http://moa.cms.waikato.ac.nz/`
GitHub: `https://github.com/Waikato/moa`

As shown in the series of screenshots from the MOA tool shown in *Figure 4* and *Figure 5*, the top-level menu lets you choose the type of learning to be done. For the classification experiments, for example, configuration of the tools consists of selecting the task to run (selected to be prequential evaluation here), and then configuring which learner and evaluator we want to use, and finally, the source of the data stream. A window width parameter shown in the **Configure Task** dialog can affect the accuracy of the model chosen, as we will see in the experiment results. Other than choosing different values for the window width, all base learner parameters were left as default values. Once the task is configured it is run by clicking the **Run** button:

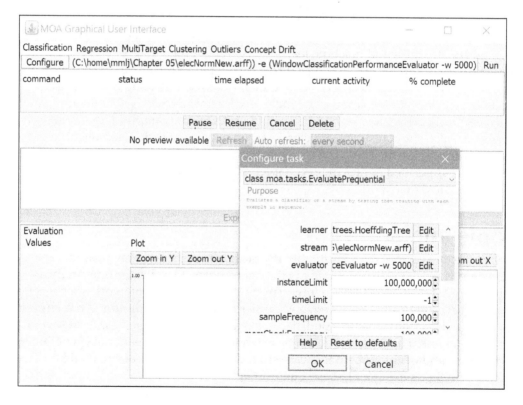

Figure 4. MOA graphical interface for configuring prequential evaluation for classification which includes setting the window width

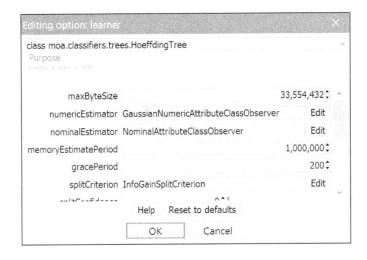

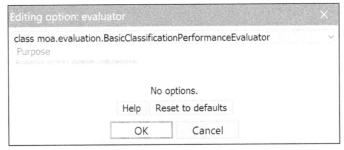

Figure 5. MOA graphical interface for prequential classification task. Within the Configure task, you must choose a learner, locate the data stream (details not shown), and select an evaluator

After the task has completed running, model evaluation results can be exported to a CSV file.

Business problem

The problem for this case study is to continuously learn from a stream of electricity market data and predict the direction of movement of the market price. We compare the accuracy and average cost of different classification methods including concept drift as well as the performance of clustering and outlier detection.

Machine learning mapping

The dataset used in this case study can be used to illustrate classical batch-based supervised and unsupervised learning techniques. However, here we treat it as a stream-based data source to show how we can employ the techniques described in this chapter to perform classification, clustering, and outlier detection tasks using the MOA framework. Within this context, we demonstrate how incremental learning can be achieved under assumptions of a stationary as well as an evolving data stream exhibiting concept drift.

Data collection

The dataset is known as the Electricity or ELEC dataset, which was collected by the New South Wales Electricity Market. The prices in this market are variable, and are adjusted every 5 minutes based on supply and demand. This dataset consists of 45,312 such data points obtained every half-hour between May 1996 and December 1998. The target is an indication of the movement of the price, whether up or down, relative to the 24-hour moving average.

> The data file is a publicly available file in the ARRF format at
> `http://downloads.sourceforge.net/project/moa-`
> `datastream/Datasets/Classification/elecNormNew.arff.`
> `zip?r=http%3A%2F%2Fmoa.cms.waikato.ac.nz%2Fdatasets%`
> `2F&ts=1483128450&use_mirror=cytranet.`

Data sampling and transformation

In the experiments conducted here, no data sampling is done; each example in the dataset is processed individually and no example is excluded. All numeric data elements have been normalized to a value between 0 and 1.

Feature analysis and dimensionality reduction

The ELEC dataset has 45,312 records with nine features, including the target class. The features class and day are nominal (categorical), all others are numeric (continuous). The features are listed in *Table 1* and *Table 2* and give descriptive statistics for the ELEC dataset:

Name	Data Type	Description
class	nominal	UP, DOWN – direction of price movement relative to 24-hour moving average
date	continuous	Date price recorded
day	nominal	Day of the week (1-7)
period	continuous	
nswprice	continuous	Electricity price in NSW
nswdemand	continuous	Electricity demand in NSW
vicprice	continuous	Electricity price in Victoria
vicdemand	continuous	Electricity demand in Victoria
transfer	integer	

Table 1. ELEC dataset features

	count	mean	std	25%	50%	75%
date	45312	0.49908	0.340308	0.031934	0.456329	0.880547
period	45312	0.5	0.294756	0.25	0.5	0.75
nswprice	45312	0.057868	0.039991	0.035127	0.048652	0.074336
nswdemand	45312	0.425418	0.163323	0.309134	0.443693	0.536001
vicprice	45312	0.003467	0.010213	0.002277	0.003467	0.003467
vicdemand	45312	0.422915	0.120965	0.372346	0.422915	0.469252
transfer	45312	0.500526	0.153373	0.414912	0.414912	0.605702

Table 2. Descriptive statistics of ELEC dataset features

The feature reduction step is omitted here as it is in most stream-based learning.

Models, results, and evaluation

The experiments are divided into classification, concept drift, clustering, and outlier detection. Details of the learning process for each set of experiments and the results of the experiments are given here.

Supervised learning experiments

For this set of experiments, a choice of linear, non-linear, and ensemble learners were chosen in order to illustrate the behavior of a variety of classifiers. **Stochastic Gradient Descent (SGD)**, which uses a linear SVM, and Naïve Bayes are the linear classifiers, while Lazy k-NN is the non-linear classifier. For ensemble learning, we use two meta-learners, **Leveraging Bagging (LB)** and OxaBag, with different linear and non-linear base learners such as SGD, Naïve Bayes, and Hoeffding Trees. The algorithm used in OxaBag is described in the section on ensemble algorithms. In LB, the weight factor used for resampling is variable (the default value of 6 is used here) whereas the weight in OxaBag is fixed at 1.

Prequential evaluation is chosen for all the classification methods, so each example is first tested against the prediction with the existing model, and then used for training the model. This requires the selection of a window width, and the performance of the various models for different values of the window width are listed in *Table 3*. Widths of 100, 500, 1,000, and 5,000 elements were used:

Algorithm	Window width	Evaluation time (CPU seconds)	Model cost (RAM-Hours)	Classifications correct (percent)	Kappa Statistic (percent)
SGD	100	0.5781	3.76E-10	67	0
SGD	500	0.5781	3.76E-10	55.6	0
SGD	1000	0.5469	3.55E-10	53.3	0
SGD	5000	0.5469	3.55E-10	53.78	0
NaiveBayes	100	0.7656	8.78E-10	86	65.7030
NaiveBayes	500	0.6094	8.00E-10	82.2	62.6778
NaiveBayes	1000	0.6719	7.77E-10	75.3	48.8583
NaiveBayes	5000	0.6406	7.35E-10	77.84	54.1966
kNN	100	34.6406	4.66E-06	74	36.3057
kNN	500	34.5469	4.65E-06	79.8	59.1424
kNN	1000	35.8750	4.83E-06	82.5	64.8049
kNN	5000	35.0312	4.71E-06	80.32	60.4594
LB-kNN	100	637.8125	2.88E-04	74	36.3057
LB-kNN	500	638.9687	2.89E-04	79.8	59.1424
LB-kNN	1000	655.8125	2.96E-04	82.4	64.5802
LB-kNN	5000	667.6094	3.02E-04	80.66	61.0965
LB-HoeffdingTree	100	13.6875	2.98E-06	91	79.1667
LB-HoeffdingTree	500	13.5781	2.96E-06	93	85.8925
LB-HoeffdingTree	1000	12.5625	2.74E-06	92.1	84.1665

Algorithm	Window width	Evaluation time (CPU seconds)	Model cost (RAM-Hours)	Classifications correct (percent)	Kappa Statistic (percent)
LB-HoeffdingTree	5000	12.7656	2.78E-06	90.74	81.3184

Table 3. Classifier performance for different window sizes

For the algorithms in *Table 4*, the performance was the same for each value of the window width used:

Algorithm	Evaluation time (CPU seconds)	Model cost (RAM-Hours)	Classifications correct (percent)	Kappa Statistic (percent)
HoeffdingTree	1.1562	3.85E-08	79.1953	57.2266
HoeffdingAdaptiveTree	2.0469	2.84E-09	83.3863	65.5569
OzaBag-NaiveBayes	2.01562	1.57E-08	73.4794	42.7636
OzaBagAdwin-HoeffdingTree	5.7812	2.26E-07	84.3485	67.5221
LB-SGD	2	1.67E-08	57.6977	3.0887
LB-NaiveBayes	3.5937	3.99E-08	78.8753	55.7639

Table 4. Performance of classifiers (same for all window widths used)

Concept drift experiments

In this experiment, we continue using EvaluatePrequential when configuring the classification task. This time we select the DriftDetectionMethodClassifier as the learner and DDM as the drift detection method. This demonstrates adapting to an evolving data stream. Base learners used and the results obtained are shown in *Table 5*:

Algorithm	Evaluation time (CPU seconds)	Model cost (RAM-Hours)	Classifications correct (percent)	Kappa Statistic (percent)	Change detected
SGD	0.307368829	1.61E-09	53.3	0	132
Naïve-Bayes	0.298290727	1.58E-09	86.6	73.03986	143
Lazy-kNN	10.34161893	1.74E-06	87.4	74.8498	12
HoeffdingTree	0.472981754	5.49E-09	86.2	72.19816	169
HoeffdingAdaptiveTree	0.598665043	7.19E-09	84	67.80878	155
LB-SGD	0.912737325	2.33E-08	53.3	0	132
LB-NaiveBayes	1.990137758	3.61E-08	85.7	71.24056	205

Algorithm	Evaluation time (CPU seconds)	Model cost (RAM-Hours)	Classifications correct (percent)	Kappa Statistic (percent)	Change detected
OzaBag-NaiveBayes	1.342189725	2.29E-08	77.4	54.017	211
LB-kNN	173.3624715	1.14E-04	87.5	75.03296	4
LB-HoeffdingTree	5.660440101	1.61E-06	91.3	82.56317	59
OzaBag-HoeffdingTree	4.306455545	3.48E-07	85.4	70.60209	125

Table 5. Performance of classifiers with concept drift detection

Clustering experiments

Almost all of the clustering algorithms implemented in the MOA tool were used in this experiment. Both extrinsic and intrinsic evaluation results were collected and are tabulated in *Table 6*. CMM, homogeneity, and completeness were defined earlier in this chapter. We have encountered Purity and Silhouette coefficients before, from the discussion in *Chapter 3, Unsupervised Machine Learning Techniques*. SSQ is the sum of squared distances of instances from their respective cluster centers; the lower the value of SSQ, the better. The use of micro-clustering is indicated by $m = 1$ in the table. How often the macro-clusters are calculated is determined by the selected time horizon h, in instances:

Algorithm	CMM	Homogeneity	Completeness	Purity	SSQ	Silhouette Coefficient
Clustream With k-Means (h = 5000; k = 2; m = 1)	0.7168	-1.0000	0.1737	0.9504	9.1975	0.5687
Clustream With k-Means (h = 1000; k = 5)	0.5391	-1.0000	0.8377	0.7238	283.6543	0.8264
Clustream (h = 1000; m = 1)	0.6241	-1.0000	0.4363	0.9932	7.2734	0.4936
Denstream With DBSCAN (h = 1000)	0.4455	-1.0000	0.7586	0.9167	428.7604	0.6682
ClusTree (h = 5000; m = 1)	0.7984	0.4874	-0.4815	0.9489	11.7789	0.6879
ClusTree (h = 1000; m = 1)	0.7090	-1.0000	0.3979	0.9072	13.4190	0.5385
AbstractC	1.0000	1.0000	-8.1354	1.0000	0.0000	0.0000
MCOD (w = 1000)	1.0000	1.0000	-8.1354	1.0000	0.0000	0.0000

Table 6. Evaluation of clustering algorithms

Outlier detection experiments

In the final set of experiments, five outlier detection algorithms were used to process the ELEC dataset. Results are given in *Table 7*:

Algorithm	Nodes always inlier	Nodes always outlier	Nodes both inlier and outlier
MCOD	42449 (93.7%)	302 (0.7%)	2561 (5.7%)
ApproxSTORM	41080 (90.7%)	358 (0.8%)	3874 (8.5%)
SimpleCOD	42449 (93.7%)	302 (0.7%)	2561 (5.7%)
AbstractC	42449 (93.7%)	302 (0.7%)	2561 (5.7%)
ExactSTORM	42449 (93.7%)	302 (0.7%)	2561 (5.7%)

Table 7. Evaluation of outlier detection

The following plots (*Figure 6*) show results for three pairs of features after running algorithm Abstract-C on the entire dataset. In each of the plots, it is easy to see the outliers identified by the circles surrounding the data points. Although it is difficult to visualize the outliers spatially in multiple dimensions simultaneously, the set bi-variate plots give some indication of the result of outlier detection methods applied in a stream-based setting:

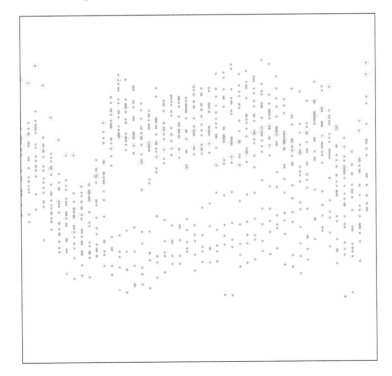

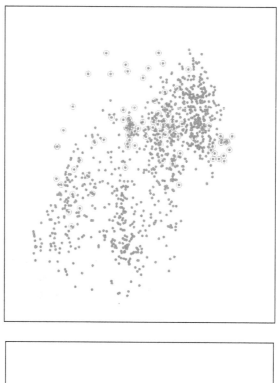

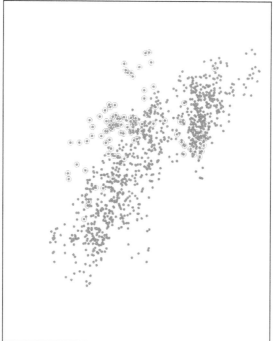

Figure 6. Outlier detection using Abstract-C, for three pairs of features, after processing all 45,300 instances

The image in *Figure 7* shows a screenshot from MOA when two algorithms, `Angiulli.ExactSTORM` and `Angiulli.ApproxSTORM`, were run simultaneously; a bivariate scatter-plot for each algorithm is shown side-by-side, accompanied by a comparison of the per-object processing time:

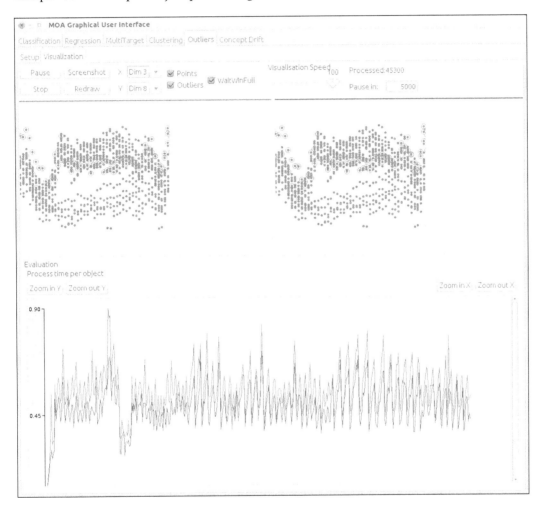

Figure 7. Visualization of outlier detection in MOA

Analysis of stream learning results

Based on the evaluation of the learned models from the classification, clustering, and outlier detection experiments, analysis reveals several interesting observations.

Classification experiments:

- Performance improves from linear to non-linear algorithms in quite a significant way as shown in Table 3. Linear SGD has the best performance using an accuracy metric of 67%, while KNN and Hoeffding Tree show 82.4 to 93%. This clearly shows that the problem is non-linear and using a non-linear algorithm will give better performance.

- K-NNs give good performance but come at the cost of evaluation time, as shown in Table 3. Evaluation time as well as memory are significantly higher — about two orders of magnitude — than the linear methods. When the model has to perform in tighter evaluation cycles, extreme caution in choosing algorithms such as KNNs must be observed.

- Hoeffding Trees gives the best classification rate and Kappa statistic. The evaluation time is also not as high as KNNs but is still in the order of seconds, which may or may not be acceptable in many real-time stream-based applications.

- The evaluation time of Naive Bayes is the lowest — though not much different from SGD — and with the right choice of window width can give performance second only to Hoeffding Trees. For example, at width 100, we have a classification rate of 86 with Naïve Bayes, which is next best to 93 of Hoeffding Trees but compared to over 13 seconds, Naïve Bayes takes only 0.76 seconds, as shown in *Table 3*.

- Keeping the window width constant, there is a clear pattern of improvement from linear (SGD, Naïve Bayes) to non-linear (Hoeffding Trees) to ensemble based (OzaBag, Adwin, Hoeffding Tree) shown in Table 4. This clearly shows that in theory, the choice of ensembles can help reduce the errors but comes at the cost of foregoing interpretability in the models.

- *Table 5*, when compared to *Table 3* and *Table 4*, shows why having drift protection and learning with automated drift detection increases robustness. Ensemble-based learning of OzaBag-NaiveBayes, OzaBag-HoeffdingTrees, and OzaBag-HoeffdingAdaptiveTree all show improvements over the non-drift protected runs as an example.

Clustering experiments:

- From the first two models in *Table 6*, we see that k-Means, with a horizon of 5,000 instances and k of 2, exhibits higher purity, higher CMM, and lower SSQ compared to the model with a smaller horizon and k of 5. In the complete set of results (available on this book's website, see link below), one can see that the effect of the larger horizon is the predominant factor responsible for the differences.

- In the clustering models using micro-clustering, the SSQ is typically significantly smaller than when no micro-clustering is used. This is understandable, as there are far more clusters and fewer instances per cluster, and SSQ is measured with respect to the cluster center.

- DBSCAN was found to be insensitive to micro-clustering, and size of the horizon. Compared to all other models, it ranks high on both intrinsic (Silhouette coefficient) as well as extrinsic measures (Completeness, Purity).

- The two ClusTree models have among the best CMM and Purity scores, with low SSQ due to micro-clusters.

- The final two outlier-based clustering algorithms have perfect CMM and Purity scores. The metrics are not significantly affected by the window size (although this impacts the evaluation time), or the value of k, the neighbor count threshold.

Outlier detection experiments:

- All the techniques in this set of experiments performed equally well, with the exception of ApproxSTORM, which is to be expected considering the reduced window used in this method compared to the exact version.

- The ratio of instances, always inlier versus those always outlier, is close to 140 for the majority of the models. Whether this implies adequate discriminatory power for a given dataset depends on the goals of the real-time learning problem.

 All MOA configuration files and results from the experiments are available at: https://github.com/mjmlbook/mastering-java-machine-learning/tree/master/Chapter5.

Summary

The assumptions in stream-based learning are different from batch-based learning, chief among them being upper bounds on operating memory and computation times. Running statistics using sliding windows or sampling must be computed in order to scale to a potentially infinite stream of data. We make the distinction between learning from stationary data, where it is assumed the generating data distribution is constant, and dynamic or evolving data, where concept drift must be accounted for. This is accomplished by techniques involving the monitoring of model performance changes or the monitoring of data distribution changes. Explicit and implicit adaptation methods are ways to adjust to the concept change.

Several supervised and unsupervised learning methods have been adapted for incremental online learning. Supervised methods include linear, non-linear, and ensemble techniques, The HoeffdingTree is introduced which is particularly interesting due largely in part to its guarantees on upper bounds on error rates. Model validation techniques such as prequential evaluation are adaptations unique to incremental learning. For stationary supervised learning, evaluation measures are similar to those used in batch-based learning. Other measures are used in the case of evolving data streams.

Clustering algorithms operating under fixed memory and time constraints typically use small memory buffers with standard techniques in a single pass. Issues specific to streaming must be considered during evaluations of clustering, such as aging, noise, and missed or misplaced points. Outlier detection in data streams is a relatively new and growing field. Extending ideas in clustering to anomaly detection has proved very effective.

The experiments in the case study in this chapter use the Java framework MOA, illustrating various stream-based learning techniques for supervised, clustering, and outlier detection.

In the next chapter, we embark on a tour of the probabilistic graph modelling techniques that are useful in representing, eliciting knowledge, and learning in various domains.

References

1. G. Cormode and S. Muthukrishnan (2010). *An improved data stream summary: The Count-Min sketch and its applications.* Journal of Algorithms, 55(1):58–75, 2005.

2. João Gama (2010). *Knowledge Discovery from Data Streams, Chapman and Hall / CRC Data Mining and Knowledge Discovery Series*, CRC Press 2010, ISBN 978-1-4398-2611-9, pp. I-XIX, 1-237.

3. B. Babcock, M. Datar, R. Motwani (2002). *Sampling from a moving window over streaming data*, in Proceedings of the thirteenth annual ACM-SIAM symposium on Discrete algorithms, pp.633–634, 2002.

4. Bifet, A. and Gavalda, R. (2007). *Learning from time-changing data with adaptive windowing.* In Proceedings of SIAM int. conf. on Data Mining. SDM. 443–448.

5. Vitter, J. (1985). *Random sampling with a reservoir. ACM Trans. Math. Softw.* 11, 1, 37–57.

6. Gama, J., Medas, P., Castillo, G., and Rodrigues, P. (2004). *Learning with drift detection.* In Proceedings of the 17th Brazilian symp. on Artif. Intell. SBIA. 286–295.

7. Gama, J., Sebastiao, R., and Rodrigues, P. 2013. *On evaluating stream learning algorithms.* Machine Learning 90, 3, 317–346.

8. Domingos, P. and Hulten, G. (2000). *Mining high-speed data streams.* In Proceedings. of the 6th ACM SIGKDD int. conference on Knowledge discovery and data mining. KDD. 71–80.

9. Oza, N. (2001). *Online ensemble learning.* Ph.D. thesis, University of California Berkeley.

10. Gama, J., Žliobaitė, I., Bifet, A., Pechenizkiy, M., Bouchachia, A. (2014). *A Survey on Concept Drift Adaptation.ACM Computing Surveys* 46(4), Article No. 44.

11. Farnstrom, F., Lewis, J., and Elkan, C. (2000). *Scalability for clustering algorithms revisited.* SIGKDD Exploration, 51–57.

12. Zhang, T., Ramakrishnan, R., and Livny, M. (1996). *BIRCH: An Efficient Data Clustering Method for Very Large Databases.* In Proceedings of the ACM SIGMOD International Conference on Management of Data. ACM Press, 103–114.

13. Aggarwal, C. (2003). *A Framework for Diagnosing Changes in Evolving Data Streams.* In ACM SIGMOD Conference. 575–586.

14. Chen, Y. and Tu, L. (2007). *Density-based clustering for real-time stream data.* In KDD '07: Proceedings of the 13th ACM SIGKDD international conference on knowledge discovery and data mining. ACM Press, 133–142.

15. Kremer, H., Kranen, P., Jansen, T., Seidl, T., Bifet, A., Holmes, G., and Pfahringer, B. (2011). *An effective evaluation measure for clustering on evolving data streams.* In proceedings of the 17th ACM SIGKDD international conference on knowledge discovery and data mining. KDD '11. ACM, New York, NY, USA, 868–876.

16. Mahdiraji, A. R. (2009). *Clustering data stream: A survey of algorithms.* International Journal of Knowledge-Based and Intelligent Engineering Systems, 39–44.

17. F. Angiulli and F. Fassetti (2007). *Detecting distance-based outliers in streams of data.* In proceedings of the Sixteenth ACM Conference on Information and Knowledge Management, CIKM '07, pages 811–820, New York, NY, USA, 2007. ACM.

18. D. Yang, E. A. Rundensteiner, and M. O. Ward (2009). *Neighbor-based pattern detection for windows over streaming data.* In Proceedings of the 12th International Conference on Extending Database Technology: Advances in Database Technology, EDBT '09, pages 529–540, New York, NY, USA, 2009. ACM.

19. M. Kontaki, A. Gounaris, A. Papadopoulos, K. Tsichlas, and Y. Manolopoulos (2011). *Continuous monitoring of distance-based outliers over data streams.* In Data Engineering (ICDE), 2011 IEEE 27th International Conference on, pages 135–146, April 2011.

Probabilistic Graph Modeling

Probabilistic graph models (PGMs), also known as graph models, capture the relationship between different variables and represent the probability distributions. PGMs capture joint probability distributions and can be used to answer different queries and make inferences that allow us to make predictions on unseen data. PGMs have the great advantage of capturing domain knowledge of experts and the causal relationship between variables to model systems. PGMs represent the structure and they can capture knowledge in a representational framework that makes it easier to share and understand the domain and models. PGMs capture the uncertainty or the probabilistic nature very well and are thus very useful in applications that need scoring or uncertainty-based approaches. PGMs are used in a wide variety of applications that use machine learning such as applications to domains of language processing, text mining and information extraction, computer vision, disease diagnosis, and DNA structure predictions.

Judea Pearl is the pioneer in the area of PGMs and was the first to introduce the topic of Bayesian Networks (*References* [2] and [7]). Although covering all there is to know about PGMs is beyond the scope of this chapter, our goal is to cover the most important aspects of PGMs — Bayes network and directed PGMs — in some detail. We will divide the subject into the areas of representation, inference, and learning and will discuss specific algorithms and sub-topics in each of these areas. We will cover Markov Networks and undirected PGMs, summarizing some differences and similarities with PGMs, and addressing related areas such as inference and learning. Finally, we will discuss specialized networks such as **tree augmented networks** (**TAN**), Markov chains and **hidden Markov models** (**HMM**). For an in-depth treatment of the subject, see *Probabilistic Graphical Models*, by Koller and Friedman (*References* [1]).

Probability revisited

Many basic concepts of probability are detailed in *Appendix B, Probability*. Some of the key ideas in probability theory form the building blocks of probabilistic graph models. A good grasp of the relevant theory can help a great deal in understanding PGMs and how they are used to make inferences from data.

Concepts in probability

In this section, we will discuss important concepts related to probability theory that will be used in the discussion later in this chapter.

Conditional probability

The essence of conditional probability, given two related events α and β, is to capture how we assign a value for one of the events when the other is known to have occurred. The conditional probability, or the conditional distribution, is represented by $P(a \mid \beta)$, that is, the probability of event a happening given that the event β has occurred (equivalently, given that β is true) and is formally defined as:

$$P(\alpha|\beta) = \frac{P(\alpha \cap \beta)}{P(\alpha)}$$

The $P(a \cap \beta)$ captures the events where both α and β occur.

Chain rule and Bayes' theorem

The conditional probability definition gives rise to the chain rule of conditional probabilities that says that when there are multiple events $\alpha_1, \alpha_2....\alpha_n$ then:

$$P(\alpha_1 \cap \alpha_2 \cap .... \cap \alpha_n) = P(\alpha_1)P(\alpha_2 \mid \alpha_1)P(\alpha_3 \mid \alpha_1 \cap \alpha_2)..P(\alpha_n \mid \alpha_1 \cap \alpha_2 \cap .... \cap \alpha_{n-1})$$

The probability of several events can be expressed as the probability of the first times the probability of the second given the first, and so on. Thus, the probability of α_n depends on everything α_1 to α_n and is independent of the order of the events.

Bayes rule also follows from the conditional probability rule and can be given formally as:

$$P(\alpha|\beta) = \frac{P(\beta|\alpha)P(\alpha)}{P(\alpha\beta)}$$

Random variables, joint, and marginal distributions

It is natural to map the event spaces and outcomes by considering them as attributes and values. Random variables are defined as attributes with different known specific values. For example, if *Grade* is an attribute associated with *Student*, and has values {A, B, C}, then P(Grade = A) represents a random variable with an outcome.

Random variables are generally denoted by capital letters, such as X, Y, and Z and values taken by them are denoted by *Val(X)* = x. In this chapter, we will primarily discuss values that are categorical in nature, that is, that take a fixed number of discrete values. In the real world, the variables can have continuous representations too. The distribution of a variable with categories {x¹, x² …xⁿ} can be represented as:

$$\sum_{i=0}^{n} P\left(X = x^{i}\right) = 1$$

Such a distribution over many categories is called a **multinomial distribution**. In the special case when there are only two categories, the distribution is said to be the **Bernoulli distribution**.

Given a random variable, a probability distribution over all the events described by that variable is known as the marginal distribution. For example, if Grade is the random variable, the marginal distribution can be defined as *(Grade = A) = 0.25, P(Grade = b) = 0.37 and P(Grade = C) = 0.38*.

In many real-world models, there are more than one random variables and the distribution that considers all of these random variable is called the **joint distribution**. For example, if *Intelligence* of student is considered as another variable and denoted by P(Intelligence) or P(I) and has binary outcomes {low, high}, then the distribution considering *Intelligence* and *Grade* represented as P(Intelligence, Grade) or P(I, G), is the joint distribution.

Marginal distribution of one random variable can be computed from the joint distribution by summing up the values over all of the other variables. The marginal distribution over grade can be obtained by summing over all the rows as shown in *Table 1* and that over the intelligence can be obtained by summation over the columns.

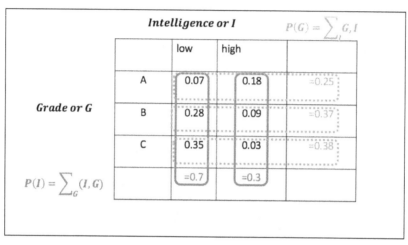

Table 1. Marginal distributions over I and G

Marginal independence and conditional independence

Marginal Independence is defined as follows. Consider two random variables X and Y; then $P(X|Y) = P(X)$ means random variable X is independent of Y. It is formally represented as $P = (X \perp Y)$ (P satisfies X is independent of Y).

This means the joint distribution can be given as:

$$P(X, Y) = P(X)P(Y)$$

If the difficulty level of the exam (D) and the intelligence of the student (I) determine the grade (G), we know that the difficulty level of the exam is independent of the intelligence of the student and ($D \perp I$) also implies $P(D, I) = P(D)P(I)$.

When two random variables are independent given a third variable, the independence is called conditional independence. Given a set of three random variables X, Y, and Z, we can say that $P = (X \perp Y|Z)$; that is, variable X is independent of Y given Z. The necessary condition for conditional independence is

$$P(X \perp Y|Z) = P(X|Z)P(Y|Z)$$

Factors

Factors are the basic building blocks for defining the probability distributions in high-dimensional (large number of variables) spaces. They give basic operations that help in manipulating the probability distributions.

A "factor" is defined as a function that takes as input the random variables known as "scope" and gives a real-value output.

Formally, a factor is represented as $\phi(X_1, X_2, \dots X_k) \phi : Val(X_1, X_2, \dots X_k) \to \mathbb{R}$ where scope is $(X_1, X_2, \dots X_k)$.

Factor types

Different types of factors are as follows:

- **Joint distribution**: For every combination of variables, you get a real-valued output.
- **Unnormalized measure**: When, in a joint distribution, one of the variables is constant, the output is also real-valued, but it is unnormalized as it doesn't sum to one. However, it is still a factor.
- **Conditional probability distribution**: A probability distribution of the form $P(G \mid I)$ is also a factor.

Various operations are performed on factors, such as:

- **Factor product**: If two factors $\phi_1(X_1, X_2)$ and $\phi_2(X_2, X_3)$ are multiplied, it gives rise to $\phi_3(X_1, X_2, X_3)$. In effect, it is taking tables corresponding to ϕ_1 and multiplying it with ϕ_2
- **Factor marginalization**: This is the same as marginalization, where $\phi_1(X_1, X_2, X_3)$ can be marginalized over a variable, say X_2, to give $\phi_2(X_1, X_3)$.
- **Factor reduction**: This is only taking the values of other variables when one of the variables is constant.

Distribution queries

Given the probability over random variables, many queries can be performed to answer certain questions. Some common types of queries are explained in the subsequent sections.

Probabilistic queries

This is one of the most common types of query and it has two parts:

- **Evidence**: A subset of variables with a well-known outcome or category. For example, a random variable **E = e**.

- **Query**: A random variable from the rest of the variables. For example, a random variable **X**.

$$P(\mathbf{X} \mid \mathbf{E} = \mathbf{e})$$

Examples of probabilistic queries are posterior marginal estimations such as $P(I = high \mid L = bad, S = low) = ?$ and evidential probability such as $P(L = bad, S = low) = ?$.

MAP queries and marginal MAP queries

MAP queries are used to find the probability assignment to the subset of variables that are most likely and hence are also called **most probable explanation** (**MPE**). The difference between these and probabilistic queries is that, instead of getting the probability, we get the most likely values for all the variables.

Formally, if we have variables $W = X - E$, where we have $E = e$ as the evidence and are interested in finding the most likely assignment to the variables in W,

$$MAP(\mathbf{W} \mid \mathbf{e}) = argmax_w P(\mathbf{w}, \mathbf{e})$$

A much more general form of marginal query is when we have a subset of variables, say given by Y that forms our query and with evidence of $E = e$, we are interested in finding most likely assignments to the variables in Y. Using the MAP definition, we get:

$$MAP(\mathbf{Y} \mid \mathbf{e}) = argmax_y P(\mathbf{y} \mid \mathbf{e})$$

Let's say, $Z = X - Y - E$, then the marginal MAP query is:

$$MAP(\mathbf{Y} \mid \mathbf{e}) = argmax_Y \sum_Z P(\mathbf{Y}, \mathbf{Z} \mid \mathbf{e})$$

Graph concepts

Next, we will briefly revisit the concepts from graph theory and some of the definitions that we will use in this chapter.

Graph structure and properties

A graph is defined as a data structure containing nodes and edges connecting these nodes. In the context of this chapter, the random variables are represented as nodes, and edges show connections between the random variables.

Formally, if $X = \{X_1, X_2,....X_k\}$ where $X_1, X_2,....X_k$ are random variables representing the nodes, then there can either be a directed edge belonging to the set ε, for example, between the nodes given by $X_i \rightarrow X_j$ or an **undirected edge** $X_i \rightarrow X_j$, and the graph is defined as a data structure $k = (x, \varepsilon)$. A graph is said to be a **directed graph** when every edge in the set ε between nodes from set **X** is directed and similarly an **undirected graph** is one where every edge between the nodes is undirected as shown in *Figure 1*. Also, if there is a graph that has both directed and undirected edges, the notation of $X_i \leftrightarrows X_j$ represents an edge that may be directed or undirected.

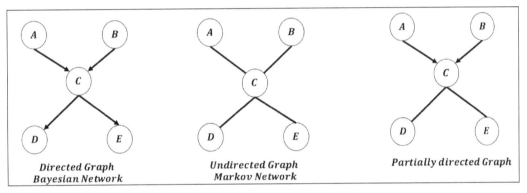

Directed Graph
Bayesian Network

Undirected Graph
Markov Network

Partially directed Graph

Figure 1. Directed, undirected, and partially-directed graphs

If a directed edge $X_i \rightarrow X_j \in \varepsilon$ exists in the graph, the node X_i is called the *parent* node and the node X_j is called the *child* node.

In the case of an undirected graph, if there is an edge $X_i - X_j$, the nodes X_i and X_j are said to be neighbors.

The set of parents of node X in a directed graph is called the boundary of the node X and similarly, adjacent nodes in an undirected graph form each other's boundary. The degree of the node X is the number of edges it participates in. The indegree of the node X is the number of edges in the directed graph that have a relationship to node X such that the edge is between node Y and node X and $X \rightarrow Y$. The degree of the graph is the maximal degree of the node in that graph.

Subgraphs and cliques

A subgraph is part of the graph that represents some of the nodes from the entire set. A **clique** is a subset of vertices in an undirected graph such that every two distinct vertices are adjacent.

Path, trail, and cycles

If there are variables $X_1, X_2, ... X_k$ in the graph $K = (X, E)$, it forms a path if, for every $i = 1, 2 ... k - 1$, we have either $X_i \rightarrow X_{i+1}$ or $X_i - X_j$; that is, there is either a directed edge or an undirected edge between the variables—recall this can be depicted as $X_i \leftrightarrows X_j$. A directed path has at least one directed edge: $X_i \rightarrow X_{i+1}$.

If there are variables $X_1, X_2, ... X_k$ in the graph $K = (X, E)$ it forms a *trail* if for every $i = 1, 2 ... k - 1$, we have either $X_i \leftrightarrows X_{i+1}$.

A graph is called a **connected** graph, if for every $X_i, ...X_j$ there is a trail between X_i and X_j.

In a graph $K = (X, \varepsilon)$, if there is a directed path between nodes X and Y, X is called the ancestor of Y and Y is called the *descendant* of X.

If a graph K has a directed path $X_1, X_2, ... X_k$ where $X_1 \leftrightarrows X_k$, the path is called a **cycle**. Conversely, a graph with no cycles is called an **acyclic** graph.

Bayesian networks

Generally, all Probabilistic Graphical Models have three basic elements that form the important sections:

- **Representation**: This answers the question of what does the model mean or represent. The idea is how to represent and store the probability distribution of $P(X_1, X_2, ... X_n)$.

- **Inference**: This answers the question: given the model, how do we perform queries and get answers. This gives us the ability to infer the values of the unknown from the known evidence given the structure of the models. Motivating the main discussion points are various forms of inferences involving trade-offs between computational and correctness concerns.

- **Learning**: This answers the question of what model is right given the data. Learning is divided into two main parts:

    ○ Learning the parameters given the structure and data

    ○ Learning the structure with parameters given the data

We will use the well-known student network as an example of a Bayesian network in our discussions to illustrate the concepts and theory. The student network has five random variables capturing the relationship between various attributes defined as follows:

- Difficulty of the exam (D)
- Intelligence of the student (I)
- Grade the student gets (G)
- SAT score of the student (S)
- Recommendation Letter the student gets based on grade (L).

Each of these attributes has binary categorical values, for example, the variable *Difficulty* (D) has two categories $(d0, d1)$ corresponding to low and high, respectively. *Grades* (G) has three categorical values corresponding to the grades (A, B, C). The arrows as indicated in the section on graphs indicate the dependencies encoded from the domain knowledge—for example, *Grade* can be determined given that we know the *Difficulty* of the exam and *Intelligence* of the student while the *Recommendation Letter* is completely determined if we know just the *Grade* (*Figure 2*). It can be further observed that no explicit edge between the variables indicates that they are independent of each other—for example, the *Difficulty* of the exam and *Intelligence* of the student are independent variables.

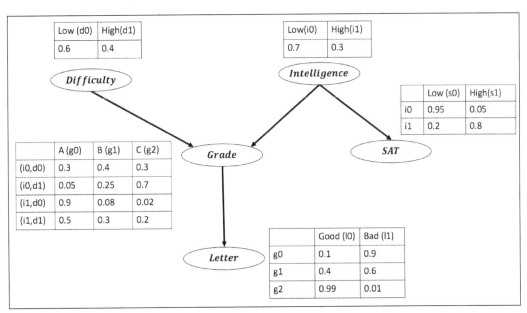

Figure 2. The "Student" network

Representation

A graph compactly represents the complex relationships between random variables, allowing fast algorithms to make queries where a full enumeration would be prohibitive. In the concepts defined here, we show how directed acyclic graph structures and conditional independence make problems involving large numbers of variables tractable.

Definition

A Bayesian network is defined as a model of a system with:

- A number of random variables $\{X_1, X_2, \dots. X_k\}$
- A **Directed Acyclic Graph** (**DAG**) with nodes representing random variables.
- A local **conditional probability distribution** (**CPD**) for each node with dependence to its parent nodes $P(X_i \mid parent(X_i))$.
- A joint probability distribution obtained using the chain rule of distribution is a factor given as:

$$P\left(X_1, X_2, \dots. X_k\right) = \prod_{i=1}^{k} P\left(X_i \mid parent\left(X_i\right)\right)$$

- For the student network defined, the joint distribution capturing all nodes can be represented as:

$$P(D,I,G,S,L) = P(D)P(I)P(G \mid D,I)P(S \mid I)P(L \mid G)$$

Reasoning patterns

The Bayesian networks help in answering various queries given some data and facts, and these reasoning patterns are discussed here.

Causal or predictive reasoning

If evidence is given as, for example, "low intelligence", then what would be the chances of getting a "good letter" as shown in *Figure 3*, in the top right quadrant? This is addressed by causal reasoning. As shown in the first quadrant, causal reasoning flows from the top down.

Evidential or diagnostic reasoning

If evidence such as a "bad letter" is given, what would be the chances that the student got a "good grade"? This question, as shown in *Figure 3* in the top left quadrant, is addressed by evidential reasoning. As shown in the second quadrant, evidential reasoning flows from the bottom up.

Intercausal reasoning

Obtaining interesting patterns from finding a "related cause" is the objective of intercausal reasoning. If evidence of "grade C" and "high intelligence" is given, then what would be the chance of course difficulty being "high"? This type of reasoning is also called "explaining away" as one cause explains the reason for another cause and this is illustrated in the third quadrant, in the bottom-left of *Figure 3*.

Combined reasoning

If a student takes an "easy" course and has a "bad letter", what would be the chances of him getting a "grade C" ? This is explained by queries with combined reasoning patterns. Note that it has mixed information and does not a flow in a single fixed direction as in the case of other reasoning patterns and is shown in the bottom-right of the figure, in quadrant 4:

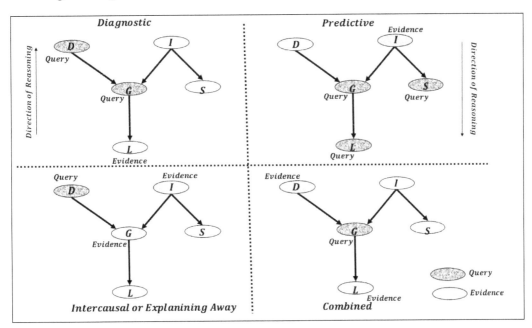

Figure 3. Reasoning patterns

Independencies, flow of influence, D-Separation, I-Map

The conditional independencies between the nodes can be exploited to reduce the computations when performing queries. In this section, we will discuss some of the important concepts that are associated with independencies.

Flow of influence

Influence is the effect of how the condition or outcome of one variable changes the value or the belief associated with another variable. We have seen this from the reasoning patterns that influence flows from variables in direct relationships (parent/child), causal/evidential (parent and child with intermediates) and in combined structures.

The only case where the influence doesn't flow is when there is a "v-structure". That is, given edges between three variables $X_{i-1} \rightarrow X_i \leftarrow X_{i+1}$ there is a v-structure and no influence flows between X_{i-1} and X_{i+1}. For example, no influence flows between the Difficulty of the course and the Intelligence of the student.

D-Separation

Random variables X and Y are said to be d-separated in the graph **G**, given there is no active trail between **X** and **Y** in **G** given **Z**. It is formally denoted by:

$$dsep_G (X, Y \mid Z)$$

The point of d-separation is that it maps perfectly to the conditional independence between the points. This gives to an interesting property that in a Bayesian network any variable is independent of its non-descendants given the parents of the node.

In the Student network example, the node/variable Letter is d-separated from Difficulty, Intelligence, and SAT given the grade.

I-Map

From the d-separation, in graph **G**, we can collect all the independencies from the d-separations and these independencies are formally represented as:

$$I(G) = \left\{ \left(X \perp Y \mid Z \right) : dsep_G \left(X, Y \mid Z \right) \right\}$$

If P satisfies $I(G)$ then we say the **G** is an independency-map or I-Map of P.

The main point of I-Map is it can be formally proven that a factorization relationship to the independency holds. The converse can also be proved.

In simple terms, one can read in the Bayesian network graph G, all the independencies that hold in the distribution *P* regardless of any parameters!

Consider the student network — its whole distribution can be shown as:

$$P(D,I,G,S,L) = P(D)P(I \mid D)P(G \mid D,I)P(S \mid D,I,G)P(L \mid D,I,G,S)$$

Now, consider the independence from I-Maps:

- Variables *I* and *D* are non-descendants and not conditional on parents so $P(I \mid D) = P(I)$

- Variable *S* is independent of its non-descendants *D* and *G*, given its parent *I*. $P(S \mid D,I,G)=P(S \mid I)$

- Variable *L* is independent of its non-descendants *D*, *I*, and *S*, given its parent *G*. $P(L \mid D,I,G,S)=P(L \mid G)$

$$(D,I,G,S,L)=P(D)P(I)P(G \mid D,I)P(S \mid I)P(L \mid G)$$

Thus, we have shown that I-Map helps in factorization given just the graph network!

Inference

The biggest advantage of probabilistic graph models is their ability to answer probability queries in the form of conditional or MAP or marginal MAP, given some evidence.

Formally, the probability of evidence **E** = **e** is given by:

$$P\left(E = e\right) = \sum_{X/E} \prod_{i=1}^{n} P\left(X_i \mid parent\left(Xi\right)\right)\Big|_{E=e}$$

But the problem has been shown to be NP-Hard (*Reference* [3]) or specifically, #P-complete. This means that it is intractable when there are a large number of trees or variables. Even for a tree-width (number of variables in the largest clique) of 25, the problem seems to be intractable — most real-world models have tree-widths larger than this.

So if the exact inference discussed before is intractable, can some approximations be used so that within some bounds of the error, we can make the problem tractable? It has been shown that even an approximate algorithm to compute inferences with an error $\epsilon < 0.5$, so that we find a number *p* such that $|P(E = e) - p| < \epsilon$, is also NP-Hard.

But the good news is that this is among the "worst case" results that show exponential time complexity. In the "general case" there can be heuristics applied to reduce the computation time both for exact and approximate algorithms.

Some of the well-known techniques for performing exact and approximate inferencing are depicted in *Figure 4*, which covers most probabilistic graph models in addition to Bayesian networks.

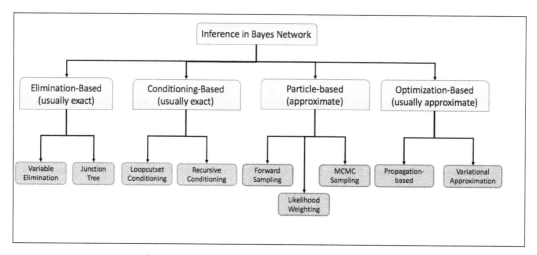

Figure 4. Exact and approximate inference techniques

It is beyond the scope of this chapter to discuss each of these in detail. We will explain a few of the algorithms in some detail accompanied by references to give the reader a better understanding.

Elimination-based inference

Here we will describe two techniques, the variable elimination algorithm and the clique-tree or junction-tree algorithm.

Variable elimination algorithm

The basics of the **Variable elimination** (VE) algorithm lie in the distributive property as shown:

$$(ab+ac+ad)= a\ (b+c+d)$$

In other words, five arithmetic operations of three multiplications and two additions can be reduced to four arithmetic operations of one multiplication and three additions by taking a common factor *a* out.

Let us understand the reduction of the computations by taking a simple example in the student network. If we have to compute a probability query such as the difficulty of the exam given the letter was good, that is, $P(D \mid L=good)=?$.

Using Bayes theorem:

$$P\big(D\big|L=good\big)=\frac{P\big(D,L=good\big)}{P\big(L=good\big)}$$

To compute $P(D \mid L=good)=?$ we can use the chain rule and joint probability:

$$P\big(D,L=good\big)=\sum_{G,I,S}P\big(S\big|I\big)P\big(I\big)P\big(G\big|I,D\big)P\big(L=good\big|G\big)$$

If we rearrange the terms on the right-hand side:

$$P\big(D,L=good\big)=\sum_{G,I}P\big(I\big)P\big(G\big|I,D\big)P\big(L=good\big|G\big)\sum_{S}P\big(S\big|I\big)$$

If we now replace $\sum_{S}P\big(S\big|I\big)=\phi_I\big(S\big)$ since the factor is independent of the variable I that S is conditioned on, we get:

$$P\big(D,L=good\big)=\sum_{G,I}P\big(I\big)P\big(G\big|I,D\big)P\big(L=good\big|G\big)\phi_I\big(S\big)$$

Thus, if we proceed carefully, eliminating one variable at a time, we have effectively converted $O(2^n)$ factors to $O(nk^2)$ factors where n is the number of variables and k is the number of observed values for each.

Thus, the main idea of the VE algorithm is to impose an order on the variables such that the query variable comes last. A list of factors is maintained over the ordered list of variables and summation is performed. Generally, we use dynamic programming in the implementation of the VE algorithm (*References* [4]).

Input and output

Inputs:

- List of Condition Probability Distribution/Table **F**
- List of query variables **Q**
- List of observed variables **E** and the observed value **e**

Output:

- $P(\mathbf{Q} \mid \mathbf{E} = e)$

How does it work?

The algorithm calls the `eliminate` function in a loop, as shown here:

VariableElimination:

1. While ρ, the set of all random variables in the Bayesian network is not empty
    1. Remove the first variable $\mathbf{Z}$ from ρ
    2. *eliminate*(F, $\mathbf{Z}$)

2. end loop.
3. Set ϕ product of all factors in F
4. Instantiate observed variables in ϕ to their observed values.
5. return $\phi_I(\mathbf{Q}) / \sum_Q \phi(\mathbf{Q})$ (renormalization)

eliminate (F, $\mathbf{Z}$)

1. Remove from the F all functions, for example, X_1, X_2, ... X_k that involve $\mathbf{Z}$.
2. Compute new function $g = \prod_{i=0}^{k} X_i$
3. Compute new function $\phi = \sum_Z g$
4. Add new function ϕ to F
5. Return F

Consider the same example of the student network with $P(D, L = good)$ as the goal.

1. Pick a variable ordering list: $S, I, L, G,$ and D
2. Initialize the active factor list and introduce the evidence:
   List: $P(S \mid I)P(I)P(D)P(G \mid I,D)P(L \mid G)\delta(L = good)$

3. Eliminate the variable SAT or **S** off the list

$$\phi_1(I) = \sum_S P(S \mid I)$$

   List: $P(I)P(D)P(G \mid I,D)P(L \mid G)\delta(L = good)\phi_1(I)$

4. Eliminate the variable Intelligence or I

$$\phi_2(G,D) = \sum_I P(I)P(G|I,D)\phi_1(I)$$

List: $P(D)P(L \mid G)\delta(L = good)\phi_2(G,D)$

5. Eliminate the variable Letter or L

$$\phi(G) = \sum_L P(L|G)\delta(L = good)$$

List: $P(D)\ \phi_3(G)\ \phi_2(G,D)$

6. Eliminate the variable Grade or G

$$\phi_4(D) = \sum_G \phi_3(G)\phi_2(G,D)$$

List: $P(D)\ \phi_4(D)$

Thus with two values, $P(D=high)\ \phi_4(D=high)$ and $P(D=low)\ \phi_4(D=low)$, we get the answer.

Advantages and limitations

The advantages and limitations are as follows:

- The main advantage of the VE algorithm is its simplicity and generality that can be applied to many networks.
- The computational reduction advantage of VE seems to go away when there are many connections in the network.
- The choice of optimal ordering of variables is very important for the computational benefit.

Clique tree or junction tree algorithm

Junction tree or Clique Trees are more efficient forms of variable elimination-based techniques.

Input and output

Inputs:

- List of Condition Probability Distribution/Table **F**
- List of query variables **Q**
- List of observed variables **E** and the observed value **e**

Output:

- $P(\mathbf{Q}|E = e)$

How does it work?

The steps involved are as follows:

1. **Moralization**: This is a process of converting a directed graph into an undirected graph with the following two steps:

   1. Replace directed edges with undirected edges between the nodes.

   2. If there are two nodes or vertices that are not connected but have a common child, add an edge connecting them. (Note the edge between V_4 and V_5 and V_2 and V_3 in *Figure 5*):

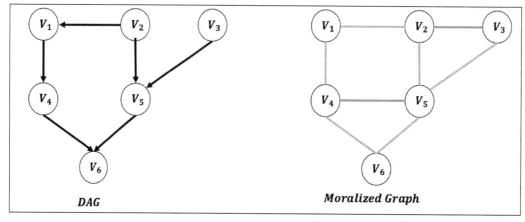

Figure 5. Graph moralization of DAG showing in green how the directional edges are changed and red edges showing new additions.

2. **Triangulation**: For understanding triangulation, chords must be formed. The chord of a cycle is a pair of vertices V_i and V_j of non-consecutive vertices that have an edge between them. A graph is called a **chordal or triangulated graph** if every cycle of length ≥ 4 has chords. Note the edge between V_1 and V_5 in *Figure 6* forming chords to make the moralized graph a chordal/triangulated graph:

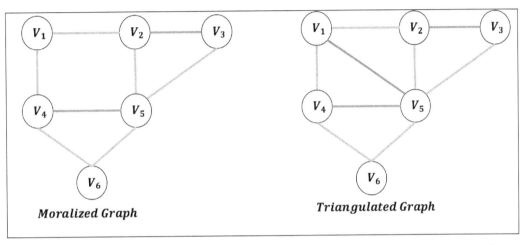

Figure 6. Graph triangulation with blue edge addition to convert a moralized graph to a chordal graph.

3. **Junction Tree**: From the chordal graphs a junction tree is formed using the following steps:

    1. Find all the cliques in the graph and make them nodes with the cluster of all vertices. A clique is a subgraph where an edge exists between each pair of nodes. If two nodes have one or more common vertices create an edge consisting of the intersecting vertices as a separator or sepset. For example, the cycle with edges V_1, V_4, V_5 and V_6, V_4, V_5 that have a common edge between V_4, V_5 can be reduced to a clique as shown with the common edge as separator.

If the preceding graph contains a cycle, all separators in the cycle contain the same variable. Remove the cycle in the graph by creating a minimum spanning tree, while including maximum separators. The entire transformation process is shown in Figure 7:

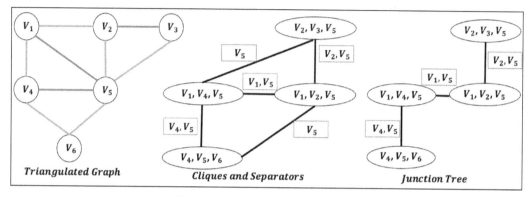

Figure 7. Formation of a Junction Tree

4. **Run the Message Passing algorithm on Junction Tree**: Junction tree can be used to compute the joint distribution using factorization of cliques and separators as

$$P(V) = \frac{\Pi_C \varphi_C(V_C)}{\Pi_S \varphi_S(V_S)}$$

5. **Compute the parameters of Junction Tree**: The junction tree parameters can be obtained per node using the parent nodes in the original Bayesian network and are called clique potentials, as shown here:

   1. $(\phi_1(V_2, V_3, V_5) = P(V_5 \mid V_2, V_3)P(V_3)$(Note in the original Bayesian network edge V_5 is dependent on V_2, V_3, whereas V_3 is independent)

   2. $\varphi_2(V_1, V_2, V_5) = P(V_1 \mid V_2)$

   3. $\varphi_3(V_1, V_4, V_5) = P(V_4 \mid V_1)$

   4. $\varphi_3(V_4, V_5, V_6) = P(V_6 \mid V_4, V_5)$

6. **Message Passing between nodes/cliques in Junction Tree**: A node in the junction tree, represented by clique C_i, multiplies all incoming messages from its neighbors with its own clique potential, resulting in a factor φ_i whose scope is the clique. It then sums out all the variables except the ones on sepset or separators $S_{i,j}$ between C_i and C_j and then sends the resulting factor as a message to C_j.

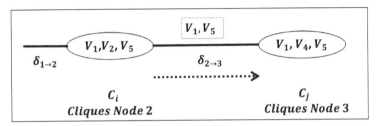

Figure 8. Message passing between nodes/cliques in Junction Tree

$$\delta_{i \to j} = \sum_{C_i - S_{i,j}} \varphi_i \prod_{k \in (Nb_i - \{j\})} \delta_{k \to i}$$

Thus, when the message passing reaches the tree root, the joint probability distribution is completed.

Advantages and limitations

The advantages and limitaions are as follows:

*   The algorithm has a theoretical upper bound on the computations that are related to the tree width in the junction tree.

*   Multiplication of each potential in the cliques can result in numeric overflow and underflow.

Propagation-based techniques

Here we discuss belief propagation, a commonly used message passing algorithm for doing inference by introducing factor graphs and the messages that can flow in these graphs.

Belief propagation

Belief propagation is one of the most practical inference techniques that has applicability across most probabilistic graph models including directed, undirected, chain-based, and temporal graphs. To understand the belief propagation algorithm, we need to first define factor graphs.

Factor graph

We know from basic probability theory that the entire joint distribution can be represented as a factor over a subset of variables as

$$p(X) = \Pi_S f_s(X_s)$$

In DAG or Bayesian networks $f_s(X_s)$ is a conditional distribution. Thus, there is a great advantage in expressing the joint distribution over factors over the subset of variables.

Factor graph is a representation of the network where the variables and the factors involving the variables are both made into explicit nodes (*References* [11]). In a simplified student network from the previous section, the factor graph is shown in *Figure 9*.

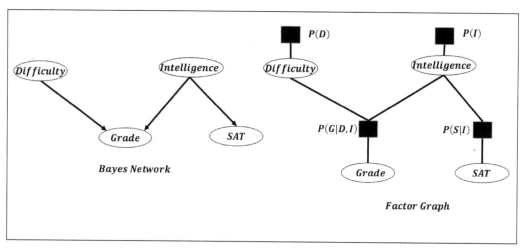

Figure 9. Factor graph of simplified "Student" network

A factor graph is a bipartite graph, that is, it has two types of nodes, variables and factors.

The edges flow between two opposite types, that is, from variables to factors and vice versa.

Converting the Bayesian network to a factor graph is a straightforward procedure as shown previously where you start adding variable nodes and conditional probability distributions as factor nodes. The relationship between the Bayesian network and factor graphs is one-to-many, that is, the same Bayesian network can be represented in many factor graphs and is not unique.

Messaging in factor graph

There are two distinct messages that flow in these factor graphs that form the bulk of all computations through communication.

- **Message from factor nodes to variable nodes**: The message that is sent from a factor node to the variable node can be mathematically represented as follows:

$$P(X) = \prod_{S \in Nb(x)} \sum_{X_s} F_s(x, X_s)$$

X_s = set of variables connected in subtree to x via factor f_s

$F_s(x, X_s)$ = product of all factors in group associated with f_s

$S \in Nb(x)$ = set of nodes (factors) that are neighbors of x

$$P(X) = \prod_{S \in Nb(x)} \mu_{f_s \to x}(x) \text{ where } \mu_{f_s \to x}(x) = \sum_{X_s} F_s(x, X_s)$$

Thus, $\mu_{f_s \to x}(x)$ is the message from factor node f_s to x and the product of all such messages from neighbors of x to x gives the combined probability to x:

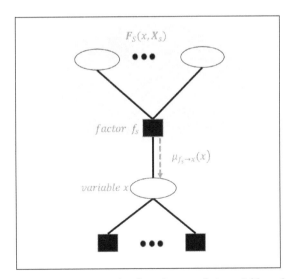

Figure 10. Message-passing from factor node to variable node

- **Message from variable nodes to factor nodes**: Similar to the previous example, messages from variable to factor can be shown to be

$$\mu_{x_m \to f_s}\left(x_m\right) = \prod_{l \in Nb\left(x_m\right)\setminus fs} \mu_{f_l \to x_m}\left(x_m\right)$$

$$Nb\left(x_m\right)\setminus f_s = all\ neighbors\ of\ x_m\ except\ f_s$$

Thus, all the factors coming to the node x_m are multiplied except for the factor it is sending to.

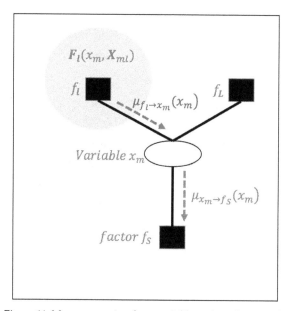

Figure 11. Message-passing from variable node to factor node

Input and output

Inputs:

- List of Condition Probability Distribution/Table (CPD/CPT) F
- List of query variables **Q**
- List of observed variables **E** and the observed value **e**

Output:

- $P(\mathbf{Q}|\mathrm{E} = e)$

How does it work?

1. Create a factor graph from the Bayesian network as discussed previously.
2. View the node **Q** as the root of the graph.
3. Initialize all the leaf nodes, that is:

$$\mu_{x \to f} = 1 \text{ and } \mu_{f \to x} = f(x)$$

4. Apply message passing from a leaf to the next node in a recursive manner.
5. Move to the next node, until root is reached.
6. Marginal at the root node gives the result.

Advantages and limitations

The advantages and limitaions are as follows:

*   This algorithm as discussed is very generic and can be used for most graph models. This algorithm gives exact inference in directed trees when there are no cycles.
*   This can be easily implemented in parallel and helps in scalability. Based on connectivity, the memory requirement can be very high.

Sampling-based techniques

We will discuss a simple approach using particles and sampling to illustrate the process of generating the distribution $P(X)$ from the random variables. The idea is to repeatedly sample from the Bayesian network and use the samples with counts to approximate the inferences.

Forward sampling with rejection

The key idea is to generate i.i.d. samples iterating over the variables using a topological order. In case of some evidence, for example, $P(X|E = e)$ that contradicts the sample generated, the easiest way is to reject the sample and proceed.

Input and output

Inputs:

*   List of Condition Probability Distribution/Table F
*   List of query variables **Q**
*   List of observed variables **E** and the observed value **e**

Output:

* $P(\mathbf{Q}|\mathbf{E} = e)$

How does it work?

1. For $j = 1$ to m // number of samples
    1. Create a topological order of variables, say $\mathbf{X}_1, \mathbf{X}_2, \ldots \mathbf{X}_n$.
    2. For $i = 1$ to n
        1. $\mathbf{u}_i \leftarrow \mathbf{X}(parent(\mathbf{X}_i))$ // assign $parent(\mathbf{X}_i)$ to variables
        2. $sample(\mathbf{x}_i, P(\mathbf{X}_i \mid \mathbf{u}_i)$ // sample $\mathbf{X}_i$ given parent assignments
        3. if($\mathbf{x}_i \neq, P(\mathbf{X}_i \mid \mathbf{E} = \mathbf{e})$ reject and go to 1.1.2. // reject sample if it doesn't agree with the evidence.
    3. Return $(\mathbf{X}_1, \mathbf{X}_2, \ldots \mathbf{X}_n)$ as sample.
2. Compute $P(\mathbf{Q} \mid \mathbf{E} = \mathbf{e})$ using counts from the samples.

An example of one sample generated for the student network can be by sampling Difficulty and getting Low, next, sampling Intelligence and getting High, next, sampling grade using the CPD table for Difficulty=low and Intelligence=High and getting Grade=A, sampling SAT using CPD for Intelligence=High and getting SAT=good and finally, using Grade=A to sample from Letter and getting Letter=Good. Thus, we get first sample (Difficulty=low, Intelligence=High, Grade=A, SAT=good, Letter=Good)

Advantages and limitations

The advantages and limitations are as follows:

- This technique is fairly simple to implement and execute. It requires a large number of samples to be approximate within the bounds.

- When evidence set is large, the rejection process becomes costly.

Learning

The idea behind learning is to generate either a structure or find parameters or both, given the data and the domain experts.

The goals of learning are as follows:

- To facilitate inference in Bayesian networks. The pre-requisite of inferencing is that the structure and parameters are known, which are the output of learning.

- To facilitate prediction using Bayesian networks. Given observed variables $\mathbf{X}$, predict the target variables $\mathbf{Y}$.

- To facilitate knowledge discovery using Bayesian networks. This means understanding causality, relationships, and other features from the data.

Learning, in general, can be characterized by *Figure 12*. The assumption is that there is a known probability distribution P^* that may or may not have been generated from a Bayesian network G^*. The observed data samples are assumed to be generated or sampled from that known probability distribution P^*. The domain expert may or may not be present to include the knowledge or prior beliefs about the structure. Bayesian networks are one of the few techniques where domain experts' inputs in terms of relationships in variables or prior probabilities can be used directly, in contrast to other machine learning algorithms. At the end of the process of knowledge elicitation and learning from data, we get as an output a Bayesian network with defined structure and parameters (CPTs).

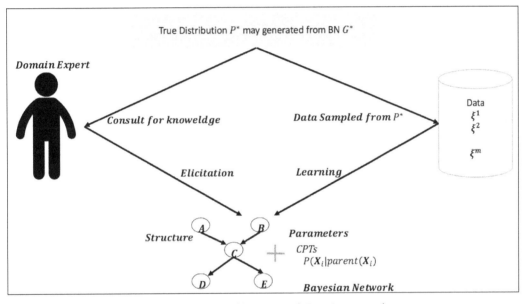

Figure 12. Elements of learning with Bayesian networks

Based on data quality (missing data or complete data) and knowledge of structure from the expert (unknown and known), the following are four classes that Learning in Bayesian networks fall into, as shown in *Table 2*:

Data	Structure	
	Known Structure (Learn Parameters)	Unknown Structure (Learn Structure and Parameters)
Complete Data	Parameter Estimation (Maximum Likelihood, Bayesian Estimation)	Optimization (Search and Scoring Techniques)
Incomplete Data	Non-Linear Parametric Optimization (Expectation Maximization, Gradient Descent)	Structure and Parameter Optimization (Structural EM, Mixture Models)

Table 2. Classes of Bayesian network learning

Learning parameters

In this section, we will discuss two broadly used methodologies to estimate parameters given the structure. We will discuss only with the complete data and readers can refer to the discussion in (*References* [8]) for incomplete data parameter estimation.

Maximum likelihood estimation for Bayesian networks

Maximum likelihood estimation (**MLE**) is a very generic method and it can be defined as: given a data set D, choose parameters $\hat{\theta}$ that satisfy:

- $L\left(\hat{\boldsymbol{\theta}}:\mathcal{D}\right)=\max_{\theta\in\theta} L\left(\boldsymbol{\theta}:\mathcal{D}\right)$

- $\theta = set\ of\ parameters$

- $\Theta = parameter\ space\ of\ all\ parameters$

Maximum likelihood is the technique of choosing parameters of the Bayesian network given the training data. For a detailed discussion, see (*References* [6]).

Given the known Bayesian network structure of graph G and training data $\mathcal{D} = \xi[1], \xi[2]....\xi[M]$, we want to learn the parameters or CPDs – or CPTs to be precise. This can be formulated as:

$$L(\boldsymbol{\theta}:\mathcal{D}) = \prod_m P_G\big(\xi[m]:\boldsymbol{\theta}\big)$$

Now each example or instance ξ can be written in terms of variables. If there are i variables represented by x_i and the parents of each is given by $parent_{Xi}$ then:

$$L(\boldsymbol{\theta}:\mathcal{D}) = \prod_m \prod_i P\big(x_i[m]|\ parent_{X_i}[m]:\boldsymbol{\theta}\big)$$

Interchanging the variables and instances:

$$L(\boldsymbol{\theta}:\mathcal{D}) = \prod_i \left[\prod_m P\big(x_i[m]|\ parent_{X_i}[m]:\boldsymbol{\theta}\big)\right]$$

The term is:

$$L_i(\boldsymbol{\theta}:\mathcal{D}) = \prod_m P\big(x_i[m]|\ parent_{X_i}[m]:\boldsymbol{\theta}\big)$$

This is the conditional likelihood of a particular variable x_i given its parents $parent_{Xi}$. Thus, parameters for these conditional likelihoods are a subset of parameters given by $\boldsymbol{\theta}_{X_i|parent_{X_i}}$. Thus:

$$L(\boldsymbol{\theta}:\mathcal{D}) = \prod_m L_i\big(\boldsymbol{\theta}_{X_i|parent_{X_i}}:\mathcal{D}\big)$$

Here, $L_i\big(\boldsymbol{\theta}_{X_i|parent_{X_i}}:\mathcal{D}\big) = \prod_m P\big(x_i[m]|\ parent_{X_i}[m]:\boldsymbol{\theta}_{X_i|parent_{X_i}}\big)$ is called the local likelihood function. This becomes very important as the total likelihood decomposes into independent terms of local likelihood and is known as the global decomposition property of the likelihood function. The idea is that these local likelihood functions can be further decomposed for a tabular CPD by simply using the count of different outcomes from the training data.

Let N_{ijk} be the number of times we observe variable or node i in the state k, given the parent node configuration j:

$$N_{ij} = \sum_{k=1}^{r_i} N_{ijk}$$

$$\hat{\theta}_{ijk} = \frac{N_{ijk}}{N_{ij}}$$

For example, we can have a simple entry corresponding to $X_i = a$ and $parent_{Xi} = b$ by estimating the likelihood function from the training data as:

$$L_i\left(\theta_{X_i = a | parent_{X_i} = b} : \mathcal{D}\right) = \frac{Count\left(X_i = a, parent_{X_i} = b\right)}{Count\left(parent_{X_i} = b\right)}$$

Consider two cases, as an example. In the first, $X_i = a, parent_{X_i} = b$ is satisfied by 10 instances with $parent_{Xi} = b = 100$. In the second, $X_i = a, parent_{X_i} = b$ is satisfied by 100 when $parent_{Xi} = b = 1000$. Notice both probabilities come to the same value, whereas the second has 10 times more data and is the "more likely" estimate! Similarly, familiarity with domain or prior knowledge, or lack of it due to uncertainty, is not captured by MLE. Thus, when the number of samples are limited or when the domain experts are aware of the priors, then this method suffers from serious issues.

Bayesian parameter estimation for Bayesian network

This technique overcomes the issue of MLE by encoding prior knowledge about the parameter θ with a probability distribution. Thus, we can encode our beliefs or prior knowledge about the parameter space as a probability distribution and then the joint distribution of variables and parameters are used in estimation.

Let us consider single variable parameter learning where we have instances $x[1]$, $x[2]$ … $x[M]$ and they all have parameter θ_X.

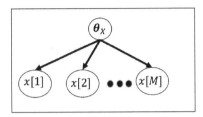

Figure 13. Single variable parameter learning

$$P\big(x[1],x[2]…..x[m],\theta\big)= P\big(x[1],x[2]…..x[m]|\theta\big)P(\theta)$$

$$P\big(x[1],x[2]…..x[m],\theta\big)= P(\theta)\prod_{m=1}^{M}P\big(x[m]|\theta\big)$$

Thus, the network is a joint probability model over parameters and data. The advantage is we can use it for the posterior distribution:

$$P\big(\theta\,|\,x[1],x[2]…..x[m]\big)=\frac{P\big(x[1],x[2]…..x[m]|\theta\big)P(\theta)}{P\big(x[1],x[2]…..x[m]\big)}$$

$P\big(x[1],x[2]…..x[m]|\theta\big)= Likelihood$, $P(\theta) = prior,$

$P\big(x[1],x[2]…..x[m]\big)= normalizing\ constant$ Thus, the difference between the

maximum likelihood and Bayesian estimation is the use of the priors.

Generalizing it to a Bayesian network G given the dataset D:

$$P\big(\theta\,|\,D\big)=\frac{P(D\,|\,\theta)P(\theta)}{P(D)}$$

$$P\big(D\,|\,\theta\big)=\prod_{i}L_{i}\Big(\theta_{X_i|parent_{X_i}}:D\Big)$$

If we assume global independence of parameters

$$P(\boldsymbol{\theta}) = \prod_i P\left(\boldsymbol{\theta}_{X_i|parent_{X_i}}\right)$$

Thus, we get

$$P(\boldsymbol{\theta} \mid \mathcal{D}) = \frac{1}{\mathcal{D}} \prod_i L_i\left(\boldsymbol{\theta}_{X_i|parent_{X_i}} : \mathcal{D}\right) P\left(\boldsymbol{\theta}_{X_i|parent_{X_i}}\right)$$

Again, as before, subset $\boldsymbol{\theta}_{Xi} \mid parent_{Xi}$ of $\boldsymbol{\theta}$ is local and thus the entire posterior can be computed in local terms!

Prior and posterior using the Dirichlet distribution

Often, in practice, a continuous probability distribution known as Dirichlet distribution—which is a Beta distribution—is used to represent priors over the parameters.

$$\left(\theta_{ij1}, \theta_{ij2} \ldots \theta_{ijr_i}\right) \sim Dirichlet\left(\alpha_{ij1}, \alpha_{ij2}, \ldots \alpha_{ijr_i}\right)$$

Probability Density Function:

$$f\left(\theta_{ij1}, \theta_{ij2} \ldots \theta_{ijr_i}\right) = \frac{1}{B\left(\alpha_{ij}\right)} \prod_{k=1}^{r_i} \theta_{\alpha_{ijr_i}}^{\alpha_{ijr_i}-1}$$

Here, $\theta_{ijr_i} \geq 0$, $\sum_i \theta_{ijr_i} = 1$ The alpha terms are known as hyperparameters and $a_{ijri} > 0$. The $\alpha_{ij} = \sum_k \alpha_{ijk}$ is the pseudo count, also known as equivalent sample size and it gives us a measure of the prior.

The Beta function, $B(a_{ij})$ is normally expressed in terms of gamma function as follows

$$B\left(\alpha_{ij}\right) = \frac{\prod_{k=1}^{r_i} \Gamma\left(\alpha_{ijr_i}\right)}{\Gamma\left(\alpha_{ij}\right)}$$

The advantage of using Dirichlet distribution is it is conjugate in nature, that is, irrespective of the likelihood, the posterior is also a Dirichlet if the prior is Dirichlet!

It can be shown that the posterior distribution for the parameters θ_{ijk} is a Dirichlet with updated hyperparameters and has a closed form solution!

$$a_{ijk} = a_{ijk} + N_{ijk}$$

If we use maximum a posteriori estimate and posterior means they can be shown to be:

$$\tilde{\theta}_{ijk} = \frac{\alpha_{ijk} + N_{ijk} - 1}{\alpha_{ijk} + N_{ijk} - r_i}$$

$$\overline{\theta}_{ijk} = \frac{\alpha_{ijk} + N_{ijk}}{\alpha_{ijk} + N_{ijk}}$$

Learning structures

Learning Bayesian network without any domain knowledge or understanding of structures includes learning the structure and the parameters. We will first discuss some measures that are used for evaluating the network structures and then discuss a few well-known algorithms for building optimal structures.

Measures to evaluate structures

The measures used to evaluate a Bayes network structure, given the dataset, can be broadly divided into the following categories and details of many are available here (*References* [14]).

- **Deviance-Threshold Measure**: The two common techniques to measure deviance between two variables used in the network and structure are Pearson's chi-squared statistic and the Kullback-Leibler distance.

  Given the dataset D of M samples, consider two variables X_i and X_j, the Pearson's chi-squared statistic measuring divergence is

$$d_{\chi^2}(D) = \sum_{X_i, X_j} \frac{\left(M[X_i, X_j] - M \cdot \hat{P}(X_i) \cdot \hat{P}(X_j)\right)^2}{M \cdot \hat{P}(X_i) \cdot \hat{P}(X_j)}$$

$$M\left[X_i, X_j\right] = joint\ count\ of\ X_i, X_j$$

$$\hat{P}\left(X_i\right) = expected\ count\ of\ X_i$$

$$\hat{P}\left(X_j\right) = expected\ count\ of\ X_j$$

$d_{\chi^2}(D)$ is 0; when the variables are independent and larger values indicate there is dependency between the variables.

Kullback-Leibler divergence is:

$$d_I\left(\mathcal{D}\right) = \frac{1}{M} \sum_{X_i, X_j} M\left[X_i, X_j\right] \log \frac{M\left[X_i, X_j\right]}{M\left[X_i\right]M\left[X_i\right]}$$

$d_I(D)$ is again 0, it shows independence and the larger values indicates dependency. Using various statistical hypothesis tests, a threshold can be used to determine the significance.

- **Structure Score Measure**: There are various measures to give scores to a structure in a Bayes network. We will discuss the most commonly used measures here. A log-likelihood score discussed in parameter learning can be used as a score for the structure:

$$score_L\left(G:\theta:D\right) = l\left(\hat{\theta}_G : \mathcal{D}\right) = \sum_{\mathcal{D}} \sum_{i=1}^{m} \log \hat{P}\left(X_i \mid parent\left(X_i\right)\right)$$

- **Bayesian information score (BIC)** is also quite a popular scoring technique as it avoids overfitting by taking into consideration the penalty for complex structures, as shown in the following equation

$$score_{BIC}\left(G:\theta:D\right) = l\left(\hat{\theta}_G : \mathcal{D}\right) - \frac{\log M}{2} Dim\left(G\right)$$

$$Dim\left(G\right) = number\ of\ independent\ parameters\ in\ G$$

The penalty function is logarithmic in *M*, so, as it increases, the penalty is less severe for complex structures.

The Akaike information score (AIC), similar to BIC, has similar penalty based scoring and is:

$$score_{AIC}(G:\theta:\mathcal{D}) = l\left(\hat{\theta}_G : \mathcal{D}\right) - c \cdot Dim(G)$$

Bayesian scores discussed in parameter learning are also employed as scoring measures.

Methods for learning structures

We will discuss a few algorithms that are used for learning structures in this section; details can be found here (*References* [15]).

Constraint-based techniques

Constraint-based algorithms use independence tests of various variables, trying to find different structural dependencies that we discussed in previous sections such as the d-separation, v-structure, and so on, by following the step-by-step process discussed here.

Inputs and outputs

The input is the dataset D with all the variables $\{X,Y..\}$ known for every instance $\{1,2, ... m\}$, and no missing values. The output is a Bayesian network graph G with all edges, directions known in **E** and the CPT table.

How does it work?

1. Create an empty set of undirected edge **E**.

2. Test for conditional independence between two variables independent of directions to have an edge.

    1. If for all subset **S** = U – $\{X, Y\}$, if X is independent of Y, then add it to the set of undirected edge **E'**.

3. Once all potential undirected edges are identified, directionality of the edge is inferred from the set **E'**.

    1. Considering a triplet $\{X, Y, Z\}$, if there is an edge X – Z and Y – Z, but no edge between X – Y using all variables in the set, and further, if X is not independent of Y given all the edges **S** = U – $\{X, Y, Z\}$, this implies the direction of $X \rightarrow Y$ and $Y \rightarrow Z$.

    2. Add the edges $X \rightarrow Y$ and $Y \rightarrow Z$ to set **E**.

    3. Update the CPT table using local calculations.

4. Return the Bayes network G, edges **E**, and the CPT tables.

Advantages and limitations

- Lack of robustness is one of the biggest drawbacks of this method. A small error in data can cause a big impact on the structure due to the assumptions of independence that will creep into the individual independence tests.

- Scalability and computation time is a major concern as every subset of variables are tested and is approximately 2^n. As the number of variables increase to the 100s, this method fails due to computation time.

Search and score-based techniques

The search and score method can be seen as a heuristic optimization method where iteratively, structure is changed through small perturbations, and measures such as BIC or MLE are used to give score to the structures to find the optimal score and structure. Hill climbing, depth-first search, genetic algorithms, and so on, have all been used to search and score.

Inputs and outputs

Input is dataset D with all the variables *{X,Y..}* known for every instance {1,2, ... *m*} and no missing values. The output is a Bayesian network graph G with all edges and directions known in **E**.

How does it work?

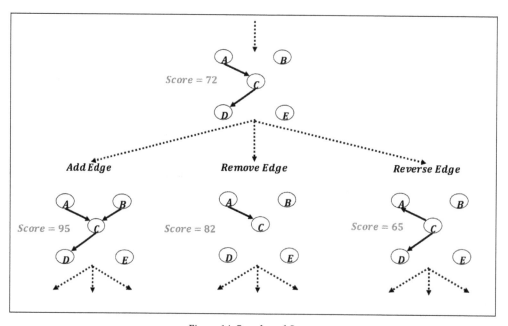

Figure 14. Search and Score

1. Initialize the Graph G, either based on domain knowledge or empty or full. Initialize the Edge set **E** based on the graph and initialize the CPT tables T based on the graph G, **E**, and the data D. Normally terminating conditions are also mentioned such as *maxIterations*:

2. *maxScore= -∞, score=computeScore(G,**E**, T)*

3. Do

    1. *maxScore=score*

    2. For each variable pair (X, Y)

        1. For each
           $$E' \in \{E \cup \{X \to Y\}, E - \{X \to Y\}, E - \{X \to Y\} \cup \{Y \to X\}\}$$

        2. New Graph G' based on parents and variables with edge changes.

        3. Compute new CPTs $T' \leftarrow computeCPT(G',E',D)$.

        4. *currentScore = computeScore(G',**E**',T')*

        5. If *currentScore > score*:

            1. *score = currentScore*

            2. $G' = G$, **E'** = **E**

4. Repeat 3 while $(score > maxScore)$ *or numIterations < maxIterations*

Advantages and limitations

- Getting stuck in a local optimum, which is the drawback of most of these heuristic search methods, is one of the biggest disadvantages.

- Convergence or theoretical guarantees are not available in heuristic search, so searching for termination is very much by guess work.

Markov networks and conditional random fields

So far, we have covered directed acyclic graphs in the area of probabilistic graph models, including every aspect of representation, inference, and learning. When the graphs are undirected, they are known as **Markov networks (MN)** or **Markov random field (MRF)**. We will discuss some aspects of Markov networks in this section covering areas of representation, inference, and learning, as before. Markov networks or MRF are very popular in various areas of computer vision such as segmentation, de-noising, stereo, recognition, and so on. For further reading, see (*References* [10]).

Representation

Even though a Markov network, like Bayesian networks, has undirected edges, it still has local interactions and distributions. We will first discuss the concept of parameterization, which is a way to capture these interactions, and then the independencies in MN.

Parameterization

The affinities between the variables in MN are captured through three alternative parameterization techniques discussed in the following sections.

Gibbs parameterization

The probability distribution function is said to be in Gibb's distribution or parameterized by Gibb's distribution if

$$P_\phi\left(X_1, X_2, \ldots X_k\right) = \frac{1}{Z}\left(\phi_1\left(\boldsymbol{D}_1\right), \phi_2\left(\boldsymbol{D}_2\right)\ldots \phi_m\left(\boldsymbol{D}_m\right)\right)$$

Z is called the partitioning function defined as:

$$Z = \sum_{X_1, X_2, \ldots X_k} \phi_1\left(\boldsymbol{D}_1\right), \phi_2\left(\boldsymbol{D}_2\right)\ldots \phi_m\left(\boldsymbol{D}_m\right)$$

Note that interaction between variables are captured by factors $\phi_1(D_1), \phi_2(D_2)....\phi_m(D_m)$ and are not the marginal probabilities, but contribute to the joint probability. The factors that parameterize a Markov network are called clique potentials. By choosing factors over maximal cliques in the graph, the number of parameters are reduced substantially.

Factor graphs

Graph structure of Markov network does not reveal properties such as whether the factors involve maximal cliques or their subsets when using Gibbs parameterization. Factor graphs discussed in the section of inferencing in Bayesian networks have a step to recognize maximal cliques and thus can capture these parameterizations. Please refer to the section on factor graphs in BN.

Log-linear models

Another form of parameterization is to use the energy model representation from statistical physics.

The potential is represented as a set of features and a potential table is generally represented by features with weights associated with them.

If D is a set of variables, $\phi(D)$ is a factor then:

$$\in(D) = -\ln\phi(D)$$

Thus, as the energy increases, the probability decreases and vice versa. The logarithmic cell frequencies captured in $\phi(D)$ are known as log-linear in statistical physics. The joint probability can be represented as:

$$P(X_1, X_2,....X_k : \theta) = \frac{1}{Z(\theta)} \exp\left[\sum_{i=1}^{m} \theta_i f_i(D_i)\right]$$

$\mathcal{F} = \{(f_i(D_i))\}^m$ is the feature function defined over the variables in D_i.

Independencies

Like Bayesian networks, Markov networks also encode a set of independence assumptions governing the flow of influence in undirected graphs.

Global

A set of nodes **Z** separates sets of nodes **X** and **Y**, if there is no active path between any node in $X \in \mathbf{X}$ and $Y \in \mathbf{Y}$ given **Z**. Independence in graph G is:

$$\mathcal{J}(G) = \{(\mathbf{X} \perp \mathbf{Y} \mid \mathbf{Z}): sep_G((\mathbf{X}; \mathbf{Y} \mid \mathbf{Z})\}$$

Pairwise Markov

Two nodes, X and Y, are independent given all other nodes if there is no direct edge between them. This property is of local independence and is weakest of all:

$$\mathcal{J}_p(G) = \{(X \perp Y \mid x - \{X, Y\}): X - Y \notin x\}$$

Markov blanket

A node is independent of all other nodes in the graph, given its Markov blanket, which is an important concept in Markov networks:

$$\mathcal{J}_l(G) = \{X \perp x - \{X\} - \mathbf{U} \mid \mathbf{U}): X \notin x\}$$

Here **U** = *markov blanket of* X.

Figure 15 shows a Markov blanket for variable X as its parents, children, and children's parents:

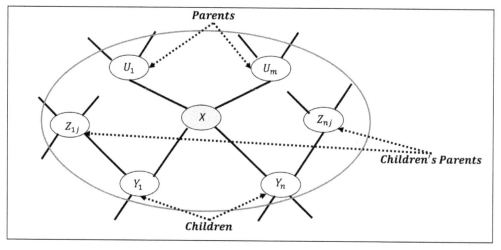

Figure 15. Markov blanket for Node X - its Parents, Children, and Children's Parents.

Inference

Inference in MNs is similarly #P-complete problem and hence similar approximations or heuristics get applied. Most exact and approximate inferencing techniques, such as variable elimination method, junction tree method, belief propagation method, and so on, which were discussed in Bayes network, are directly applicable to Markov networks. The marginals and conditionals remain similar and computed over the potential functions over the cliques as

$$P(X) = \frac{1}{Z} \prod_c \phi_c(X)_c$$

$$Z = \sum_X \prod_C \phi_c(X)_c$$

Markov blankets simplify some of the computations.

Learning

Learning the parameters in Markov networks is complex and computationally expensive due to the entanglement of all the parameters in the partitioning function. The advantageous step of decomposing the computations into local distributions cannot be done because of the partitioning function needing the factor coupling of all the variables in the network.

Maximum likelihood estimation in MN does not have a closed–form solution and hence incremental techniques such as gradient descent are used for optimizing over the entire parameter space. The optimization function can be shown to be a concave function, thus ensuring a global optimum, but each step of the iterations in gradient descent requires inferencing over the entire network, making it computationally expensive and sometimes intractable.

Bayesian parameter estimation requires integration over the entire space of parameters, which again has no closed-form solution and is even harder. Thus, most often, approximate learning methods such as **Markov Chain Monte Carlo (MCMC)** are used for MNs.

Structure learning in the MNs is similar or even harder than parameter learning and has been shown to be NP-hard. In the constraint-based approach, for a given dataset, conditional independence between the variables is tested. In MNs, each pair of variables is tested for conditional independence using mutual information between the pair. Then, based on a threshold, an edge is either considered to be existing between the pair or not. One disadvantage of this is it requires extremely large numbers of samples to refute any noise present in the data. Complexity of the network due to occurrence of pairwise edges is another limitation.

In search and score-based learning, the goal is similar to BNs, where search is done for structures and scoring — based on various techniques — is computed to help and adjust the search. In the case of MNs, we use features described in the log-linear models rather than the potentials. The weighting of the features is considered during optimization and scoring.

Conditional random fields

Conditional random fields (CRFs) are a specialized form of Markov network where the hidden and observables are mostly modeled for labeled sequence prediction problems (*References* [16]). Sequence prediction problems manifest in many text mining areas such as next word/letter predictions, **Part of speech (POS)** tagging, and so on, and in bioinformatics domain for DNA or protein sequence predictions.

The idea behind CRFs is the conditional distribution of sequence is modeled as feature functions and the labeled data is used to learn using optimization the empirical distribution, as shown in the following figure.

The conditional distribution is expressed as follows where $Z(\mathbf{x})$ is the normalizing constant. Maximum likelihood is used for parameter estimation for λ and is generally a convex function in log-linear obtained through iterative optimization methods such as gradient descent.

$$P(\mathbf{y}\mid \mathbf{x},\lambda)=\frac{1}{Z(\mathbf{x})}\exp\sum_{i=1}^{n}\sum_{j}\lambda_j f\left(y_{i-1},y_i,\mathbf{x},i\right)$$

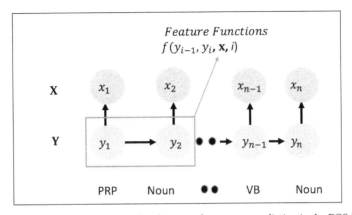

Figure 16: Conditional random fields mapped to the area of sequence prediction in the POS tagging domain.

Specialized networks

In this section, we will cover some basic specialized probabilistic graph models that are very useful in different machine learning applications.

Tree augmented network

In *Chapter 2, Practical Approach to Real-World Supervised Learning*, we discussed the Naïve Bayes network, which makes the simplified assumption that all variables are independent of each other and only have dependency on the target or the class variable. This is the simplest Bayesian network derived or assumed from the dataset. As we saw in the previous sections, learning complex structures and parameters in Bayesian networks can be difficult or sometimes intractable. The **tree augmented network** or **TAN** (*References* [9]) can be considered somewhere in the middle, introducing constraints on how the trees are connected. TAN puts a constraint on features or variable relationships. A feature can have only one other feature as parent in addition to the target variable, as illustrated in the following figure:

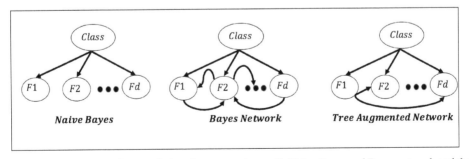

Figure 17. Tree augmented network showing comparison with Naïve Bayes and Bayes network and the constraint of one parent per node.

Input and output

Inputs are the training dataset D with all the features as variables $\{X, Y..\}$. The features have discrete outcomes, if they don't need to be discretized as a pre-processing step.

Outputs are TAN as Bayesian network with CPTs.

How does it work?

1. Compute mutual information between every pair of variables from the training dataset.

2. Build an undirected graph with each node being the variable and edge being the mutual information between them.

3. Create a maximum weighted spanning tree.

4. Transform the spanning tree to a directed graph by selecting the outcome or the target variable as the root and having all the edges flowing in the outwards direction.

5. If there is no directed edge between the class variable and other features, add it.

6. Compute the CPTs based on the DAG or TAN constructed previously.

Advantages and limitations

- It is more accurate than Naïve Bayes in many practical models. It is less complex and faster to build and compute than complete Bayes networks.

Markov chains

Markov Chains are specialized probabilistic graph models, with directed graphs containing loops. Markov chains can be seen as extensions of automata where the weights are probabilities of transition. Markov chains are useful to model temporal or sequence of changes that are directly observable. See (*References* [12]) for further study.

Figure 17 represents a Markov chain (first order) and the general definition can be given as a stochastic process consisting of

Nodes as states, $Q = \{q_1, q_2 \ldots q_L\} \ and \ |Q| = N$.

Edges representing transition probabilities between the states or nodes. It is generally represented as a matrix $\mathbf{A} = a_{kl}$, which is a $N \times N$ matrix where N is the number of nodes or states. The value of a_{kl} captures the transition probability to node q_l given the state q_k. The rows of matrix add to 1 and the values of $0 \le a_{kl} \le 1$.

Initial probabilities of being in the state, $\pi = \{\pi_1, \pi_2, \ldots \pi_N\}$.

Thus, it can be written as a triple $M = (Q, \mathbf{A}, \pi)$ and the probability of being in any state only depends on the last state (first order):

$$P\left(q_i = k_i \mid q_1 = k_1, q_2 = k_2, \ldots q_{i-1} = k_{i-1}\right) = P\left(q_i = k_i \mid q_{i-1} = k_{i-1}\right)$$

The joint probability:

$$P\left(q_1, q_2, \ldots q_L\right) = \pi_{q_1} \prod_{i=2}^{L} a_{q_i} a_{q_{i-1}}$$

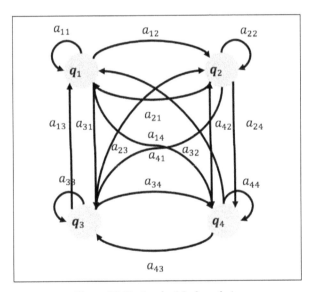

Figure 18. First-order Markov chain

Hidden Markov models

In many real-world situations, the events we are interested in are not directly observable. For example, the words in sentences are observable, but the part-of-speech that generated the sentence is not. **Hidden Markov models (HMM)** help us in modeling such states where there are observable events and hidden states (*References* [13]). HMM are widely used in various modeling applications for speech recognition, language modeling, time series analysis, and bioinformatics applications such as DNA/protein sequence predictions, to name a few.

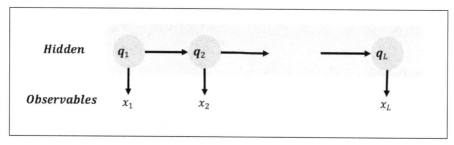

Figure 19. Hidden Markov model showing hidden variables and the observables.

Hidden Markov models can be defined again as a triple $\mathcal{H} = (\Sigma, Q, \Theta)$, where:

- Σ is a set of finite states or symbols that are observed. $\Sigma = \{x_1, x_2, \ldots x_L\}$
- Q is a set of finite states that are not observed $|Q| = N$.
- Θ are the parameters.

The state transition matrix, given as $\mathbf{A} = (a_{kl}) k, l \in Q$ captures the probability of transition from state q_k to q_l.

Emission probabilities capturing relationships between the hidden and observed state, given as $e_k(b), k \in Q$ and $b \in \Sigma$. $e_k(b) = P(x_i = b \mid q_i = k)$.

Initial state distribution $\pi = \{\pi_1, \pi_2, \ldots \pi_N\}$.

Thus, a path in HMM consisting of a sequence of hidden states $Q = \{q_1, q_2, \ldots q_L\}$ is a first order Markov chain $M = (Q, \mathbf{A}, \pi)$. This path in HMM emits a sequence of symbols, x_1, x_2, x_L, referred to as the observations. Thus, knowing both the observations and hidden states the joint probability is:

$$P(x, q) = \pi_{q_1} e_{q_1}(x_1) \prod_{i=2}^{L} a_{q_i} a_{q_{i-1}} e_{q_i}(x_i)$$

In real-world situations, we only know the observations x and do not know the hidden states q. HMM helps us to answer the following questions:

- What is the most likely path that could have generated the observation x?
- What is the probability of x?
- What is the probability of being in state $q_i = k$ given the observation ?

Most probable path in HMM

Let us assume the observations $x = x_1, x_2, x_L$ and we want to find the path q^* that generated the observations. This can be given as:

$$q^* = \operatorname{argmax} P(x,q)$$

The path q^* need not be unique, but for computation and explanation the assumption of the unique path is often made. In a naïve way, we can compute all possible paths of length L of q and chose the one(s) with the highest probability giving exponential computing terms or speed. More efficient is using Viterbi's algorithm using the concept of dynamic programming and recursion. It works on the simple principle of breaking the equation into simpler terms as:

$V_k(i) = highest\ probability\ of\ path\ q_1, q_2 ....q_i\ emitting\ observables\ x_1, x_2, ...x_i$

$$P(x,q^*) = \max \{V_k(L) \mid k \in Q\}$$

$$V_k(i) = e_k(x_i) \max V_l(i-1) a_{lk}$$

Here, $e_k(x_i) = probability\ of\ stake\ k\ emitting\ x_i$ and

$V_l(i-1) a_{lk} = probability\ of\ best\ path\ that\ ends\ in\ l\ and\ transitions\ to\ k.$ Given the initial condition $e_k(x_1)\pi_1$ and using dynamic programming with keeping pointer to the path, we can efficiently compute the answer.

Posterior decoding in HMM

The probability of being in a state $q_i = k$ given the observation x can be written using Bayes theorem as:

$$P(q_i = k \mid x) = \frac{P(q_i = k, x)}{P(x)}$$

The numerator can be rewritten as:

$$P(q_i = k \mid x) = P(q_i = k, x_1, x_2 \ldots x_i, x_{i+1}, x_{i+2} \ldots x_L)$$

$$P(q_i = k, x) = P(x_1, x_2 \ldots x_i, q_i = k) P(x_{i+1}, x_{i+2} \ldots x_L \mid x_1, x_2 \ldots x_i, q_i = k)$$

$$P(q_i = k, x) = F_k(i) B_k(i)$$

$$P(q_i = k \mid x) = \frac{F_k(i) B_k(i)}{P(x)}$$

Where $F_k(i) = P(x_1, x_2 \ldots x_i, q_i = k)$ is called a Forward variable and $B_k(i) = P(x_{i+1}, x_{i+2} \ldots x_L \mid x_1, x_2 \ldots x_i, q_i = k)$ is called a Backward variable.

The computation of the forward variable is similar to Viterbi's algorithm using dynamic programming and recursion where summation is done instead:

$$F_k(i) = P(x_1, x_2 \ldots x_i, q_i = k)$$

$$F_k(i) = e_k(x_i) \sum_{l \in Q} P(x_1, x_2 \ldots x_{i-1}, q_{i-1} = l) a_{lk}$$

$$F_k(i) = e_k(x_i) \sum_{l \in Q} F_l(i-1) a_{lk}$$

The probability of observing x can be, then

$$P(x) = \sum_{k \in Q} F_k(L)$$

The forward variable is the joint probability and the backward variable is a conditional probability:

$$B_k(i) = P\left(x_{i+1}, x_{i+2} \ldots x_L \mid x_1, x_2 \ldots x_i, q_i = k\right)$$

$$B_k(i) = \sum_l a_{kl} e_l(x_{i+1}) P\left(x_{i+2} \ldots x_L \mid q_{i+1} = l\right)$$

$$B_k(i) = \sum_l a_{kl} e_l(x_{i+1}) B_l(i+1)$$

It is called a backward variable as the dynamic programming table is filled starting with the Lth column to the first in a backward manner. The backward probabilities can also be used to compute the probability of observing x as:

$$P(x) = \sum_{k \in Q} B_k(1) e_k(x_1) \pi_k$$

Tools and usage

In this section, we will introduce two tools in Java that are very popular for probabilistic graph modeling.

OpenMarkov

OpenMarkov is a Java-based tool for PGMs and here is the description from `www.openmarkov.org`:

> OpenMarkov is a software tool for probabilistic graphical models (PGMs) developed by the Research Centre for Intelligent Decision-Support Systems of the UNED in Madrid, Spain.
>
> It has been designed for: editing and evaluating several types of PGMs, such as Bayesian networks, influence diagrams, factored Markov models, and so on, learning Bayesian networks from data interactively, and cost-effectiveness analysis.

OpenMarkov is very good in performing interactive and automated learning from the data. It has capabilities to preprocess the data (discretization using frequency and value) and perform structure and parameter learning using a few search algorithms such as search-based Hill Climbing and score-based PC. OpenMarkov stores the models in a format known as pgmx. To apply the models in most traditional packages there may be a need to convert the pgmx models to XMLBIF format. Various open source tools provide these conversions.

Here we have some screenshots illustrating the usage of OpenMarkov to learn the structure and parameters from the data.

In *Figure 20*, we see the screen for interactive learning where you select the data file and algorithm to use:

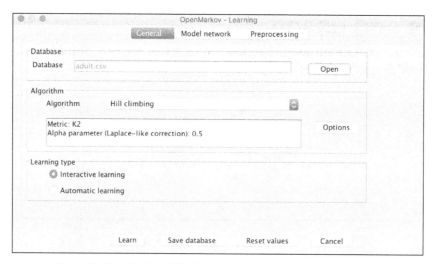

Figure 20. OpenMarkov GUI – Interactive learning, algorithm selection

The next step is the **Preprocessing** tab (*Figure 21*) where we can select how discretization is done:

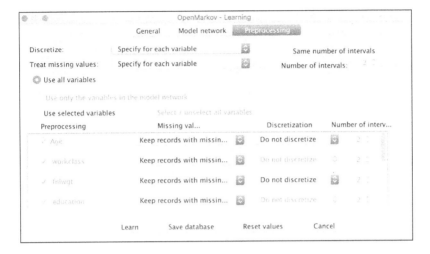

Figure 21. OpenMarkov GUI – Preprocessing screen

Finally, in *Figure 22*, we see the display of the learned Bayes network structure:

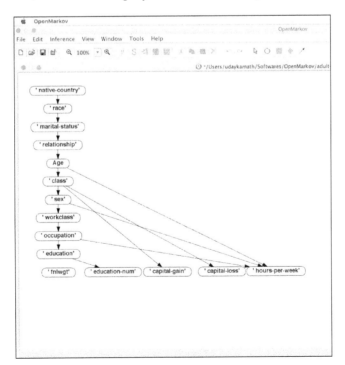

Figure 22. OpenMarkov GUI – Structure output

Weka Bayesian Network GUI

Weka's Bayes Network editor for interactive and automated learning has a large number of options for Bayes network representation, inference and learning as compared to OpenMarkov. The advantage in using Weka is the availability of a number of well-integrated preprocessing and transformation filters, algorithms, evaluation, and experimental metrics.

In *Figure 23*, we see the Bayes Network Editor where the search algorithm is selected and various options can be configured:

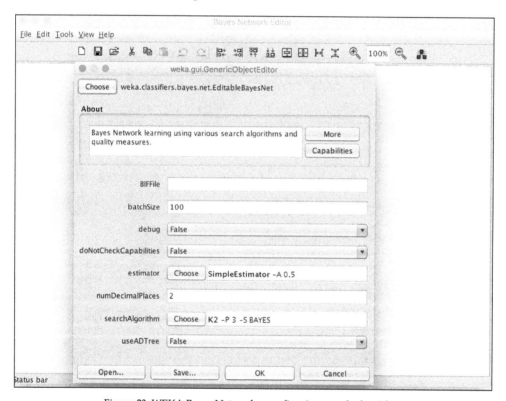

Figure 23. WEKA Bayes Network – configuring search algorithm

The learned structure and parameters of the BayesNet are shown in the output screen in *Figure 24*:

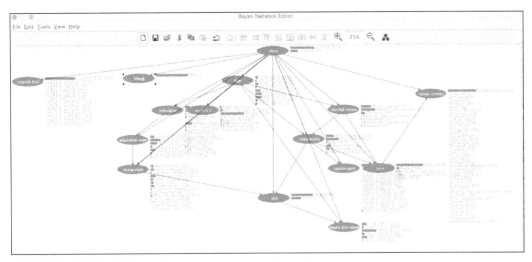

Figure 24. WEKA Bayes Network – Learned parameter and structure

Case study

In this section, we will perform a case study with real-world machine learning datasets to illustrate some of the concepts from Bayesian networks.

We will use the UCI Adult dataset, also known as the *Census Income* dataset (http://archive.ics.uci.edu/ml/datasets/Census+Income). This dataset was extracted from the United States Census Bureau's 1994 census data. The donors of the data is Ronny Kohavi and Barry Becker, who were with Silicon Graphics at the time. The dataset consists of 48,842 instances with 14 attributes, with a mix of categorical and continuous types. The target class is binary.

Business problem

The problem consists of predicting the income of members of a population based on census data, specifically, whether their income is greater than $50,000.

Machine learning mapping

This is a problem of classification and this time around we will be training Bayesian graph networks to develop predictive models. We will be using linear, non-linear, and ensemble algorithms, as we have done in experiments in previous chapters.

Data sampling and transformation

In the original dataset, there are 3,620 examples with missing values and six duplicate or conflicting instances. Here we include only examples with no missing values. This set, without unknowns, is divided into 30,162 training instances and 15,060 test instances.

Feature analysis

The features and their descriptions are given in *Table 3*:

Feature	Type information
age	continuous.
workclass	Private, Self-emp-not-inc, Self-emp-inc, Federal-gov, Local-gov, State-gov, Without-pay, Never-worked.
fnlwgt	continuous.
education	Bachelors, Some-college, 11th, HS-grad, Prof-school, Assoc-acdm, Assoc-voc, 9th, 7th-8th, 12th, Masters, 1st-4th, 10th, Doctorate, 5th-6th, Preschool.
education-num	continuous.
marital-status	Married-civ-spouse, Divorced, Never-married, Separated, Widowed, Married-spouse-absent, Married-AF-spouse.
occupation	Tech-support, Craft-repair, Other-service, Sales, Exec-managerial, Prof-specialty, Handlers-cleaners, Machine-op-inspct, Adm-clerical, Farming-fishing, Transport-moving, Priv-house-serv, Protective-serv, Armed-Forces.
relationship	Wife, Own-child, Husband, Not-in-family, Other-relative, Unmarried.
race	White, Asian-Pac-Islander, Amer-Indian-Eskimo, Other, Black.
sex	Female, Male.
capital-gain	continuous.
capital-loss	continuous.
hours-per-week	continuous.
native-country	United-States, Cambodia, England, Puerto-Rico, Canada, Germany, Outlying-US(Guam-USVI-etc), India, Japan, Greece, South, China, Cuba, Iran, Honduras, Philippines, Italy, Poland, Jamaica, Vietnam, Mexico, Portugal, Ireland, France, Dominican-Republic, Laos, Ecuador, Taiwan, Haiti, Columbia, Hungary, Guatemala, Nicaragua, Scotland, Thailand, Yugoslavia, El-Salvador, Trinadad&Tobago, Peru, Hong, Holand-Netherlands.

Table 3. UCI Adult dataset – features

The dataset is split by label as 24.78% (>50K) to 75.22% (<= 50K). Summary statistics of key features are given in *Figure 25*:

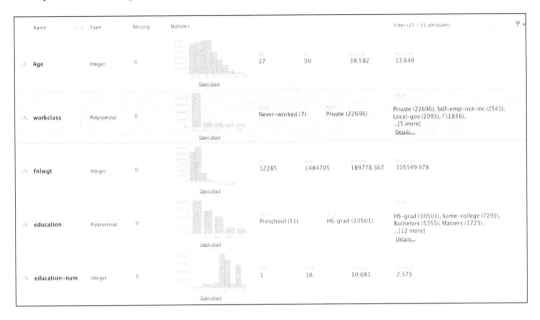

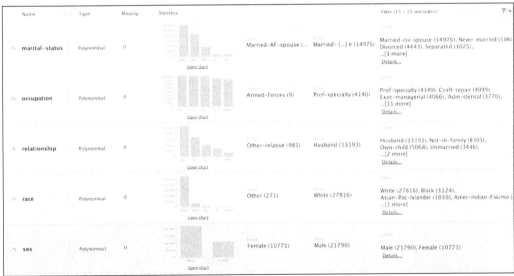

Figure 25. Feature summary statistics

Models, results, and evaluation

We will perform detailed analysis on the Adult dataset using different flavors of Bayes network structures and with regular linear, non-linear, and ensemble algorithms. Weka also has an option to visualize the graph model on the trained dataset using the menu item, as shown in *Figure 26*. This is very useful when the domain expert wants to understand the assumptions and the structure of the graph model. If the domain expert wants to change or alter the network, it can be done easily and saved using the Bayes Network editor.

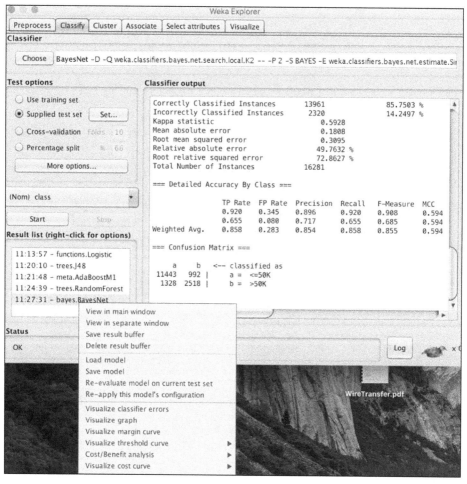

Figure 26. Weka Explorer – visualization menu

Figure 27 shows the visualization of the trained Bayes Network model's graph structure:

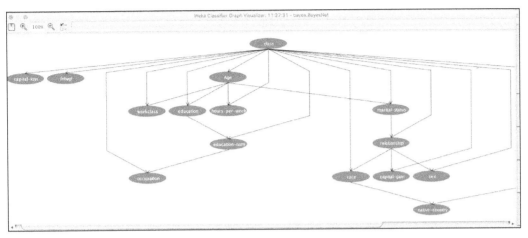

Figure 27: Visualization of learned structure of the Bayesian network.

The algorithms used for experiments are:

- Bayesian network Classifiers
- Naïve Bayes with default Kernel estimation on continuous data
- Naïve Bayes with supervised discretization on continuous data
- Tree augmented network (TAN) with search-score structure parameter learning using the K2 algorithm and a choice of three parents per node
- Bayesian network with search and score
- Searching using Hill Climbing and K2
- Scoring using Simple Estimation
- Choice of parents changed from two to three to illustrate the effect on metrics
- Non-Bayesian algorithms
- Logistic Regression (default parameters)
- KNN (IBK with 10 Neighbors)
- Decision Tree (J48, default parameters)
- AdaBoostM1 (DecisionStump and default parameters)
- Random Forest (default parameters)

Table 4 presents the evaluation metrics for all the learners used in the experiments, including Bayesian network classifiers as well as the non-Bayesian algorithms:

Algorithms	TP Rate	FP Rate	Precision	Recall	F-Measure	MCC	ROC Area	PRC Area
Naïve Bayes (Kernel Estimator)	0.831	0.391	0.821	0.831	0.822	0.494	0.891	0.906
Naïve Bayes (Discretized)	0.843	0.191	0.861	0.843	0.848	0.6	0.917	0.93
TAN (K2, 3 Parents, Simple Estimator)	0.859	0.273	0.856	0.859	0.857	0.6	0.916	0.931
BayesNet (K2, 3 Parents, Simple Estimator)	0.863	0.283	0.858	0.863	0.86	0.605	0.934	0.919
BayesNet (K2, 2 Parents, Simple Estimator)	0.858	0.283	0.854	0.858	0.855	0.594	0.917	0.932
BayesNet (Hill Climbing, 3 Parents, Simple Estimator)	0.862	0.293	0.857	0.862	0.859	0.602	0.918	0.933
Logistic Regression	0.851	0.332	0.844	0.851	0.845	0.561	0.903	0.917
KNN (10)	0.834	0.375	0.824	0.834	0.826	0.506	0.867	0.874
Decision Tree (J48)	0.858	0.300	0.853	0.858	0.855	0.590	0.890	0.904
AdaBoostM1	0.841	0.415	0.833	0.841	0.826	0.513	0.872	0.873
Random Forest	0.848	0.333	0.841	0.848	0.843	0.555	0.896	0.913

Table 4. Classifier performance metrics

Analysis of results

Naïve Bayes with supervised discretization shows relatively better performance than kernel estimation. This gives a useful hint that discretization, which is needed in most Bayes networks, will play an important role.

The results in the table show continuous improvement when Bayes network complexity is increased. For example, Naïve Bayes with discretization assumes independence from all features and shows a TP rate of 84.3, the TAN algorithm where there can be one more parent shows a TP rate of 85.9, and BN with three parents shows the best TP rate of 86.2. This clearly indicates that a complex BN with some nodes having no more than three parents can capture the domain knowledge and encode it well to predict on unseen test data.

Bayes network where structure is learned using search and score (with K2 search with three parents and scoring using Bayes score) and estimation is done using simple estimation, performs the best in almost all the metrics of the evaluation, as shown in the highlighted values.

There is a very small difference between Bayes Networks—where structure is learned using search and score of Hill Climbing—and K2, showing that even local search algorithms can find an optimum.

Bayes network with a three-parent structure beats most linear, non-linear, and ensemble methods such as AdaBoostM1 and Random Forest on almost all the metrics on unseen test data. This shows the strength of BNs in not only learning the structure and parameters on small datasets with large number of missing values as well as predicting well on unseen data, but in beating other sophisticated algorithms too.

Summary

PGMs capture domain knowledge as relationships between variables and represent joint probabilities. They are used in a range of applications.

Probability maps an event to a real value between 0 and 1 and can be interpreted as a measure of the frequency of occurrence (frequentist view) or as a degree of belief in that occurrence (Bayesian view). Concepts of random variables, conditional probabilities, Bayes' theorem, chain rule, marginal and conditional independence and factors form the foundations to understanding PGMs. MAP and Marginal Map queries are ways to ask questions about the variables and relationships in the graph.

The structure of graphs and their properties such as paths, trails, cycles, sub-graphs, and cliques are vital to the understanding of Bayesian networks. Representation, Inference, and Learning form the core elements of networks that help us capture, extract, and make predictions using these methods. From the representation of graphs, we can reason about the flow of influence and detect independencies that help reduce the computational load when querying the model. Junction trees, variable elimination, and belief propagation methods likewise make inference from queries more tractable by reductive steps. Learning from Bayesian networks involves generating the structure and model parameters from the data. We discussed several methods of learning parameters and structure.

Markov networks (MN), which have undirected edges, also contain interactions that can be captured using parameterization techniques such as Gibbs parameterization, Factor Graphs, and Log-Linear Models. Independencies in MN govern flows of influence, as in Bayesian networks. Inference techniques are also similar. Learning of parameters and structure in MN is hard, and approximate methods are used. Specialized networks such as **Tree augmented networks (TAN)** make assumptions of independence amongst nodes and are very useful in some applications. Markov Chains and hidden Markov models are other specialty networks that also find application in a range of fields.

Open Markov and Weka Bayesian Network GUI are introduced as Java-based tools for PGMs. The case study in this chapter used Bayesian Networks to learn from the UCI Adult census dataset and its performance was compared to other (non-PGM) classifiers.

References

1. Daphne Koller and Nir Friedman (2009). *Probabilistic Graphical Models*. MIT Press. ISBN 0-262-01319-3.

2. T. Verma and J. Pearl (1988), In proceedings for fourth workshop on Uncertainty in Artificial Intelligence, Montana, Pages 352-359. Causal Networks- Semantics and expressiveness.

3. Dagum, P., and Luby, M. (1993). *Approximating probabilistic inference in Bayesian belief networks is NP hard*. Artificial Intelligence 60(1):141–153.

4. U. Bertele and F. Brioschi, *Nonserial Dynamic Programming*, Academic Press. New York, 1972.

5. Shenoy, P. P. and G. Shafer (1990). *Axioms for probability and belief-function propagation*, in Uncertainty in Artificial Intelligence, 4, 169-198, North-Holland, Amsterdam

6. Bayarri, M.J. and DeGroot, M.H. (1989). *Information in Selection Models*. Probability and Bayesian Statistics, (R. Viertl, ed.), Plenum Press, New York.

7. Spiegelhalter and Lauritzen (1990). *Sequential updating of conditional probabilities on directed graphical structures*. Networks 20. Pages 579-605.

8. David Heckerman, Dan Geiger, David M Chickering (1995). In journal of Machine Learning. *Learning Bayesian networks: The combination of knowledge and statistical data*.

9. Friedman, N., Geiger, D., & Goldszmidt, M. (1997). *Bayesian network classifiers*. Machine Learning, 29, 131– 163.

10. Isham, V. (1981). *An introduction to spatial point processes and Markov random fields*. International Statistical Rewview, 49(1):21–43

11. Frank R. Kschischang, Brendan J. Frey, and Hans-Andrea Loeliger, *Factor graphs and sum-product algorithm*, IEEE Trans. Info. Theory, vol. 47, pp. 498–519, Feb. 2001.

12. Kemeny, J. G. and Snell, J. L. *Finite Markov Chains*. New York: Springer-Verlag, 1976.

13. Baum, L. E.; Petrie, T. (1966). *Statistical Inference for Probabilistic Functions of Finite State Markov Chains*. The Annals of Mathematical Statistics. 37 (6): 1554–1563.

14. Gelman, A., Hwang, J. and Vehtar, A. (2004). *Understanding predictive information criteria for Bayesian models*. Statistics and Computing Journal 24: 997. doi:10.1007/s11222-013-9416-2

15. Dimitris. Margaritis (2003). *Learning Bayesian Network Model Structure From Data*. Ph.D Thesis Carnegie Mellon University.

16. John Lafferty, Andrew McCallum, Fernando C.N. Pereira (2001). *Conditional Random Fields: Probabilistic Models for Segmenting and Labeling Sequence Data*, International Conference on Machine Learning 2001 (ICML 2001), pages 282-289.

7
Deep Learning

In *Chapter 2, Practical Approach to Real-World Supervised Learning*, we discussed different supervised classification techniques that are general and can be used in a wide range of applications. In the area of supervised non-linear techniques, especially in computer-vision, deep learning and its variants are having a remarkable impact. We find that deep learning and associated methodologies can be applied to image-recognition, image and object annotation, movie descriptions, and even areas such as text classification, language modeling, translations, and so on. (*References* [1, 2, 3, 4, and 5])

To set the stage for deep learning, we will start with describing what neurons are and how they can be arranged to build multi-layer neural networks, present the core elements of these networks, and explain how they work. We will then discuss the issues and problems associated with neural networks that gave rise to advances and structural changes in deep learning. We will learn about some building blocks of deep learning such as Restricted Boltzmann Machines and Autoencoders. We will then explore deep learning through different variations in supervised and unsupervised learning. Next, we will take a tour of Convolutional Neural Networks (CNN) and by means of a use case, illustrate how they work by deconstructing an application of CNNs in the area of computer-vision. We will introduce Recurrent Neural Networks (RNN) and its variants and how they are used in the text/sequence mining fields. We will finally present a case study using real-life data of MNIST images and use it to compare/contrast different techniques. We will use DeepLearning4J as our Java toolkit for performing these experiments.

Multi-layer feed-forward neural network

Historically, artificial neural networks have been largely identified by multi-layer feed-forward perceptrons, and so we will begin with a discussion of the primitive elements of the structure of such networks, how to train them, the problem of overfitting, and techniques to address it.

Inputs, neurons, activation function, and mathematical notation

A single neuron or perceptron is the same as the unit described in the Linear Regression topic in *Chapter 2, Practical Approach to Real-World Supervised Learning*. In this chapter, the data instance vector will be represented by x and has d dimensions, and each dimension can be represented as $x_1, x_2 \ldots x_d$. The weights associated with each dimension are represented as a weight vector w that has d dimensions, and each dimension can be represented as $w_1, w_2 \ldots w_d$. Each neuron has an extra input b, known as the bias, associated with it.

Neuron pre-activation performs the linear transformation of inputs given by:

$$a(\mathbf{x}) = b + \sum_i w_i x_i = b + \mathbf{w}^T \mathbf{x}$$

The activation function is given by $g(\cdot)$, which transforms the neuron input $a(x)$ as follows:

$$h(x) = g\big(a(\mathbf{x})\big) = g\Big(b + \sum_i w_i x_i\Big)$$

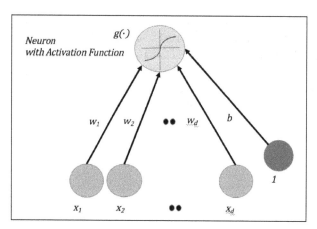

Figure 1. Perceptron with inputs, weights, and bias feeding to generate outputs.

Multi-layered neural network

Multi-layered neural networks are the first step to understanding deep learning networks as the fundamental concepts and primitives of multi-layered nets form the basis of all deep neural nets.

Structure and mathematical notations

We introduce the generic structure of neural networks in this section. Most neural nets are variants of the structure outlined here. We also present the relevant notation that we will use in the rest of the chapter.

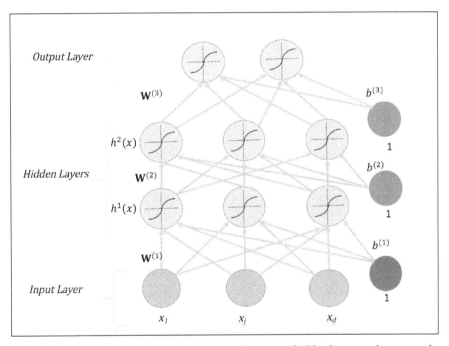

Figure 2. Multilayer neural network showing an input layer, two hidden layers, and an output layer.

The most common supervised learning algorithms pertaining to neural networks use multi-layered perceptrons. The Input Layer consists of several neurons, each connected independently to the input, with its own set of weights and bias. In addition to the Input Layer, there are one or more layers of neurons known as Hidden Layers. The input layer neurons are connected to every neuron in the first hidden layer, that layer is similarly connected to the next hidden layer, and so on, resulting in a fully connected network. The layer of neurons connected to the last hidden layer is called the Output Layer.

Each hidden layer is represented by $h^k(x)$ where k is the layer. The pre-activation for layer $0 < k < l$ is given by:

$$\mathbf{a}^k(x) = \mathbf{b}^k(x) + \mathbf{W}^k \mathbf{h}^{k-1}(x)$$

The hidden layer activation for $1 < k \leq L$:

$$\mathbf{h}^k(x) = \mathbf{g}\left(\mathbf{a}^k(x)\right)$$

The final output layer activation is:

$$\mathbf{h}^{l+1}(x) = \mathbf{o}\left(\mathbf{a}^{l+1}(x)\right)$$

The output is generally one class per neuron and it is tuned in such a way that only one neuron activates and all others have 0 as the output. A softmax function with $\mathbf{o}(\mathbf{a}) = \mathbf{softmax}(\mathbf{a})$ is used for giving the result.

Activation functions in NN

Some of the most well-known activation functions that are used in neural networks are given in the following sections and they are used because the derivatives needed in learning can be expressed in terms of the function itself.

Sigmoid function

Sigmoid activation functions are given by the following equation:

$$g(a) = sigma(a) = \frac{1}{1 + \exp(-a)}$$

It can be seen as a bounded, strictly increasing and positive transformation function that squashes the values between 0 and 1.

Hyperbolic tangent ("tanh") function

The Tanh function is given by the following equation:

$$g(a) = \tanh(a) = \frac{\exp(a) - \exp(-a)}{\exp(a) + \exp(-a)}$$

It can be seen as bounded, strictly increasing, but as a positive or negative transformation function that squashes the values between -1 and 1.

Training neural network

In this section, we will discuss the key elements of training neural networks from input training sets, in much the same fashion as we did in *Chapter 2, Practical Approach to Real-World Supervised Learning*. The dataset is denoted by D and consists of individual data instances. The instances are normally represented as the set $\{x^1, x^2 .. x^n\}$. The labels for each instance are represented as the set $\{y^1, y^2 ... y^n\}$. The entire labeled dataset with numeric or real-valued features is represented as paired elements in a set as given by $\mathcal{D} = \{(x^1, y^1), (x^2, y^2), ... (x^n, y^n)\}$.

Empirical risk minimization

Empirical risk minimization is a general machine learning concept that is used in many classifications or supervised learning. The main idea behind this technique is to convert a training or learning problem into an optimization problem (*References* [13]).

Given the parameters for a neural network as $\theta = (\{W^1, W^2, ... W^{l+1}\}, \{b^1, b^2, ...b^{L+1}\})$ the training problem can be seen as finding the best parameters (θ)such that

$$\arg\min_{\theta} \frac{1}{n} \sum_{t=1}^{n} l\left(f\left(x^t; \theta\right), y^t \right) + \lambda\Omega(\theta)$$

Where $\sum_{t=1}^{n} l\left(f\left(x^t; \theta\right), y^t\right) = Average\ Loss\ using\ Loss\ function\ and\ \Omega(\theta)\ is\ penalty\ function\ or\ Regularizer$ Stochastic gradient descent (SGD) discussed in *Chapter 2, Practical Approach to Real-World Supervised Learning* and *Chapter 5, Real-Time Stream Machine Learning,* is commonly used as the optimization procedure. The SGD applied to training neural networks is:

1. initialize $\theta = (\{W^1, W^2, ... W^{l+1}\}, \{b^1, b^2, ...b^{L+1}\})$
2. for i=1 to N epochs

    1. for each training sample (x^t, y^t)

        1 $\Delta = -\nabla_{\theta}\left(l\left(f\left(x^t; \theta\right), y^t\right)\right) - \lambda\nabla_{\theta}\Omega(\theta)$ // find the gradient of function

        2 $\theta = \theta + \alpha\Delta$ //move in direction

The learning rate used here (α) will impact the algorithm convergence by reducing the oscillation near the optimum; choosing the right value of α is often a hyper parameter search that needs the validation techniques described in *Chapter 2, Practical Approach to Real-World Supervised Learning*.

Thus, to learn the parameters of a neural network, we need to choose a way to do parameter initialization, select a loss function $\left(l\left(f\left(\mathbf{x}';\boldsymbol{\theta} \right), y' \right) \right)$, compute the parameter gradients $\nabla_{\theta} \left(l\left(\mathbf{f}\left(\mathbf{x}';\boldsymbol{\theta} \right), y' \right) \right)$, propagate the losses back, select the regularization/penalty function $\Omega(\theta)$, and compute the gradient of regularization $\nabla_{\theta}\Omega(\boldsymbol{\theta})$. In the next few sections, we will describe this step by step.

Parameter initialization

The parameters of neural networks are the weights and biases of each layer from the input layer, through hidden layers, to the output layer. There has been much research in this area as the optimization depends on the start or initialization. Biases are generally set to value 0. The weight initialization depends on the activation functions as some, such as tanh, value 0, cannot be used. Generally, the way to initialize the weights of each layer is by random initialization using a symmetric function with a user-defined boundary.

Loss function

The loss function's main role is to maximize how well the predicted output label matches the class of the input data vector.

Thus, maximization $f\left(x \right)_{c} = p\left(y = c \middle| \mathbf{x} \right)$ is equivalent to minimizing the negative of the log-likelihood or cross-entropy:

$$l\left(\mathbf{f}\left(\mathbf{x} \right), y \right) = -\log\left(f\left(\mathbf{x} \right)_{y} \right)$$

Gradients

We will describe gradients at the output layer and the hidden layer without going into the derivation as it is beyond the scope of this book. Interested readers can see the derivation in the text by Rumelhart, Hinton and Williams (*References* [6]).

Gradient at the output layer

Gradient at the output layer can be calculated as:

$$= \nabla_{\mathbf{f(x)}} - \log\left(f(\mathbf{x})_y \right)$$

$$= \frac{-1}{f(\mathbf{x})_y} \begin{bmatrix} 1_{(y-0)} \\ .. \\ 1_{(y=c-1)} \end{bmatrix}$$

$$= \frac{-\mathbf{e}(y)}{f(\mathbf{x})_y}$$

Where *e(y)* is called the "one hot vector" where only one value in the vector is 1 corresponding to the right class *y* and the rest are 0.

The gradient at the output layer pre-activation can be calculated similarly:

$$= \nabla_{a^{l+1}(\mathbf{x})} - \log\left(f(\mathbf{x})_y \right)$$

$$= -\,(\mathbf{e}(y) - \mathbf{f}(\mathbf{x}))$$

Gradient at the Hidden Layer

A hidden layer gradient is computed using the chain rule of partial differentiation.

Gradient at the hidden layer $= \nabla_{\mathbf{h}^k(\mathbf{x})} - \log\left(f(\mathbf{x})_y \right)$

$$= \mathbf{W}^{k+1} \left(\nabla_{a^{k+1}(x)} - \log\left(f(\mathbf{x})_y \right) \right)$$

Gradient at the hidden layer pre-activation can be shown as:

$$= \left(\nabla_{\mathbf{h}^k(\mathbf{x})} - \log\left(f(\mathbf{x})_y \right) \right)^T \nabla_{\mathbf{a}^k(\mathbf{x})} \mathbf{h}^k(\mathbf{x})$$

$$= \left(\nabla_{\mathbf{h}^k(\mathbf{x})} - \log\left(f(\mathbf{x})_y \right) \right) \odot \left[.., g'\left(a^k \mathbf{x}_j \right) ... \right]$$

Since the hidden layer pre-activation needs partial derivatives of the activation functions as shown previously ($g'(a^k\mathbf{x}_j)$), some of the well-known activation functions described previously have partial derivatives in terms of the equation itself, which makes computation very easy.

For example, the partial derivative of the sigmoid function is $g'(a) = g(a)(1 - g(a))$ and, for the tanh function, it is $1 - g(a)^2$.

Parameter gradient

The loss gradient of parameters must be computed using gradients of weights and biases. Gradient of weights can be shown as:

$$= \nabla_{\mathbf{w}^k} - \log\left(f(\mathbf{x})_y \right)$$

$$= \left(\nabla_{\mathbf{a}^k(\mathbf{x})} - \log\left(f(\mathbf{x})_y \right) \right) \mathbf{h}^{k-1}(\mathbf{x})^T$$

Gradient of biases can be shown as:

$$= \nabla_{\mathbf{b}^k} - \log\left(f(\mathbf{x})_y \right)$$

$$= \nabla_{2^k(\mathbf{x})} - \log\left(f(\mathbf{x}) \right)_y$$

Feed forward and backpropagation

The aim of neural network training is to adjust the weights and biases at each layer so that, based on the feedback from the output layer and the loss function that estimates the difference between the predicted output and the actual output, that difference is minimized.

The neural network algorithm based on initial weights and biases can be seen as forwarding the computations layer by layer as shown in the acyclic flow graph with one hidden layer to demonstrate the flow:

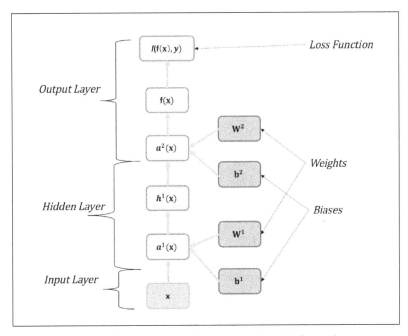

Figure 3: Neural network flow as a graph in feed forward.

From the input vector and pre-initialized values of weights and biases, each subsequent element is computed: the pre-activation, hidden layer output, final layer pre-activation, final layer output, and loss function with respect to the actual label. In backward propagation, the flow is exactly reversed, from the loss at the output down to the weights and biases of the first layer, as shown in the following figure:

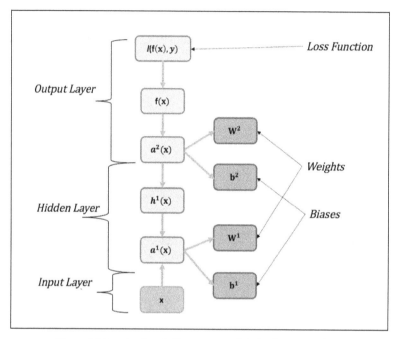

Figure 4: Neural network flow as a graph in back propagation.

How does it work?

The backpropagation algorithm (*References* [6 and 7]) in its entirety can be summarized as follows:

Compute the output gradient before activation:

$$= \nabla_{a^{l+1}(x)} - \log\left(f(x)_y\right) = -\left(e(y) - f(x)\right)$$

For hidden layers *k=l+1 to 1*:

Compute the gradient of hidden layer parameters:

$$\nabla_{\mathbf{W}^k} - \log\left(f(\mathbf{x})_y\right) = \left(\nabla_{a^k(\mathbf{x})} - \log\left(f(\mathbf{x})_y\right)\right)\mathbf{h}^{k-1}(\mathbf{x})^T$$

$$\nabla_{b^k} - \log\left(f(\mathbf{x})_y\right) = \nabla_{a^k(\mathbf{x})} - \log\left(f(\mathbf{x})_y\right)$$

Compute the gradient of the hidden layer below the current:

$$\nabla_{\mathbf{h}^{k-1}(\mathbf{x})} - \log\left(f(\mathbf{x})_y\right) = \mathbf{W}^k\left(\nabla_{a^k(\mathbf{x})} - \log\left(f(\mathbf{x})_y\right)\right)$$

Compute the gradient of the layer before activation:

$$\left(\nabla_{\mathbf{h}^{k-1}(\mathbf{x})} - \log\left(f(\mathbf{x})_y\right)\right)^T \nabla_{a^{k-1}(\mathbf{x})}\mathbf{h}^k(\mathbf{x})$$

$$= \left(\nabla_{\mathbf{h}^{k-1}(\mathbf{x})} - \log\left(f(\mathbf{x})_y\right)\right)\odot\left[..,g'\left(a^{k-1}\mathbf{x}_j\right)...\right]$$

Regularization

In the empirical risk minimization objective defined previously, regularization is used to address the over-fitting problem in machine learning as introduced in *Chapter 2, Practical Approach to Real-World Supervised Learning*. The well-known regularization functions are given as follows.

L2 regularization

This is applied only to the weights and not to the biases and is given for layers connecting *(i,j)* components as:

$$\Omega(\boldsymbol{\theta}) = \sum_k\sum_i\sum_j\left(W_{i,j}^k\right)^2$$

$$= \sum_k\left\|\mathbf{W}^k\right\|_F^2$$

Also, the gradient of the regularizer can be computed as $\nabla_\theta \Omega(\theta) = 2\mathbf{W}^k$. They are often interpreted as the "Gaussian Prior" over the weight distribution.

L1 regularization

This is again applied only to the weights and not to the biases and is given for layers connecting *(i,j)* components as:

$$\Omega(\theta) = \sum_k \sum_i \sum_j \left| W_{i,j}^k \right|$$

And the gradient of this regularizer can be computed as $\nabla_\theta \Omega(\theta) = sign(\mathbf{W}^k)$. It is often interpreted as the "Laplacian Prior" over the weight distribution.

Limitations of neural networks

In this section, we will discuss in detail the issues faced by neural networks, which will become the stepping stone for building deep learning networks.

Vanishing gradients, local optimum, and slow training

One of the major issues with neural networks is the problem of "vanishing gradient" (*References* [8]). We will try to give a simple explanation of the issue rather than exploring the mathematical derivations in depth. We will choose the sigmoid activation function and a two-layer neural network, as shown in the following figure, to demonstrate the issue:

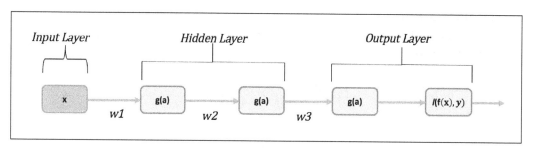

Figure 5: Vanishing Gradient issue.

As we saw in the activation function description, the sigmoid function squashes the output between the range 0 and 1. The derivative of the sigmoid function $g'(a) = g(a)(1 - g(a))$ has a range between 0 and 0.25. The goal of learning is to minimize the output loss, that is, $\dfrac{\delta l(f(x), y)}{\delta x} \to 0$. In general, the output error does not go to 0, so maximum iterations; a user-specified parameter determines the quality of learning and backpropagation of the errors.

Simplifying to illustrate the effect of output error on the input weight layer:

$$\frac{\delta l(f(x), y)}{\delta w1} = \frac{\delta l(f(x), y)}{\delta output} * \frac{\delta output}{\delta hidden2} * \frac{\delta hidden2}{\delta hidden1} * \frac{\delta hidden1}{\delta w1}$$

Each of the transformations, for instance, from output to hidden, involves multiplication of two terms, both less than 1:

$$\frac{\delta output}{\delta hidden2} = w3 * g'(a)$$

Thus, the value becomes so small when it reaches the input layer that the propagation of the gradient has almost vanished. This is known as the vanishing gradient problem.

A paradoxical situation arises when you need to add more layers to make features more interesting in the hidden layers. But adding more layers also increases the errors. As you add more layers, the input layers become "slow to train," which causes the output layers to be more inaccurate as they are dependent on the input layers; further, and for the same number of iterations, the errors increase with the increase in the number of layers.

With a fixed number of maximum iterations, more layers and slow propagation of errors can lead to a "local optimum."

Another issue with basic neural networks is the number of parameters. Finding effective size and weights for each hidden layer and bias becomes more challenging with the increase in the number of layers. If we increase the number of layers, the parameters increase in polynomials. Fitting the parameters for the data requires a large number of data samples. This can result in the problem discussed before, that is, overfitting.

In the next few sections, we will start learning about the building blocks of deep learning that help overcome these issues.

Deep learning

Deep learning includes architectures and techniques for supervised and unsupervised learning with the capacity to internalize the abstract structure of high-dimensional data using networks composed of building blocks to create discriminative or generative models. These techniques have proved enormously successful in recent years and any reader interested in mastering them must become familiar with the basic building blocks of deep learning first and understand the various types of networks in use by practitioners. Hands-on experience building and tuning deep neural networks is invaluable if you intend to get a deeper understanding of the subject. Deep learning, in various domains such as image classification and text learning, incorporates feature generation in its structures thus making the task of mining the features redundant in many applications. The following sections provide a guide to the concepts, building blocks, techniques for composing architectures, and training deep networks.

Building blocks for deep learning

In the following sections, we introduce the most important components used in deep learning, including Restricted Boltzmann machines, Autoencoders, and Denoising Autoencoders, how they work, and their advantages and limitations.

Rectified linear activation function

The Reclin function is given by the equation:

$$g(a) = reclin\ (a) = max\ (0,a)$$

It can be seen as having a lower bound of 0 and no upper bound, strictly increasing, and a positive transformation function that just does linear transformation of positives.

It is easier to see that the rectified linear unit or ReLu has a derivative of 1 or identity for values greater than 0. This acts as a significant benefit as the derivatives are not squashed and do not have diminishing values when chained. One of the issues with ReLu is that the value is 0 for negative inputs and the corresponding neurons act as "dead", especially when a large negative value is learned for the bias term. ReLu cannot recover from this as the input and derivative are both 0. This is generally solved by having a "leaky ReLu". These functions have a small value for negative inputs and are given by $g(a) = reclin(a) = max(\in a, a)$ where $\in = 0.01$, typically.

Restricted Boltzmann Machines

Restricted Boltzmann Machines (RBM) is an unsupervised learning neural network (*References* [11]). The idea of RBM is to extract "more meaningful features" from labeled or unlabeled data. It is also meant to "learn" from the large quantity of unlabeled data available in many domains when getting access to labeled data is costly or difficult.

Definition and mathematical notation

In its basic form RBM assumes inputs to be binary values 0 or 1 in each dimension. RBMs are undirected graphical models having two layers, a visible layer represented as x and a hidden layer h, and connections W.

RBM defines a distribution over the visible layer that involves the latent variables from the hidden layer. First an energy function is defined to capture the relationship between the visible and the hidden layers in vector form as:

$$E(\mathbf{x},\mathbf{h}) = -\mathbf{h}^T\mathbf{W}\mathbf{x} - \mathbf{c}^T\mathbf{x} - \mathbf{b}^T\mathbf{h}$$

In scalar form the energy function can be defined as:

$$E(\mathbf{x},\mathbf{h}) = -\sum_j\sum_k W_{j,k}h_jx_k - \sum_k c_kx_k - \sum_j b_jh_j$$

The probability of the distribution is given by $p(\mathbf{x},\mathbf{h}) = \exp(-E(\mathbf{x},\mathbf{h}))/Z$ where Z is called the "partitioning function", which is an enumeration over all the values of x *and* h, which are binary, resulting in exponential terms and thus making it intractable!

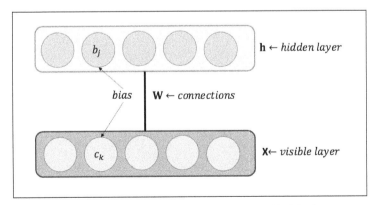

Figure 6: Connection between the visible layer and hidden layer.

The Markov network view of the same in scalar form can be represented using all the pairwise factors, as shown in the following figure. This also makes it clear why it is called a "restricted" Boltzmann machine as there is no connection among units within a given hidden layer or in the visible layers:

$$p(\mathbf{x},\mathbf{h}) = \frac{1}{Z}\prod_j\prod_k \exp\left(W_{j,k}h_j x_k\right)\prod_j \exp\left(c_k x_k\right)\prod_k \exp\left(b_j h_j\right)$$

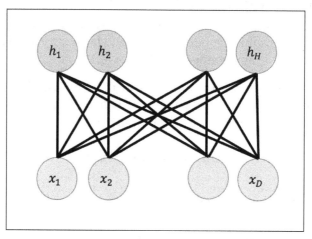

Figure 7: Input and hidden layers as scalars

We have seen that the whole probability distribution function $p(\mathbf{x},\mathbf{h}) = \exp\left(-E(\mathbf{x},\mathbf{h})\right)/Z$ is intractable. We will now derive the basic conditional probability distributions for x, h.

Conditional distribution

Although computing the whole $p(x, h)$ is intractable, the conditional distribution of $p(x\,|\,h)$ or $p(h\,|\,x)$ can be easily defined and shown to be a Bernoulli distribution and tractable:

$$p(\mathbf{h}|\mathbf{x}) = \prod_j p\left(h_j|\mathbf{x}\right)$$

$$p\left(h_j = 1|\mathbf{x}\right) = sigmoid\left(b_j + \mathbf{W}_j\mathbf{x}\right)$$

$$= \frac{1}{1 + \exp\left(-\left(b_j + \mathbf{W}_j\mathbf{x}\right)\right)}$$

Similarly, being symmetric and undirected:

$$p(\mathbf{x}|\mathbf{h}) = \prod_k p(x_k|\mathbf{h})$$

$$p(x_k = 1|\mathbf{h}) = sigmoid\left(c_k + \mathbf{h}^{\mathrm{T}}\mathbf{W}_k\right)$$

$$= \frac{1}{1 + \exp\left(-\left(c_k + \mathbf{h}^{\mathrm{T}}\mathbf{W}_k\right)\right)}$$

Free energy in RBM

The distribution of input or the observed variable is:

$$p(\mathbf{x}) = \sum_h p(\mathbf{x}, \mathbf{h})$$

$$p(\mathbf{x}) = \sum_h \exp\left(-E(\mathbf{x}, \mathbf{h})\right)/Z$$

$$p(\mathbf{x}) = \exp\left(\mathbf{c}^{\mathrm{T}}\mathbf{x} + \sum_{h=1}^{H} \log\left(1 + \exp\left(b_j + \mathbf{W}_j\mathbf{x}\right)\right)\right)\Big/ Z$$

$$p(\mathbf{x}) = \exp\left(-\mathcal{F}(\mathbf{x})\right)\Big/ Z$$

The function $F(x)$ is called free energy.

Training the RBM

RBMs are trained using the optimization objective of minimizing the average negative log-likelihood over the entire training data. This can be represented as:

$$\mathcal{L}(\theta, \mathcal{D}) = \frac{1}{T}\sum_t -\log\left(\mathbf{x}^t\right) \text{ where } \theta \text{ are the parameters}$$

The optimization is carried out by using stochastic gradient descent:

$$\frac{\partial - \log p(\mathbf{x}^t)}{\partial \theta} = E_{\mathbf{h}}\left[\frac{\partial E(\mathbf{x}^t, \mathbf{h})}{\partial \theta}\Big|\mathbf{x}^t\right] - E_{\mathbf{x},\mathbf{h}}\left[\frac{\partial E(\mathbf{x}, \mathbf{h})}{\partial \theta}\right]$$

The term $E_{\mathbf{h}}\left[\dfrac{\partial E(\mathbf{x}^t, \mathbf{h})}{\partial \theta}\Big|\mathbf{x}^t\right]$ is called the "positive phase" and the term

$E_{\mathbf{x},\mathbf{h}}\left[\dfrac{\partial E(\mathbf{x}, \mathbf{h})}{\partial \theta}\right]$ is called the "negative phase" because of how they affect the

probability distributions – the positive phase, because it increases the probability of training data by reducing the free energy, and the negative phase, as it decreases the probability of samples generated by the model.

It has been shown that the overall gradient is difficult to compute analytically because of the "negative phase", as it is computing the expectation over all possible configurations of the input data under the distribution formed by the model and making it intractable!

To make the computation tractable, estimation is carried out using a fixed number of model samples and they are referred to as "negative particles" denoted by N.

The gradient can be now written as the approximation:

$$\frac{\partial - \log p(\mathbf{x}^t)}{\partial \theta} \approx \frac{\partial \mathcal{F}(\mathbf{x})}{\partial \theta} - \frac{1}{N}\sum_{\tilde{\mathbf{x}} \in \mathcal{N}} \frac{\partial F(\tilde{\mathbf{x}})}{\partial \theta}$$

Where particles $\tilde{\mathbf{x}}$ are sampled using some sampling techniques such as the Monte Carlo method.

Sampling in RBM

Gibbs sampling is often the technique used to generate samples and learn the probability of $p(x,h)$ in terms of $p(x \mid h)$ and $p(h \mid x)$, which are relatively easy to compute, as shown previously.

Gibbs sampling for joint sampling of N random variables $S = (S_1, \ldots S_N)$ is done using N sampling sub-steps of the form $S_i \sim p(S_i | S_{-i})$ where S_{-i} contains samples up to and excluding step S_i. Graphically, this can be shown as follows:

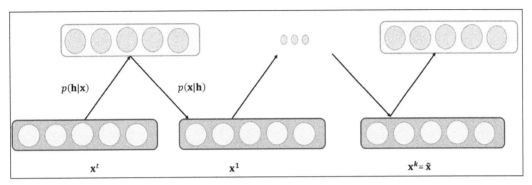

Figure 8: Graphical representation of sampling done between hidden and input layers.

As $t \to \infty$ it can be shown that the sampling represents the actual distribution $p(x,h)$.

Contrastive divergence

Contrastive divergence (CD) is a trick used to expedite the Gibbs sampling process described previously so it stops at step k of the process rather than continuing for a long time to guarantee convergence. It has been seen that even $k=1$ is reasonable and gives good performance (*References* [10]).

Inputs and outputs

These are the inputs to the algorithm:

- Training dataset
- Number of steps for Gibbs sampling, k
- Learning rate α
- The output is the set of updated parameters

How does it work?

The complete training pseudo-code using CD with the free energy function and partial derivatives can be given as:

1. For each instance in training $\mathbf{x}^t$:

    1. Generate a negative particle $\tilde{\mathbf{x}}$ using k steps of Gibbs Sampling.

    2. Update the parameters:

$$W \Leftarrow W + \alpha \left(h\left(x^t\right) x^{t^T} - h\left(\tilde{x}\right) \tilde{x}^T \right)$$

$$b \Leftarrow b + \alpha \left(h\left(x^t\right) - h\left(\tilde{x}\right) \right)$$

$$c \Leftarrow c + \alpha \left(x^t - \tilde{x} \right)$$

Persistent contrastive divergence

Persistent contrastive divergence is another trick used to compute the joint probability $p(x,h)$. In this method, there is a single chain that does not reinitialize after every observed sample to find the negative particle $\tilde{\mathbf{x}}$. It persists its state and parameters are updated just through running these k states by using the particle from the previous step.

Autoencoders

An autoencoder is another form of unsupervised learning technique in neural networks. It is very similar to the feed-forward neural network described at the start with the only difference being it doesn't generate a class at output, but tries to replicate the input at the output layer (*References* [12 and 23]). The goal is to have hidden layer(s) capture the latent or hidden information of the input as features that can be useful in unsupervised or supervised learning.

Definition and mathematical notations

A single hidden layer example of an Autoencoder is shown in the following figure:

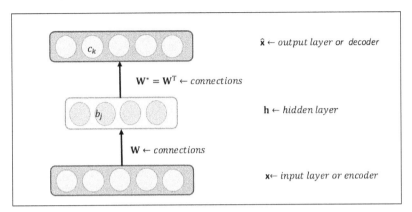

Figure 9: Autoencoder flow between layers

The input layer and the output layer have the same number of neurons similar as feed-forward, corresponding to the input vector, x. Each hidden layer can have greater, equal, or fewer neurons than the input or output layer and an activation function that does a non-linear transformation of the signal. It can be seen as using the unsupervised or latent hidden structure to "compress" the data effectively.

The encoder or input transformation of the data by the hidden layer is given by:

$$\mathbf{h}(\mathbf{x}) = g\big(a(\mathbf{x})\big)$$

And the decoder or output transformation of the data by the output layer is given by:

$$\hat{\mathbf{x}} = o\big(\hat{a}(\mathbf{x})\big)$$

Generally, a sigmoid function with linear transformation of signals as described in the neural network section is popularly used in the layers:

$$\mathbf{h}(\mathbf{x}) = sigma(\mathbf{b} + \mathbf{W}\mathbf{x}) \text{ and } \hat{x} = sigma\big(c + W * h(x)\big)$$

Loss function

The job of the loss function is to reduce the training error as before so that an optimization process such as a stochastic gradient function can be used.

In the case of binary valued input, the loss function is generally the average cross-entropy given by:

$$l\left(f\left(\mathbf{x}\right)\right) = \sum_{k}\left(x_k \log \hat{x}_k + \left(1 - x_k\right)\log\left(1 - \hat{x}_k\right)\right) where \, k = dimension$$

It can be easily verified that, when the input signal and output signal match either 0 or 1, the error is 0. Similarly, for real-valued input, a squared error is used:

$$l\left(f\left(\mathbf{x}\right)\right) = \frac{1}{2}\sum_{k}\left(x_k - \hat{x}_k\right)^2$$

The gradient of the loss function that is needed for the stochastic gradient procedure is similar to the feed-forward neural network and can be shown through derivation for both real-valued and binary as follows:

$$\nabla_{\hat{a}\left(\mathbf{x}^{(t)}\right)}l\left(f\left(\mathbf{x}\right)\right) = \hat{\mathbf{x}}^{(t)} - \mathbf{x}^{(t)}$$

Parameter gradients are obtained by back-propagating the $\nabla_{\hat{a}\left(\mathbf{x}^{(t)}\right)}l\left(f\left(\mathbf{x}\right)\right)$ exactly as in the neural network.

Limitations of Autoencoders

Autoencoders have some known drawbacks that have been addressed by specialized architectures that we will discuss in the sections to follow. These limitations are:

When the size of the Autoencoder is equal to the number of neurons in the input, there is a chance that the weights learned by the Autoencoders are just the identity vectors and that the whole representation simply passes on the inputs exactly as outputs with zero loss. Thus, they emulate "rote learning" or "memorization" without any generalization.

When the size of the Autoencoder is greater than the number of neurons in the input, the configuration is called an "overcomplete" hidden layer and can have similar problems to the ones mentioned previously. Some of the units can be turned off and others can become identity making it just the copy unit.

When the size of the Autoencoder is less than the number of neurons in the input, known as "undercomplete", the latent structure in the data or important hidden components can be discovered.

Denoising Autoencoder

As mentioned previously, when the Autoencoder has a hidden layer size greater than or equal to that of the input, it is not guaranteed to learn the weights and can become simply a unit switch to copy input to output. This issue is addressed by the Denoising Autoencoder. Here there is another layer added between input and the hidden layer. This layer adds some noise to the input using either a well-known distribution $p(\tilde{x}|x)$ or using stochastic noise such as turning a bit to 0 in binary input. This "noisy" input then goes through learning from the hidden layer to the output layer exactly like the Autoencoder. The loss function of the Denoising Autoencoder compares the output with the actual input. Thus, the added noise and the larger hidden layer enable either learning latent structures or adding/removing redundancy to produce the exact signal at the output. This architecture — where non-zero features at the noisy layer generate features at the hidden layer that are themselves transformed by the activation layer as the signal advances forward — lends a robustness and implicit structure to the learning process (*References* [15]).

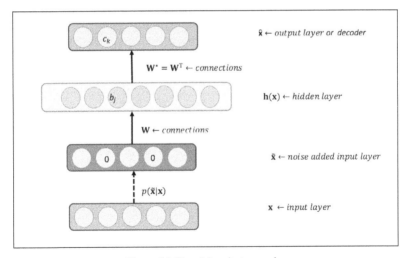

Figure 10: Denoising Autoencoder

Unsupervised pre-training and supervised fine-tuning

As we discussed in the issues section on neural networks, the issue with over-training arises especially in deep learning as the number of layers, and hence parameters, is large. One way to account for over-fitting is to do data-specific regularization. In this section, we will describe the "unsupervised pre-training" method done in the hidden layers to overcome the issue of over-fitting. Note that this is generally the "initialization process" used in many deep learning algorithms.

The algorithm of unsupervised pre-training works in a layer-wise greedy fashion. As shown in the following figure, one layer of a visible and hidden structure is considered at a given time. The weights of this layer are learned for a few iterations using unsupervised techniques such as RBM, described previously. The output of the hidden layer is then used as a "visible" or "input" layer and the training proceeds to the next, and so on.

Each learning of layers can be thought of as a "feature extraction or feature generation" process. The real data inputs when transformed form higher-level features at a given layer and then are further combined to form much higher-level features, and so on.

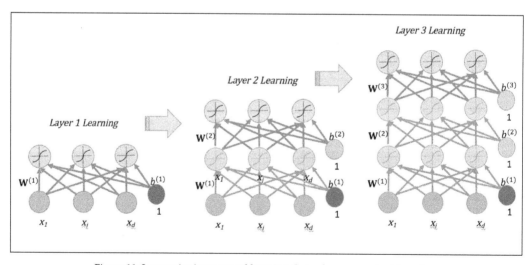

Figure 11: Layer wise incremental learning through unsupervised learning.

Once all the hidden layer parameters are learned in pre-training using unsupervised techniques as described previously, a supervised fine-tuning process follows. In the supervised fine-tuning process, a final output layer is added and, just like in a neural network, training is done with forward and backward propagation. The idea is that most weights or parameters are almost fully tuned and only need a small change for producing a discriminative class mapping at the output.

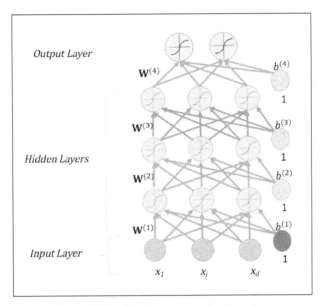

Figure 12: Final tuning or supervised learning.

Deep feed-forward NN

A deep feed-forward neural network involves using the stages pre-training, and fine-tuning.

Depending on the unsupervised learning technique used—RBM, Autoencoders, or Denoising Autoencoders—different algorithms are formed: Stacked RBM, Stacked Autoencoders, and Stacked Denoising Autoencoders, respectively.

Input and outputs

Given an architecture for the deep feed-forward neural net, these are the inputs for training the network:

- Number of layers L
- Dataset without labels D
- Dataset with labels D
- Number of training iterations n

How does it work?

The generalized learning/training algorithm for all three is given as follows:

1. For layers $l=1$ to L (Pre-Training):

    1. Dataset without Labels $\mathcal{D} = \left\{ \mathbf{h}^{l-1}\left(\mathbf{x}^{(t)} \right) \right\}_{t=1}^{T}$
    2. Perform Step-wise Layer Unsupervised Learning (RBM, Autoencoders, or Denoising Autoencoders)
    3. Finalize the parameters $\mathbf{W}^l$, $\mathbf{b}^l$ from the preceding step

2. For the output layer $(L+1)$ perform random initialization of parameters $\mathbf{W}^{L+1}$, $\mathbf{b}^{L+1}$.

3. For layers $l=1$ to $L+1$ (Fine-Tuning):

    1. Dataset with Labels $\mathcal{D} = \left\{ \mathbf{h}^{l-1}\left(\mathbf{x}^{(t)} \right), y^{(t)} \right\}_{t=1}^{T}$.
    2. Use the pre-initialized weights from 1. ($\mathbf{W}^l$, $\mathbf{b}^l$).
    3. Perform forward-backpropagation for n iterations.

Deep Autoencoders

Deep Autoencoders have many layers of hidden units, which shrink to a very small dimension and then symmetrically grow to the input size.

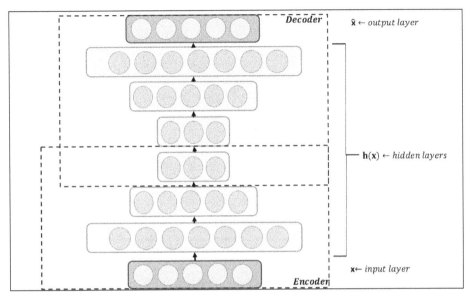

Figure 13: Deep Autoencoders

The idea behind Deep Autoencoders is to create features that capture latent complex structures of input using deep networks and at the same time overcome the issue of gradients and underfitting due to the deep structure. It was shown that this methodology generated better features and performed better than PCA on many datasets (*References* [13]).

Deep Autoencoders use the concept of pre-training, encoders/decoders, and fine-tuning to perform unsupervised learning:

In the pre-training phase, the RBM methodology is used to learn greedy stepwise parameters of the encoders, as shown in the following figure, for initialization:

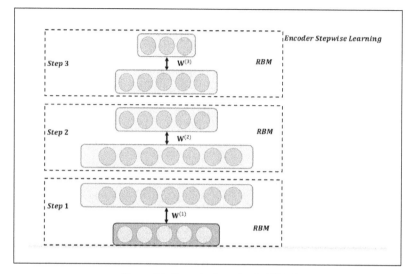

Figure 14: Stepwise learning in RBM

In the unfolding phase the same parameters are symmetrically applied to the decoder network for initialization.

Finally, fine-tuning backpropagation is used to adjust the parameters across the entire network.

Deep Belief Networks

Deep Belief Networks (DBNs) are the origin of the concept of unsupervised pre-training (*References* [9]). Unsupervised pre-training originated from DBNs and then was found to be equally useful and effective in the feed-forward supervised deep networks.

Deep belief networks are not supervised feed-forward networks, but a generative model to generate data samples.

Inputs and outputs

The input layer is the instance of data, represented by one neuron for each input feature. The output of a DBN is a reconstruction of the input from a hierarchy of learned features of increasingly greater abstraction.

How does it work?

How a DBN learns the joint distribution of the input data is explained here using a three-layer DBN architecture as an example.

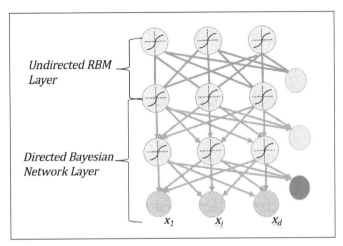

Figure 15: Deep belief network

The three-hidden-layered DBN as shown has a first layer of undirected RBM connected to a two-layered Bayesian network. The Bayesian network with a sigmoid activation function is called a sigmoid Bayesian network (SBN).

The goal of a generative model is to learn the joint distribution as given by $p(\mathbf{x},\mathbf{h}^{(1)},\mathbf{h}^{(2)},\mathbf{h}^{(3)})$

$$p(\mathbf{x},\mathbf{h}^{(1)},\mathbf{h}^{(2)},\mathbf{h}^{(3)}) = p(\mathbf{h}^{(2)},\mathbf{h}^{(3)})p(\mathbf{h}^{(1)}\,|\,\mathbf{h}^{(2)})\,p(\mathbf{x}\,|\,\mathbf{h}^{(1)})$$

RBM computation as seen before gives us:

$$p\left(\mathbf{h}^{(2)},\mathbf{h}^{(3)}\right) = \exp\left(\mathbf{h}^{(2)}\mathbf{W}^3\mathbf{h}^{(2)} + \mathbf{b}^{2^\mathrm{T}}\mathbf{h}^{(2)} + \mathbf{b}^{3^\mathrm{T}}\mathbf{h}^{(3)}\right)\Big/Z$$

The Bayesian Network in the next two layers is:

$$p\left(\mathbf{h}^{(1)}\Big|\mathbf{h}^{(2)}\right) = \exp\prod_j p\left(\mathbf{h}^{(1)}_j\Big|\mathbf{h}^{(2)}\right)$$

$$p\left(\mathbf{x}\Big|\mathbf{h}^{(1)}\right) = \prod_i p\left(x_i\Big|\mathbf{h}^{(2)}\right)$$

For binary data:

$$p\left(h_j^{(1)} = 1 \mid \mathbf{h}^{(2)}\right) = sigm\left(\mathbf{b}^{(2)} + {\mathbf{W}^{(2)}}^{\mathrm{T}} \mathbf{h}^{(2)}\right)$$

$$p\left(h_j^{(1)} = 1 \mid \mathbf{h}^{(2)}\right) = sigm\left(\mathbf{b}^{(2)} + {\mathbf{W}^{(2)}}^{\mathrm{T}} \mathbf{h}^{(2)}\right)$$

Deep learning with dropouts

Another technique used to overcome the "overfitting" issues mentioned in deep neural networks is using the dropout technique to learn the parameters. In the next sections, we will define, illustrate, and explain how deep learning with dropouts works.

Definition and mathematical notation

The idea behind dropouts is to "cripple" the deep neural network structure by stochastically removing some of the hidden units as shown in the following figure after the parameters are learned. The units are set to 0 with the dropout probability generally set as *p=0.5*

The idea is similar to adding noise to the input, but done in all the hidden layers. When certain features (or a combination of features) are removed stochastically, the neural network has to learn latent features in a more robust way, without the interdependence of some features.

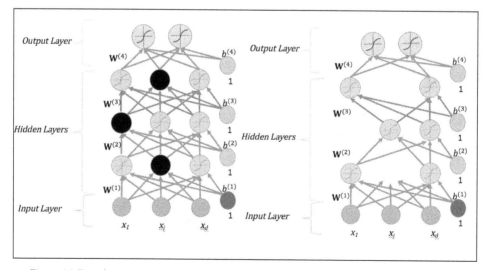

Figure 16: Deep learning with dropout indicated by dropping certain units with dark shading.

Each hidden layer is represented by $h^k(x)$ where k is the layer. The pre-activation for layer $0<k<l$ is given by:

$$\mathbf{a}^k\left(x\right) = \mathbf{b}^k\left(x\right) + \mathbf{W}^k \mathbf{h}^{k-1}\left(x\right)$$

The hidden layer activation for $1 < k < l$. Binary masks are represented by $\mathbf{m}^k$ at each hidden layer:

$$\mathbf{h}^k\left(x\right) = \mathbf{g}\left(\mathbf{a}^k\left(x\right)\right) \odot \mathbf{m}^k$$

The final output layer activation is:

$$\mathbf{h}^{l+1}\left(x\right) = \mathbf{o}\left(\mathbf{a}^{l+1}\left(x\right)\right)$$

Inputs and outputs

For training with dropouts, inputs are:

- Network architecture
- Training dataset
- Dropout probability p (typically 0.5)

The output is a trained deep neural net that can be applied for predictive use.

How does it work?

We will now describe the different parts of how deep learning with dropouts works.

Learning Training and testing with dropouts

The backward propagation learning of weights and biases from the output loss function using gradients is very similar to traditional neural network learning. The only difference is that masks are applied appropriately as follows:

Compute the output gradient before activation:

$$= \nabla_{a^{l+1}(x)} - \log\left(f\left(\mathbf{x}\right)_y\right) = -\left(\mathbf{e}\left(y\right) - \mathbf{f}\left(\mathbf{x}\right)\right)$$

For hidden layers $k=l+1$ *to 1*:

Compute the gradient of hidden layer parameters:

$$\nabla_{W^k} - \log\left(f(\mathbf{x})_y\right) = \left(\nabla_{a^k(\mathbf{x})} - \log\left(f(\mathbf{x})_y\right)\right)\mathbf{h}^{k-1}(\mathbf{x})^T$$

$$\nabla_{b^k} - \log\left(f(\mathbf{x})_y\right) = \nabla_{a^k(\mathbf{x})} - \log\left(f(\mathbf{x})_y\right)$$

$\mathbf{h}^{k-1}$ computation has taken into account the binary mask $\mathbf{m}^{k-1}$ applied.

Compute the gradient of the hidden layer below the current:

$$\nabla_{\mathbf{h}^{k-1}(\mathbf{x})} - \log\left(f(\mathbf{x})_y\right) = \mathbf{W}^k\left(\nabla_{a^k(\mathbf{x})} - \log\left(f(\mathbf{x})_y\right)\right)$$

Compute the gradient of the layer below before activation:

$$\left(\nabla_{\mathbf{h}^{k-1}(\mathbf{x})} - \log\left(f(\mathbf{x})_y\right)\right)^T \nabla_{a^{k-1}(\mathbf{x})}\mathbf{h}^k(\mathbf{x})$$

$$= \left(\nabla_{\mathbf{h}^{k-1}(\mathbf{x})} - \log\left(f(\mathbf{x})_y\right)\right) \odot \left[..,g'\left(a^{k-1}\mathbf{x}_j\right)...\right] \odot \mathbf{m}^{k-1}$$

When testing the model, we cannot use the binary mask as it is stochastic; the "expectation" value of the mask is used. If the dropout probability is $p=0.5$, the same value 0.5 is used as the expectation for the unit at test or model application time.

Sparse coding

Sparse coding is another neural network used for unsupervised learning and feature generation (*References* [22]). It works on the principle of finding latent structures in high dimensions that capture the patterns, thus performing feature extraction in addition to unsupervised learning.

Formally, for every input $\mathbf{x}^{(t)}$ a latent representation $\mathbf{h}^{(t)}$ is learned, which has a sparse representation (most values are 0 in the vector). This is done by optimization using the following objective function:

$$\min_{D} \frac{1}{T} \sum_{t-1}^{T} \min_{\mathbf{h}^{(t)}} \left(\frac{1}{2} \left\| \mathbf{x}^{(t)} - \mathbf{D}\mathbf{h}^{(t)} \right\|_{2}^{2} + \lambda \left\| \mathbf{h}^{(t)} \right\|_{1} \right)$$

Where the first term $\frac{1}{2} \left\| \mathbf{x}^{(t)} - \mathbf{D}\mathbf{h}^{(t)} \right\|_{2}^{2}$ is to control the reconstruction error and the second term, which uses a regularizer λ, is for sparsity control. The matrix $\mathbf{D}$ is also known as a Dictionary as it has equivalence to words in a dictionary and $\mathbf{h}^{(t)}$ is similar to word frequency; together they capture the impact of words in extracting patterns when performing text mining.

Convolutional Neural Network

Convolutional Neural Networks or CNNs have become prominent and are widely used in the computer vision domain. Computer vision involves processing images/videos for capturing knowledge and patterns. Annotating images, classifying images/videos, correcting them, story-telling or describing images, and so on, are some of the broad applications in computer vision [16].

Computer vision problems most generally have to deal with unstructured data that can be described as:

Inputs that are 2D images with single or multiple color channels or 3D videos that are high-dimensional vectors.

The features in these 2D or 3D representations have a well-known spatial topology, a hierarchical structure, and some repetitive elements that can be exploited.

The images/videos have a large number of transformations or variants based on factors such as illumination, noise, and so on. The same person or car can look different based on several factors.

Deep Learning

Next, we will describe some building blocks used in CNNs. We will use simple images such as the letter X of the alphabet to explain the concept and mathematics involved. For example, even though the same character X is represented in different ways in the following figure due to translation, scaling, or distortion, the human eye can easily read it as X, but it becomes tricky for the computer to see the pattern. The images are shown with the author's permission (*References* [19]):

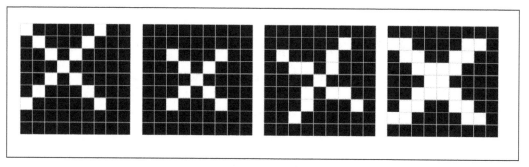

Figure 17: Image of character X represented in different ways.

The following figure illustrates how a simple grayscale image of X has common features such as a diagonal from top left, a diagonal from top right, and left and right intersecting diagonals repeated and combined to form a larger X:

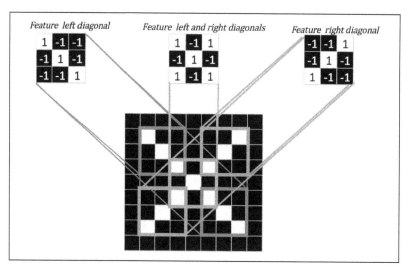

Figure 18: Common features represented in the image of character X.

[346]

Local connectivity

This is the simple concept of dividing the whole image into "patches" or "recipient fields" and giving each patch to the hidden layers. As shown in the figure, instead of 9 X 9 pixels of the complete sample image, a 3 X 3 patch of pixels from the top left goes to the first hidden unit, the overlapping second patch goes to second, and so on.

Since the fully connected hidden layer would have a huge number of parameters, having smaller patches completely reduces the parameter or high-dimensional space problem!

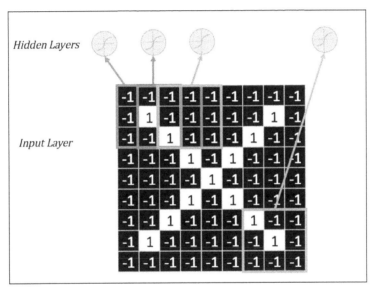

Figure 19: Concept of patches on the whole image.

Parameter sharing

The concept of parameter sharing is to construct a weight matrix that can be reused over different patches or recipient fields as constructed in the preceding figure in the local sharing. As shown in the following figure, the Feature map with same parameters $W_{1,1}$ and $W_{1,4}$ creates two different feature maps, Feature Map 1 and 4, both capturing the same features, that is, diagonal edges on either side. Thus, feature maps capture "similar regions" in the images and further reduce the dimensionality of the input space.

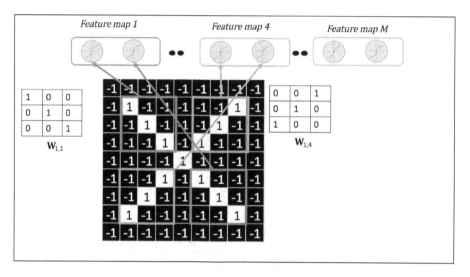

Discrete convolution

We will explain the steps in discrete convolution, taking a simple contrived example with simplified mathematics to illustrate the operation.

Suppose the kernel representing the diagonal feature is scanned over the entire image as a patch of 3 X 3. If this kernel lands on the self-same feature in the input image and we have to compute the center value through what we call the convolution operator, we get the exact value of 1 because of the matching as shown:

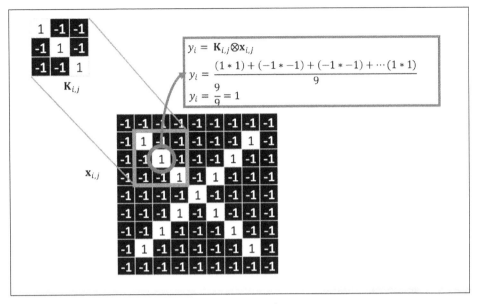

Figure 21: Discrete convolution step.

The entire image when run through this kernel and convolution operator gives a matrix of values as follows:

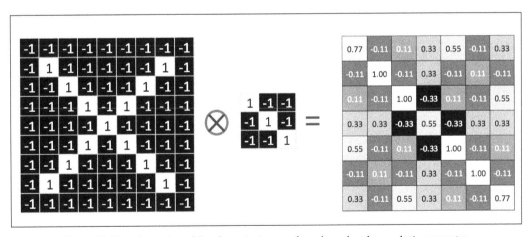

Figure 22: Transformation of the character image after a kernel and convolution operator.

We can see how the left diagonal feature gets highlighted by running this scan. Similarly, by running other kernels, as shown in the following figure, we can get a "stack of filtered images":

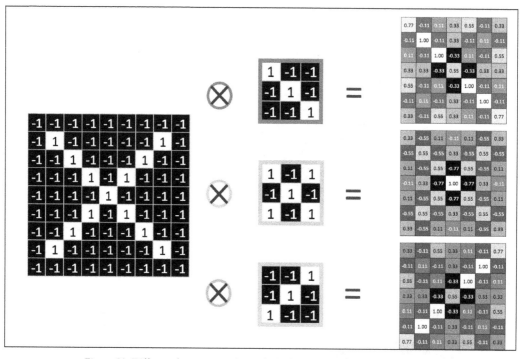

Figure 23: Different features run through the kernel giving a stack of images.

Each cell in the filtered images can be given as:

$$y_j = g_j \tanh\left(\sum_i \mathbf{K}_{i,j}\mathbf{x}_i\right)$$

$$\mathbf{K}_{i,j} = \text{convolution kernel}$$

$$\mathbf{x}_i = \text{feature map or patch} \quad g_j = \text{scaling factor}$$

Pooling or subsampling

Pooling or subsampling works on the stack of filtered images to further shrink the image or compress it, while keeping the pattern as-is. The main steps carried out in pooling are:

1. Pick a window size (for example, 2 X 2) and a stride size (for example, 2).

2. Move the window over all the filtered images at stride.

3. At each window, pick the "maximum" value.

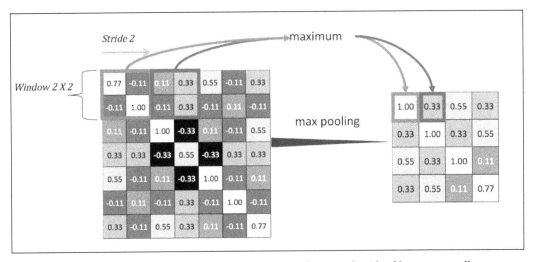

Figure 24: Max pooling, done using a window size of 2 X 2 and stride of 2, computes cell values with maximum for first as 1.0, 0.33 for next, and so on.

Pooling also plays an important part where the same features if moved or scaled can still be detected due to the use of maximum. The same set of stacked filtered images gets transformed into pooled images as follows:

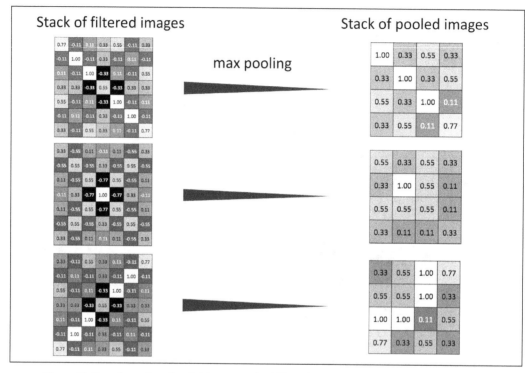

Figure 25: Transformation showing how a stack of filtered images is converted to pooled images.

Normalization using ReLU

As we discussed in the building blocks of deep learning, ReLUs remove the negative by squashing it to 0 and keep the positives as-is. They also play an important role in gradient computation in the backpropagation, removing the vanishing gradient issue of vanishing gradient.

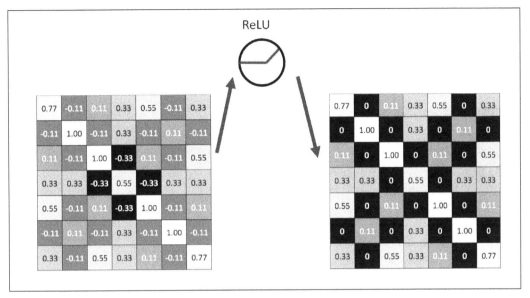

Figure 26: Transformation using ReLu.

CNN Layers

In this section, we will put together the building blocks discussed earlier to form the complete picture of CNNs. Combining the layers of convolution, ReLU, and pooling to form a connected network yielding shrunken images with patterns captured in the final output, we obtain the next composite building block, as shown in the following figure:

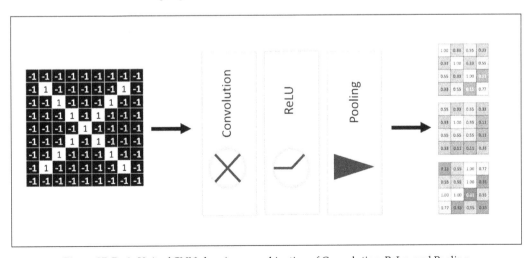

Figure 27: Basic Unit of CNN showing a combination of Convolution, ReLu, and Pooling.

Thus, these layers can be combined or "deep-stacked", as shown in the following figure, to form a complex network that gives a small pool of images as output:

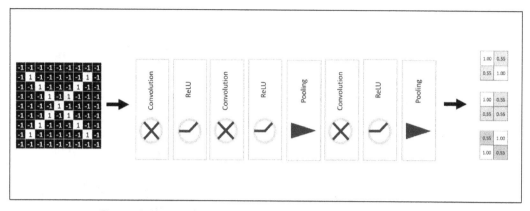

Figure 28: Deep-stacking the basic units repeatedly to form CNN layers.

The output layer is a fully connected network as shown, which uses a voting technique and learns the weights for the desired output. The fully connected output layer can be stacked too.

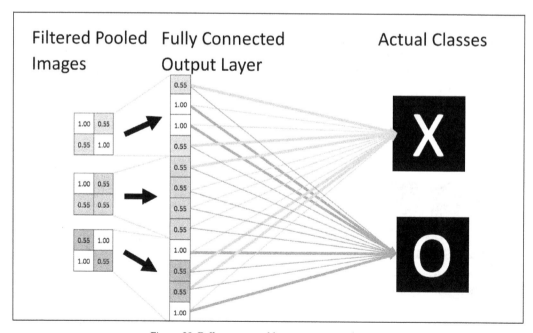

Figure 29: Fully connected layer as output of CNN.

Thus, the final CNNs can be completely illustrated as follows:

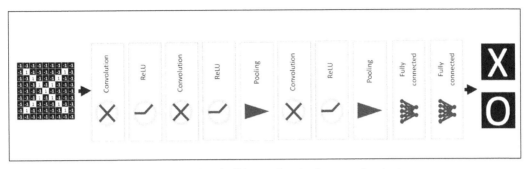

Figure 30: CNNS with all layers showing inputs and outputs.

As before, gradient descent is selected as the learning technique using the loss functions to compute the difference and propagate the error backwards.

CNN's can be used in other domains such as voice pattern recognition, text mining, and so on, if the mapping of the data to the "image" can be successfully done and "local spatial" patterns exist. The following figure shows one of the ways of mapping sound and text to images for CNN usage:

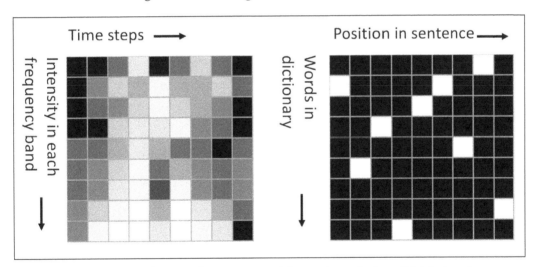

Figure 31: Illustration of mapping between temporal data, such as voice to spatial data, to an image.

Recurrent Neural Networks

Normal deep networks are used when you have finite inputs and there is no interdependence between the input examples or instances. When there are variable length inputs and there are temporal dependencies between them, that is, sequence related data, neural networks must be modified to handle such data. Recurrent Neural Networks (RNN) are examples of neural networks that are used widely to solve such problems, and we will discuss them in the following sections. RNNs are used in many sequence-related problems such as text mining, language modeling, bioinformatics data modeling, and so on, to name a few areas that fit this meta-level description (*References* [18 and 21]).

Structure of Recurrent Neural Networks

We will describe the simplest unit of the RNN first and then shown how it is combined to understand it functionally and mathematically and illustrate how different components interact and work.

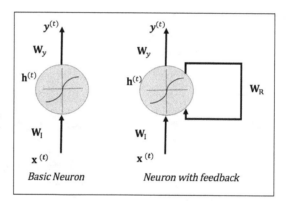

Figure 32: Difference between an artificial neuron and a neuron with feedback.

Let's consider the basic input, a neuron with activation, and its output at a given time *t*:

$$\mathbf{h}^{(t)} = g_h\left(\mathbf{W}_{\mathrm{I}}\mathbf{x}^{(t)} + b_h\right)$$

$$\mathbf{y}^{(t)} = g_y\left(\mathbf{W}_y\mathbf{h}^{(t)} + b_y\right)$$

A neuron with feedback keeps a matrix $\mathbf{W}_R$ to incorporate previous output at time *t-1* and the equations are:

$$\mathbf{h}^{(t)} = g_h\left(\mathbf{W}_I\mathbf{x}^{(t)} + \mathbf{W}_R\mathbf{h}^{(t-1)} + b_h\right)$$

$$\mathbf{y}^{(t)} = g_y\left(\mathbf{W}_y\mathbf{h}^{(t)} + b_y\right)$$

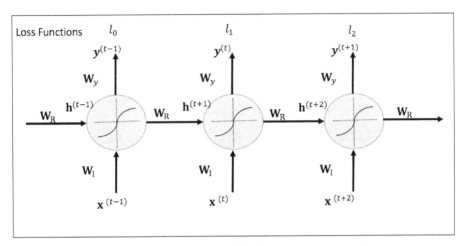

Figure 33: Chain of neurons with feedbacks connected together.

The basic RNN stacks the structure of hidden units as shown with feedback connected from the previous layer. At activation at time *t*, it depends not only on $\mathbf{x}^{(t)}$ as input, but also on the previous unit given by $\mathbf{W}_R\mathbf{h}^{(t-1)}$. The weights in the feedback connection of RNN are generally the same across all the units, $\mathbf{W}_R$. Also, instead of emitting output at the very end of the feed-forward neural network, each unit continuously emits an output that can be used in the loss function calculation.

Learning and associated problems in RNNs

Working with RNNs presents some challenges that are specific to them but there are common problems that are also encountered in other types of neural net.

1. The gradient used from the output loss function at any time *t* of the unit has dependency going back to the first unit or *t=0*, as shown in the following figure. This is because the partial derivative at the unit is dependent on the previous unit, since:

$$\mathbf{h}^{(t)} = g_h\left(\mathbf{W}_I\mathbf{x}^{(t)} + \mathbf{W}_R\mathbf{h}^{(t-1)} + b_h\right)$$

Backpropagation through time (BPTT) is the term used to illustrate the process.

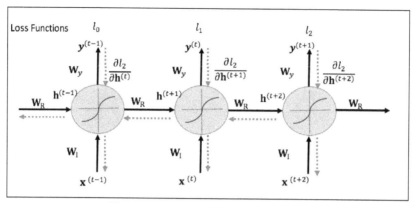

Figure 34: Backpropagation through time.

2. Similar to what we saw in the section on feed-forward neural networks, the cases of exploding and vanishing gradient become more pronounced in RNNs due to the connectivity of units as discussed previously.

3. Some of the solutions for exploding gradients are:

    1. Truncated BPTT is a small change to the BPTT process. Instead of propagating the learning back to time $t=0$, it is truncated to a fixed time backward to $t=k$.

    2. Gradient Clipping to cut the gradient above a threshold when it shoots up.

    3. Adaptive Learning Rate. The learning rate adjusts itself based on the feedback and values.

4. Some of the solutions for vanishing gradients are:

    1. Using ReLU as the activation function; hence the gradient will be 1.

    2. Adaptive Learning Rate. The learning rate adjusts itself based on the feedback and values.

    3. Using extensions such as Long Short Term Memory (LSTM) and Gated Recurrent Units (GRUs), which we will describe next.

There are many applications of RNNs, for example, in next letter predictions, next word predictions, language translation, and so on.

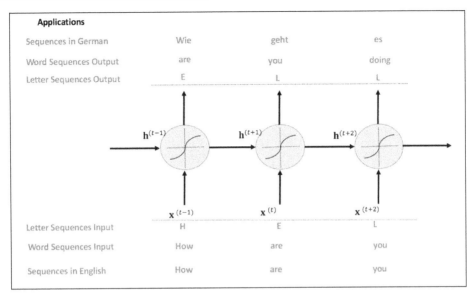

Figure 35: Showing some applications in next letter/word predictions using RNN structures.

Long Short Term Memory

One of the neural network architectures or modifications to RNNs that addresses the issue of vanishing gradient is known as long short term memory or LSTM. We will explain some building blocks of LSTM and then put it together for our readers.

The first modification to RNN is to change the feedback learning matrix to 1, that is, $W_R = 1$, as shown in the following figure:

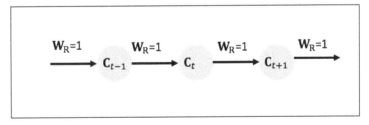

Figure 36: Building blocks of LSTM where the feedback matrix is set to 1.

This will ensure the inputs from older cell or memory units are passed as-is to the next unit. Hence some modifications are needed.

The output gate, as shown in the following figure, combines two computations. The first is the output from the individual unit, passed through an activation function, and the second is the output of the older unit that has been passed through a sigmoid using scaling.

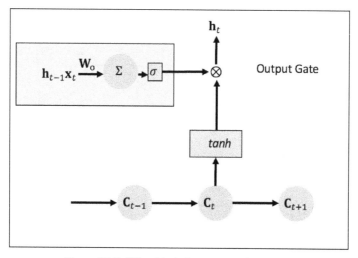

Figure 37: Building block Output Gate for LSTM.

Mathematically, the output gate at the unit is given by:

$$\mathbf{h}_t = \sigma\left(\mathbf{W}_o \cdot [\mathbf{h}_{t-1} \mathbf{x}_t] + b_0\right) \odot \tanh\left(C_t\right)$$

$$\mathbf{h}_t = \mathbf{o}_t \odot \tanh\left(\mathbf{C}_t\right)$$

The forget gate is between the two memory units. It generates 0 or 1 based on learned weights and transformations. The forget gate is shown in the following figure:

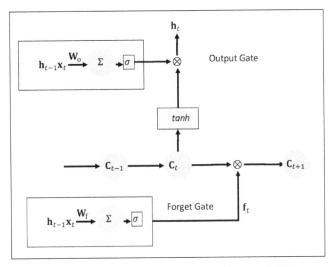

Figure 38: Building block Forget Gate addition to LSTM.

Mathematically, $\mathbf{f}_t = \sigma\left(\mathbf{W}_f \cdot \left[\mathbf{h}_{t-1} \mathbf{x}_t\right] + b_f\right)$ can be seen as the representation of the forget gate. Next, the input gate and the new gate are combined, as shown in the following figure:

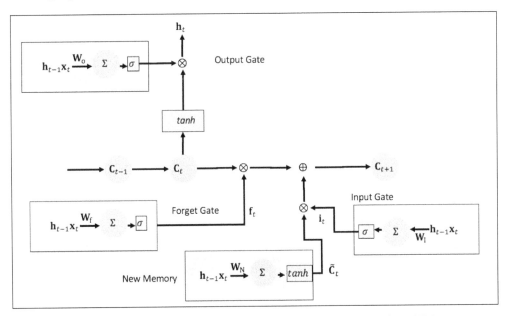

Figure 39: Building blocks New Gate and Input Gate added to complete LSTM.

The new memory generation unit uses the current input x_t and the old state h_{t-1} through an activation function and generates a new memory C_t. The input gate combines the input and the old state and determines whether the new memory or the input should be preserved.

Thus, the update equation looks like this:

$$\mathbf{C}_{t+1} = \mathbf{f}_t \odot \mathbf{C}_t + \mathbf{i}_t \odot \tilde{\mathbf{C}}_t$$

Gated Recurrent Units

Gated Recurrent Units (GRUs) are simplified LSTMs with modifications. Many of the gates are simplified by using one "update" unit as follows:

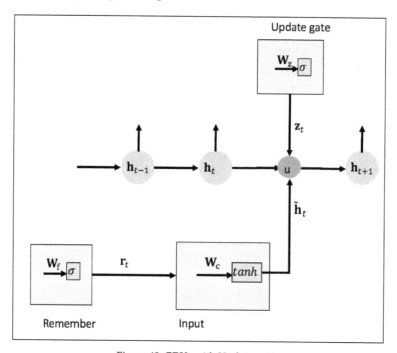

Figure 40: GRUs with Update unit.

The changes made to the equations are:

$$z_t = \sigma\left(\mathbf{W}_z \cdot \left[\mathbf{h}_{t-1}, \mathbf{x}_t\right] + b_z\right)$$

$$\mathbf{r}_t = \sigma\left(\mathbf{W}_f \cdot \left[\mathbf{h}_{t-1}, \mathbf{x}_t\right] + b_f\right)$$

$$\overset{\propto}{\mathbf{h}}_t = \tanh\left(\mathbf{W}_c \cdot \left[\mathbf{r}_t\mathbf{h}_{t-1}, \mathbf{x}_t\right] + b_c\right)$$

$$\mathbf{h}_t = \left(1 - \mathbf{z}_t\right) \odot \mathbf{h}_{t-1} + \mathbf{z}_t \odot \overset{\propto}{\mathbf{h}}_t$$

Case study

Several benchmarks exist for image classification. We will use the MNIST image database for this case study. When we used MNIST in *Chapter 3, Unsupervised Machine Learning Techniques* with clustering and outlier detection techniques, each pixel was considered a feature. In addition to learning from the pixel values as in previous experiments, with deep learning techniques we will also be learning new features from the structure of the training dataset. The deep learning algorithms will be trained on 60,000 images and tested on a 10,000-image test dataset.

Tools and software

In this chapter, we introduce the open-source Java framework for deep learning called DeepLearning4J (DL4J). DL4J has libraries implementing a host of deep learning techniques and they can be used on distributed CPUs and GPUs.

DeepLearning4J: `https://deeplearning4j.org/index.html`

We will illustrate the use of some DL4J libraries in learning from the MNIST training images and apply the learned models to classify the images in the test set.

Business problem

Image classification is a particularly attractive test-bed to evaluate deep learning networks. We have previously encountered the MNIST database, which consists of greyscale images of handwritten digits. This time, we will show how both unsupervised and supervised deep learning techniques can be used to learn from the same dataset. The MNIST dataset has 28-by-28 pixel images in a single channel. These images are categorized into 10 labels representing the digits 0 to 9. The goal is to train on 60,000 data points and test our deep learning classification algorithm on the remaining 10,000 images.

Machine learning mapping

This includes supervised and unsupervised methods applied to a classification problem in which there are 10 possible output classes. Some techniques use an initial pre-training stage, which is unsupervised in nature, as we have seen in the preceding sections.

Data sampling and transformation

The dataset is available at: `https://yann.lecun.com/exdb/mnist`

In the experiments in this case study, the MNIST dataset has been standardized such that pixel values in the range 0 to 255 have been normalized to values from 0.0 to 1.0. The exception is in the experiment using stacked RBMs, where the training and test data have been binarized, that is, set to 1 if the standardized value is greater than or equal to 0.3 and 0 otherwise. Each of the 10 classes is equally represented in both the training set and the test set. In addition, examples are shuffled using a random number generator seed supplied by the user.

Feature analysis

The input data features are the greyscale values of the pixels in each image. This is the raw data and we will be using the deep learning algorithms to learn higher-level features out of the raw pixel values. The dataset has been prepared such that there are an equal number of examples of each class in both the training and the test sets.

Models, results, and evaluation

We will perform different experiments starting with simple MLP, Convolutional Networks, Variational Autoencoders, Stacked RBMS, and DBNs. We will walk through important parts of code that highlight the network structure or specialized tunings, give parameters to help readers, reproduce the experiments, and give the results for each type of network.

Basic data handling

The following snippet of code shows:

How to generically read data from a CSV with a structure enforced by delimiters.

How to iterate the data and get records.

How to shuffle data in memory and create training/testing or validation sets:

```
RecordReader recordReader = new  ] CSVRecordReader(numLinesToSkip,del
imiter);
recordReader.initialize(new FileSplit(new ClassPathResource(fileName).
getFile()));
DataSetIterator iterator = new RecordReaderDataSetIterator(recordReade
r,batchSize,labelIndex,numClasses);
DataSet allData = iterator.next();
allData.shuffle();
SplitTestAndTrain testAndTrain = allData.splitTestAndTrain(trainPerce
nt);
DataSet trainingData = testAndTrain.getTrain();
DataSet testData = testAndTrain.getTest();
```

DL4J has a specific MNIST wrapper for handling the data that we have used, as shown in the following snippet:

```
DataSetIterator mnistTrain = new MnistDataSetIterator(batchSize, true,
randomSeed);
DataSetIterator mnistTest = new MnistDataSetIterator(batchSize, false,
randomSeed);
```

Multi-layer perceptron

In the first experiment, we will use a basic multi-layer perceptron with an input layer, one hidden layer, and an output layer. A detailed list of parameters that are used in the code is given here:

Parameters used for MLP

Parameter	Variable	Value
Number of iterations	m	1
Learning rate	rate	0.0015
Momentum	momentum	0.98
L2 regularization	regularization	0.005
Number of rows in input	numRows	28
Number of columns in input	numColumns	28
Layer 0 output size, Layer 1 input size	outputLayer0, inputLayer1	500
Layer 1 output size, Layer 2 input size	outputLayer1, inputLayer2	300
Layer 2 output size, Layer 3 input size	outputLayer2, inputLayer3	100
Layer 3 output size,	outputNum	10

Code for MLP

In the listing that follows, we can see how we first configure the MLP by passing in the hyperarameters using the Builder pattern.

```
MultiLayerConfiguration conf = new NeuralNetConfiguration.Builder()
.seed(randomSeed) .optimizationAlgo(OptimizationAlgorithm.STOCHASTIC_
GRADIENT_DESCENT) // use SGD
.iterations(m)//iterations
.activation(Activation.RELU)//activation function
.weightInit(WeightInit.XAVIER)//weight initialization
.learningRate(rate) //specify the learning rate
.updater(Updater.NESTEROVS).momentum(momentum)//momentum
.regularization(true).l2(rate * regularization) //
.list()
.layer(0,
new DenseLayer.Builder() //create the first input layer.
.nIn(numRows * numColumns)
.nOut(firstOutput)
.build())
.layer(1, new DenseLayer.Builder() //create the second input layer
.nIn(secondInput)
```

```
.nOut(secondOutput)
.build())
.layer(2, new OutputLayer.Builder(LossFunction.NEGATIVELOGLIKELIHOOD)
//create hidden layer
.activation(Activation.SOFTMAX)
.nIn(thirdInput)
.nOut(numberOfOutputClasses)
.build())
.pretrain(false).backprop(true) //use backpropagation to adjust
weights
.build();
```

Training, evaluation, and testing the MLP are shown in the following snippet. Notice the code that initializes the visualization backend enabling you to monitor the model training in your browser, particularly the model score (the training error after each iteration) and updates to parameters:

```
MultiLayerNetwork model = new MultiLayerNetwork(conf);
model.init();
model.setListeners(new ScoreIterationListener(5));  //print the score
with every iteration
//Initialize the user interface backend
UIServer uiServer = UIServer.getInstance();
//Configure where the network information (gradients, activations,
score vs. time etc) is to be stored
//Then add the StatsListener to collect this information from the
network, as it trains
StatsStorage statsStorage = new InMemoryStatsStorage();          //
Alternative: new FileStatsStorage(File) - see UIStorageExample
int listenerFrequency = 1;
net.setListeners(new StatsListener(statsStorage, listenerFrequency));
//Attach the StatsStorage instance to the UI: this allows the contents
of the StatsStorage to be visualized
uiServer.attach(statsStorage);
log.info(""Train model....."");
for( int i=0; i<numEpochs; i++ ){
log.info(""Epoch "" + i);
model.fit(mnistTrain);
        }
log.info(""Evaluate model....."");
Evaluation eval = new Evaluation(numberOfOutputClasses);
while(mnistTest.hasNext()){
DataSet next = mnistTest.next();
INDArray output = model.output(next.getFeatureMatrix()); //get the
networks prediction
```

```
eval.eval(next.getLabels(), output); //check the prediction against
the true class
        }
log.info(eval.stats());
```

The following plots show the training error against training iteration for the MLP model. This curve should decrease with iterations:

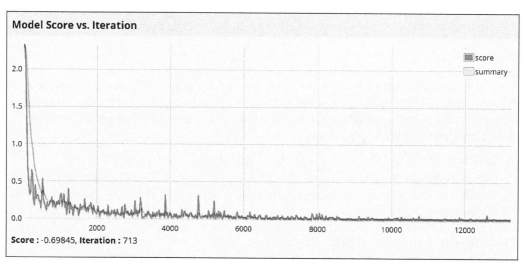

Figure 41: Training error as measured with number of iterations of training for the MLP model.

In the following figure, we see the distribution of parameters in Layer 0 of the MLP as well as the distribution of updates to the parameters. These histograms should have an approximately Gaussian (Normal) shape, which indicates good convergence. For more on how to use charts to tune your model, see the DL4J Visualization page (https://deeplearning4j.org/visualization):

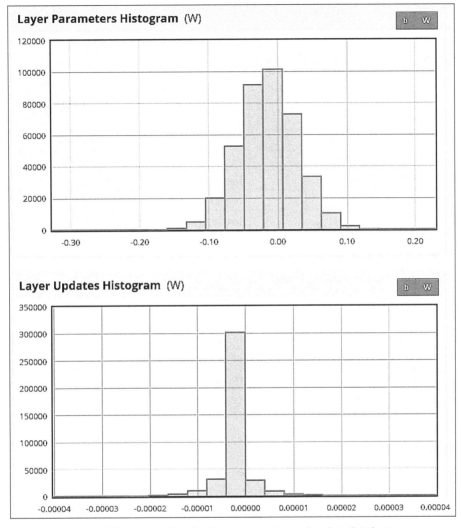

Figure 42: Histograms showing Layer parameters and update distribution.

Convolutional Network

In the second experiment, we configured a Convolutional Network (ConvNet) using the built-in MultiLayerConfiguration. The architecture of the network consists of a total of five layers, as can be seen from the following code snippet. Following the input layer, two convolution layers with 5-by-5 filters alternating with Max pooling layers are followed by a fully connected dense layer using the ReLu activation layer, ending with Softmax activation in the final output layer. The optimization algorithm used is Stochastic Gradient Descent, and the loss function is Negative Log Likelihood.

The various configuration parameters (or hyper-parameters) for the ConvNet are given in the table.

Parameters used for ConvNet

Parameter	Variable	Value
Seed	seed	123
Input size	numRows, numColumns	28, 28
Number of epochs	numEpochs	10
Number of iterations	iterations	1
L2 regularization	regularization	0.005
Learning rate	learningRate	0.1
Momentum	momentum	0.9
Convolution filter size	xsize, ysize	5, 5
Convolution layers stride size	x, y	1, 1
Number of input channels	numChannels	1
Subsampling layer stride size	sx, sy	2, 2
Layer 0 output size	nOut0	20
Layer 2 output size	nOut1	50
Layer 4 output size	nOut2	500
Layer 5 output size	outputNum	10

Code for CNN

As you can see, configuring multi-layer neural networks with the DL4J API is similar whether you are building MLPs or CNNs. Algorithm-specific configuration is simply done in the definition of each layer.

```
MultiLayerConfiguration conf = new NeuralNetConfiguration.Builder()
.seed(seed)
.iterations(iterations) .regularization(true).l2(regularization)
.learningRate(learningRate)
.weightInit(WeightInit.XAVIER) .optimizationAlgo(OptimizationAlg
orithm.STOCHASTIC_GRADIENT_DESCENT) .updater(Updater.NESTEROVS).
momentum(momentum)
.list()
.layer(0, new ConvolutionLayer.Builder(xsize, ysize)
.nIn(nChannels)
.stride(x,y)
.nOut(nOut0)
```

```
.activation(Activation.IDENTITY)
.build())
.layer(1, new SubsamplingLayer
.Builder(SubsamplingLayer.PoolingType.MAX)
.kernelSize(width, height)
.stride(sx,sy)
.build())
.layer(2, new ConvolutionLayer.Builder(xsize, ysize)
.stride(x,y)
.nOut(nOut2)
.activation(Activation.IDENTITY)
.build())
.layer(3, new SubsamplingLayer
.Builder(SubsamplingLayer.PoolingType.MAX)
.kernelSize(width, height)
.stride(sx,sy)
.build())
.layer(4, new DenseLayer.Builder()
.activation(Activation.RELU)
.nOut(nOut4).build())
.layer(5, new OutputLayer. Builder(LossFunctions.LossFunction.
NEGATIVELOGLIKELIHOOD)
.nOut(outputNum)
.activation(Activation.SOFTMAX)
.build())
.setInputType(InputType.convolutionalFlat(numRows,numColumns,1))
.backprop(true).pretrain(false).build();
```

Variational Autoencoder

In the third experiment, we configure a Variational Autoencoder as the classifier.

Parameters used for the Variational Autoencoder

The parameters used to configure the VAE are shown in the table.

Parameter	Variable	Values
Seed for RNG	rngSeed	12345
Number of iterations	Iterations	1
Learning rate	learningRate	0.001
RMS decay	rmsDecay	0.95
L2 regularization	regularization	0.0001
Output layer size	outputNum	10

Parameter	Variable	Values
VAE encoder layers size	vaeEncoder1, vaeEncoder2	256, 256
VAE decoder layers size	vaeDecoder1, vaeDecoder2	256, 256
Size of latent variable space	latentVarSpaceSize	128

Code for Variational Autoencoder

We have configured two layers each of encoders and decoders and are reconstructing the input using a Bernoulli distribution.

```
MultiLayerConfiguration conf = new NeuralNetConfiguration.Builder()
.seed(rngSeed)
.iterations(iterations)
.optimizationAlgo(
OptimizationAlgorithm.STOCHASTIC_GRADIENT_DESCENT)
.learningRate(learningRate)
.updater(Updater.RMSPROP).rmsDecay(rmmsDecay)
.weightInit(WeightInit.XAVIER)
.regularization(true).l2(regularization)
.list()
.layer(0, new VariationalAutoencoder.Builder()
.activation(Activation.LEAKYRELU)
            .encoderLayerSizes(vaeEncoder1, vaeEncoder2)
//2 encoder layers
            .decoderLayerSizes(vaeDecoder1, vaeDecoder2)
//2 decoder layers
.pzxActivationFunction(""identity"")  //p(z|data) activation function
.reconstructionDistribution(new BernoulliReconstructionDistribut
ion(Activation.SIGMOID.getActivationFunction()))    //Bernoulli
distribution for p(data|z) (binary or 0 to 1 data only)
.nIn(numRows * numColumns) //Input size
.nOut(latentVarSpaceSize) //Size of the latent variable space: p(z|x).
.build())
.layer(1, new OutputLayer.Builder(LossFunction.NEGATIVELOGLIKELIHOOD).
activation(Activation.SOFTMAX)
.nIn(latentVarSpaceSize).nOut(outputNum).build())
.pretrain(true).backprop(true).build();
```

DBN

The parameters used in DBN are shown in the following table:

Parameter	Variable	Value
Input data size	numRows, numColumns	28, 28
Seed for RNG	seed	123
Number of training iterations	iterations	1
Momentum	momentum	0.5
Layer 0 (input)	numRows * numColumns	28 * 28
Layer 0 (output)	nOut0	500
Layer 1 (input, output)	nIn1, nOut1	500, 250
Layer 2 (input, output)	nIn2, nOut2	250, 200
Layer 3 (input, output)	nIn3, outputNum	200, 10

Configuring the DBN using the DL4J API is shown in the example used in this case study. The code for the configuration of the network is shown here.

```
MultiLayerConfiguration conf = new NeuralNetConfiguration.Builder()
.seed(seed)
.gradientNormalization(GradientNormalization.
ClipElementWiseAbsoluteValue)
.gradientNormalizationThreshold(1.0)
.iterations(iterations)
.updater(Updater.NESTEROVS)
.momentum(momentum)
.optimizationAlgo(OptimizationAlgorithm.CONJUGATE_GRADIENT)
.list()
.layer(0, new RBM.Builder().nIn(numRows*numColumns).nOut(nOut0)
.weightInit(WeightInit.XAVIER).lossFunction(LossFunction.KL_
DIVERGENCE)
.visibleUnit(RBM.VisibleUnit.BINARY)
.hiddenUnit(RBM.HiddenUnit.BINARY)
.build())
.layer(1, new RBM.Builder().nIn(nIn1).nOut(nOut1)
.weightInit(WeightInit.XAVIER).lossFunction(LossFunction.KL_
DIVERGENCE)
.visibleUnit(RBM.VisibleUnit.BINARY)
.hiddenUnit(RBM.HiddenUnit.BINARY)
.build())
.layer(2, new RBM.Builder().nIn(nIn2).nOut(nOut2)
```

```
.weightInit(WeightInit.XAVIER).lossFunction(LossFunction.KL_
DIVERGENCE)
.visibleUnit(RBM.VisibleUnit.BINARY)
.hiddenUnit(RBM.HiddenUnit.BINARY)
.build())
.layer(3, new OutputLayer.Builder().nIn(nIn3).nOut(outputNum)
.weightInit(WeightInit.XAVIER).activation(Activation.SOFTMAX)
.build())
.pretrain(true).backprop(true)
.build();
MultiLayerNetwork model = new MultiLayerNetwork(conf);
model.init();
model.setListeners(new ScoreIterationListener(listenerFreq));
```

Parameter search using Arbiter

DeepLearning4J provides a framework for fine-tuning hyper-parameters by taking the burden of hand-tuning away from the modeler; instead, it allows the specification of the parameter space to search. In the following example code snippet, the configuration is specified using a MultiLayerSpace instead of a MutiLayerConfiguration object, in which the ranges for the hyper-parameters are specified by means of ParameterSpace objects in the Arbiter DL4J package for the parameters to be tuned:

```
ParameterSpace<Double> learningRateHyperparam = new
ContinuousParameterSpace(0.0001, 0.1);  //Values will be generated
uniformly at random between 0.0001 and 0.1 (inclusive)
ParameterSpace<Integer> layerSizeHyperparam = new
IntegerParameterSpace(16,256);              //Integer values will be
generated uniformly at random between 16 and 256 (inclusive)
MultiLayerSpace hyperparameterSpace = new MultiLayerSpace.Builder()
//These next few options: fixed values for all models
.optimizationAlgo(OptimizationAlgorithm.STOCHASTIC_GRADIENT_DESCENT)
.iterations(1)
.regularization(true)
.l2(0.0001)
//Learning rate: this is something we want to test different values
for
.learningRate(learningRateHyperparam)
.addLayer( new DenseLayerSpace.Builder()
//Fixed values for this layer:
.nIn(784)  //Fixed input: 28x28=784 pixels for MNIST
.activation(""relu"")
//One hyperparameter to infer: layer size
```

```
.nOut(layerSizeHyperparam)
.build())
.addLayer( new OutputLayerSpace.Builder()
//nIn: set the same hyperparemeter as the nOut for the last layer.
.nIn(layerSizeHyperparam)
//The remaining hyperparameters: fixed for the output layer
.nOut(10)
.activation(""softmax"")
.lossFunction(LossFunctions.LossFunction.MCXENT)
.build())
.pretrain(false).backprop(true).build();
```

Results and analysis

The results of evaluating the performance of the four networks on the test data are given in the following table:

	MLP	**ConvNet**	**VAE**	**DBN**
Accuracy	0.9807	0.9893	0.9743	0.7506
Precision	0.9806	0.9893	0.9742	0.7498
Recall	0.9805	0.9891	0.9741	0.7454
F1 score	0.9806	0.9892	0.9741	0.7476

The goal of the experiments was not to match benchmark results in each of the neural network structures, but to give a comprehensive architecture implementation in the code with detailed parameters for the readers to explore.

Tuning the hyper-parameters in deep learning Networks is quite a challenge and though Arbiter and online resources such as gitter (`https://gitter.im/deeplearning4j/deeplearning4j`) help with DL4J, the time and cost of running the hyper-parameter search is quite high as compared to other classification techniques including SVMs.

The benchmark results on the MNIST dataset and corresponding papers are available here:

- `http://yann.lecun.com/exdb/mnist/`
- `http://rodrigob.github.io/are_we_there_yet/build/classification_datasets_results.html#4d4e495354`

As seen from the benchmark result, Linear 1 Layer NN gets an error rate of 12% and adding more layers reduces it to about 2. This shows the non-linear nature of the data and the need for a complex algorithm to fit the patterns.

As compared to the benchmark best result on neural networks ranging from a 2.5% to 1.6% error rate, our results are very much comparable with the 2% error rate.

Most of the benchmark results show Convolutional Network architectures having error rates in the range of 1.1% to 0.5% and our hyper-parameter search has matched the best of those models with an error rate of just under 1.1%.

Our results for DBN fall far short of the benchmarks at just over 25%. There is no reason to doubt that further tuning can improve performance bringing it to the range of 3-5%.

Summary

The history of Deep Learning is intimately tied to the limitations of earlier attempts at using neural networks in machine learning and AI, and how these limitations were overcome with newer techniques, technological improvements, and the availability of vast amounts of data.

The perceptron is the basic neural network. Multi-layer networks are used in supervised learning and are built by connecting several hidden layers of neurons to propagate activations forward and using backpropagation to reduce the training error. Several activation functions are used, most commonly, the sigmoid and tanh functions.

The problems of neural networks are vanishing or exploding gradients, slow training, and the trap of local minima.

Deep learning successfully addresses these problems with the help of several effective techniques that can be used for unsupervised as well as supervised learning.

Among the building blocks of deep learning networks are Restricted Boltzmann Machines (RBM), Autoencoders, and Denoising Autoencoders. RBMs are two-layered undirected networks that are able to extract high-level features from their input. Contrastive divergence is used to speed up the training. Autoencoders are also deep learning networks used in unsupervised learning—they attempt to replicate the input by first encoding learned features in the encoding layer and then reconstructing the input via a set of decoding layers. Denoising Autoencoders address some limitations of Autoencoders, which can sometimes cause them to trivially learn the identity function.

Deep learning networks are often pretrained in an unsupervised fashion and then their parameters are fine-tuned via supervised fine-tuning. Stacked RBMs or Autoencoders are used in the pretraining phase and the fine-tuning is typically accomplished with a softmax activation in the output layer in the case of classification.

Deep Autoencoders are good at learning complex latent structures in data and are used in unsupervised learning by employing pre-training and fine-tuning with Autoencoder building blocks. Deep Belief Networks (DBN) are generative models that can be used to create more samples. It is constructed using a directed Bayesian network with an undirected RBM layer on top. Overfitting in deep learning networks can be addressed by learning with dropouts, where some nodes in the network are randomly "turned off".

Convolutional Neural Networks (CNNs) have a number of applications in computer vision. CNNs can learn patterns in the data translation-invariant and robust to linear scaling in the data. They reduce the dimensionality of the data using convolution filters and pooling layers and can achieve very effective results in classification tasks. A use case involving the classification of digital images is presented.

When the data arrives as sequences and there are temporal relationships among data, Recurrent Neural Networks (RNN) are used for modeling. RNNs use feedback from previous layers and emit output continually. The problem of vanishing and exploding gradients recurs in RNNs, and are addressed by several modifications to the architecture, such as Long Short Term Memory (LSTM) and Gated Recurrent Networks (GRU).

In this chapter's case study, we present the experiments done with various deep learning networks to learn from MNIST handwritten digit image datasets. Results using MLP, ConvNet, Variational Autoencoder, and Stacked RBM are presented.

We think that deep neural networks are able to approximate a significant and representative sub-set of key structures that the underlying data is based on. In addition, the hierarchic structures of the data can be easily captured with the help of different hidden layers. Finally, the invariance against rotation, translation, and the scale of images, for instance, is the last key elements of the performance of deep neural networks. The invariance allows us to reduce the number of possible states to be captured by the neural network (*References* [19]).

References

1. Behnke, S. (2001). Learning iterative image reconstruction in the neural abstraction pyramid. International Journal of Computational Intelligence and Applications, 1(4), 427–438.

2. Behnke, S. (2002). Learning face localization using hierarchical recurrent networks. In Proceedings of the 12th international conference on artificial neural networks (pp. 1319–1324).

3. Behnke, S. (2003). Discovering hierarchical speech features using convolutional non-negative matrix factorization. In Proceedings of the international joint conference on neural networks, vol. 4 (pp. 2758–2763).

4. Behnke, S. (2003). LNCS, Lecture notes in computer science: Vol. 2766. Hierarchical neural networks for image interpretation. Springer. Behnke, S. (2005). Face localization and tracking in the neural abstraction pyramid. Neural Computing and Applications, 14(2), 97–103.

5. Casey, M. P. (1996). The dynamics of discrete-time computation, with application to recurrent neural networks and finite state machine extraction. Neural Computation, 8(6), 1135–1178.

6. Rumelhart, D. E., Hinton, G. E., and Williams, R. J. (1986). Learning internal representations by error propagation. In Rumelhart, D. E. and McClelland, J. L., editors, Parallel Distributed Processing, volume 1, pages 318–362. MIT Press.

7. Goller, C.; Küchler, A (1996). ""Learning task-dependent distributed representations by backpropagation through structure"". Neural Networks, IEEE. doi:10.1109/ICNN.1996.548916

8. Hochreiter, Sepp. The vanishing gradient problem during learning recurrent neural nets and problem solutions. International Journal of Uncertainty, Fuzziness and Knowledge-Based Systems, 6(02): 107–116, 1998.

9. G. E. Hinton, S. Osindero, and Y. The (2006). "A fast learning algorithm for deep belief nets," Neural Comput., vol. 18, pp. 1527–1554.

10. G. E. Hinton (2002). "Training products of experts by minimizing contrastive divergence," Neural Comput., vol. 14, pp. 1771–1800.

11. G. E. Hinton and R. R. Salakhutdinov (2006). "Reducing the dimensionality of data with neural networks," Science, vol. 313, no. 5786, pp. 504–507.

12. Hinton, G. E., & Zemel, R. S. (1994). Autoencoders, minimum description length, and Helmholtz free energy. Advances in Neural Information Processing Systems, 6, 3–10.

13. Y. Bengio, P. Lamblin, D. Popovici, and H. Larochelle. (2007). "Greedy layer-wise training of deep networks," in Advances in Neural Information Processing Systems 19 (NIPS'06) pp. 153–160.

14. H. Larochelle, D. Erhan, A. Courville, J. Bergstra, and Y. Bengio (2007). "An empirical evaluation of deep architectures on problems with many factors of variation," in Proc. 24th Int. Conf. Machine Learning (ICML'07) pp. 473–480.

15. P. Vincent, H. Larochelle, Y. Bengio, and P.-A. Manzagol (2008), "Extracting and composing robust features with denoising autoencoders," in Proc. 25th Int. Conf. Machine Learning (ICML'08), pp. 1096–1103.

16. F.-J. Huang and Y. LeCun (2006). "Large-scale learning with SVM and convolutional nets for generic object categorization," in Proc. Computer Vision and Pattern Recognition Conf. (CVPR'06).

17. F. A. Gers, N. N. Schraudolph, and J. Schmidhuber (2003). Learning precise timing with LSTM recurrent networks. The Journal of Machine Learning Research.

18. Kyunghyun Cho et. al (2014). Learning Phrase Representations using RNN Encoder-Decoder for Statistical Machine Translation. `https://arxiv.org/pdf/1406.1078.pdf`.

19. `https://brohrer.github.io/how_convolutional_neural_networks_work.html`

20. Henry W. Lin, Max Tegmark, David Rolnick (2016). Why does deep and cheap learning work so well? `https://arxiv.org/abs/1608.08225`

21. Mike Schuster and Kuldip K. Paliwal (1997). Bidirectional Recurrent Neural Networks, Trans. on Signal Processing.

22. H Lee, A Battle, R Raina, AY Ng (2007). Efficient sparse coding algorithms, In Advances in Neural Information Processing Systems

23. Bengio Y. (2009). Learning deep architectures for AI, Foundations and Trends in Machine Learning 1(2) pages 1-127.

8
Text Mining and Natural Language Processing

Natural language processing (**NLP**) is ubiquitous today in various applications such as mobile apps, ecommerce websites, emails, news websites, and more. Detecting spam in e-mails, characterizing e-mails, speech synthesis, categorizing news, searching and recommending products, performing sentiment analysis on social media brands — these are all different aspects of NLP and mining text for information.

There has been an exponential increase in digital information that is textual in content — in the form of web pages, e-books, SMS messages, documents of various formats, e-mails, social media messages such as tweets and Facebook posts, now ranges in exabytes (an exabyte is 1,018 bytes). Historically, the earliest foundational work relying on automata and probabilistic modeling began in the 1950s. The 1970s saw changes such as stochastic modeling, Markov modeling, and syntactic parsing, but their progress was limited during the 'AI Winter' years. The 1990s saw the emergence of text mining and a statistical revolution that included ideas of corpus statistics, supervised Machine Learning, and human annotation of text data. From the year 2000 onwards, with great progress in computing and Big Data, as well as the introduction of sophisticated Machine Learning algorithms in supervised and unsupervised learning, the area has received rekindled interest and is now among the hottest topics in research, both in academia and the R&D departments of commercial enterprises. In this chapter, we will discuss some aspects of NLP and text mining that are essential in Machine Learning.

The chapter begins with an introduction to the key areas within NLP, and it then explains the important processing and transformation steps that make the documents more suitable for Machine Learning, whether supervised or unsupervised. The concept of topic modeling, clustering, and named entity recognition follow, with brief descriptions of two Java toolkits that offer powerful text processing capabilities. The case study for this chapter uses another widely-known dataset to demonstrate several techniques described here through experiments using the tools KNIME and Mallet.

The chapter is organized as follows:

- NLP, subfields, and tasks:
    - Text categorization
    - POS tagging
    - Text clustering
    - Information extraction and named entity recognition
    - Sentiment analysis
    - Coreference resolution
    - Word-sense disambiguation
    - Machine translation
    - Semantic reasoning and inferencing
    - Summarization
    - Questions and answers
    - Issues with mining and unstructured data

- Text processing components and transformations:
    - Document collection and standardization
    - Tokenization
    - Stop words removal
    - Stemming/Lemmatization
    - Local/Global dictionary
    - Feature extraction/generation
    - Feature representation and similarity
    - Feature selection and dimensionality reduction

- Topics in text mining:
    ◦ Topic modeling
    ◦ Text clustering
    ◦ Named entity recognition
    ◦ Deep learning and NLP

- Tools and usage:
    ◦ Mallet
    ◦ KNIME

- Case study

NLP, subfields, and tasks

Information about the real world exists in the form of structured data, typically generated by automated processes, or unstructured data, which, in the case of text, is created by direct human agency in the form of the written or spoken word. The process of observing real-world situations and using either automated processes or having humans perceive and convert that information into understandable data is very similar in both structured and unstructured data. The transformation of the observed world into unstructured data involves complexities such as the language of the text, the format in which it exists, variances among different observers in interpreting the same data, and so on. Furthermore, the ambiguity caused by the syntax and semantics of the chosen language, subtlety in expression, the context in the data, and so on, make the task of mining text data very difficult.

Next, we will discuss some high-level subfields and tasks that involve NLP and text mining. The subject of NLP is quite vast, and the following topics is in no way comprehensive.

Text categorization

This field is one of the most well-established, and in its basic form classifies documents with unstructured text data into predefined categories. This can be viewed as a direct extension of supervised Machine Learning in the unstructured text world, learning from historic documents to predict categories of unseen documents in the future. Basic methods in spam detection in e-mails or news categorization are among some of the most prominent applications of this task.

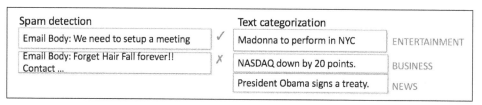

Figure 1: Text Categorization showing classification into different categories

Part-of-speech tagging (POS tagging)

Another subtask in NLP that has seen a lot of success is associating parts-of-speech of the language—such as nouns, adjectives, verbs—to words in a text, based on context and relationship to adjacent words. Today, instead of manual POS tagging, automated and sophisticated POS taggers perform the job.

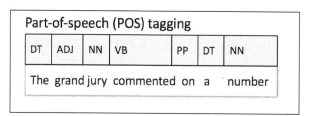

Figure 2: POS Tags associated with segment of text

Text clustering

Clustering unstructured data for organization, retrieval, and groupings based on similarity is the subfield of text clustering. This field is also well-developed with advancements in different clustering and text representations suited for learning.

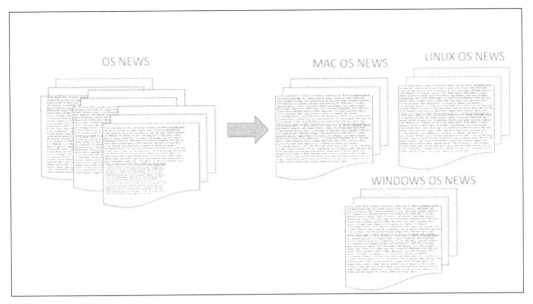

Figure 3: Clustering of OS news documents to various OS specific clusters

Information extraction and named entity recognition

The task of extracting specific elements, such as time, location, organization, entities, and so on, comes under the topic of information extraction. Named entity recognition is a sub-field that has wide applications in different domains, from reviews of historical documents to bioinformatics with gene and drug information.

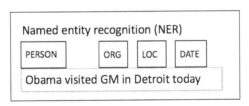

Figure 4: Named Entity Recognition in a sentence

Sentiment analysis and opinion mining

Another sub-field in the area of NLP involves inferring the sentiments of observers in order to categorize them with an understandable metric or to give insights into their opinions. This area is not as advanced as some of the ones mentioned previously, but much research is being done in this direction.

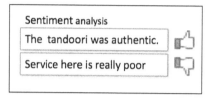

Figure 5: Sentiment Analysis showing positive and negative sentiments for sentences

Coreference resolution

Understanding references to multiple entities existing in the text and disambiguating that reference is another popular area of NLP. This is considered as a stepping stone in doing more complex tasks such as question answering and summarization, which will be discussed later.

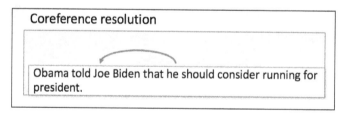

Figure 6: Coreference resolution showing how pronouns get disambiguated

Word sense disambiguation

In a language such as English, since the same word can have multiple meanings based on the context, deciphering this automatically is an important part of NLP, and the focus of **word sense disambiguation (WSD)**.

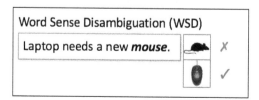

Figure 7: Showing how word "mouse" is associated with right word using the context

Machine translation

Translating text from one language to another or from speech to text in different languages is broadly covered in the area of **machine translation** (**MT**). This field has made significant progress in the last few years, with the usage of Machine Learning algorithms in supervised, unsupervised, and semi-supervised learning. Deep learning with techniques such as LSTM has been proved to be the most effective technique in this area, and is widely used by Google for its translation.

Figure 8: Machine Translation showing English to Chinese conversion

Semantic reasoning and inferencing

Reasoning, deriving logic, and inferencing from unstructured text is the next level of advancement in NLP.

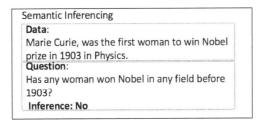

Figure 9: Semantic Inferencing answering complex questions

Text summarization

A subfield that is growing in popularity in NLP is the automated summarization of large documents or passages of text to a small representative text that can be easily understood. This is one of the budding research areas in NLP. Search engines' usage of summaries, multi-document summarizations for experts, and so on, are some of the applications that are benefiting from this field.

Automating question and answers

Answering questions posed by humans in natural language, ranging from questions specific to a certain domain to generic, open-ended questions is another emerging field in the area of NLP.

Issues with mining unstructured data

Humans can read, parse, and understand unstructured text/documents more easily than computer-based programs. Some of the reasons why text mining is more complicated than general supervised or unsupervised learning are given here:

- Ambiguity in terms and phrases. The word *bank* has multiple meanings, which a human reader can correctly associate based on context, yet this requires preprocessing steps such as POS tagging and word sense disambiguation, as we have seen. According to the Oxford English Dictionary, the word *run* has no fewer than 645 different uses in the verb form alone and we can see that such words can indeed present problems in resolving the meaning intended (between them, the words run, put, set, and take have more than a thousand meanings).

- Context and background knowledge associated with the text. Consider a sentence that uses a neologism with the suffix *gate* to signify a political scandal, as in, *With cries for impeachment and popularity ratings in a nosedive, Russiagate finally dealt a deathblow to his presidency*. A human reader can surmise what is being referred to by the coinage *Russiagate* as something that recalls the sense of high-profile intrigue, by association via an affix, of another momentous scandal in US political history, *Watergate*. This is particularly difficult for a machine to make sense of.

- Reasoning, that is, inferencing from documents is very difficult as mapping unstructured information to knowledge bases is itself a big hurdle.

- Ability to perform supervised learning needs labeled training documents and based on the domain, performing labeling on the documents can be time consuming and costly.

Text processing components and transformations

In this section, we will discuss some common preprocessing and transformation steps that are done in most text mining processes. The general concept is to convert the documents into structured datasets with features or attributes that most Machine Learning algorithms can use to perform different kinds of learning.

We will briefly describe some of the most used techniques in the next section. Different applications of text mining might use different pieces or variations of the components shown in the following figure:

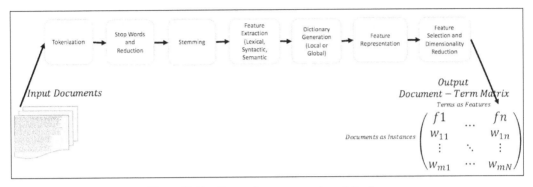

Figure 10: Text Processing components and the flow

Document collection and standardization

One of the first steps in most text mining applications is the collection of data in the form of a body of documents—often referred to as a *corpus* in the text mining world. These documents can have predefined categorization associated with them or it can simply be an unlabeled corpus. The documents can be of heterogeneous formats or standardized into one format for the next process of tokenization. Having multiple formats such as text, HTML, DOCs, PDGs, and so on, can lead to many complexities and hence one format, such as XML or **JavaScript Object Notation (JSON)** is normally preferred in most applications.

Inputs and outputs

Inputs are vast collections of homogeneous or heterogeneous sources and outputs are a collection of documents standardized into one format, such as XML.

How does it work?

Standardization involves ensuring tools and formats are agreed upon based on the needs of the application:

1. Agree to a standard format, such as XML, with predefined tags that provide information on meta-attributes of documents (`<author>`, `<title>`, `<date>`, and so on) and actual content, such as `<document>`.

2. Most document processors can either be transformed into XML or transformation code can be written to perform this.

Tokenization

The task of tokenization is to extract words or meaningful characters from the text containing a stream of these words. For example, the text *The boy stood up. He then ran after the dog* can be tokenized into tokens such as *{the, boy, stood, up, he, ran, after, the, dog}*.

Inputs and outputs

An input is a collection of documents in a well-known format as described in the last section and an output is a document with tokens of words or characters as needed in the application.

How does it work?

Any automated system for tokenization must address the particular challenges presented by the language(s) it is expected to handle:

- In languages such as English, tokenization is relatively simple due to the presence of white space, tabs, and newline for separating the words.

- There are different challenges in each language—even in English, abbreviations such as *Dr.*, alphanumeric characters (*B12*), different naming schemes (*O'Reilly*), and so on, must be tokenized appropriately.

- Language-specific rules in the form of if-then instructions are written to extract tokens from the documents.

Stop words removal

This involves removing high frequency words that have no discriminatory or predictive value. If every word can be viewed as a feature, this process reduces the dimension of the feature vector by a significant number. Prepositions, articles, and pronouns are some of the examples that form the stop words that are removed without affecting the performance of text mining in many applications.

Inputs and outputs

An input is a collection of documents with the tokens extracted and an output is a collection of documents with tokens reduced by removing stop words.

How does it work?

There are various techniques that have evolved in the last few years ranging from manually precompiled lists to statistical elimination using either term-based or mutual information.

- The most commonly used technique for many languages is a manually precompiled list of stop words, including prepositions (in, for, on), articles (a, an, the), pronouns (his, her, they, their), and so on.

- Many tools use Zipf's law (*References* [3]), where high frequency words, singletons, and unique terms are removed. Luhn's early work (*References* [4]), as represented in the following figure 11, shows thresholds of the upper bound and lower bound of word frequency, which give us the significant words that can be used for modeling:

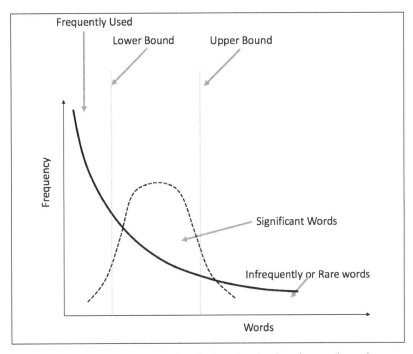

Figure 11: Word Frequency distribution, showing how frequently used, significant and rare words exist in corpus

Stemming or lemmatization

The idea of normalizing tokens of similar words into one is known as stemming or lemmatization. Thus, reducing all occurrences of "talking", "talks", "talked", and so on in a document to one root word "talk" in the document is an example of stemming.

Inputs and outputs

An input is documents with tokens and an output is documents with reduced tokens normalized to their stem or root words.

How does it work?

1. There are basically two types of stemming: inflectional stemming and stemming to the root.

2. Inflectional stemming generally involves removing affixes, normalizing the verb tenses and removing plurals. Thus, "ships" to "ship", "is", "are" and "am" to "be" in English.

3. Stemming to the root is generally a more aggressive form than inflectional stemming, where words are normalized to their roots. An example of this is "applications", "applied", "reapply", and so on, all reduced to the root word "apply".

4. Lovin's stemmer was one of the first stemming algorithms (*References* [1]). Porter's stemming, which evolved in the 1980s with around 60 rules in 6 steps, is still the most widely used form of stemming (*References* [2]).

5. Present-day applications drive a wide range of statistical techniques based on stemming, including those using n-grams (a contiguous sequence of n items, either letters or words from a given sequence of text), **hidden Markov models (HMM)**, and context-sensitive stemming.

Local/global dictionary or vocabulary

Once the preprocessing task of converting documents into tokens is performed, the next step is the creation of a corpus or vocabulary as a single dictionary, using all the tokens from all documents. Alternatively, several dictionaries are created based on category, using specific tokens from fewer documents.

Many applications in topic modeling and text categorization perform well when dictionaries are created per topic/category, which is known as a local dictionary. On the other hand, many applications in document clustering and information extraction perform well when one single global dictionary is created from all the document tokens. The choice of creating one or many specific dictionaries depends on the core NLP task, as well as on computational and storage requirements.

Feature extraction/generation

A key step in converting the document(s) with unstructured text is to transform them into datasets with structured features, similar to what we have seen so far in Machine Learning datasets. Extracting features from text so that it can be used in Machine Learning tasks such as supervised, unsupervised, and semi-supervised learning depends on many factors, such as the goals of the applications, domain-specific requirements, and feasibility. There are a wide variety of features, such as words, phrases, sentences, POS-tagged words, typographical elements, and so on, that can be extracted from any document. We will give a broad range of features that are commonly used in different Machine Learning applications.

Lexical features

Lexical features are the most frequently used features in text mining applications. Lexical features form the basis for the next level of features. They are the simple character- or word- level features constructed without trying to capture information about intent or the various meanings associated with the text. Lexical features can be further broken down into character-based features, word-based features, part-of-speech features, and taxonomies, for example. In the next section, we will describe some of them in greater detail.

Character-based features

Individual characters (unigram) or a sequence of characters (n-gram) are the simplest forms of features that can be constructed from the text document. The bag of characters or unigram characters have no positional information, while higher order n-grams capture some amount of context and positional information. These features can be encoded or given numeric values in different ways, such as binary 0/1 values, or counts, for example, as discussed later in the next section.

Let us consider the memorable Dr. Seuss rhyme as the text content—"the Cat in the Hat steps onto the mat". While the bag-of-characters (1-gram or unigram features) will generate unique characters {"t","h", "e", "c","a","i","n","s","p","o","n","m"} as features, the 3-gram features are { "\sCa" ,"\sHa", "\sin" , "\sma", "\son", "\sst", "\sth", "Cat", "Hat", "at\s", "e\sC", "e\sH", "e\sm", "eps", "he\s", "in\s ", "mat", "n\st", "nto", "o\st", "ont", "ps\s", "s\so" , "ste" , t\si"," t\ss" , "tep", "the", "to\s "}. As can be seen, as "n" increases, the number of features increases exponentially and soon becomes unwieldy. The advantage of n-grams is that at the cost of increasing the total number of features, the assembled features often seem to capture combinations of characters that are more interesting than the individual characters themselves.

Word-based features

Instead of generating features from characters, features can similarly be constructed from words in a unigram and n-gram manner. These are the most popular feature generation techniques. The unigram or 1-word token is also known as the bag of words model. So the example of "the Cat in the Hat steps onto the mat" when considered as unigram features is {"the", "Cat", "in", "Hat", "steps", "onto", "mat"}. Similarly, bigram features on the same text would result in {"the Cat", "Cat in", "in the", "the Hat", "Hat step", "steps onto", "onto the", "the mat"}. As in the case of character-based features, by going to higher "n" in the n-grams, the number of features increases, but so does the ability to capture word sense via context.

Part-of-speech tagging features

The input is text with words and the output is text where every word is associated with the grammatical tag. In many applications, part-of-speech gives a context and is useful in identification of named entities, phrases, entity disambiguation, and so on. In the example "the Cat in the Hat steps onto the mat" , the output is {"the\Det", "Cat\Noun", "in\Prep", "the\Det", "Hat\Noun", "steps\Verb", "onto\Prep", "the\Det", "mat\Noun"}. Language specific rule-based taggers or Markov chain–based probabilistic taggers are often used in this process.

Taxonomy features

Creating taxonomies from the text data and using it to understand relationships between words is also useful in different contexts. Various taxonomical features such as hypernyms, hyponyms, is-member, member-of, is-part, part-of, antonyms, synonyms, acronyms, and so on, give lexical context that proves useful in searches, retrieval, and matching in many text mining scenarios.

Syntactic features

The next level of features that are higher than just characters or words in text documents are the syntax-based features. Syntactical representation of sentences in text is generally in the form of syntax trees. Syntax trees capture nodes as terms used in sentences, and relationships between the nodes are captured as links. Syntactic features can also capture more complex features about sentences and usage — such as aggregates — that can be used for Machine Learning. It can also capture statistics about syntax trees — such as sentences being left-heavy, right-heavy, or balanced — that can be used to understand signatures of different content or writers.

Two sentences can have the same characters and words in the lexical analysis, but their syntax trees or intent could be completely different. Breaking the sentences in the text into different phrases — **Noun Phrase (NP)**, **Prepositional Phrase (PP)**, **Verbal** (or Gerund) **Phrase (VP)**, and so on — and capturing phrase structure trees for the sentences are part of this processing task. The following is the syntactic parse tree for our example sentence:

```
(S (NP (NP the cat)
       (PP in
           (NP the hat)))
   (VP steps
       (PP onto
           (NP the mat)))))
```

Syntactic Language Models (SLM) are about determining the probability of a sequence of terms. Language model features are used in machine translation, spelling correction, speech translation, summarization, and so on, to name a few of the applications. Language models can additionally use parse trees and syntax trees in their computation as well.

The chain rule is applied to compute the joint probability of terms in the sentence:

$$P(w_1, w_2, \ldots w_n) = \prod_i P(w_i | w_1, w_2, \ldots w_{i-1})$$

In the example "the cat in the hat steps onto the mat":

$$P(the, cat, in, the, hat, steps, onto, the, mat)$$
$$= P(the) \times P(cat \setminus the) \times P(in \setminus the\, cat)..$$
$$\times P(mat \setminus the, cat, in, the, hat, steps, onto, the))$$

Generally, the estimation of the probability of long sentences based on counts using any corpus is difficult due to the need for many examples of such sentences. Most language models use the Markov assumption of independence and n-grams (2-5 words) in practical implementations (*References* [8]).

Semantic features

Semantic features attempt to capture the "meaning" of the text, which is then used for different applications of text mining. One of the simplest forms of semantic features is the process of adding annotations to the documents. These annotations, or metadata, can have additional information that describes or captures the intent of the text or documents. Adding tags using collaborative tagging to capture tags as keywords describing the text is a common semantic feature generation process.

Another form of semantic feature generation is the process of ontological representation of the text. Generic and domain specific ontologies that capture different relationships between objects are available in knowledge bases and have well-known specifications, such as Semantic Web 2.0. These ontological features help in deriving complex inferencing, summarization, classification, and clustering tasks in text mining. The terms in the text or documents can be mapped to "concepts" in ontologies and stored in knowledge bases. These concepts in ontologies have semantic properties, and are related to other concepts in a number of ways, such as generalization/specialization, member-of/isAMember, association, and so on, to name a few. These attributes or properties of concepts and relationships can be further used in search, retrieval, and even in predictive modeling. Many semantic features use the lexical and syntactic processes as pre-cursors to the semantic process and use the outputs, such as nouns, to map to concepts in ontologies, for example. Adding the concepts to an existing ontology or annotating it with more concepts makes the structure more suitable for learning. For example, in the "the cat in the .." sentence, "cat" has properties such as {age, eats, ...} and has different relationships, such as { "isA Mammal", "hasChild", "hasParent", and so on}.

Feature representation and similarity

Lexical, syntactic, and semantic features, described in the last section, often have representations that are completely different from each other. Representations of the same feature type, that is, lexical, syntactic, or semantic, can differ based on the computation or mining task for which they are employed. In this section, we will describe the most common lexical feature-based representation known as vector space models.

Vector space model

The **vector space model (VSM)** is a transformation of the unstructured document to a numeric vector representation where terms in the corpus form the dimensions of the vector and we use some numeric way of associating value with these dimensions.

As discussed in the section on dictionaries, a corpus is formed out of unique words and phrases from the entire collection of documents in a domain or within local sub-categories of one. Each of the elements of such a dictionary are the dimensions of the vector. The terms—which can be single words or phrases, as in n-grams—form the dimensions and can have different values associated with them in a given text/document. The goal is to capture the values in the dimensions in a way that reflects the relevancy of the term(s) in the entire corpus (*References* [11]). Thus, each document or file is represented as a high-dimensional numeric vector. Due to the sparsity of terms, the numeric vector representation has a sparse representation in numeric space. Next, we will give some well-known ways of associating values to these terms.

Binary

This is the simplest form of associating value to the terms, or dimensions. In binary form, each term in the corpus is given a 0 or 1 value based on the presence or absence of the term in the document. For example, consider the following three documents:

- Document 1: "The Cat in the Hat steps onto the mat"
- Document 2: "The Cat sat on the Hat"
- Document 3: "The Cat loves to step on the mat"

After preprocessing by removing stop words {on, the, in, onto} and stemming {love/loves, steps/step} using a unigram or bag of words, {cat, hat, step, mat, sat, love} are the features of the corpus. Each document is now represented in a binary vector space model as follows:

Terms	cat	hat	step	mat	sat	love
Document 1	1	1	1	1	0	0
Document 2	1	1	0	0	1	0
Document 3	1	0	1	1	0	1

Term frequency (TF)

In **term frequency** (**TF**), as the name suggests, the frequency of terms in the entire document forms the numeric value of the feature. The basic assumption is that the higher the frequency of the term, the greater the relevance of that term for the document. Counts of terms or normalized counts of terms are used as values in each column of terms:

$tf(t) = count(D, t)$

The following table gives term frequencies for the three documents in our example:

TF/Terms	cat	hat	step	mat	sat	love
Document 1	1	1	1	1	0	0
Document 2	1	1	0	0	1	0
Document 3	1	0	1	1	0	1

Inverse document frequency (IDF)

Inverse document frequency (IDF) has various flavors, but the most common way of computing it is using the following:

$$Idf(t) = \log\left(\frac{N}{n_j}\right)$$

Here, N = *total number of documents*, n_j = *number of documents containing term j*. IDF favors mostly those terms that occur relatively infrequently in the documents. Some empirically motivated improvements to IDF have also been proposed in the research (*References* [7]).

TF for our example corpus:

Terms	cat	hat	step	mat	sat	love
N/nj	3/3	3/2	3/2	3/2	3/1	3/1
IDF	0.0	0.40	0.40	0.40	1.10	1.10

Term frequency-inverse document frequency (TF-IDF)

Combining both term frequencies and inverse document frequencies in one metric, we get the term frequency-inverse document frequency values. The idea is to value those terms that are relatively uncommon in the corpus (high IDF), but are reasonably relevant for the document (high TF). TF-IDF is the most common form of value association in many text mining processes:

$$tfIdf(t) = tf(t) \times Idf(t)$$

This gives us the TF-IDF for all the terms in each of the documents:

TF-IDF/Terms	cat	hat	step	mat	sat	love
Document 1	0.0	0.40	0.40	0.40	1.10	1.10
Document 2	0.0	0.40	0.0	0.0	1.10	0.0
Document 3	0.0	0.0	0.40	0.40	0.0	1.10

Similarity measures

Many techniques in supervised, unsupervised, and semi-supervised learning use "similarity" measures in their underlying algorithms to find similar patterns or to separate different patterns. Similarity measures are tied closely to the representation of the data. In the VSM representation of documents, the vectors are very high dimensional and sparse. This poses a serious issue in most traditional similarity measures for classification, clustering, or information retrieval. Angle-based similarity measures, such as cosine distances or Jaccard coefficients, are more often used in practice. Consider two vectors represented by $\mathbf{t}_1$ and $\mathbf{t}_2$ corresponding to two text documents.

Euclidean distance

This is the L2 norm in the feature space of the documents:

$$d_{EUC}\left(\mathbf{t}_1, \mathbf{t}_2\right) = \left[\left(\mathbf{t}_1 - \mathbf{t}_2\right)\left(\left(\mathbf{t}_1 - \mathbf{t}_2\right)\right)\right]^{1/2}$$

Cosine distance

This angle-based similarity measure considers orientation between vectors only and not their lengths. It is equal to the cosine of the angle between the vectors. Since the vector space model is a positive space, cosine distance varies from 0 (orthogonal, no common terms) to 1 (all terms are common to both, but not necessarily with the same term frequency):

$$S_{cos}\left(\mathbf{t}_1, \mathbf{t}_2\right) = \frac{\mathbf{t}_1 \cdot \mathbf{t}_2}{\|\mathbf{t}_1\|\|\mathbf{t}_2\|}$$

Pairwise-adaptive similarity

This measure the distance in a reduced feature space by only considering the features that are most important in the two documents:

$$d_{PAIR}(\mathbf{t}_1, \mathbf{t}_2) = \frac{\mathbf{t}_{1,K} \cdot \mathbf{t}_{2,K}}{\|\mathbf{t}_{1,K}\| \|\mathbf{t}_{2,K}\|}$$

Here, $\mathbf{t}_{i,k}$ is a vector formed from a subset of the features of $\mathbf{t}_i$ ($i = 1, 2$) containing the union of the K largest features appearing in $\mathbf{t}_1$ and $\mathbf{t}_2$.

Extended Jaccard coefficient

This measure is computed as a ratio of the shared terms to the union of the terms between the documents:

$$S_{EJ}(\mathbf{t}_1, \mathbf{t}_2) = \frac{\mathbf{t}_1 \cdot \mathbf{t}_2}{\mathbf{t}_1 \cdot \mathbf{t}_1 + \mathbf{t}_2 \cdot \mathbf{t}_2 - \mathbf{t}_1 \cdot \mathbf{t}_2}$$

Dice coefficient

The Dice coefficient is given by the following:

$$S_{DICE}(\mathbf{t}_1, \mathbf{t}_2) = \frac{2(\mathbf{t}_1 \cdot \mathbf{t}_2)}{\mathbf{t}_1 \cdot \mathbf{t}_1 + \mathbf{t}_2 \cdot \mathbf{t}_2}$$

Feature selection and dimensionality reduction

The goal is the same as in *Chapter 2, Practical Approach to Real-World Supervised Learning* and *Chapter 3, Unsupervised Machine Learning Techniques*. The problem of the curse of dimensionality becomes even more pronounced with text mining and high dimensional features.

Feature selection

Most feature selection techniques are supervised techniques that depend on the labels or the outcomes for scoring the features. In the majority of cases, we perform filter-based rather than wrapper-based feature selection, due to the lower performance cost. Even among filter-based methods, some, such as those involving multivariate techniques such as **Correlation based Feature selection (CFS)**, as described in *Chapter 2, Practical Approach to Real-World Supervised Learning*, can be quite costly or result in suboptimal performance due to high dimensionality (*References* [9]).

Information theoretic techniques

As shown in *Chapter 2, Practical Approach to Real-World Supervised Learning*, filter-based univariate feature selection methods, such as **Information gain (IG)** and **Gain Ratio (GR)**, are most commonly used once preprocessing and feature extraction is done.

In their research, Yang and Pederson (*References* [10]) clearly showed the benefits of feature selection and reduction using IG to remove close to 98% of terms and yet improve the predictive capability of the classifiers.

Many of the information theoretic or entropy-based methods have a stronger influence resulting from the marginal probabilities of the tokens. This can be an issue when the terms have equal conditional probability $P(t|class)$, the rarer terms may have better scores than the common terms.

Statistical-based techniques

χ^2 feature selection is one of the most common statistical-based techniques employed to perform feature selection in text mining. χ^2 statistics, as shown in *Chapter 2, Practical Approach to Real-World Supervised Learning*, give the independence relationship between the tokens in the text and the classes.

It has been shown that χ^2 statistics for feature selection may not be effective when there are low-frequency terms (*References* [19]).

Frequency-based techniques

Using the term frequency or the document frequency described in the section on feature representation, a threshold can be manually set, and only terms above or below a certain threshold can be allowed used for modeling in either classification or clustering tasks. Note that **term frequency (TF)** and **document frequency (DF)** methods are biased towards common words while some of the information theoretic or statistical-based methods are biased towards less frequent words. The choice of selection of features depends on the domain, the particular application of predictive learning, and more importantly, on how models using these features are evaluated, especially on the unseen dataset.

Dimensionality reduction

Another approach that we saw in *Chapter 3, Unsupervised Machine Learning Techniques,* was to use unsupervised techniques to reduce the features using some form of transformation to decide their usefulness.

Principal component analysis (PCA) computes a covariance or correlation matrix from the document-term matrix. It transforms the data into linear combinations of terms in the inputs in such a way that the transformed combination of features or terms has higher discriminating power than the input terms. PCA with cut-off or thresholding on the transformed features, as shown in *Chapter 3, Unsupervised Machine Learning Techniques,* can bring down the dimensionality substantially and even improve or give comparable performance to the high dimensional input space. The only issue with using PCA is that the transformed features are not interpretable, and for domains where understanding which terms or combinations yield better predictive models, this technique has some limitations.

Latent semantic analysis (LSA) is another way of using the input matrix constructed from terms and documents and transforming it into lower dimensions with latent concepts discovered through combinations of terms used in documents (*References* [5]). The following figure captures the process using the **singular value decomposition (SVD)** method for factorizing the input document-term matrix:

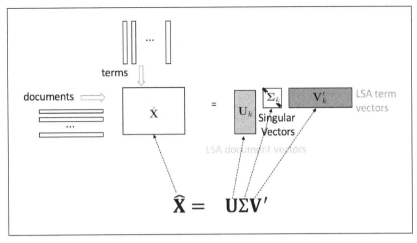

Figure 12: SVD factorization of input document-terms into LSA document vectors and LSA term vectors

LSA has been shown to be a very effective way of reducing the dimensions and also of improving the predictive performance in models. The disadvantage of LSA is that storage of both vectors U and V is needed for performing retrievals or queries. Determining the lower dimension k is hard and needs some heuristics similar to k-means discussed in *Chapter 3, Unsupervised Machine Learning Techniques*.

Topics in text mining

As we saw in the first section, the area of text mining and performing Machine Learning on text spans a wide range of topics. Each topic discussed has some customizations to the mainstream algorithms, or there are specific algorithms that have been developed to perform the task called for in that area. We have chosen four broad topics, namely, text categorization, topic modeling, text clustering, and named entity recognition, and will discuss each in some detail.

Text categorization/classification

The text classification problem manifests itself in different applications, such as document filtering and organization, information retrieval, opinion and sentiment mining, e-mail spam filtering, and so on. Similar to the classification problem discussed in *Chapter 2, Practical Approach to Real-World Supervised Learning*, the general idea is to train on the training data with labels and to predict the labels of unseen documents.

As discussed in the previous section, the preprocessing steps help to transform the unstructured document collection into well-known numeric or categorical/ binary structured data arranged in terms of a document-term matrix. The choice of performing some preprocessing steps, such as stemming or customizing stop words, depends on the data and applications. The feature choice is generally basic lexical features, n-grams of words as terms, and only in certain cases do we use the entire text as a string without breaking it into terms or tokens. It is common to use binary feature representation or frequency-based representation for document-term structured data. Once this transformation is complete, we do feature selection using univariate analysis, such as information gain or chi-square, to choose discriminating features above certain thresholds of scores. One may also perform feature transformation and dimensionality reduction such as PCA or LSA in many applications.

There is a wide range in the choice of classifiers once we get structured data from the preceding process. In the research as well as in commercial applications, we see the use of most of the common modeling techniques, including linear (linear regression, logistic regression, and so on), non-linear (SVM, neural networks, KNN), generative (naïve bayes, bayesian networks), interpretable (decision trees, rules), and ensemble-based (bagging, boosting, random forest) classifiers. Many algorithms use similarity or distance metrics, of which cosine distance is the most popular choice. In certain classifiers, such as SVM, the string representation of the document can be used as is, with the right choice of string kernels and similarity-based metrics on strings to compute the dot products.

Validation and evaluation methods are similar to supervised classification methodologies—splitting the data into train/validation/test, training on training data, tuning parameters of algorithm(s) on validation data, and estimating the performance of the models on hold-out or test data.

Since most of text classification involves a large number of documents, and the target classes are rare, the metrics used for evaluation, tuning, or choosing algorithms are in most cases precision, recall, and F-score measure, as follows:

$$precision(p) = \frac{Count(\{relevant \cap retrieved\})}{Count(retrieved)}$$

$$recall(r) = \frac{Count(\{relevant \cap retrieved\})}{Count(relevant)}$$

$$F-score = \frac{2}{1/precision + 1/recall}$$

Topic modeling

A topic is a distribution over a fixed vocabulary. Topic modeling can be defined as an ability to capture different core ideas or themes in various documents. This has a wide range of applications, such as the summarization of documents, understanding reasons for sentiments, trends, the news, and many others. The following figure shows how topic modeling can discern a user-specified number k of topics from a corpus and then, for every document, assign proportions representing how much of each topic is found in the document:

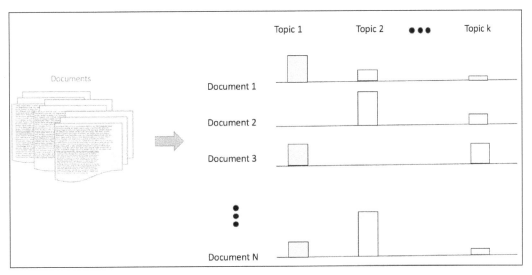

Figure 13: Probabilistic topic weights assignment for documents

There are quite a few techniques for performing topic modeling using supervised and unsupervised learning in the literature (*References* [13]). We will discuss the most common technique known as **probabilistic latent semantic index** (PLSI).

Probabilistic latent semantic analysis (PLSA)

The idea of PLSA, as in the LSA for feature reduction, is to find latent concepts hidden in the corpus by discovering the association between co-occurring terms and treating the documents as mixtures of these concepts. This is an unsupervised technique, similar to dimensionality reduction, but the idea is to use it to model the mixture of topics or latent concepts in the document (*References* [12]).

As shown in the following figure, the model may associate terms occurring together often in the corpus with a latent concept, and each document can then be said to exhibit that topic to a smaller or larger extent:

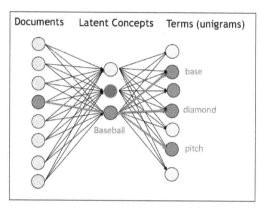

Figure 14: Latent concept of Baseball capturing the association between documents and related terms

Input and output

The inputs are:

- A collection of documents following a certain format and structure. We will give the notation:

$$c = \{d_1, d_2, \dots ..d_n\}$$

- The number of topics that need to be modeled or discovered as k.

The output is:

- k topics identified T = $\{T_1, T_2, \dots T_k\}$.
- For each document, coverage of the topic given in the document d_i can be written as = $\{\pi_{i1}, \pi_{i2}, \dots \pi_{ik}\}$, where π_{ij} is the probability of the document d_i covering the topic T_j.

How does it work?

Implementations of PLSA generally follow the steps described here:

1. Basic preprocessing steps as discussed previously, such as tokenization, stop words removal, stemming, dictionary of words formation, feature extraction (unigrams or n-grams, and so on), and feature selection (unsupervised techniques) are carried out, if necessary.

2. The problem can be reduced to estimating the distribution of terms in a document, and, given the distribution, choosing the topic based on the maximum terms corresponding to the topic.

3. Introducing a "latent variable" z helps us to select whether the term belongs to a topic. Note that z is not "observed", but we assume that it is related to picking the term from the topic. Thus, the probability of the term t given the document t can be expressed in terms of this latent variable as:

$$p(t|d) = \sum_z p(t|z) p(z|d)$$

4. By using two sets of variables (θ, π) the equation can be written as:

$$p(t|d) = \sum_z p(t|z;\theta) p(d;\pi)$$

Here, $p(t|z; \theta)$ is the probability of latent concepts in terms and $p(z|d; \pi)$ is the probability of latent concepts in document-specific mixtures.

5. Using log-likelihood to estimate the parameters to maximize:

$$l(\theta,\pi;N) = \sum_{d,t} count(d,t) \log\left(\sum_z p(t|z;\theta) p(z|d;\pi) \right)$$

6. Since this equation involves nonconvex optimization, the EM algorithm is often used to find the parameters iteratively until convergence is reached or the total number of iterations are completed (*References* [6]):

    1. The E-step of the EM algorithm is used to determine the posterior probability of the latent concepts. The probability of term t occurring in the document d, can be explained by the latent concept z as:

$$p(z|d,t) = \frac{p(z|d;\pi) p(t|z;\theta)}{\sum_{z'} p(t|z';\theta) p(z'|d;\pi)}$$

2. The M-step of the EM algorithm uses the values obtained from the E-step, that is, p(z | d, t) and does parameter estimation as:

$$p(t \mid z; \theta) \propto \sum_d count(d,t) \, p(z \mid d, t)$$

3. $\sum_d count(d,t) p(z \mid d,t)$ = how often the term *t* is associated with concept *z*:

$$p(z \mid d, t) \propto \sum_t count(d,t) \, p(z \mid d, t)$$

4. $\sum_t count(d,t) \, p(z \mid d,t)$ = how often document *d* is associated with concept *z*.

Advantages and limitations

The advantages and limitations are as follows:

- Though widely used, PLSA has some drawbacks that have been overcome by more recent techniques.
- The unsupervised nature of the algorithm and its general applicability allows it to be used in a wide variety of similar text mining applications, such as clustering documents, associating topics related to authors/time, and so on.
- PLSA with EM algorithms, as discussed in previous chapters, face the problem of getting "stuck in local optima", unlike other global algorithms, such as evolutionary algorithms.
- PLSA algorithms can only do topic identification in known documents, but cannot do any predictive modeling. PLSA has been generalized and is known as **latent dirichlet allocation (LDA)** to overcome this (*References* [14]).

Text clustering

The goal of clustering, as seen in *Chapter 3, Unsupervised Machine Learning Techniques*, is to find groups of data, text, or documents that are similar to one another within the group. The granularity of unstructured data can vary from small phrases or sentences, paragraphs, and passages of text to a collection of documents. Text clustering finds its application in many domains, such as information retrieval, summarization, topic modeling, and document classification in unsupervised situations, to name a few. Traditional techniques in clustering can be employed once the unstructured text data is transformed into structured data via preprocessing. The difficulty with traditional clustering techniques is the high-dimensional and sparse nature of the dataset obtained using the transformed document-term matrix representation. Many traditional clustering algorithms work only on numeric values of features. Because of this constraint, categorical or binary representation of terms cannot be used and often TF or TF-IDF are used for representation of the document-term matrix.

In this section, we will discuss some of the basic processes and techniques in clustering. We will start with pre-processing and transformations and then discuss some techniques that are widely used and the modifications made to them.

Feature transformation, selection, and reduction

Most of the pre-processing steps discussed in this section are normally used to get either unigram or n-gram representation of terms in documents. Dimensionality reduction techniques, such as LSA, are often employed to transform the features into smaller latent space.

Clustering techniques

The techniques for clustering in text include probabilistic models, as well as those that use distance-based methods, which are familiar to us from when we learned about structured data. We will also discuss **Non-negative Matrix Factorization (NMF)** as an effective technique with good performance and interpretability.

Generative probabilistic models

There is commonality between topic modeling and text clustering in generative methods. As shown in the following figure, clustering associates a document with a single cluster (generally), compared to topic modeling where each document can have a probability of coverage in multiple topics. Every word in topic modeling can be generated by multiple topics in an independent manner, whereas in clustering all the words are generated from the same cluster:

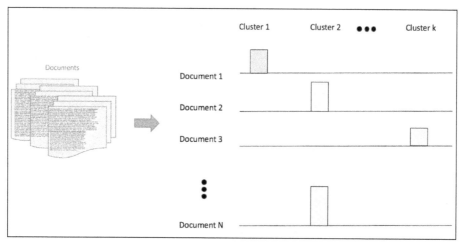

Figure 15: Exclusive mapping of documents to K-Clusters

Mathematically, this can be explained using two topics $T = \{T_1, T_2\}$ and two clusters $c = \{c_1, c_2\}$.

In clustering, the likelihood of the document can be given as:

$$p(d) = p(c_1) p(d \mid c_1) + p(c_2) p(d \mid c_2)$$

If the document has, say, L terms, this can be further expanded as:

$$p(d) = p(t_1, t_2..t_L) = p(c_1) \prod_{i=1}^{L} p(t_i \mid c_1) + p(c_2) \prod_{i=1}^{L} p(t_i \mid c_2)$$

Thus, once you "assume" a cluster, all the words come from that cluster. The product of all terms is computed, followed by the summation across all clusters.

In topic modeling, the likelihood of the document can be given as:

$$p(d) = p(t_1, t_2..t_L) = \prod_{i=1}^{L} \left[p(T_1) p(t_i \mid T_1) + p(T_2) p(t_i \mid T_2) \right]$$

Thus, each term t_i can be picked independently from topics and hence summation is done inside and the product is done outside.

Input and output

The inputs are:

- A collection of documents following a certain format and structure expressed with the following notation:

$$D = \{d_1, d_2, \ldots d_n\}$$

- The number of clusters that need to be modeled or discovered as k.

The output is:

- k clusters identified $c = \{c_1, c_2, \ldots c_k\}$.
- For each document, $p(d_i)$ is mapped to one of the clusters k.

How does it work?

Here are the steps:

1. Basic preprocessing steps as discussed previously, such as tokenization, stop words removal, stemming, dictionary of words formation, feature extraction (unigrams or n-grams, and so on) of terms, feature transformations (LSA), and even feature selection. Let t be the terms in the final feature set; they correspond to the dictionary or vocabulary $\mathbb{V}$.

2. Similar to PLSA, we introduce a "latent variable", z, which helps us to select whether the document belonging to the cluster falls in the range of $z = \{1, 2, \ldots k\}$ corresponding to the clusters. Let the θ parameter be the parameter we estimate for each latent variable such that $p(\theta_i)$ corresponds to the probability of cluster $z = i$.

3. The probability of a document belonging to a cluster is given by $p(\theta_j)$, and every term in the document generated from that cluster is given by $p(t \mid \theta_j)$. The likelihood equation can be written as:

$$p(d \mid \Lambda) = \sum_{i=1}^{k} p(\theta_i) \prod_{t \in vp} \left(t \mid \theta_i\right)^{count(t,d)} ; \Lambda = \left\{\theta_i \mid i = 1..k\right\}$$

Note that instead of going through the documents, it is rewritten with terms t in the vocabulary $\mathbb{V}$ raised to the number of times that term appears in the document.

4. Perform the EM algorithm in a similar way to the method we used previously to estimate the parameters as follows:

   1. The E-step of the EM algorithm is used to infer the cluster from which the document was generated:

   $$p(z_d = i \mid d) \propto p(\theta_i) \prod_{t \in \mathbb{V}} p(t \mid \theta_i)^{count(t,d)} ; \sum_{i=1}^{k} p(z_d = i \mid d) = 1$$

   2. The M-step of the EM algorithm is used to re-estimate the parameters using the result of the E-step, as shown here:

   $$p(\theta_i) \alpha \sum_{j=1}^{N} p(z_{dj} = i \mid d_j); \sum_{i=1}^{k} p(\theta_i) = 1$$

   $$p(t \mid \theta_i) \propto \sum_{j=1}^{N} count(t, d_j) p(z_{d_j} = i \mid d_j); \sum_{t \in \mathbb{V}} p(t \mid \theta_i) = 1$$

5. The final probability estimate for each document can be done using either the maximum likelihood or by using a Bayesian algorithm with prior probabilities, as shown here:

$$c_d = \text{argmax}_i \left(p(d \mid \theta_i)\right) \text{ or } c_d = \text{argmax}_i \left(p(d \mid \theta_i) p(\theta_i)\right)$$

Advantages and limitations

- Generative-based models have similar advantages to LSA and PLSA, where we get a probabilistic score for documents in clusters. By applying domain knowledge or priors using cluster size, the assignments can be further fine-tuned.

- The disadvantages of the EM algorithm having to do with getting stuck in local optima and being sensitive to the starting point are still true here.

Distance-based text clustering

Most distance-based clustering algorithms rely on the similarity or the distance measure used to determine how far apart instances are from each other in feature space. Normally in datasets with numeric values, Euclidean distance or its variations work very well. In text mining, even after converting unstructured text to structured features of terms with numeric values, it has been found that the cosine and Jaccard similarity functions perform better.

Often, Agglomerative or Hierarchical clustering, discussed in *Chapter 3, Unsupervised Machine Learning Techniques*, are used, which can merge documents based on similarity, as discussed previously. Merging the documents or groups is often done using single linkage, group average linkage, and complete linkage techniques. Agglomerative clustering also results in a structure that can be used for information retrieval and the searching of documents.

The partition-based clustering techniques k-means and k-medoids accompanied by *h* a suitable similarity or distance method are also employed. The issue with k-means, as indicated in the discussion on clustering techniques, is the sensitivity to starting conditions along with computation space and time. k-medoids are sensitive to the sparse data structure and also have computation space and time constraints.

Non-negative matrix factorization (NMF)

Non-negative matrix factorization is another technique used to factorize a large data-feature matrix into two non-negative matrices, which not only perform the dimensionality reduction, but are also easier to inspect. NMF has gained popularity for document clustering, and many variants of NMF with different optimization functions have now been shown to be very effective in clustering text (*References* [15]).

Input and output

The inputs are:

- A collection of documents following a certain format and structure given by the notation:

$$D = \{d_1, d_2, \ldots d_n\}$$

- Number of clusters that need to be modeled or discovered as *k*.

The output is:

- k clusters identified $c = \{c_1, c_2, \ldots c_k\}$ with documents assigned to the clusters.

How does it work?

The mathematical details and interpretation of NMF are given in the following:

1. The basic idea behind NMF is to factorize the input matrix using low-rank approximation, as follows:

    $$\mathbf{A} \cong \mathbf{A}_k = \mathbf{W}_k \mathbf{H}_k$$

2. A non-linear optimization function is used as:

    $$\min \|\mathbf{A} - \mathbf{W}\mathbf{H}\| ; \mathbf{W}, \mathbf{H} \geq \mathbf{0}$$

    This is convex in W or H, but not in both, resulting in no guarantees of a global minimum. Various algorithms that use constrained least squares, such as mean-square error and gradient descent, are used to solve the optimization function.

3. The interpretation of NMF, especially in understanding the latent topics based on terms, makes it very useful. The input $A_{m \times n}$ of terms and documents, can be represented in low rank approximation as $W_{m \times k} H_{k \times n}$ matrices, where $W_{m \times k}$ is the term-topic representation whose columns are NMF basis vectors. The non zero elements of column 1 of W, given by W_1, correspond to particular terms. Thus, the w_{ij} can be interpreted as a basis vector W_i about the terms j. The H_{i1} can be interpreted as how much the document given by doc 1 has affinity towards the direction of the topic vector W_i.

4. From the paper (*References* [18]) it was clearly shown how the basis vectors obtained for the medical abstracts, known as the Medlars dataset, creates highly interpretable basis vectors. The highest weighted terms in these basis vectors directly correspond to the concept, for example, W_1 corresponds to the topic related to "heart" and W_5 is related to "developmental disability".

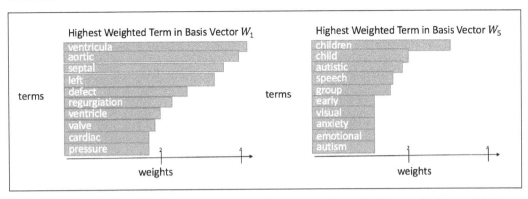

Figure 16: From Langville et al (2006) showing some basis vectors for medical datasets for interpretability.

Advantages and limitations

NMF has been shown to be almost equal in performance with top algorithms, such as LSI, for information retrieval and queries:

- Scalability, computation, and storage is better in NMF than in LSA or LSI using SVD.

- NMF has a problem with optimization not being global and getting stuck in local minima.

- NMF generation of factors depends on the algorithms for optimization and the parameters chosen, and is not unique.

Evaluation of text clustering

In the case of labeled datasets, all the external measures discussed in *Chapter 3, Unsupervised Machine Learning Techniques,* such as F-measure and Rand Index are useful in evaluating the clustering techniques. When the dataset doesn't have labels, some of the techniques described as the internal measures, such as the Davies–Bouldin Index, R-Squared, and Silhouette Index, can be used.

The general good practice is to adapt and make sure similarity between the documents, as discussed in this section, is used for measuring closeness, remoteness, and spread of the cluster when applied to text mining data. Similarly usage depends on the algorithm and some relevance to the problem too. In distance-based partition algorithms, the similarity of the document can be computed with the mean vector or the centroid. In hierarchical algorithms, similarity can be computed with most similar or dissimilar documents in the group.

Named entity recognition

Named entity recognition (**NER**) is one of the most important topics in information retrieval for text mining. Many complex mining tasks, such as the identification of relations, annotations of events, and correlation between entities, use NER as the initial component or basic preprocessing step.

Historically, manual rules-based and regular expression-based techniques were used for entity recognition. These manual rules relied on basic pre processing, using POS tags as features, along with hand-engineered features, such as the presence of capital words, usage of punctuations prior to words, and so on.

Statistical learning-based techniques are now used more for NER and its variants. NER can be mapped to sequence labeling and prediction problems in Machine Learning. BIO notation, where each entity type T has two labels B-T and I-T corresponding to beginning and intermediate, respectively, is labeled, and learning involves finding the pattern and predicting it in unseen data. The O represents an outside or unrelated entity in the sequence of text. The entity type T is further classified into Person, Organization, Data, and location in the most basic form.

In this section, we will discuss the two most common algorithms used: generative-based hidden Markov models and discriminative-based maximum entropy models.

Though we are discussing these algorithms in the context of Named Entity Recognition, the same algorithms and processes can be used for other NLP tasks such as POS Tagging, where tags are associated with a sequence rather than associating the NER classes.

Hidden Markov models for NER

Hidden Markov models, as explained in *Chapter 6, Probabilistic Graph Modeling*, are the sequence-based generative models that assume an underlying distribution that generates the sequences. The training data obtained by labeling sequences with the right NER classes can be used to learn the distribution and parameters, so that for unseen future sequences, effective predictions can be performed.

Input and output

The training data consists of text sequences $x = \{x_1, x_2, \dots x_n\}$ where each x_i is a word in the text sequence and labels for each word are available as $y = \{y_1, y_2, \dots y_n\}$. The algorithm generates a model so that on testing on unseen data, the labels for new sequences can be generated.

How does it work?

1. In the simplest form, a Markov assumption is made, which is that the hidden states and labels of the sequences are only dependent on the previous state. An adaptation to the sequence of words with labels is shown in the following figure:

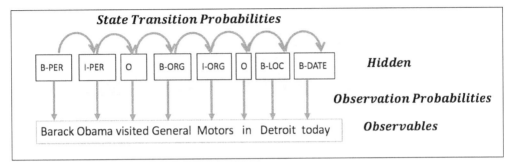

Figure 17: Text sequence and labels corresponding to NER in Hidden Markov Chain

2. The HMM formulation of the sequence classification helps in estimating the joint probability maximized on training data:

$$p(\mathbf{x}, \mathbf{y}) = \prod_i p(x_i \mid y_i) p(y_i \mid y_{i-1})$$

3. Each y_i is assumed to be generated based on y_{i-1} and x_i. The first word in the entity is generated conditioned on current and previous labels, that is, y_i and y_{i-1}. If the instance is already a Named entity, then conditioning is only on previous instances, that is, x_{i-1}. Outside words such as "visited" and "in" are considered "not a name class".

4. The HMM formulation with the forward-backward algorithm can be used to determine the likelihood of a sequence of observations with parameters learned from the training data.

Advantages and limitations

The advantages and limitations are as follows:

*   HMMs are good for short sequences, as shown, with one word or term and independence assumption. For sequences with entities that have a longer span, the results will violate these assumptions.
*   The HMM needs a large set of training data to estimate the parameters.

Maximum entropy Markov models for NER

Maximum entropy Markov model (MEMM) is a popular NER technique that uses the concept of Markov chains and maximum entropy models to learn and predict the named entities (*References* [16] and [17]).

Input and output

The training data consists of text sequences $x = \{x_1, x_2, \ldots x_n\}$ where each x_i is a word in the text sequence and labels for each word are available as $y = \{y_1, y_2, \ldots y_n\}$. The algorithm generates models so that, on testing on unseen data, the labels for new sequences can be generated.

How does it work?

The following illustrates how the MEMM method is used for learning named entities.

1. The features in MEMM can be word features or other types of features, such as "isWordCapitalized", and so on, which gives it a bit more context and improves performance compared to HMM, where it is only word-based.

2. Next, let us look at a maximum entropy model known as a MaxEnt model, which is an exponential probabilistic model, but which can also be seen as a multinomial logistic regression model. In basic MaxEnt models, given the features $\{f_1, f_2 \ldots f_N\}$ and classes $c_1, c_2 \ldots c_C$, weights for these features are learned $\{w_{c1}, w_{c2} \ldots w_{cN}\}$ per class using optimization methods from the training data, and the probability of a particular class can be estimated as:

$$p(c \mid x) = \frac{\exp\left(\sum_{i=0}^{N} w_{ci} f_i\right)}{\sum_{c' \in c} \exp\left(\sum_{i=0}^{N} w_{ci} f_i\right)}$$

3. The feature f_i is formally written as $f_i(c, x)$, which means the feature f_i for class c and observation x. The $f_i(c, x)$ is generally binary with values 1/0 in most NER models. Thus, it can be written as:

$$p(c \mid x) = \frac{\exp\left(\sum_{i=0}^{N} w_{ci} f_i(c, x),\right)}{\sum_{c' \in C} \exp\left(\sum_{i=0}^{N} w_{ci} f_i(c, x),\right)}$$

Maximum likelihood based on the probability of prediction across class can be used to select a single class:

$$\hat{c} = \operatorname{argmax}_{c \in C} p(c \mid x)$$

4. For every word, we use the current word, the features from "nearby" words, and the predictions on the nearby words to create a joint probability model. This is also called local learning as the chunks of test and distribution are learned around local features corresponding to the word.

    Mathematically, we see how a discriminative model is created from current word and last prediction as:

    $$\hat{c} = \operatorname{argmax}_{C} p(y \mid x)$$

    $$\hat{c} = \operatorname{argmax}_{C} \prod_{i} p(y_i \mid y_{i-1}, x_i)$$

    Generalizing for the k features:

    $$\hat{c} = \operatorname{argmax}_{C} \prod_{i} p\left(y_i \mid y_{i-k}^{i-1}, x_{i-1}^{i+1}\right)$$

5. Thus, in MEMM we compute the probability of the state, which is the class in NER, and even though we condition on prediction of nearby words given by y_{i-1}, in general we can use more features, and that is the advantage over the HMM model discussed previously:

    $$p(y_i \mid x_i) = \prod_{i} p(y_i \mid y_{i-1}, x_i)$$

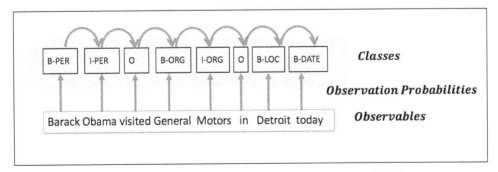

Figure 18 : Text Sequences and observation probabilities with labels

6. The Viterbi algorithm is used to perform the estimation of class for the word or decoding/inferencing in HMM, that is, to get estimates for $p(y_i | y_{i-1}, X_i)$

7. Finally, the MaxEnt model is used to estimate the weights as before using the optimization methods for state changes in general:

$$p\left(y_i | y_{i-1}, x_i\right) = \frac{\exp\left(\sum_{i=0}^{N} w_{ci} f_i\left(x_i, y_i, y_{i-1}\right)\right)}{\sum_{c' \in C} \exp\left(\sum_{i=0}^{N} w_{ci} f_i\left(x_i, y_i, y_{i-1}\right)\right)}$$

Advantages and limitations

*   MEMM has more flexibility in using features that are not just word-based or even human-engineered, giving it more richness and enabling its models to be more predictive.

*   MEMM can have a range of more than just close words, giving it an advantage of detection over larger spans compared to HMM.

Deep learning and NLP

In the last few years, Deep Learning and its application to various areas of NLP has shown huge success and is considered the cutting edge of technology these days. The main advantage of using Deep Learning lies in a small subset of tools and methods, which are useful in a wide variety of NLP problems. It solves the basic issue of feature engineering and carefully created manual representations by automatically learning them, and thus solves the issue of having a large number of language experts dealing with a wide range of problems, such as text classification, sentiment analysis, POS tagging, and machine translation, to name a few. In this section, we will try to cover important concepts and research in the area of Deep Learning and NLP.

In his seminal paper, Bengio introduced one of the most important building blocks for deep learning known as word embedding or word vector (*References* [20]). Word embedding can be defined as a parameterized function that maps words to a high dimensional vector (usually 25 to 500 dimensions based on the application).

Formally, this can be written as $W : \text{words} \rightarrow \mathbb{R}^n$.

For example, $W(\text{"cat"}) = (0.2, -0.4, 0.3, \ldots 0.6)$ and $W(\text{"hat"}) = (0.1, 0.2, 0.7, \ldots 0.1)$, and so on.

A neural network (R) whose inputs are the words from sentences or n-grams of sentences with binary classification, such as whether the sequence of words in n-grams are valid or not, is used to train and learn the W and R:

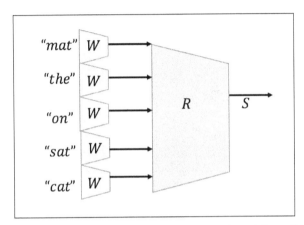

Figure 19: A modular neural network learning 5-gram words for valid–invalid classification

For example:

- $R(W(cat), W(sat), W(on), W(the), W(mat)) = 1(valid)$
- $R(W(cat), W(sat), W(on), W(the), W(mat)) = 0 \ (Invalid)$

The idea of training these sentences or n-grams is not only to learn the correct structure of the phrases, but also the right parameters for W and R. The word embeddings can also be projected on to a lower dimensional space, such as a 2D space, using various linear and non linear feature reduction/visualization techniques introduced in *Chapter 3, Unsupervised Machine Learning Techniques*, which humans can easily visualize. This visualization of word embeddings in two dimensions using techniques such as t-SNE discovers important information about the closeness of words based on semantic meaning and even clustering of words in the area, as shown in the following figure:

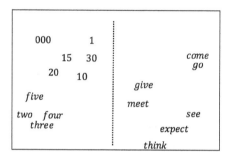

Figure 20: t-SNE representation of a small section of the entire word mappings. Numbers in Roman numerals and words are shown clustered together on the left, while semantically close words are clustered together on the right.

Further extending the concepts, both Collobert and Mikolov showed that the side effects of learning the word embeddings can be very useful in a variety of NLP tasks, such as similar phrase learning (for example, $W("the\ color\ is\ red")) \cong W("the\ color\ is\ yellow"))$, finding synonyms (for example, $W("nailed")) \cong W("smashed"))$, analogy mapping (for example, $W("man") \to W("woman")$ then $W("king") \to W("queen"))$, and even complex relationship mapping (for example, $W("Paris") \to W("France")$ then $W("Tokyo") \to W("Japan"))$ (*References* [21 and 22]).

The extension of word embedding concepts towards a generalized representation that helps us reuse the representation with various NLP problems (with minor extensions) has been the main reason for many recent successes of Deep Learning in NLP. Socher, in his research, extended the word embeddings concept to produce bilingual word embeddings, that is, embed words from two different languages, such as Chinese (Mandarin) and English into a shared space (*References* [23]). By learning two language word embeddings independently of each other and then projecting them in a same space, his work gives us interesting insights into word similarities across languages that can be extended for Machine Translation. Socher also did interesting work on projecting the images learned from CNNs with the word embedding in to the same space for associating words with images as a basic classification problem (*References* [24]). Google, around the same time, has also been working on similar concepts, but at a larger scale for word-image matching and learning (*References* [26]).

Extending the word embedding concept to have combiners or association modules that can help combine the words, words-phrases, phrases-phrases in all combinations to learn complex sentences has been the idea of Recursive Neural Networks. The following figure shows how complex association *((the cat)(sat(on (the mat))))* can be learned using Recursive Neural Networks. It also removes the constraint of a "fixed" number of inputs in neural networks because of the ability to recursively combine:

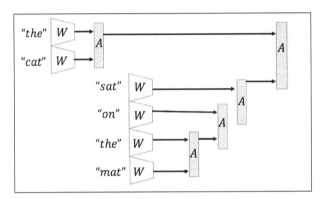

Figure 21: Recursive Neural Network showing how complex phrases can be learned.

Recursive Neural Networks have been showing great promise in NLP tasks, such as sentiment analysis, where association of one negative word at the start of many positive words has an overall negative impact on sentences, as shown in the following figure:

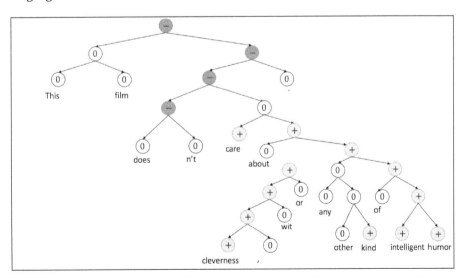

Figure 22: A complex sentence showing words with negative (as red circle), positive (green circle), and neutral (empty with 0) connected through RNN with overall negative sentiment.

The concept of recursive neural networks is now extended using the building blocks of encoders and decoders to learn reversible sentence representation—that is, reconstructing the original sentence with roughly the same meaning from the input sentence (*References* [27]). This has become the central core theme behind Neural Machine Translation. Modeling conversations using the encoder-decoder framework of RNNs has also made huge breakthroughs (*References* [28]).

Tools and usage

We will now discuss some of the most well-known tools and libraries in Java that are used in various NLP and text mining applications.

Mallet

Mallet is a Machine Learning toolkit for text written in Java, which comes with several natural language processing libraries, including those some for document classification, sequence tagging, and topic modeling, as well as various Machine Learning algorithms. It is open source, released under CPL. Mallet exposes an extensive API (see the following screenshots) to create and configure sequences of "pipes" for pre-processing, vectorizing, feature selection, and so on, as well as to extend implementations of classification and clustering algorithms, plus a host of other text analytics and Machine Learning capabilities.

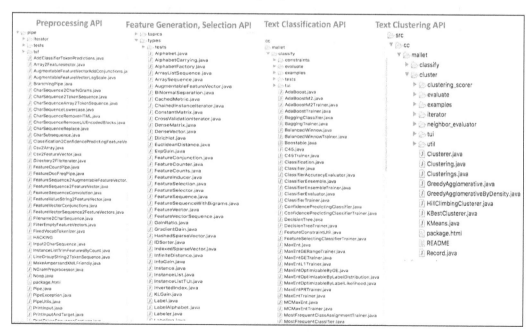

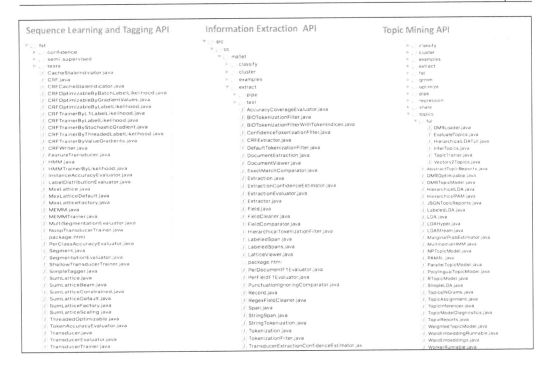

KNIME

KNIME is an open platform for analytics with Open GL licensing with a number of powerful tools for conducting all aspects of data science. The Text Processing module is available for separate download from KNIME Labs. KNIME has an intuitive drag and drop UI with downloadable examples available from their workflow server.

KNIME: https://www.knime.org/
KNIME Labs: https://tech.knime.org/knime-text-processing

The platform includes a Node repository that contains all the necessary tools to compose your workflow with a convenient nesting of nodes that can easily be reused by copying and pasting. The execution of the workflows is simple. Debugging errors can take some getting used to, so our recommendation is to take the text mining example, use a different dataset as input, and make the workflow execute without errors. This is the quickest way to get familiar with the platform.

Topic modeling with mallet

We will now illustrate the usage of API and Java code to implement Topic Modeling to give the user an illustration on how to build a text learning pipeline for a problem in Java:

```
//create pipeline
ArrayList<Pipe> pipeList = new ArrayList<Pipe>();
  // Pipes: lowercase, tokenize, remove stopwords, map to features
pipeList.add( new CharSequenceLowercase() );
pipeList.add( new CharSequence2TokenSequence(Pattern.compile("\\p{L}
[\\p{L}\\p{P}]+\\p{L}")) );
pipeList.add( new TokenSequenceRemoveStopwords(new File("stopReuters/
en.txt"), "UTF-8", false, false, false) );
//add all
pipeList.add( new TokenSequence2FeatureSequence() );
InstanceList instances = new InstanceList (new SerialPipes(pipeList));
//read the file
Reader fileReader = new InputStreamReader(new FileInputStream(new
File(reutersFile)), "UTF-8");
instances.addThruPipe(new CsvIterator (fileReader, Pattern.
compile("^(\\S*)[\\s,]*(\\S*)[\\s,]*(.*)$"),
3, 2, 1)); // name fields, data, label
```

ParallelTopicModel in Mallet has an API with parameters such as the number of topics, alpha, and beta that control the underlying parameter for tuning the LDA using Dirichlet distribution. Parallelization is very well supported, as seen by the increased number of threads available in the system:

```
ParallelTopicModel model = new ParallelTopicModel(10, 1.0, 0.01);//10
topics using LDA method
model.addInstances(instances);//add instances
model.setNumThreads(3);//parallelize with threading
model.setNumIterations(1000);//gibbs sampling iterations
model.estimate();//perform estimation of probability
```

Topic and term association is shown in the following screenshot as the result of running the ParallelTopicModel in Mallet. Clearly, the top terms and association of the topics are very well discovered in many cases, such as the classes of exec, acq, wheat, crude, corn, and earning:

Topic (class)	Probability	Terms(Weights)
0(exc)	0.091	bank (1990) pct (1540) market (1250) rate (1093) rates (897) mln (852) stg (723) money (676) banks (626) billion (622)
1(exc)	0.097	trade (1733) u.s (1718) japan (1017) japanese (695) dollar (681) foreign (583) told (522) economic (485) exchange (479) government (462)
2(acq)	0.229	cts (4879) mln (4855) net (4802) loss (4271) shr (4024) dlrs (2684) march (2405) revs (2321) qtr (2307) profit (2264)
3	0.120	shares (1576) pct (1135) stock (1083) offer (1050) company (1010) dlrs (993) march (798) share (795) group (673) common (626)
4(wheat)	0.065	tonnes (2104) mln (1721) wheat (1298) corn (720) u.s (647) grain (568) pct (532) march (528) april (463) export (432)
5	0.041	u.s (466) gulf (437) oil (361) iran (249) iranian (246) march (201) shipping (188) ships (181) strike (167) spokesman (164)
6(crude)	0.050	oil (2082) crude (579) mln (499) prices (489) gas (470) dlrs (466) opec (408) bpd (385) barrels (354) production (340)
7(corn)	0.046	u.s (918) wheat (472) farm (391) trade (356) washington (341) corn (340) bill (330) agriculture (327) march (289) program (254)
8(earning)	0.121	mln (3374) dlrs (2395) billion (1883) year (1639) pct (1553) company (870) quarter (770) earnings (666) march (663) share (569)
9(acq)	0.139	mln (1055) company (946) march (878) corp (871) dlrs (796) sale (508) sell (421) unit (407) acquisition (391) agreement (377)

Business problem

The Reuters corpus labels each document with one of 10 categories. The aim of the experiments in this case study is to employ the techniques of text processing learned in this chapter to give structure to these documents using vector space modeling. This is done in three different ways, and four classification algorithms are used to train and make predictions using the transformed dataset in each of the three cases. The open source Java analytics platform KNIME was used for text processing and learning.

Machine Learning mapping

Among the learning techniques for unstructured data, such as text or images, classification of the data into different categories given a training set with labels is a supervised learning problem. However, since the data is unstructured, some statistical or information theoretic means are necessary to extract learnable features from the data. In the design of this study, we performed feature representation and selection on the documents before using linear, non-linear, and ensemble methods for classification.

Data collection

The dataset used in the experiments is a version of the Reuters-21578 Distribution 1.0 Text Categorization Dataset available from the UCI Machine Learning Repository:

Reuters-21578 dataset: `https://archive.ics.uci.edu/ml/ datasets/Reuters-21578+Text+Categorization+Collection`

This dataset is a Modified-Apte split containing 9,981 documents, each with a class label indicating the category of the document. There are 10 distinct categories in the dataset.

Data sampling and transformation

After importing the data file, we performed a series of pre-processing steps in order to enrich and transform the data before training any models on the documents. These steps can be seen in the screenshot of the workflow created in KNIME. They include:

- Punctuation erasure
- N char filtering (removes tokens less than four characters in length)
- Number filtering
- Case conversion – convert all to lower case
- Stop word filtering
- Stemming

Prior to the learning step, we sampled the data randomly into a 70-30 split for training and testing, respectively. We used five-fold cross-validation in each experiment.

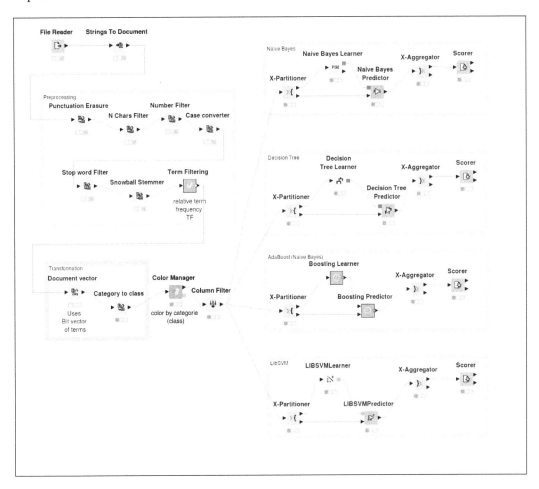

The preceding screenshot shows the workflow for the first experiment set, which uses a binary vector of features. Data import is followed by a series of pre processing nodes, after which the dataset is transformed into a document vector. After adding back the target vector, the workflow branches out into four classification tasks, each using a five-fold cross-validation setup. Results are gathered in the Scorer node.

Feature analysis and dimensionality reduction

We conducted three sets of experiments in total. In the first set, after pre processing, we used binary vectorization of the terms, which adds a representation indicating whether or not a term appeared in the document:

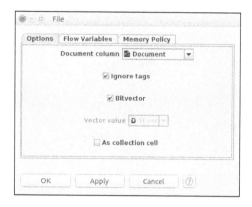 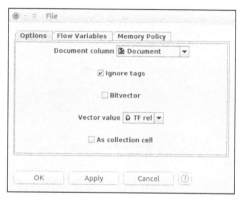

In the second experiment, we used the values for relative **Term Frequency (TF)** for each term, resulting in a value between 0 and 1.

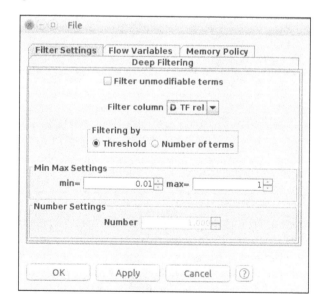

In the third, we performed feature selection by filtering out terms that had a relative TF score of less than 0.01.

Models, results, and evaluation

For each of the three sets of experiments, we used two linear classifiers (naïve Bayes and SVM using linear kernel) and two non-linear classifiers (Decision Tree and AdaBoost with Naïve Bayes as base learner). In text mining classification, precision/recall metrics are generally chosen as the evaluation metric over accuracy, which is more common in traditional, balanced classification problems.

The results from the three sets of experiments are given in the tables. Scores are averages over all the classes:

Binary Term Vector:

Classifier	Recall	Precision	Sensitivity	Specificity	F-measure	Accuracy	Cohen's kappa
Naïve Bayes	0.5079	0.5281	0.5079	0.9634	0.5087	0.7063	0.6122
Decision Tree	0.4989	0.5042	0.4989	0.9518	0.5013	0.7427(2)	0.6637(2)
AdaBoost(NB)	0.5118(2)	0.5444(2)	0.5118(2)	0.9665(2)	0.5219(2)	0.7285	0.6425
LibSVM	0.6032(1)	0.5633(1)	0.6032(1)	0.9808(1)	0.5768(1)	0.8290(1)	0.7766(1)

Relative TF vector:

Classifier	Recall	Precision	Sensitivity	Specificity	F-measure	Accuracy	Cohen's kappa
Naïve Bayes	0.4853	0.5480(2)	0.4853	0.9641	0.5113(2)	0.7248	0.6292
Decision Tree	0.4947(2)	0.4954	0.4947(2)	0.9703(2)	0.4950	0.7403(2)	0.6612(2)
AdaBoost(NB)	0.4668	0.5326	0.4668	0.9669	0.4842	0.6963	0.6125
LibSVM	0.6559(1)	0.6651(1)	0.6559(1)	0.9824(1)	0.6224(1)	0.8433(1)	0.7962(1)

Relative TF vector with threshold filtering (rel TF > 0.01):

Classifier	Recall	Precision	Sensitivity	Specificity	F-measure	Accuracy	Cohen's kappa
Naïve Bayes	0.4689	0.5456(2)	0.4689	0.9622	0.4988	0.7133	0.6117
Decision Tree	0.5008(2)	0.5042	0.5008(2)	0.9706(2)	0.5022(2)	0.7439(2)	0.6657(2)
AdaBoost(NB)	0.4435	0.4992	0.4435	0.9617	0.4598	0.6870	0.5874
LibSVM	0.6438(1)	0.6326(1)	0.6438(1)	0.9810(1)	0.6118(1)	0.8313(1)	0.7806(1)

Analysis of text processing results

The analysis of results obtained from our experiments on the Reuters dataset is presented here with some key observations:

- As seen in the first table, with the binary representation of terms, Naïve Bayes scores around 0.7, which indicates that the features generated have good discriminating power. AdaBoost on the same configuration of Naïve Bayes further improves all the metrics, such as precision, recall, F1-measure, and accuracy, by about 2%, indicating the advantage of boosting and meta-learning.

- As seen in the first table, non-linear classifiers, such as Decision Tree, do only marginally better than linear Naïve Bayes in most metrics. SVM with a linear classifier increases accuracy by 17% over linear Naïve Bayes and has better metrics similarly in almost all measures. SVM and kernels, which have no issues with higher dimensional data, the curse of text classification, are thus one of the better algorithms for modeling, and the results confirm this.

- Changing the representation from binary to TF improves many measures, such as accuracy, for linear Naïve Bayes (from 0.70 to 0.72) and SVM (0.82 to 0.84). This indeed confirms that TF-based representation in many numeric-based algorithms, such as SVM. AdaBoost performance with Naïve Bayes drops in most metrics when the underlying classifier Bayes gets stronger in performance, as shown in many theoretical and empirical results.

- Finally, by reducing features using threshold TF > 0.01, as used here, we get almost similar or somewhat reduced performance in most classifiers, indicating that although certain terms seem rare, they have discriminating power, and reducing them has a negative impact.

Summary

A large proportion of information in the digital world is textual. Text mining and NLP are areas concerned with extracting information from this unstructured form of data. Several important sub areas in the field are active topics of research today and an understanding of these areas is essential for data scientists.

Text categorization is concerned with classifying documents into pre-determined categories. Text may be enriched by annotating words, as with POS tagging, in order to give it more structure for subsequent processing tasks to act on. Unsupervised techniques such as clustering can be applied to documents as well. Information extraction and named entity recognition help identify information-rich specifics such as location, person or organization name, and so on. Summarization is another important application for producing concise abstracts of larger documents or sets of documents. Various ambiguities of language and semantics such as context, word sense, and reasoning make the tasks of NLP challenging.

Transformations of the contents of text include tokenization, stop words removal, and word stemming, all of which prepare the corpus by standardizing the content so Machine Learning techniques can be applied productively. Next, lexical, semantic, and syntactic features are extracted so numerical values can represent the document structure more conventionally with a vector space model. Similarity and distance measures can then be applied to effectively compare documents for sameness. Dimensionality reduction is key due to the large number of features that are typically present. The details of the techniques for topic modeling, PLSA and text clustering, and named entity recognition are described in this chapter. Finally, the recent techniques employing deep learning in various fields of NLP are introduced to the readers.

Mallet and KNIME are two open source Java-based tools that provide powerful NLP and Machine Learning capabilities. The case study examines performance of different classifiers on the Reuters corpus using KNIME.

References

1. J. B. Lovins (1968). *Development of a stemming algorithm*, Mechanical Translation and Computer Linguistic, vol.11, no.1/2, pp. 22-31.

2. Porter M.F, (1980). *An algorithm for suffix stripping*, Program; 14, 130-137.

3. ZIPF, H.P., (1949). *Human Behaviour and the Principle of Least Effort*, Addison-Wesley, Cambridge, Massachusetts.

4. LUHN, H.P., (1958). *The automatic creation of literature abstracts'*, IBM Journal of Research and Development, 2, 159-165.

5. Deerwester, S., Dumais, S., Furnas, G., & Landauer, T. (1990), *Indexing by latent semantic analysis*, Journal of the American Society for Information Sciences, 41, 391–407.

6. Dempster, A. P., Laird, N. M., & Rubin, D. B. (1977), *Maximum likelihood from incomplete data via the EM algorithm*. Journal of the Royal Statistic Society, Series B, 39(1), 1–38.

7. Greiff, W. R. (1998). *A theory of term weighting based on exploratory data analysis.* In 21st Annual International ACM SIGIR Conference on Research and Development in Information Retrieval, New York, NY. ACM.

8. P. F. Brown, P. V. deSouza, R. L. Mercer, V. J. Della Pietra, and J/ C. Lai (1992), *Class-based n-gram models of natural language,* Computational Linguistics, 18, 4, 467-479.

9. T. Liu, S. Lin, Z. Chen, W.-Y. Ma (2003), *An Evaluation on Feature Selection for Text Clustering,* ICML Conference.

10. Y. Yang, J. O. Pederson (1995). *A comparative study on feature selection in text categorization,* ACM SIGIR Conference.

11. Salton, G. & Buckley, C. (1998). *Term weighting approaches in automatic text retrieval.* Information Processing & Management, 24(5), 513–523.

12. Hofmann, T. (2001). *Unsupervised learning by probabilistic latent semantic analysis.* Machine Learning Journal, 41(1), 177–196.

13. D. Blei, J. Lafferty (2006). *Dynamic topic models.* ICML Conference.

14. D. Blei, A. Ng, M. Jordan (2003). *Latent Dirichlet allocation,* Journal of Machine Learning Research, 3: pp. 993–1022.

15. W. Xu, X. Liu, and Y. Gong (2003). *Document-Clustering based on Non-negative Matrix Factorization.* Proceedings of SIGIR'03, Toronto, CA, pp. 267-273,

16. Dud´ık M. and Schapire (2006). R. E. *Maximum entropy distribution estimation with generalized regularization.* In Lugosi, G. and Simon, H. (Eds.), COLT, Berlin, pp. 123–138, Springer-Verlag,.

17. McCallum, A., Freitag, D., and Pereira, F. C. N. (2000). *Maximum Entropy Markov Models for Information Extraction and Segmentation.* In ICML, pp. 591–598..

18. Langville, A. N, Meyer, C. D., Albright, R. (2006). *Initializations for the Nonnegative Factorization.* KDD, Philadelphia, USA

19. Dunning, T. (1993). *Accurate Methods for the Statistics of Surprise and Coincidence. Computational Linguistics,* 19, 1, pp. 61-74.

20. Y. Bengio, R. Ducharme, P. Vincent and C. Jauvin (2003). *A Neural Probabilistic Language Model.* Journal of Machine Learning Research.

21. R. Collobert, J. Weston, L. Bottou, M. Karlen, K. Kavukcuoglu, and P. Kuksa. (2011). *Natural language processing (almost) from scratch.* Journal of Machine Learning Research, 12:2493–2537.

22. T. Mikolov, K. Chen, G. Corrado and J. Dean (2013). *Efficient Estimation of Word Representations in Vector Space.* arXiv:1301.3781v1.

23. R. Socher, Christopher Manning, and Andrew Ng. (2010). *Learning continuous phrase representations and syntactic parsing with recursive neural networks*. In NIPS 2010 Workshop on Deep Learning and Unsupervised Feature Learning.

24. R. Socher, J. Pennington, E. H. Huang, A. Y. Ng, and C. D. Manning. (2011). *Semi-supervised recursive autoencoders for predicting sentiment distributions*. In EMNLP.

25. M. Luong, R. Socher and C. Manning (2013). *Better word representations with recursive neural networks for morphology*. CONLL.

26. A. Frome, G. S. Corrado, J. Shlens, S. Bengio, J. Dean, T. Mikolov, et al (2013). *Devise: A deep visual-semantic embedding model*. In NIPS Proceedings.

27. Léon Bottou (2011). From Machine Learning to Machine Reasoning. `https://arxiv.org/pdf/1102.1808v3.pdf`.

28. Cho, Kyunghyun, et al (2014). *Learning phrase representations using rnn encoder-decoder for statistical machine translation*. arXiv preprint arXiv:1406.1078.

Big Data Machine Learning –
The Final Frontier

In recent years, we have seen an exponential growth in data generated by humans and machines. Varied sources, including home sensors, healthcare-related monitoring devices, news feeds, conversations on social media, images, and worldwide commerce transactions — an endless list — contribute to the vast volumes of data generated every day.

Facebook had 1.28 billion daily active users in March 2017 sharing close to four million pieces of unstructured information as text, images, URLs, news, and videos (Source: Facebook). 1.3 billion Twitter users share approximately 500 million tweets a day (Source: Twitter). **Internet of Things (IoT)** sensors in lights, thermostats, sensor in cars, watches, smart devices, and so on, will grow from 50 billion to 200 billion by 2020 (Source: IDC estimates). YouTube users upload 300 hours of new video content every five minutes. Netflix has 30 million viewers who stream 77,000 hours of video daily. Amazon has sold approximately 480 million products and has approximately 244 million customers. In the financial sector, the volume of transactional data generated by even a single large institution is enormous — approximately 25 million households in the US have Bank of America, a major financial institution, as their primary bank, and together produce petabytes of data annually. Overall, it is estimated that the global Big Data industry will be worth 43 billion US dollars in 2017 (Source: www.statista.com).

Each of the aforementioned companies and many more like them face the real problem of storing all this data (structured and unstructured), processing the data, and learning hidden patterns from the data to increase their revenue and to improve customer satisfaction. We will explore how current methods, tools and technology can help us learn from data in Big Data-scale environments and how as practitioners in the field we must recognize challenges unique to this problem space.

This chapter has the following structure:

- What are the characteristics of Big Data?
- Big Data Machine Learning
  - ° General Big Data Framework:
    - ° Big data cluster deployments frameworks
    - ° HortonWorks Data Platform (HDP)
    - ° Cloudera CDH
    - ° Amazon Elastic MapReduce (EMR)
    - ° Microsoft HDInsight
  - ° Data acquisition:
    - ° Publish-subscribe framework
    - ° Source-sink framework
    - ° SQL framework
    - ° Message queueing framework
    - ° Custom framework
  - ° Data storage:
    - ° Hadoop Distributed File System (HDFS)
    - ° NoSQL
  - ° Data processing and preparation:
    - ° Hive and Hive Query Language (HQL)
    - ° Spark SQL
    - ° Amazon Redshift
    - ° Real-time stream processing
  - ° Machine Learning
  - ° Visualization and analysis
- Batch Big Data Machine Learning
  - ° H2O:
  - ° H2O architecture
    - ° Machine learning in H2O
    - ° Tools and usage
    - ° Case study

- ° Business problems
- ° Machine Learning mapping
- ° Data collection
- ° Data sampling and transformation
- ° Experiments, results, and analysis
  - ° Spark MLlib:
    - ° Spark architecture
    - ° Machine Learning in MLlib
    - ° Tools and usage
    - ° Experiments, results, and analysis

- Real-time Big Data Machine Learning
  - ° Scalable Advanced Massive Online Analysis (SAMOA):
    - ° SAMOA architecture
    - ° Machine Learning algorithms
    - ° Tools and usage
    - ° Experiments, results, and analysis
    - ° The future of Machine Learning

What are the characteristics of Big Data?

There are many characteristics of Big Data that are different than normal data. Here we highlight them as four *V*s that characterize Big Data. Each of these makes it necessary to use specialized tools, frameworks, and algorithms for data acquisition, storage, processing, and analytics:

- **Volume**: One of the characteristic of Big Data is the size of the content, structured or unstructured, which doesn't fit the storage capacity or processing power available on a single machine and therefore needs multiple machines.
- **Velocity**: Another characteristic of Big Data is the rate at which the content is generated, which contributes to volume but needs to be handled in a time sensitive manner. Social media content and IoT sensor information are the best examples of high velocity Big Data.

- **Variety**: This generally refers to multiple formats in which data exists, that is, structured, semi-structured, and unstructured and furthermore, each of them has different forms. Social media content with images, video, audio, text, and structured information about activities, background, networks, and so on, is the best example of where data from various sources must be analyzed.

- **Veracity**: This refers to a wide variety of factors such as noise, uncertainty, biases, and abnormality in the data that must be addressed, especially given the volume, velocity, and variety of data. One of the key steps, as we will discuss in the context of Big Data Machine Learning, is processing and cleaning such "unclean" data.

Many have added other characteristics such as value, validity, and volatility to the preceding list, but we believe they are largely derived from the previous four.

Big Data Machine Learning

In this section, we will discuss the general flow and components that are required for Big Data Machine Learning. Although many of the components, such as data acquisition or storage, are not directly related to Machine Learning methodologies, they inevitably have an impact on the frameworks and processes. Giving a complete catalog of the available components and tools is beyond the scope of this book, but we will discuss the general responsibilities of the tasks involved and give some information on the techniques and tools available to accomplish them.

General Big Data framework

The general Big Data framework is illustrated in the following figure:

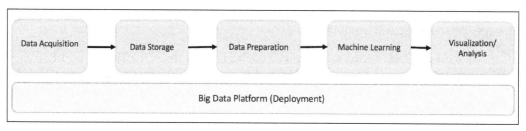

Figure 1: Big data framework

The choice of how the Big Data framework is set up and deployed in the cluster is one of the decisions that affects the choice of tools, techniques, and cost. The data acquisition or collection component is the first step and it consists of several techniques, both synchronous and asynchronous, to absorb data into the system. Various techniques ranging from publish-subscribe, source-sink, relational database queries, and custom data connectors are available in the components.

Data storage choices ranging from distributed filesystems such as HDFS to non-relational databases (NoSQL) are available based on various other functional requirements. NoSQL databases are described in the section on *Data Storage*.

Data preparation, or transforming the large volume of stored data so that it is consumable by the Machine Learning analytics, is an important processing step. This has some dependencies on the frameworks, techniques, and tools used in storage. It also has some dependency on the next step: the choice of Machine Learning analytics/frameworks that will be used. There are a wide range of choices for processing frameworks that will be discussed in the following sub-section.

Recall that, in batch learning, the model is trained simultaneously on a number of examples that have been previously collected. In contrast to batch learning, in real-time learning model training is continuous, each new instance that arrives becoming part of a dynamic training set. See *Chapter 5, Real-Time Stream Machine Learning* for details. Once the data is collected, stored, and transformed based on the domain requirements, different Machine Learning methodologies can be employed, including batch learning, real-time learning, and batch-real-time mixed learning. Whether one selects supervised learning, unsupervised learning, or a combination of the two also depends on the data, the availability of labels, and label quality. These will be discussed in detail later in this chapter.

The results of analytics during the development stage as well as the production or runtime stage also need to be stored and visualized for humans and automated tasks.

Big Data cluster deployment frameworks

There are many frameworks that are built on the core Hadoop (*References* [3]) open source platform. Each of them provides a number of tools for the Big Data components described previously.

Hortonworks Data Platform

Hortonworks Data Platform (HDP) provides an open source distribution comprising various components in its stack, from data acquisition to visualization. Apache Ambari is often the user interface used for managing services and provisioning and monitoring clusters. The following screenshot depicts Ambari used for configuring various services and the health-check dashboard:

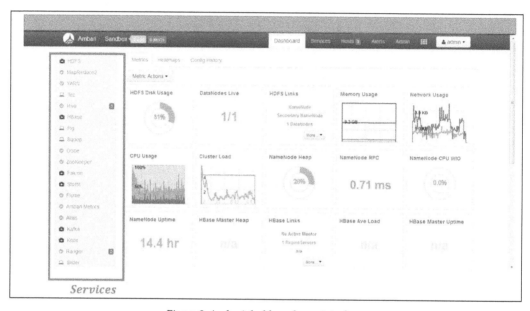

Figure 2: Ambari dashboard user interface

Cloudera CDH

Like HDP, Cloudera CDH (*References* [4]) provides similar services and Cloudera Services Manager can be used in a similar way to Ambari for cluster management and health checks, as shown in the following screenshot:

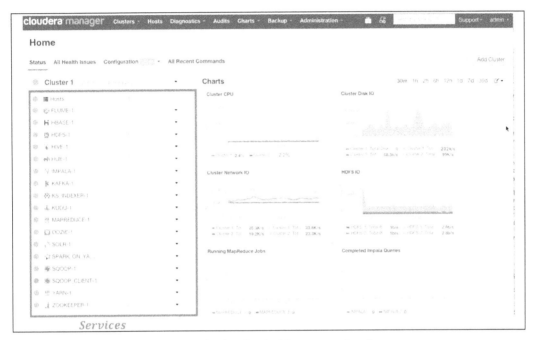

Figure 3: Cloudera Service Manager user interface

Amazon Elastic MapReduce

Amazon Elastic MapReduce (EMR) (*References* [5]) is another Big Data cluster, platform similar to HDP and Cloudera, which supports a wide variety of frameworks. EMR has two modes — **cluster mode** and **step execution mode**. In cluster mode, you choose the Big Data stack vendor EMR or MapR and in step execution mode, you give jobs ranging from JARs to SQL queries for execution. In the following screenshot, we see the interface for configuring a new cluster as well as defining a new job flow:

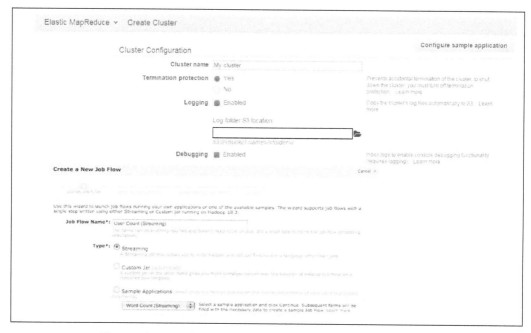

Figure 4: Amazon Elastic MapReduce cluster management user interface

Microsoft Azure HDInsight

Microsoft Azure HDInsight (*References* [6]) is another platform that allows cluster management with most of the services that are required, including storage, processing, and Machine Learning. The Azure portal, as shown in the following screenshot, is used to create, manage, and help in learning the statuses of the various components of the cluster:

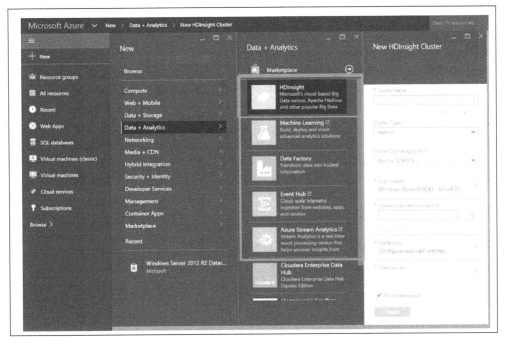

Figure 5: Microsoft Azure HDInsight cluster management user interface

Data acquisition

In the Big Data framework, the acquisition component plays an important role in collecting the data from disparate source systems and storing it in Big Data storage. Based on types of source and volume, velocity, functional, and performance-based requirements, there are a wide variety of acquisition frameworks and tools. We will describe a few of the most well-known frameworks and tools used to give readers some insight.

Publish-subscribe frameworks

In publish-subscribe based frameworks, the publishing source pushes the data in different formats to the broker, which has different subscribers waiting to consume them. The publisher and subscriber are unaware of each other, with the broker mediating in between.

Apache Kafka (*References* [9]) and **Amazon Kinesis** are two well-known implementations that are based on this model. Apache Kafka defines the concepts of publishers, consumers, and topics—on which things get published and consumed— and a broker to manage the topics. Amazon Kinesis is built on similar concepts with producers and consumers connected through Kinesis streams, which are similar to topics in Kafka.

Source-sink frameworks

In source-sink models, sources push the data into the framework and the framework pushes the system to the sinks. Apache Flume (*References* [7]) is a well-known implementation of this kind of framework with a variety of sources, channels to buffer the data, and a number of sinks to store the data in the Big Data world.

SQL frameworks

Since many traditional data stores are in the form of SQL-based RDBMS, SQL-based frameworks provide a generic way to import the data from RDBMS and store it in Big Data, mainly in the HDFS format. Apache Sqoop (*References* [10]) is a well-known implementation that can import data from any JDBC-based RDBMS and store it in HDFS-based systems.

Message queueing frameworks

Message queueing frameworks are push-pull based frameworks similar to publisher-subscriber systems. Message queues separate the producers and consumers and can store the data in the queue, in an asynchronous communication pattern. Many protocols have been developed on this such as Advanced Message Queueing Protocol (AMQP) and ZeroMQ Message Transfer Protocol (ZMTP). RabbitMQ, ZeroMQ, Amazon SQS, and so on, are some well-known implementations of this framework.

Custom frameworks

Specialized connectors for different sources such as IoT, HTTP, WebSockets, and so on, have resulted in many specific connectors such as Amazon IoT Hub, REST-connectors, WebSocket, and so on.

Data storage

The data storage component plays a key part in connecting the acquisition and the rest of the components together. Performance, impact on data processing, cost, high-availability, ease of management, and so on, should be taken into consideration while deciding on data storage. For pure real-time or near real-time systems there are in-memory based frameworks for storage, but for batch-based systems there are mainly distributed File Systems such as HDFS or NoSQL.

HDFS

HDFS can run on a large cluster of nodes and provide all the important features such as high-throughput, replications, fail-over, and so on.

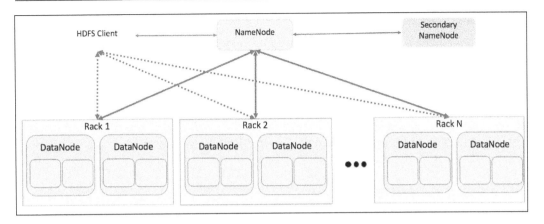

The basic architecture of HDFS has the following components:

- **NameNode**: The HDFS client always sends the request to the NameNode, which keeps the metadata of the file while the real data is distributed in blocks on the DataNodes. NameNodes are only responsible for handling opening and closing a file while the remaining interactions of reading, writing, and appending happen between clients and the data nodes. The NameNode stores the metadata in two files: `fsimage` and `edit` files. The `fsimage` contains the filesystem metadata as a snapshot, while edit files contain the incremental changes to the metadata.

- **Secondary NameNode**: Secondary NameNode provides redundancy to the metadata in the NameNode by keeping a copy of the `fsimage` and `edit` files at every predefined checkpoint.

- **DataNode**: DataNodes manage the actual blocks of data and facilitate read-write operation on these datablocks. DataNodes keep communicating with the NameNodes using heartbeat signals indicating they are alive. The data blocks stored in DataNodes are also replicated for redundancy. Replication of the data blocks in the DataNodes is governed by the rack-aware placement policy.

NoSQL

Non-relational databases, also referred to as NoSQL databases, are gaining enormous popularity in the Big Data world. High throughput, better horizontal scaling, improved performance on retrieval, and storage at the cost of weaker consistency models are notable characteristics of most NoSQL databases. We will discuss some important forms of NoSQL database in this section along with implementations.

Key-value databases

Key-value databases are the most prominent NoSQL databases used mostly for semi-structured or unstructured data. As the name suggests, the structure of storage is quite basic, with unique keys associating the data values that can be of any type including string, integer, double precision, and so on—even BLOBS. Hashing the keys for quick lookup and retrieval of the values together with partitioning the data across multiple nodes gives high throughput and scalability. The query capabilities are very limited. Amazon DynamoDB, Oracle NoSQL, MemcacheDB, and so on, are examples of key-value databases.

Document databases

Document databases store semi-structured data in the form of XML, JSON, or YAML documents, to name some of the most popular formats. The documents have unique keys to which they are mapped. Though it is possible to store documents in key-value stores, the query capabilities offered by document stores are greater as the primitives making up the structure of the document—which may include names or attributes—can also be used for retrieval. When the data is ever-changing and has variable numbers or lengths of fields, document databases are often a good choice. Document databases do not offer join capabilities and hence all information needs to be captured in the document values. MongoDB, ElasticSearch, Apache Solr, and so on, are some well-known implementations of document databases.

Columnar databases

The use of columns as the basic unit of storage with name, value, and often timestamp, differentiates columnar databases from traditional relational databases. Columns are further combined to form column families. A row is indexed by the row key and has multiple column families associated with the row. Certain rows can use only column families that are populated, giving it a good storage representation in sparse data. Columnar databases do not have fixed schema-like relational databases; new columns and families can be added at any time, giving them a significant advantage. **HBase, Cassandra**, and **Parquet** are some well-known implementations of columnar databases.

Graph databases

In many applications, the data has an inherent graph structure with nodes and links. Storing such data in graph databases makes it more efficient for storage, retrieval, and queries. The nodes have a set of attributes and generally represent entities, while links represent relationships between the nodes that can be directed or undirected. **Neo4J, OrientDB**, and **ArangoDB** are some well-known implementations of graph databases.

Data processing and preparation

The data preparation step involves various preprocessing steps before the data is ready to be consumed by analytics and machine learning algorithms. Some of the key tasks involved are:

- **Data cleansing**: Involves everything from correcting errors, type matching, normalization of elements, and so on, on the raw data.

- **Data scraping and curating**: Converting data elements and normalizing the data from one structure to another.

- **Data transformation**: Many analytical algorithms need features that are aggregates built on raw or historical data. Transforming and computing those extra features are done in this step.

Hive and HQL

Apache Hive (*References* [11]) is a powerful tool for performing various data preparation activities in HDFS systems. Hive organizes the underlying HDFS data a of structure that is similar to relational databases. HQL is like SQL and helps in performing various aggregates, transformations, cleanup, and normalization, and the data is then serialized back to HDFS. The logical tables in Hive are partitioned across and sub-divided into buckets for speed-up. Complex joins and aggregate queries in Hive are automatically converted into MapReduce jobs for throughput and speed-up.

Spark SQL

Spark SQL, which is a major component of Apache Spark (*References* [1] and [2]), provides SQL-like functionality — similar to what HQL provides — for performing changes to the Big Data. Spark SQL can work with underlying data storage systems such as Hive or NoSQL databases such as Parquet. We will touch upon some aspects of Spark SQL in the section on Spark later.

Amazon Redshift

Amazon Redshift provides several warehousing capabilities especially on Amazon EMR setups. It can process petabytes of data using its **massively parallel processing (MPP)** data warehouse architecture.

Real-time stream processing

In many Big Data deployments, processing and performing the transformations specified previously must be done on the stream of data in real time rather than from stored batch data. There are various **Stream Processing Engines** (**SPE**) such as Apache Storm (*References* [12]) and Apache Samza, and in-memory processing engines such as Spark-Streaming that are used for stream processing.

Machine Learning

Machine learning helps to perform descriptive, predictive, and prescriptive analysis on Big Data. There are two broad extremes that will be covered in this chapter:

- Machine learning can be done on batch historical data and then the learning/models can be applied to new batch/real-time data
- Machine learning can be done on real-time data and applied simultaneously to the real-time data

Both topics are covered at length in the remainder of this chapter.

Visualization and analysis

With batch learning done at modeling time and real-time learning done at runtime, predictions—the output of applying the models to new data—must be stored in some data structure and then analyzed by the users. Visualization tools and other reporting tools are frequently used to extract and present information to the users. Based on the domain and the requirements of the users, the analysis and visualization can be static, dynamic, or interactive.

Lightning is a framework for performing interactive visualizations on the Web with different binding APIs using REST for Python, R, Scala, and JavaScript languages.

Pygal and Seaborn are Python-based libraries that help in plotting all possible charts and graphs in Python for analysis, reporting, and visualizations.

Batch Big Data Machine Learning

Batch Big Data Machine Learning involves two basic steps, as discussed in *Chapter 2, Practical Approach to Real-World Supervised Learning, Chapter 3, Unsupervised Machine Learning Techniques,* and *Chapter 4, Semi-Supervised and Active Learning,* learning or training data from historical datasets and applying the learned models to unseen future data. The following figure demonstrates the two environments along with the component tasks and some technologies/frameworks that accomplish them:

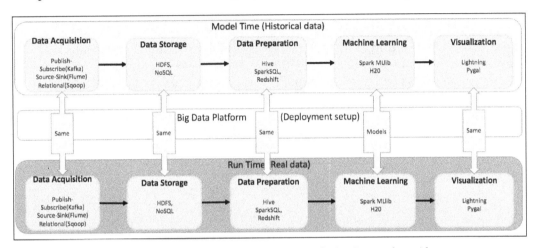

Figure 6: Model time and run time components for Big Data and providers

We will discuss two of the most well-known frameworks for doing Machine Learning in the context of batch data and will use the case study to highlight either the code or tools to perform modeling.

H2O as Big Data Machine Learning platform

H2O (*References* [13]) is a leading open source platform for Machine Learning at Big Data scale, with a focus on bringing AI to the enterprise. The company was founded in 2011 and counts several leading lights in statistical learning theory and optimization among its scientific advisors. It supports programming environments in multiple languages. While the H2O software is freely available, customer service and custom extensions to the product can be purchased.

H2O architecture

The following figure gives a high-level architecture of H2O with important components. H2O can access data from various data stores such as HDFS, SQL, NoSQL, and Amazon S3, to name a few. The most popular deployment of H2O is to use one of the deployment stacks discussed earlier with Spark or to run it in a H2O cluster itself.

The core of H2O is an optimized way of handling Big Data in memory, so that iterative algorithms that go through the same data can be handled efficiently and achieve good performance. Important Machine Learning algorithms in supervised and unsupervised learning are implemented specially to handle horizontal scalability across multiple nodes and JVMs. H2O provides not only its own user interface, known as flow, to manage and run modeling tasks, but also has different language bindings and connector APIs to Java, R, Python, and Scala.

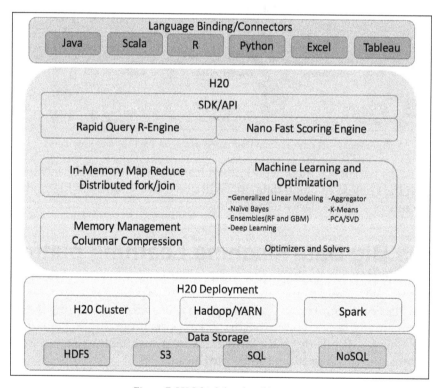

Figure 7: H2O high level architecture

Most Machine Learning algorithms, optimization algorithms, and utilities use the concept of fork-join or MapReduce. As shown in *Figure 8*, the entire dataset is considered as a **Data Frame** in H2O, and comprises vectors, which are features or columns in the dataset. The rows or instances are made up of one element from each Vector arranged side-by-side. The rows are grouped together to form a processing unit known as a **Chunk**. Several chunks are combined in one JVM. Any algorithmic or optimization work begins by sending the information from the topmost JVM to fork on to the next JVM, then on to the next, and so on, similar to the map operation in MapReduce. Each JVM works on the rows in the chunks to establish the task and finally the results flow back in the reduce operation:

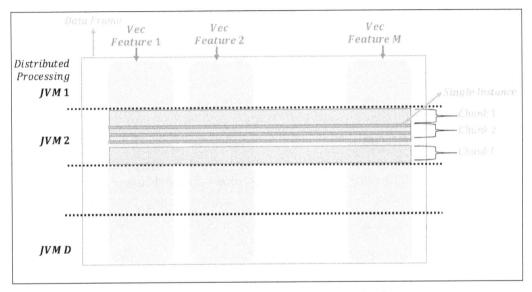

Figure 8: H2O distributed data processing using chunking

Machine learning in H2O

The following figure shows all the Machine Learning algorithms supported in H2O v3 for supervised and unsupervised learning:

Data Science Algorithms

Supervised Learning	Unsupervised Learning
Generalized Linear Modeling (GLM)	Generalized Low Rank Models (GLRM)
Gradient Boosting Machine (GBM)	K-Means Clustering
Deep Learning	Principal Components Analysis (PCA)
Distributed Random Forest	
Naive Bayes	
Ensembles (Stacking)	

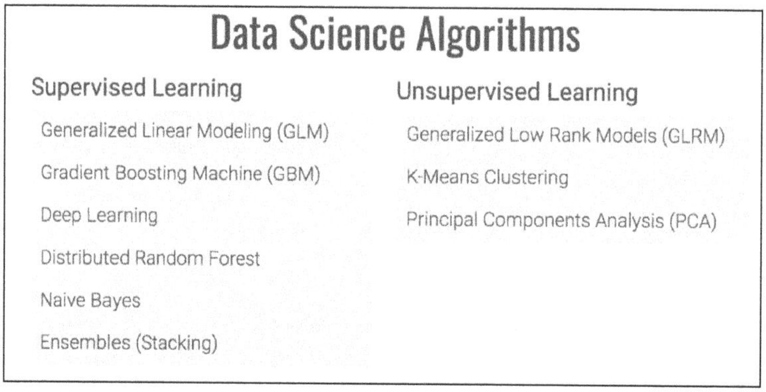

Figure 9: H2O v3 Machine learning algorithms

Tools and usage

H2O Flow is an interactive web application that helps data scientists to perform various tasks from importing data to running complex models using point and click and wizard-based concepts.

H2O is run in local mode as:

```
java -Xmx6g -jar h2o.jar
```

The default way to start Flow is to point your browser and go to the following URL: http://192.168.1.7:54321/. The right-side of Flow captures every user action performed under the tab **OUTLINE**. The actions taken can be edited and saved as named flows for reuse and collaboration, as shown in *Figure 10*:

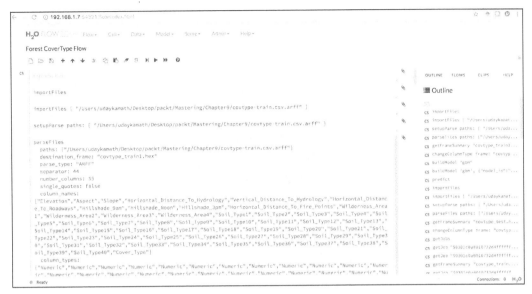

Figure 10: H2O Flow in the browser

Figure 11 shows the interface for importing files from the local filesystem or HDFS and displays detailed summary statistics as well as next actions that can be performed on the dataset. Once the data is imported, it gets a data frame reference in the H2O framework with the extension of .hex. The summary statistics are useful in understanding the characteristics of data such as **missing**, **mean**, **max**, **min**, and so on. It also has an easy way to transform the features from one type to another, for example, numeric features with a few unique values to categorical/nominal types known as enum in H2O.

The actions that can be performed on the datasets are:

1. Visualize the data.
2. Split the data into different sets such as training, validation, and testing.
3. Build supervised and unsupervised models.
4. Use the models to predict.

5. Download and export the files in various formats.

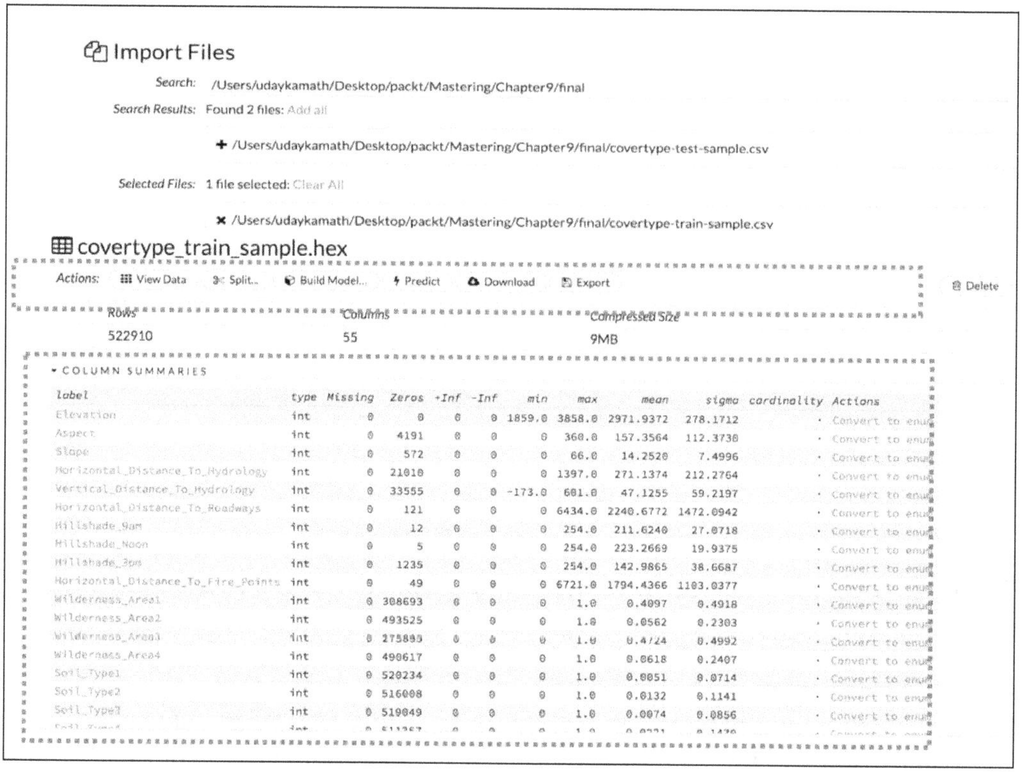

Figure 11: Importing data as frames, summarizations, and actions that can be performed

Building supervised or unsupervised models in H2O is done through an interactive screen. Every modeling algorithm has its parameters classified into three sections: basic, advanced, and expert. Any parameter that supports hyper-parameter searches for tuning the model has a checkbox grid next to it, and more than one parameter value can be used.

Some basic parameters such as **training_frame**, **validation_frame**, and **response_column**, are common to every supervised algorithm; others are specific to model types, such as the choice of solver for GLM, the activation function for deep learning, and so on. All such common parameters are available in the basic section. Advanced parameters are settings that afford greater flexibility and control to the modeler if the default behavior must be overridden. Several of these parameters are also common across some algorithms—two examples are the choice of method for assigning the fold index (if cross-validation was selected in the basic section), and selecting the column containing weights (if each example is weighted separately), and so on.

Expert parameters define more complex elements such as how to handle the missing values, model-specific parameters that need more than a basic understanding of the algorithms, and other esoteric variables. In *Figure 12*, GLM, a supervised learning algorithm, is being configured with 10-fold cross-validation, binomial (two-class) classification, efficient LBFGS optimization algorithm, and stratified sampling for cross-validation split:

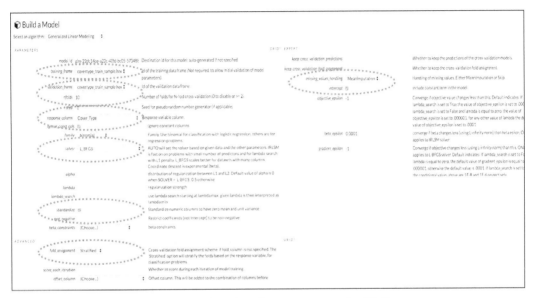

Figure 12: Modeling algorithm parameters and validations

The model results screen contains a detailed analysis of the results using important evaluation charts, depending on the validation method that was used. At the top of the screen are possible actions that can be taken, such as to run the model on unseen data for prediction, download the model as POJO format, export the results, and so on.

Some of the charts are algorithm-specific, like the scoring history that shows how the training loss or the objective function changes over the iterations in GLM—this gives the user insight into the speed of convergence as well as into the tuning of the iterations parameter. We see the ROC curves and the Area Under Curve metric on the validation data in addition to the gains and lift charts, which give the cumulative capture rate and cumulative lift over the validation sample respectively.

Figure 13 shows **SCORING HISTORY, ROC CURVE,** and **GAINS/LIFT** charts for GLM on 10-fold cross-validation on the `CoverType` dataset:

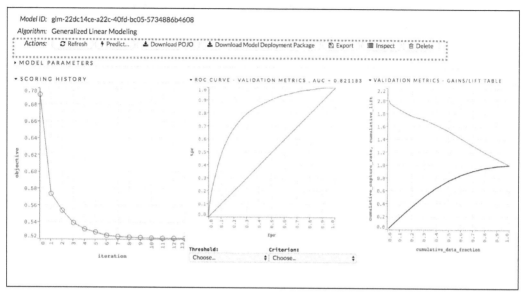

Figure 13: Modeling and validation ROC curves, objective functions, and lift/gain charts

The output of validation gives detailed evaluation measures such as accuracy, AUC, err, errors, f1 measure, MCC (Mathews Correlation Coefficient), precision, and recall for each validation fold in the case of cross-validation as well as the mean and standard deviation computed across all.

▾ OUTPUT - CROSS-VALIDATION METRICS SUMMARY

	mean	sd	cv_1_valid	cv_2_valid	cv_3_valid	cv_4_valid	cv_5_valid	cv_6_valid	cv_7_valid	cv_8_valid	cv_9_valid	c
accuracy	0.7411992	0.0020919477	0.73774326	0.7429334	0.7448235	0.7381085	0.7430922	0.7459533	0.73845685	0.7381071	0.7431965	
auc	0.8211171	0.0011226425	0.81931686	0.82393146	0.8218799	0.82080626	0.8215902	0.82210237	0.8197568	0.8186006	0.82291764	
err	0.25880077	0.0020919477	0.26225677	0.2570666	0.25517648	0.26189148	0.25690782	0.25404665	0.26154318	0.26189288	0.2568035	
err_count	13532.7	101.7846	13801.0	13487.0	13396.0	13616.0	13398.8	13372.0	13657.0	13664.0	13362.0	
f0point5	0.7140929	0.0025237158	0.70960116	0.714942	0.71712357	0.71209085	0.7179527	0.71962744	0.7101482	0.7093464	0.7170292	
f1	0.75218046	0.001344509	0.75220394	0.755657	0.7514657	0.75472856	0.7509017	0.75085706	0.7507892	0.7490542	0.753505	
f2	0.79461336	0.004883693	0.8002491	0.80128044	0.7892624	0.8027975	0.78702044	0.78492016	0.79636425	0.7934711	0.79389083	
lift_top_group	2.0038874	0.0143965315	1.9922546	2.040354	2.012063	1.9806873	1.9791358	2.0059962	1.9857894	2.0164146	2.0331407	
logloss	0.5208205	0.0013281262	0.5231053	0.51792485	0.51960087	0.5214477	0.5202888	0.5187702	0.5226515	0.52344406	0.5189758	
max_per_class_error	0.33552998	0.009792185	0.3514494	0.34064615	0.31948155	0.3546882	0.32055646	0.31096375	0.34422165	0.34093636	0.32979506	
mcc	0.49442172	0.002846507	0.4905058	0.499489	0.4993631	0.49085903	0.49499753	0.49987337	0.4906272	0.48938003	0.49720892	
mean_per_class_accuracy	0.7450862	0.0018750997	0.74219555	0.7471276	0.7485821	0.7418539	0.7462687	0.74920785	0.7428648	0.74259645	0.7467569	
mean_per_class_error	0.2549138	0.0018750997	0.25780442	0.2528724	0.25141785	0.2581461	0.25373128	0.25079215	0.25713524	0.25740358	0.2532431	
mse	0.17293216	5.2172324E-4	0.17375539	0.1715806	0.17254509	0.17318714	0.17266512	0.17245334	0.17356905	0.17399642	0.17212443	
null_deviance	72367.18	215.07042	72833.43	72612.14	72618.93	72002.8	72178.836	72816.945	72254.55	72179.43	72019.37	
precision	0.69079375	0.003936701	0.6837827	0.6901516	0.6959211	0.68624496	0.6975475	0.700212	0.6854135	0.6851335	0.6946126	
r2	0.30661532	0.0021007422	0.30340376	0.3120748	0.30770847	0.30620724	0.3077754	0.30816406	0.30394053	0.30199826	0.31000972	
recall	0.82570237	0.0066806898	0.8358405	0.83490133	0.81664586	0.83839595	0.8130939	0.8093995	0.82995117	0.82612926	0.8233089	
residual_deviance	54468.254	192.93034	55055.793	54345.855	54554.977	54221.18	54258.812	54611.98	54582.586	54620.344	54006.695	
rmse	0.4158502	6.274607E-4	0.41683978	0.41423255	0.41538548	0.4161576	0.4155299	0.415275	0.4166162	0.41712877	0.41487882	
specificity	0.66447	0.009792185	0.64855057	0.65935385	0.68051845	0.64531183	0.67944354	0.6890163	0.65577835	0.65906364	0.67020494	

Figure 14: Validation results and summary

The prediction action runs the model using unseen held-out data to estimate the out-of-sample performance. Important measures such as errors, accuracy, area under curve, ROC plots, and so on, are given as the output of predictions that can be saved or exported.

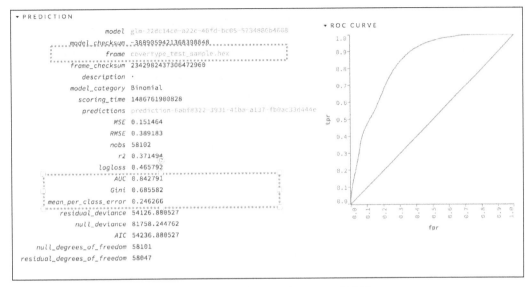

Figure 15: Running test data, predictions, and ROC curves

Case study

In this case study, we use the `CoverType` dataset to demonstrate classification and clustering algorithms from H2O, Apache Spark MLlib, and SAMOA Machine Learning libraries in Java.

Business problem

The `CoverType` dataset available from the UCI machine learning repository (`https://archive.ics.uci.edu/ml/datasets/Covertype`) contains unscaled cartographic data for 581,012 cells of forest land 30 x 30 m² in dimension, accompanied by actual forest cover type labels. In the experiments conducted here, we use the normalized version of the data. Including one-hot encoding of two categorical types, there are a total of 54 attributes in each row.

Machine Learning mapping

First, we treat the problem as one of classification using the labels included in the dataset and perform several supervised learning experiments. With the models generated, we make predictions about the forest cover type of an unseen held out test dataset. For the clustering experiments that follow, we ignore the data labels, determine the number of clusters to use, and then report the corresponding cost using various algorithms implemented in H2O and Spark MLLib.

Data collection

This dataset was collected using cartographic measurements only and no remote sensing. It was derived from data originally collected by the **US Forest Service** (**USFS**) and the **US Geological Survey** (**USGS**).

Data sampling and transformation

Train and test data — The dataset was split into two sets in the ratio 20% for testing and 80% for training.

The categorical Soil Type designation was represented by 40 binary variable attributes. A value of 1 indicates the presence of a soil type in the observation; a 0 indicates its absence.

The wilderness area designation is likewise a categorical attribute with four binary columns, with 1 indicating presence and 0 absence.

All continuous value attributes have been normalized prior to use.

Experiments, results, and analysis

In the first set of experiments in this case study, we used the H2O framework.

Feature relevance and analysis

Though H2O doesn't have explicit feature selection algorithms, many learners such as GLM, random forest, GBT, and so on, give feature importance metrics based on training/validation of the models. In our analysis, we have used GLM for feature selection, as shown in *Figure 16*. It is interesting that the feature **Elevation** emerges as the most discriminating feature along with some categorical features that are converted into numeric/binary such as **Soil_Type2**, **Soil_Type4**, and so on. Many of the soil type categorical features have no relevance and can be dropped from the modeling perspective.

Learning algorithms included in this set of experiments were: **Generalized Linear Models (GLM)**, **Gradient Boosting Machine (GBM)**, **Random Forest (RF)**, **Naïve Bayes (NB)**, and **Deep Learning (DL)**. The deep learning model supported by H2O is the **multi-layered perceptron (MLP)**.

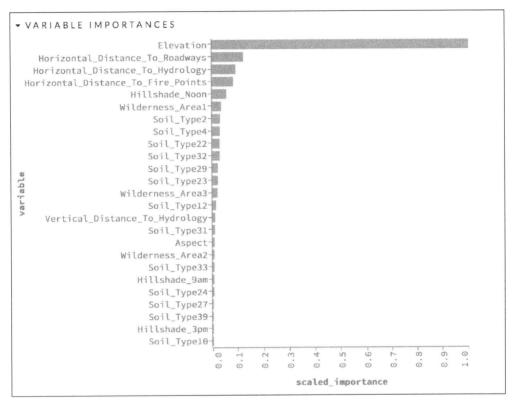

Figure 16: Feature selection using GLM

Evaluation on test data

The results using all the features are shown in the table:

Algorithm	Parameters	AUC	Max Accuracy	Max F1	Max Precision	Max Recall	Max Specificity
GLM	Default	0.84	0.79	0.84	0.98	1.0(1)	0.99
GBM	Default	0.86	0.82	0.86	1.0(1)	1.0(1)	1.0(1)
Random Forest (RF)	Default	0.88(1)	0.83(1)	0.87(1)	0.97	1.0(1)	0.99
Naïve Bayes (NB)	Laplace=50	0.66	0.72	0.81	0.68	1.0(1)	0.33

Algorithm	Parameters	AUC	Max Accuracy	Max F1	Max Precision	Max Recall	Max Specificity
Deep Learning (DL)	Rect,300, 300,Dropout	0.	0.78	0.83	0.88	1.0(1)	0.99
Deep Learning (DL)	300, 300,MaxDropout	0.82	0.8	0.84	1.0(1)	1.0(1)	1.0(1)

Table 1: Model evaluation results with all features included

The results after removing features not scoring well in feature relevance were:

Algorithm	Parameters	AUC	Max Accuracy	Max F1	Max Precision	Max Recall	Max Specificity
GLM	Default	0.84	0.80	0.85	1.0	1.0	1.0
GBM	Default	0.85	0.82	0.86	1.0	1.0	1.0
Random Forest (RF)	Default	0.88	0.83	0.87	1.0	1.0	1.0
Naïve Bayes (NB)	Laplace=50	0.76	0.74	0.81	0.89	1.0	0.95
Deep Learning (DL)	300,300, RectDropout	0.81	0.79	0.84	1.0	1.0	1.0
Deep Learning (DL)	300, 300, MaxDropout	0.85	0.80	0.84	0.89	0.90	1.0

Table 2: Model evaluation results with only relevant features included

Analysis of results

The main observations from an analysis of the results obtained are quite instructive and are presented here.

1. The feature relevance analysis shows how the **Elevation** feature is a highly discriminating feature, whereas many categorical attributes converted to binary features, such as **SoilType_10**, and so on, have near-zero to no relevance.

2. The results for experiments with all features included, shown in *Table 1*, clearly indicate that the non-linear ensemble technique Random Forest is the best algorithm as shown by the majority of the evaluation metrics including accuracy, F1, AUC, and recall.

3. *Table 1* also highlights the fact that whereas the faster, linear Naive Bayes algorithm may not be best-suited, GLM, which also falls in the category of linear algorithms, demonstrates much better performance—this points to some inter-dependence among features!

4. As we saw in *Chapter 7, Deep Learning,* algorithms used in deep learning typically need a lot of tuning; however, even with a few small tuning changes, the results from DL are comparable to Random Forest, especially with MaxDropout.

5. *Table 2* shows the results of all the algorithms after removing low-relevance features from the training set. It can be seen that Naive Bayes—which has the most impact due to multiplication of probabilities based on the assumption of independence between features—gets the most benefit and highest uplift in performance. Most of the other algorithms such as Random Forest have inbuilt feature selection as we discussed in *Chapter 2, Practical Approach to Real-World Supervised Learning,* and as a result removing the unimportant features has little or no effect on their performance.

Spark MLlib as Big Data Machine Learning platform

Apache Spark, started in 2009 at AMPLab at UC Berkley, was donated to Apache Software Foundation in 2013 under Apache License 2.0. The core idea of Spark was to build a cluster computing framework that would overcome the issues of Hadoop, especially for iterative and in-memory computations.

Spark architecture

The Spark stack as shown in *Figure 17* can use any kind of data stores such as HDFS, SQL, NoSQL, or local filesystems. It can be deployed on Hadoop, Mesos, or even standalone.

The most important component of Spark is the Spark Core, which provides a framework to handle and manipulate the data in a high-throughput, fault-tolerant, and scalable manner.

Built on top of Spark core are various libraries each meant for various functionalities needed in processing data and doing analytics in the Big Data world. Spark SQL gives us a language for performing data manipulation in Big Data stores using a querying language very much like SQL, the *lingua franca* of databases. Spark GraphX provides APIs to perform graph-related manipulations and graph-based algorithms on Big Data. Spark Streaming provides APIs to handle real-time operations needed in stream processing ranging from data manipulations to queries on the streams.

Spark-MLlib is the Machine Learning library that has an extensive set of Machine Learning algorithms to perform supervised and unsupervised tasks from feature selection to modeling. Spark has various language bindings such as Java, R, Scala, and Python. MLlib has a clear advantage running on top of the Spark engine, especially because of caching data in memory across multiple nodes and running MapReduce jobs, thus improving performance as compared to Mahout and other large-scale Machine Learning engines by a significant factor. MLlib also has other advantages such as fault tolerance and scalability without explicitly managing it in the Machine Learning algorithms.

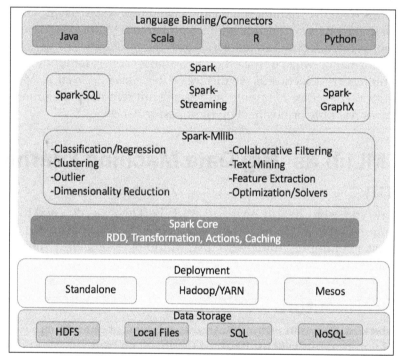

Figure 17: Apache Spark high level architecture

The Spark core has the following components:

- **Resilient Distributed Datasets (RDD)**: RDDs are the basic immutable collection of objects that Spark Core knows how to partition and distribute across the cluster for performing tasks. RDDs are composed of "partitions", dependent on parent RDDs and metadata about data placement.

- Two distinct operations are performed on RDDs:
    - **Transformations**: Operations that are lazily evaluated and transform one RDD into another. Lazy evaluation defers evaluation as long as possible, which makes some resource optimizations possible.
    - **Action**: The actual operation that triggers transformations and returns output values

- **Lineage graph**: The pipeline or flow of data describing the computation for a particular task, including different RDDs created in transformations and actions is known as the lineage graph of the task. The lineage graph plays a key role in fault tolerance.

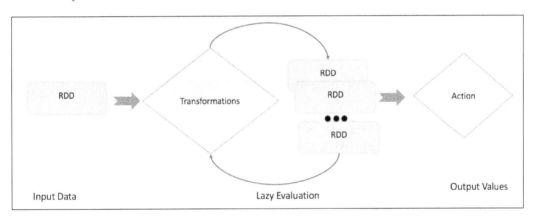

Figure 18: Apache Spark lineage graph

Spark is agnostic to the cluster management and can work with several implementations—including YARN and Mesos—for managing the nodes, distributing the work, and communications. The distribution of tasks in Transformations and Actions across the cluster is done by the scheduler, starting from the driver node where the Spark context is created, to the many worker nodes as shown in *Figure 19*. When running with YARN, Spark gives the user the choice of the number of executors, heap, and core allocation per JVM at the node level.

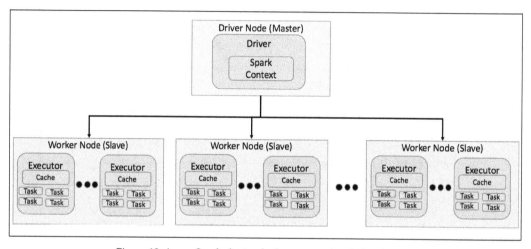

Figure 19: Apace Spark cluster deployment and task distribution

Machine Learning in MLlib

Spark MLlib has a comprehensive Machine Learning toolkit, offering more algorithms than H2O at the time of writing, as shown in *Figure 20*:

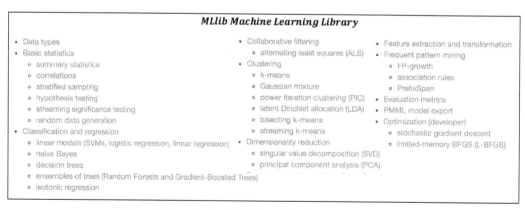

Figure 20: Apache Spark MLlib machine learning algorithms

Many extensions have been written for Spark, including Spark MLlib, and the user community continues to contribute more packages. You can download third-party packages or register your own at `https://spark-packages.org/`.

Tools and usage

Spark MLlib provides APIs for other languages in addition to Java, including Scala, Python, and R. When a `SparkContext` is created, it launches a monitoring and instrumentation web console at port `4040`, which lets us see key information about the runtime, including scheduled tasks and their progress, RDD sizes and memory use, and so on. There are also external profiling tools available for use.

Experiments, results, and analysis

The business problem we tackled here is the same as the one described earlier for experiments using H2O. We employed five learning algorithms using MLlib, in all. The first was k-Means with all features using a *k* value determined from computing the cost—specifically, the **Sum of Squared Errors (SSE)**—over a large number of values of *k* and selecting the "elbow" of the curve. Determining the optimal value of *k* is typically not an easy task; often, evaluation measures such as silhouette are compared in order to pick the best *k*. Even though we know the number of classes in the dataset is *7*, it is instructive to see where experiments like this lead if we pretend we did not have labeled data. The optimal *k* found using the elbow method was 27. In the real world, business decisions may often guide the selection of *k*.

In the following listings, we show how to use different models from the MLlib suite to do cluster analysis and classification. The code is based on examples available in the MLlib API Guide (`https://spark.apache.org/docs/latest/mllib-guide.html`). We use the normalized UCI `CoverType` dataset in CSV format. Note that it is more natural to use `spark.sql.Dataset` with the newer `spark.ml` package, whereas the `spark.mllib` package works more closely with `JavaRDD`. This provides an abstraction over RDDs and allows for optimization of the transformations beneath the covers. In the case of most unsupervised learning algorithms, this means the data must be transformed such that the dataset to be used for training and testing should have a column called features by default that contains all the features of an observation as a vector. A `VectorAssembler` object can be used for this transformation. A glimpse into the use of ML pipelines, which is a way to chain tasks together, is given in the source code for training a Random Forest classifier.

k-Means

The following code fragment for the k-Means experiment uses the algorithm from the `org.apache.spark.ml.clustering` package. The code includes minimal boilerplate for setting up the `SparkSession`, which is the handle to the Spark runtime. Note that eight cores have been specified in local mode in the setup:

```
SparkSession spark = SparkSession.builder()
    .master("local[8]")
    .appName("KMeansExpt")
    .getOrCreate();

// Load and parse data
String filePath =
    "/home/kchoppella/book/Chapter09/data/covtypeNorm.csv";
// Selected K value
int k =  27;

// Loads data.
Dataset<Row> inDataset = spark.read()
    .format("com.databricks.spark.csv")
    .option("header", "true")
    .option("inferSchema", true)
    .load(filePath);
ArrayList<String> inputColsList = new
  ArrayList<String>(Arrays.asList(inDataset.columns()));

//Make single features column for feature vectors
inputColsList.remove("class");
String[] inputCols = inputColsList.parallelStream()
  .toArray(String[]::new);

//Prepare dataset for training with all features in "features"
  column
VectorAssembler assembler = new VectorAssembler().
  setInputCols(inputCols).setOutputCol("features");
Dataset<Row> dataset = assembler.transform(inDataset);

KMeans kmeans = new KMeans().setK(k).setSeed(1L);
KMeansModel model = kmeans.fit(dataset);

// Evaluate clustering by computing Within Set Sum of Squared
  Errors.
double SSE = model.computeCost(dataset);
System.out.println("Sum of Squared Errors = " + SSE);

spark.stop();
```

The optimal value for the number of clusters was arrived at by evaluating and plotting the sum of squared errors for several different values and choosing the one at the elbow of the curve. The value used here is *27*.

k-Means with PCA

In the second experiment, we used k-Means again, but first we reduced the number of dimensions in the data through PCA. Again, we used a rule of thumb here, which is to select a value for the PCA parameter for the number of dimensions such that at least 85% of the variance in the original dataset is preserved after the reduction in dimensionality. This produced 16 features in the transformed dataset from an initial 54, and this dataset was used in this and subsequent experiments. The following code shows the relevant code for PCA analysis:

```
int numDimensions = 16
PCAModel pca = new PCA()
    .setK(numDimensions)
    .setInputCol("features")
    .setOutputCol("pcaFeatures")
    .fit(dataset);

Dataset<Row> result = pca.transform(dataset).select("pcaFeatures");
KMeans kmeans = new KMeans().setK(k).setSeed(1L);
KMeansModel model = kmeans.fit(dataset);
```

Bisecting k-Means (with PCA)

The third experiment used MLlib's Bisecting k-Means algorithm. This algorithm is similar to a top-down hierarchical clustering technique where all instances are in the same cluster at the outset, followed by successive splits:

```
// Trains a bisecting k-Means model.
BisectingKMeans bkm = new BisectingKMeans().setK(k).setSeed(1);
BisectingKMeansModel model = bkm.fit(dataset);
```

Gaussian Mixture Model

In the next experiment, we used MLlib's **Gaussian Mixture Model (GMM)**, another clustering model. The assumption inherent to this model is that the data distribution in each cluster is Gaussian in nature, with unknown parameters. The same number of clusters is specified here, and default values have been used for the maximum number of iterations and tolerance, which dictate when the algorithm is considered to have converged:

```
GaussianMixtureModel gmm = new GaussianMixture()
    .setK(numClusters)
    .fit(result);
```

```
// Output the parameters of the mixture model
for (int k = 0; k < gmm.getK(); k++) {
  String msg = String.format("Gaussian
  %d:\nweight=%f\nmu=%s\nsigma=\n%s\n\n",
                k, gmm.weights()[k], gmm.gaussians()[k].mean(),
                gmm.gaussians()[k].cov());
  System.out.printf(msg);
  writer.write(msg + "\n");
  writer.flush();
}
```

Random Forest

Finally, we ran Random Forest, which is the only available ensemble learner that can handle multi-class classification. In the following code, we see that this algorithm needs some preparatory tasks to be performed prior to training. Pre-processing stages are composed into a pipeline of Transformers and Estimators. The pipeline is then used to fit the data. You can learn more about Pipelines on the Apache Spark website (https://spark.apache.org/docs/latest/ml-pipeline.html):

```
// Index labels, adding metadata to the label column.
// Fit on whole dataset to include all labels in index.
StringIndexerModel labelIndexer = new StringIndexer()
    .setInputCol("class")
    .setOutputCol("indexedLabel")
    .fit(dataset);
// Automatically identify categorical features, and index them.
// Set maxCategories so features with > 2 distinct values are treated
as continuous since we have already encoded categoricals with sets of
binary variables.
VectorIndexerModel featureIndexer = new VectorIndexer()
    .setInputCol("features")
    .setOutputCol("indexedFeatures")
    .setMaxCategories(2)
    .fit(dataset);

// Split the data into training and test sets (30% held out for
testing)
Dataset<Row>[] splits = dataset.randomSplit(new double[] {0.7, 0.3});
Dataset<Row> trainingData = splits[0];
Dataset<Row> testData = splits[1];

// Train a RF model.
RandomForestClassifier rf = new RandomForestClassifier()
    .setLabelCol("indexedLabel")
```

```
    .setFeaturesCol("indexedFeatures")
    .setImpurity("gini")
    .setMaxDepth(5)
    .setNumTrees(20)
    .setSeed(1234);

// Convert indexed labels back to original labels.
IndexToString labelConverter = new IndexToString()
    .setInputCol("prediction")
    .setOutputCol("predictedLabel")
    .setLabels(labelIndexer.labels());

// Chain indexers and RF in a Pipeline.
Pipeline pipeline = new Pipeline()
    .setStages(new PipelineStage[] {labelIndexer, featureIndexer, rf,
labelConverter});

// Train model. This also runs the indexers.
PipelineModel model = pipeline.fit(trainingData);

// Make predictions.
Dataset<Row> predictions = model.transform(testData);

// Select example rows to display.
predictions.select("predictedLabel", "class", "features").show(5);

// Select (prediction, true label) and compute test error.
MulticlassClassificationEvaluator evaluator = new
MulticlassClassificationEvaluator()
    .setLabelCol("indexedLabel")
    .setPredictionCol("prediction");

evaluator.setMetricName("accuracy");
double accuracy = evaluator.evaluate(predictions);
System.out.printf("Accuracy = %f\n", accuracy);
```

The sum of squared errors for the experiments using k-Means and Bisecting k-Means are given in the following table:

Algorithm	k	Features	SSE
k-Means	27	54	214,702
k-Means(PCA)	27	16	241,155
Bisecting k-Means(PCA)	27	16	305,644

Table 3: Results with k-Means

The GMM model was used to illustrate the use of the API; it outputs the parameters of the Gaussian mixture for every cluster as well as the cluster weight. Output for all the clusters can be seen at the website for this book.

For the case of Random Forest these are the results for runs with different numbers of trees. All 54 features were used here:

Number of trees	Accuracy	F1 measure	Weighted precision	Weighted recall
15	0.6806	0.6489	0.6213	0.6806
20	0.6776	0.6470	0.6191	0.6776
25	0.5968	0.5325	0.5717	0.5968
30	0.6547	0.6207	0.5972	0.6547
40	0.6594	0.6272	0.6006	0.6594

Table 4: Results for Random Forest

Analysis of results

As can be seen from *Table 3*, there is a small increase in cost when fewer dimensions are used after PCA with the same number of clusters. Varying k with PCA might suggest a better k for the PCA case. Notice also that in this experiment, for the same k, Bisecting K-Means with PCA-derived features has the highest cost of all. The stopping number of clusters used for Bisecting k-Means has simply been picked to be the one determined for basic k-Means, but this need not be so. A similar search for k that yields the best cost may be done independently for Bisecting k-Means.

In the case of Random Forest, we see the best performance when using 15 trees. All trees have a depth of three. This hyper-parameter can be varied to tune the model as well. Even though Random Forest is not susceptible to over-fitting due to accounting for variance across trees in the training stages, increasing the value for the number of trees beyond an optimum number can degrade performance.

Real-time Big Data Machine Learning

In this section, we will discuss the real-time version of Big Data Machine Learning where data arrives in large volumes and is changing at a rapid rate at the same time. Under these conditions, Machine Learning analytics cannot be applied *per* the traditional practice of "batch learning and deploy" (*References* [14]).

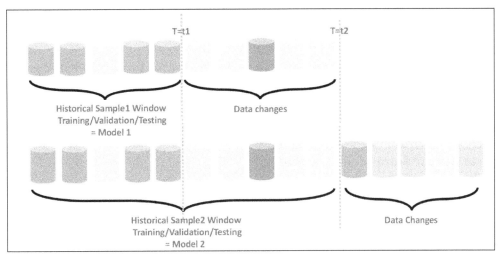

Figure 21: Use case for real-time Big Data Machine Learning

Let us consider a case where labeled data is available for a short duration, and we perform the appropriate modeling techniques on the data and then apply the most suitable evaluation methods on the resulting models. Next, we select the best model and use it for predictions on unseen data at runtime. We then observe, with some dismay, that model performance drops significantly over time. Repeating the exercise with new data shows a similar degradation in performance! What are we to do now? This quandary, combined with large volumes of data motivates the need for a different approach: real-time Big Data Machine Learning.

Like the batch learning framework, the real-time framework in big data may have similar components up until the data preparation stage. When the computations involved in data preparation must take place on streams or combined stream and batch data, we require specialized computation engines such as **Spark Streaming**. Like stream computations, Machine Learning must work across the cluster and perform different Machine Learning tasks on the stream. This adds an additional layer of complexity to the implementations of single machine multi-threaded streaming algorithms.

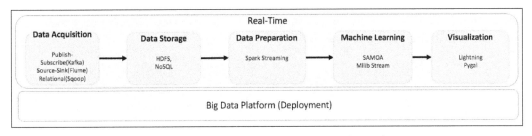

Figure 22: Real-time big data components and providers

SAMOA as a real-time Big Data Machine Learning framework

For a single machine, in *Chapter 5*, *Real-Time Stream Machine Learning*, we discussed the MOA framework at length. SAMOA is the distributed framework for performing Machine Learning on streams.

At the time of writing, SAMOA is an incubator-level open source project with Apache 2.0 license and good integration with different stream processing engines such as **Apache Storm**, **Samza**, and **S4**.

SAMOA architecture

The SAMOA framework offers several key streaming services to an extendable set of stream processing engines, with existing implementations for the most popular engines of today.

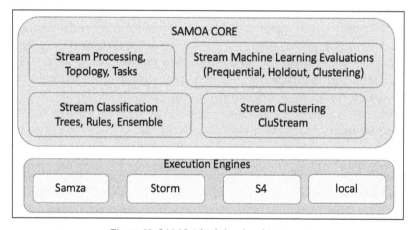

Figure 23: SAMOA high level architecture

`TopologyBuilder` is the interface that acts as a factory to create different components and connect them together in SAMOA. The core of SAMOA is in building processing elements for data streams. The basic unit for processing consists of `ProcessingItem` and the `Processor` interface, as shown in *Figure 24*. `ProcessingItem` is an encapsulated hidden element, while Processor is the core implementation where the logic for handling streams is coded.

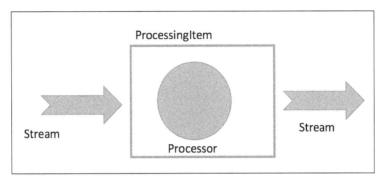

Figure 24: SAMOA processing data streams

Stream is another interface that connects various **Processors** together as the source and destination created by TopologyBuilder. A Stream can have one source and multiple destinations. Stream supports three forms of communication between source and destinations:

- **All**: In this communication, all messages from source are sent to all the destinations

- **Key**: In this communication, messages with the same keys are sent to the same processors

- **Shuffle**: In this communication, messages are randomly sent to the processors

All the messages or events in SAMOA are implementations of the interface ContentEvent, encapsulating mostly the data in the streams as a value and having some form of key for uniqueness.

Each stream processing engine has an implementation for all the key interfaces as a plugin and integrates with SAMOA. The Apache Storm implementations StormTopology, StormStream, and StormProcessingItem, and so on are shown in the API in *Figure 25*.

Task is another unit of work in SAMOA, having the responsibility of execution. All the classification or clustering evaluation and validation techniques such as prequential, holdout, and so on, are implemented as Tasks.

Learner is the interface for implementing all Supervised and Unsupervised Learning capability in SAMOA. Learners can be local or distributed and have different extensions such as ClassificationLearner and RegressionLearner.

Machine Learning algorithms

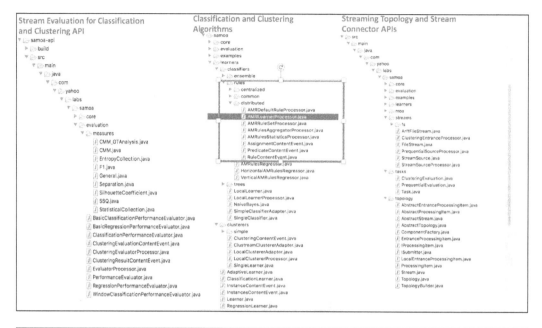

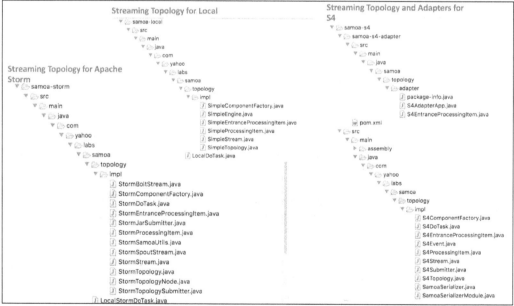

Figure 25: SAMOA machine learning algorithms

Figure 25 shows the core components of the SAMOA topology and their implementation for various engines.

Tools and usage

We continue with the same business problem as before. The command line to launch the training job for the `covtype` dataset is:

```
bin/samoa local target/SAMOA-Local-0.3.0-SNAPSHOT.jar
"PrequentialEvaluation -l classifiers.ensemble.Bagging
    -s (ArffFileStream -f covtype-train.csv.arff) -f 10000"
```

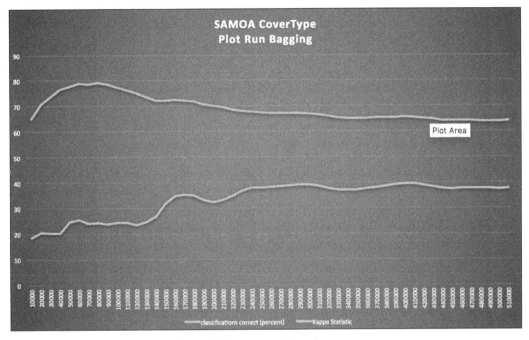

Figure 25: Bagging model performance

When running with Storm, this is the command line:

```
bin/samoa storm target/SAMOA-Storm-0.3.0-SNAPSHOT.jar
"PrequentialEvaluation -l classifiers.ensemble.Bagging
    -s (ArffFileStream -f covtype-train.csv.arff) -f 10000"
```

Experiments, results, and analysis

The results of experiments using SAMOA as a stream-based learning platform for Big Data are given in *Table 5*.

Algorithm	Best Accuracy	Final Accuracy	Final Kappa Statistic	Final Kappa Temporal Statistic
Bagging	79.16	64.09	37.52	-69.51
Boosting	78.05	47.82	0	-1215.1
VerticalHoeffdingTree	83.23	67.51	44.35	-719.51
AdaptiveBagging	81.03	64.64	38.99	-67.37

Table 5: Experimental results with Big Data real-time learning using SAMOA

Analysis of results

From an analysis of the results, the following observations can be made:

- *Table 5* shows that the popular non-linear decision tree-based VHDT on SAMOA is the best performing algorithm according to almost all the metrics.

- The adaptive bagging algorithm performs better than bagging because it employs Hoeffding Adaptive Trees in the implementation, which are more robust than basic online stream bagging.

- The online boosting algorithm with its dependency on the weak learners and no adaptability ranked the lowest as expected.

- The bagging plot in *Figure 25* shows a nice trend of stability achieved as the number of examples increased, validating the general consensus that if the patterns are stationary, more examples lead to robust models.

The future of Machine Learning

The impact of Machine Learning on businesses, social interactions, and indeed, our day-to-day lives today is undeniable, though not always immediately obvious. In the near future, it will be ubiquitous and inescapable. According to a report by McKinsey Global Institute published in December 2016 (*References* [15]), there is a vast unexploited potential for data and analytics in major industry sectors, especially healthcare and the public sector. Machine Learning is one of the key technologies poised to help exploit that potential. More compute power is at our disposal than ever before. More data is available than ever before, and we have cheaper and greater storage capacity than ever before.

Already, the unmet demand for data scientists has spurred changes to college curricula worldwide, and has caused an increase of 16% a year in wages for data scientists in the US, in the period 2012-2014. The solution to a wide swathe of problems is within reach with Machine Learning, including resource allocation, forecasting, predictive analytics, predictive maintenance, and price and product optimization.

The same McKinsey report emphasizes the increasing role of Machine Learning, including deep learning in a variety of use cases across industries such as agriculture, pharma, manufacturing, energy, media, and finance. These scenarios run the gamut: predict personalized health outcomes, identify fraud transactions, optimize pricing and scheduling, personalize crops to individual conditions, identify and navigate roads, diagnose disease, and personalize advertising. Deep learning has great potential in automating an increasing number of occupations. Just improving natural language understanding would potentially cause a USD 3 trillion impact on global wages, affecting jobs like customer service and support worldwide.

Giant strides in image and voice recognition and language processing have made applications such as personal digital assistants commonplace, thanks to remarkable advances in deep learning techniques. The symbolism of AlphaGO's success in defeating Lee Sedol, alluded to in the opening chapter of this book, is enormous, as it is a vivid example of how progress in artificial intelligence is besting our own predictions of milestones in AI advancement. Yet this is the tip of the proverbial iceberg. Recent work in areas such as transfer learning offers the promise of more broadly intelligent systems that will be able to solve a wider range of problems rather than narrowly specializing in just one. General Artificial Intelligence, where AI can develop objective reasoning, proposes a methodology to solve a problem, and learn from its mistakes, is some distance away at this point, but check back in a few years and that distance may well have shrunk beyond our current expectations! Increasingly, the confluence of transformative advances in technologies incrementally enabling each other spells a future of dizzying possibilities that we can already glimpse around us. The role of Machine Learning, it would appear, is to continue to shape that future in profound and extraordinary ways. Of that, there is little doubt.

Summary

The final chapter of this book deals with Machine Learning adapted to what is arguably one of the most significant paradigm shifts in information management and analytics to have emerged in the last few decades – Big Data. Much as many other areas of computer science and engineering have seen, AI – and Machine Learning in particular – has benefited from innovative solutions and dedicated communities adapting to face the many challenges posed by Big Data.

One way to characterize Big Data is by volume, velocity, variety, and veracity. This demands a new set of tools and frameworks to conduct the tasks of effective analytics at large.

Choosing a Big Data framework involves selecting distributed storage systems, data preparation techniques, batch or real-time Machine Learning, as well as visualization and reporting tools.

Several open source deployment frameworks are available including Hortonworks Data Platform, Cloudera CDH, Amazon Elastic MapReduce, and Microsoft Azure HDInsight. Each provides a platform with components supporting data acquisition, data preparation, Machine Learning, evaluation, and visualization of results.

Among the data acquisition components, publish-subscribe is a model offered by Apache Kafka (*References* [8]) and Amazon Kinesis, which involves a broker mediating between subscribers and publishers. Alternatives include source-sink, SQL, message queueing, and other custom frameworks.

With regard to data storage, several factors contribute to the proper choice for whatever your needs may be. HDFS offers a distributed File System with robust fault tolerance and high throughput. NoSQL databases also offer high throughput, but generally with weak guarantees on consistency. They include key-value, document, columnar, and graph databases.

Data processing and preparation come next in the flow, which includes data cleaning, scraping, and transformation. Hive and HQL provide these functions in HDFS systems. SparkSQL and Amazon Redshift offer similar capabilities. Real-time stream processing is available from products such as Storm and Samza.

The learning stage in Big Data analytics can include batch or real-time data.

A variety of rich visualization and analysis frameworks exist that are accessible from multiple programming environments.

Two major Machine Learning frameworks on Big Data are H2O and Apache Spark MLlib. Both can access data from various sources such as HDFS, SQL, NoSQL, S3, and others. H2O supports a number of Machine Learning algorithms that can be run in a cluster. For Machine Learning with real-time data, SAMOA is a big data framework with a comprehensive set of stream-processing capabilities.

The role of Machine Learning in the future is going to be a dominant one, with a wide-ranging impact on healthcare, finance, energy, and indeed on most industries. The expansion in the scope of automation will have inevitable societal effects. Increases in compute power, data, and storage per dollar are opening up great new vistas to Machine Learning applications that have the potential to increase productivity, engender innovation, and dramatically improve living standards the world over.

References

1. Matei Zaharia, Mosharaf Chowdhury, Michael J. Franklin, Scott Shenker, *Ion Stoica:Spark: Cluster Computing with Working Sets*. HotCloud 2010

2. Matei Zaharia, Reynold S. Xin, Patrick Wendell, Tathagata Das, Michael Armbrust, Ankur Dave, Xiangrui Meng, Josh Rosen, Shivaram Venkataraman, Michael J. Franklin, Ali Ghodsi, Joseph Gonzalez, Scott Shenker, *Ion Stoica:Apache Spark: a unified engine for Big Data processing*. Commun. ACM 59(11): 56-65 (2016)

3. Apache Hadoop: `https://hadoop.apache.org/`.

4. Cloudera: `http://www.cloudera.com/`.

5. Hortonworks: `http://hortonworks.com/`.

6. Amazon EC2: `http://aws.amazon.com/ec2/`.

7. Microsoft Azure: `http://azure.microsoft.com/`.

8. Apache Flume: `https://flume.apache.org/`.

9. Apache Kafka: `http://kafka.apache.org/`.

10. Apache Sqoop: `http://sqoop.apache.org/`.

11. Apache Hive: `http://hive.apache.org/`.

12. Apache Storm: `https://storm.apache.org/`.

13. H_2O: `http://h2o.ai/`.

14. Shahrivari S, Jalili S. *Beyond batch processing: towards real-time and streaming Big Data.* Computers. 2014;3(4):117–29.

15. *MGI, The Age of Analytics-—*Executive Summary `http://www.mckinsey.com/~/media/McKinsey/Business%20Functions/McKinsey%20Analytics/Our%20Insights/The%20age%20of%20analytics%20Competing%20in%20a%20data%20driven%20world/MGI-The-Age-of-Analytics-Full-report.ashx`.

A
Linear Algebra

Linear algebra is of primary importance in machine learning and it gives us an array of tools that are especially handy for the purpose of manipulating data and extracting patterns from it. Moreover, when data must be processed in batches as in much machine learning, great runtime efficiencies are gained from using the "vectorized" form as an alternative to traditional looping constructs when implementing software solutions in optimization or data pre-processing or any number of operations in analytics.

We will consider only the domain of real numbers in what follows. Thus, a vector $\vec{v} \in \mathbb{R}^n$ represents an array of n real-valued numbers. A matrix $\mathbf{A} \in \mathbb{R}^{m \times n}$ is a two-dimensional array of m rows and n columns of real-valued numbers.

Some key concepts from the foundation of linear algebra are presented here.

Vector

The vector $\mathbf{x}$ (lowercase, bold, by convention; equivalently, $\vec{x}$) can be thought of as a point in n-dimensional space. Conventionally, we mean column-vector when we say vector. The *transpose* of a column vector is a *row* vector with the same number of elements, arranged in a single row.

$$x = \begin{bmatrix} x_1 \\ x_2 \\ \cdots \\ x_n \end{bmatrix} \Rightarrow x^T = \begin{bmatrix} x & x_2 & \cdots & x_n \end{bmatrix}$$

Scalar product of vectors

Also known as the dot product, the scalar product is defined for two vectors of equal length. The result of the operation is a scalar value and is obtained by summing over the products of the corresponding elements of the vectors. Thus, given vectors **x** and **y**:

$$x = \begin{bmatrix} x_1 \\ x_2 \end{bmatrix} \quad y = \begin{bmatrix} y_1 \\ y_2 \end{bmatrix}$$

The dot product $x_T y$ is given as:

$$x^T y = \begin{bmatrix} x_1 x_2 \end{bmatrix} \begin{bmatrix} y_1 \\ y_2 \end{bmatrix} = x_1 y_1 + x_2 y_2$$

Matrix

A matrix is a two-dimensional array of numbers. Each element can be indexed by its row and column position. Thus, a 3 x 2 matrix:

$$\mathbf{A} = \begin{bmatrix} a_{11} & a_{12} \\ a_{21} & a_{22} \\ a_{31} & a_{32} \end{bmatrix}$$

Transpose of a matrix

Swapping columns for rows in a matrix produces the transpose. Thus, the transpose of *A* is a 2 x 3 matrix:

$$\mathbf{A}^T = \begin{bmatrix} a_{11} & a_{21} & a_{31} \\ a_{12} & a_{22} & a_{32} \end{bmatrix}$$

Matrix addition

Matrix addition is defined as element-wise summation of two matrices with the same shape. Let **A** and **B** be two m x n matrices. Their sum **C** can be written as follows:

$$\mathbf{C}_{i,j} = \mathbf{A}_{i,j} + \mathbf{B}_{i,j}$$

Scalar multiplication

Multiplication with a scalar produces a matrix where each element is scaled by the scalar value. Here **A** is multiplied by the scalar value d:

$$\mathbf{D}_{i,j} = d\mathbf{A}_{i,j}$$

Matrix multiplication

Two matrices **A** and **B** can be multiplied if the number of columns of **A** equals the number of rows of **B**. If **A** has dimensions m x n and **B** has dimensions n x p, then the product **AB** has dimensions m x p:

$$\mathbf{C}_{i,j} = \mathbf{AB} = \sum_{k} \mathbf{A}_{ik}\mathbf{B}_{kj}$$

Properties of matrix product

Distributivity over addition: $A(B + C) = AB + AC$

Associativity: $A(BC) = (AB)C$

Non-commutativity: $AB \neq BA$

Vector dot-product is commutative: $\mathbf{x}^T\mathbf{y} = \mathbf{y}^T\mathbf{x}$

Transpose of product is product of transposes: $(\mathbf{AB})^T = \mathbf{A}^T\mathbf{B}^T$

Linear transformation

There is a special importance to the product of a matrix and a vector in linear algebra. Consider the product of a 3 x 2 matrix **A** and a 2 x 1 vector **x** producing a 3 x 1 vector *y*:

$$y = Ax \Rightarrow \begin{bmatrix} a_{11} & a_{12} \\ a_{21} & a_{22} \\ a_{31} & a_{32} \end{bmatrix} \begin{bmatrix} x_1 \\ x_2 \end{bmatrix} = \begin{bmatrix} x_1 a_{11} + x_2 a_{12} \\ x_1 a_{21} + x_2 a_{22} \\ x_1 a_{31} + x_2 a_{32} \end{bmatrix} = \begin{bmatrix} y_1 \\ y_2 \end{bmatrix}$$

$$= x_1 \begin{bmatrix} a_{11} \\ a_{21} \\ a_{31} \end{bmatrix} + x_2 \begin{bmatrix} a_{12} \\ a_{22} \\ a_{32} \end{bmatrix} \quad \text{(C)}$$

$$= \begin{bmatrix} [a_{11}, a_{12}] \cdot \vec{x} \\ [a_{21}, a_{22}] \cdot \vec{x} \\ [a_{31}, a_{32}] \cdot \vec{x} \end{bmatrix} \quad \text{(R)}$$

It is useful to consider two views of the preceding matrix-vector product, namely, the column picture (**C**) and the row picture (**R**). In the column picture, the product can be seen as a linear combination of the column vectors of the matrix, whereas the row picture can be thought of as the dot products of the rows of the matrix with the vector $\vec{x}$.

Matrix inverse

The product of a matrix with its inverse is the Identity matrix. Thus:

$$A^{-1}A = \begin{bmatrix} 1 & \cdots & 0 \\ \vdots & \ddots & \vdots \\ 0 & \cdots & 1 \end{bmatrix} = I$$

The matrix inverse, if it exists, can be used to solve a system of simultaneous equations represented by the preceding vector-matrix product equation. Consider a system of equations:

$$x_1 + 2x_2 = 3$$

$$3x_1 + 9x_2 = 21$$

This can be expressed as an equation involving the matrix-vector product:

$$\begin{bmatrix} 1 & 2 \\ 3 & 9 \end{bmatrix} \begin{bmatrix} x_1 \\ x_2 \end{bmatrix} = \begin{bmatrix} 3 \\ 21 \end{bmatrix}$$

We can solve for the variables x_1 and x_2 by multiplying both sides by the matrix inverse:

$$\begin{bmatrix} x_1 \\ x_2 \end{bmatrix} = \begin{bmatrix} 3 & -\frac{2}{3} \\ -1 & \frac{1}{3} \end{bmatrix} \begin{bmatrix} 5 \\ 21 \end{bmatrix} = \begin{bmatrix} 1 \\ 2 \end{bmatrix}$$

The matrix inverse can be calculated by different methods. The reader is advised to view Prof. Strang's MIT lecture: `bit.ly/1OvmKcL`.

Eigendecomposition

Matrices can be decomposed to factors that can give us valuable insight into the transformation that the matrix represents. Eigenvalues and eigenvectors are obtained as the result of eigendecomposition. For a given square matrix $\mathbf{A}$, an eigenvector is a non-zero vector that is transformed into a scaled version of itself when multiplied by the matrix. The scalar multiplier is the eigenvalue. All scalar multiples of an eigenvector are also eigenvectors:

$$\mathbf{A}\mathbf{v} = \lambda\mathbf{v}$$

In the preceding example, $\mathbf{v}$ is an eigenvector and λ is the eigenvalue.

The eigenvalue equation of matrix $\mathbf{A}$ is given by:

$$(\mathbf{A} - \lambda\mathbf{I})\mathbf{v} = 0$$

The non-zero solution for the eigenvalues is given by the roots of the characteristic polynomial equation of degree n represented by the determinant:

$$|A - \lambda I| = (\lambda_1 - \lambda)(\lambda_2 - \lambda)(\lambda_3 - \lambda)...(\lambda_n - \lambda)$$

The eigenvectors can then be found by solving for v in $Av = \lambda v$.

Some matrices, called diagonalizable matrices, can be built entirely from their eigenvectors and eigenvalues. If Λ is the diagonal matrix with the eigenvalues of matrix A on its principal diagonal, and Q is the matrix whose columns are the eigenvectors of A:

$$\Lambda = \begin{bmatrix} \lambda_1 & \cdots & 0 \\ \vdots & \ddots & \vdots \\ 0 & \cdots & \lambda_n \end{bmatrix}, Q = \begin{bmatrix} v^{(1)} v^{(2)} v^{(3)} ... v^{(n)} \end{bmatrix}$$

Then $A = Q \Lambda Q^{-1}$.

Positive definite matrix

If a matrix has only positive eigenvalues, it is called a **positive definite matrix**. If the eigenvalues are positive or zero, the matrix is called a **positive semi-definite matrix**. With positive definite matrices, it is true that:

$$x^T A x \geq 0$$

Singular value decomposition (SVD)

SVD is a decomposition of any rectangular matrix A of dimensions $n \times p$ and is written as the product of three matrices:

$$A_{nxp} = U_{nxn} S_{nxp} V^T_{pxp}$$

U is defined to be $n \times n$, S is a diagonal $n \times p$ matrix, and V is $p \times p$. U and V are orthogonal matrices; that is:

$$U^T U = I_{nxn} \text{ and } V^T V = I_{pxp}$$

The diagonal values of **S** are called the singular values of **A**. Columns of **U** are called left singular vectors of **A** and those of **V** are called right singular vectors of **A**. The left singular vectors are orthonormal eigenvectors of $\mathbf{A}^\mathrm{T}\mathbf{A}$ and the right singular vectors are orthonormal eigenvectors of $\mathbf{A}\mathbf{A}^\mathrm{T}$.

The SVD representation expands the original data into a coordinate system such that the covariance matrix is a diagonal matrix.

B
Probability

Essential concepts in probability are presented here in brief.

Axioms of probability

Kolmogorov's axioms of probability can be stated in terms of the sample space S of possible events, $E_1, E_2, E_3, \ldots E_n$ and the real-valued probability $P(E)$ of an event E. The axioms are:

1. $P(E) \geq 0 \text{ for all } E \in S$
2. $P(S) = 1$
3. $\text{if } A \cap B = \varnothing \text{ then } P(A \cup B) = P(A) + P(B)$

Together, these axioms say that probabilities cannot be negative numbers — impossible events have zero probability — no events outside the sample space are possible as it is the universe of possibilities under consideration, and that the probability of either of two mutually exclusive events occurring is equal to the sum of their individual probabilities.

Bayes' theorem

The probability of an event **E** conditioned on evidence **X** is proportional to the prior probability of the event and the likelihood of the evidence given that the event has occurred. This is Bayes' Theorem:

$$P(E \mid X) = \frac{P(X \mid E) P(E)}{P(X)}$$

$P(X)$ is the normalizing constant, which is also called the marginal probability of X. $P(E)$ is the prior, and $P(X | E)$ is the likelihood. $P(E | X)$ is also called the posterior probability.

Bayes' Theorem expressed in terms of the posterior and prior odds is known as Bayes' Rule.

Density estimation

Estimating the hidden probability density function of a random variable from sample data randomly drawn from the population is known as density estimation. Gaussian mixtures and kernel density estimates are examples used in feature engineering, data modeling, and clustering.

Given a probability density function $f(X)$ for a random variable X, the probabilities associated with the values of X can be found as follows:

$$P\left(a < X < b\right) = \int_b^a f\left(x\right)dx \text{ for all } a < b$$

Density estimation can be parametric, where it is assumed that the data is drawn from a known family of distributions and $f(x)$ is estimated by estimating the parameters of the distribution, for example, μ and σ^2 in the case of a normal distribution. The other approach is non-parametric, where no assumption is made about the distribution of the observed data and the data is allowed to determine the form of the distribution.

Mean

The long-run average value of a random variable is known as the expectation or mean. The sample mean is the corresponding average over the observed data.

In the case of a discrete random variable, the mean is given by:

$$\mu = \sum xP\left(x\right)$$

For example, the mean number of pips turning up on rolling a single fair die is 3.5.

For a continuous random variable with probability density function *f(x)*, the mean is:

$$\mu = \int_{-\infty}^{\infty} xf(x)dx$$

Variance

Variance is the expectation of the square of the difference between the random variable and its mean.

In the discrete case, with the mean defined as previously discussed, and with the probability mass function *p(x)*, the variance is:

$$Var(X) = \sigma^2 = \sum_{i=1}^{n} p_i \cdot (x_i - \mu)^2 = \sum_{i=1}^{n} p_i x_i^2 - \mu^2$$

In the continuous case, it is as follows:

$$Var(X) = \sigma^2 = \int_{-\infty}^{\infty} (x - \mu)^2 f(x)dx = \int_{-\infty}^{\infty} x^2 f(x)dx - \mu^2$$

Some continuous distributions do not have a mean or variance.

Standard deviation

Standard deviation is a measure of how spread out the data is in relation to its mean value. It is the square root of variance, and unlike variance, it is expressed in the same units as the data. The standard deviation in the case of discrete and continuous random variables are given here:,

- Discrete case:

$$\sigma = \sqrt{\sum_{i=1}^{n} p_i \cdot (x_i - \mu)^2}$$

- Continuous case:

$$\sigma = \sqrt{\int (x - \mu)^2 f(x)dx}$$

Gaussian standard deviation

The standard deviation of a sample drawn randomly from a larger population is a biased estimate of the population standard deviation. Based on the particular distribution, the correction to this biased estimate can differ. For a Gaussian or normal distribution, the variance is adjusted by a value of $n/_{n-1}$.

Per the definition given earlier, the biased estimate s is given by:

$$s = \sqrt{\frac{1}{n}\sum_{i=1}^{n}(x_i - \bar{x})^2}$$

In the preceding equation, $\bar{x}$ is the sample mean.

The unbiased estimate, which uses Bessel's correction, is:

$$s = \sqrt{\frac{1}{n-1}\sum_{i=1}^{n}(x_i - \bar{x})^2}$$

Covariance

In a joint distribution of two random variables, the expectation of the product of the deviations of the random variables from their respective means is called the covariance. Thus, for two random variables **X** and **Y**, the equation is as follows:

$$cov(X,Y) = E\left[(X - \mu_X)(Y - \mu_Y)\right]$$

$$= E[XY] - \mu_x \mu_y$$

If the two random variables are independent, then their covariance is zero.

Correlation coefficient

When the covariance is normalized by the product of the standard deviations of the two random variables, we get the correlation coefficient $\rho_{X,Y}$, also known as the Pearson product-moment correlation coefficient:

$$\rho_{X,Y} = \frac{E\left[\left(X - \mu_X\right)\left(Y - \mu_Y\right)\right]}{\sigma_X \sigma_Y}$$

The correlation coefficient can take values between -1 and 1 only. A coefficient of +1 means a perfect increasing linear relationship between the random variables. -1 means a perfect decreasing linear relationship. If the two variables are independent of each other, the Pearson's coefficient is 0.

Binomial distribution

Discrete probability distribution with parameters **n** and **p**. A random variable is a binary variable, with the probability of outcome given by **p** and **1 – p** in a single trial. The probability mass function gives the probability of **k** successes out of **n** independent trials.

Parameters: n, k

PMF:

$$f\left(k \mid n, p\right) = \binom{n}{k} p^k \left(1 - p\right)^{n-k}$$

Where:

$$\binom{n}{k} = \frac{n!}{k!\left(n-k\right)!}$$

This is the Binomial coefficient.

Mean: $E[X] = np$

Variance: $Var(X) = np(1 - p)$

Poisson distribution

The Poisson distribution gives the probability of the number of occurrences of an event in a given time period or in a given region of space.

Parameter λ, is the average number of occurrences in a given interval. The probability mass function of observing k events in that interval is

PMF:

$$P(k \mid \lambda) = e^{-\lambda} \frac{\lambda^k}{k!}$$

Mean: $E[X] = \lambda$

Variance: $Var(X) = \lambda$

Gaussian distribution

The Gaussian distribution, also known as the normal distribution, is a continuous probability distribution. Its probability density function is expressed in terms of the mean and variance as follows:

$$f\left(x \mid \mu, \sigma^2\right) = \frac{1}{\sqrt{2\pi\sigma^2}} e^{\frac{-(x-\mu)^2}{2\sigma^2}}$$

Mean: μ

Standard deviation: σ

Variance: σ^2

The standard normal distribution is the case when the mean is 0 and the standard deviation is 1. The PDF of the standard normal distribution is given as follows:

$$\varphi(x) = \frac{e^{\frac{-x^2}{2}}}{\sqrt{2\pi}}$$

Central limit theorem

The central limit theorem says that when you have several independent and identically distributed random variables with a distribution that has a well-defined mean and variance, the average value (or sum) over a large number of these observations is approximately normally distributed, irrespective of the parent distribution. Furthermore, the limiting normal distribution has the same mean as the parent distribution and a variance equal to the underlying variance divided by the sample size.

Given a random sample X_1, X_2, X_3 ... X_n with $\mu = E[X_i]$ and $\sigma^2 = Var(X_i)$, the sample mean:

$$\bar{X} = \sum_{i=1}^{n} X_i \text{ is approximately normal } N\left(n\mu, \frac{\sigma^2}{n}\right).$$

There are several variants of the central limit theorem where independence or the constraint of being identically distributed are relaxed, yet convergence to the normal distribution still follows.

Error propagation

Suppose there is a random variable X, which is a function of multiple observations each with their own distributions. What can be said about the mean and variance of X given the corresponding values for measured quantities that make up X? This is the problem of error propagation.

Say x is the quantity to be determined via observations of variables u, v, and so on:

$$x = f(u, v,)$$

Let us assume that:

$$\bar{x} = f\left(\bar{u}, \bar{v}, \ldots\right)$$

The uncertainty in x in terms of the variances of u, v, and so on, can be expressed by the variance of x:

$$\sigma_x^2 = \lim_{N \to \infty} \frac{1}{N} \sum_i \left(x_i - \bar{x}\right)^2$$

From the Taylor expansion of the variance of x, we get the following:

$$\sigma_x^2 = \sigma_u^2 \left(\frac{\partial f}{\partial u}\right)_{\bar{u}}^2 + \sigma_v^2 \left(\frac{\partial f}{\partial v}\right)_{\bar{v}}^2 + 2\sigma_{uv}^2 \left.\frac{\partial f}{\partial u}\right|_{\bar{u}} \left.\frac{\partial f}{\partial v}\right|_{\bar{v}} + \cdots$$

Here, σ_{uv}^2 is the covariance.

Similarly, we can determine the propagation error of the mean. Given N measurements with x_i with uncertainties characterized by s_i, the following can be written:

$$\bar{x} = \frac{1}{N}\left(x_1 + x_2 + x_3 + \cdots x_n\right) = \frac{1}{N}\sum x_i$$

With:

$$s_i^2 = \sum_i s_i^2 \left(\frac{\partial \bar{x}}{\partial x_i}\right)_{\bar{x}}^2,$$

These equations assume that the covariance is 0.

Suppose $s_i = s$ – that is, all observations have the same error.

Then, $s_{\bar{x}}^2 = \sum_i s_i^2 \left(\frac{\partial \bar{x}}{\partial x_i}\right)_{\bar{x}}^2$.

Since $\dfrac{\partial \bar{x}}{\partial x_i} = \dfrac{\partial}{\partial x_i}\left(\dfrac{1}{N}\sum_J x_j\right) = \dfrac{1}{N} \quad \left(\dfrac{\partial x_J}{\partial x_i}\delta_{ij}\right)$

Therefore, $s_{\bar{x}}^2 = \sum_i s^2 \left(\dfrac{1}{N}\right)^2$.

$$= \frac{s^2}{N}$$

Index

B

Balanced Iterative Reducing and Clustering
    Hierarch (BIRCH)
  about 218
  advantages 219
  input 218
  limitations 219
  output 218
  working 218

Batch Big Data Machine Learning
  about 451
  used, as H2O 451

Bayesian information score (BIC) 284

Bayesian networks
  about 258, 259
  inference 258, 263
  learning 258, 276-278
  representation 258, 260

Bayes theorem
  about 491, 492
  binomial distribution 495
  central limit theorem 497
  correlation coefficient 495
  covariance 494
  density, estimation 492
  error propagation 497, 498
  Gaussian distribution 496
  Gaussian standard deviation 494
  mean 492, 493
  Poisson distribution 496
  standard deviation 493
  variance 493

Bernoulli distribution 253

Big Data
  characteristics 439
  variety 440
  velocity 439
  veracity 440
  volume 439

Big Data cluster deployment frameworks
  about 441
  Amazon Elastic MapReduce (EMR) 444
  Cloudera CDH 443
  Hortonworks Data Platform (HDP) 442
  Microsoft Azure HDInsight 444

Big Data framework
  about 441
  analysis 450
  cluster deployment frameworks 441
  data acquisition 445
  data preparation 449
  data processing 449
  data storage 446
  machine learning 450
  visualization 450

Big Data Machine Learning
  about 440
  Big Data framework 441
  framework 441
  Spark MLlib 463

binomial distribution 495

boosting
  about 67
  advantages 68
  algorithm input 67
  algorithm output 67
  limitation 68
  working 67

bootstrap aggregating (bagging)
  about 66
  advantages 66
  algorithm inputs 66
  algorithm outputs 66
  limitations 66
  Random Forest 66
  working 66

Broyden-Fletcher-Goldfarb-Shanno
  (BFGS) 55

Business Intelligence (BI) 4

business problem 77, 136

C

case study, with CoverType dataset
  about 459
  Big Data Machine Learning, used as Spark
    MLlib 463
  business problem 459
  data collection 460
  data sampling 460
  data transformation 460
  machine learning, mapping 460

MNIST database
  reference link 136
MOA 24
model
  building 52
  linear models 52
model assessment 68, 69
model comparison
  about 68, 72
  algorithms, comparing 73
  multiple algorithms, comparing 75
model evaluation 68
model evaluation metrics
  about 69, 89
  confusion matrix 71
  Confusion Metrics, evaluation 89
  Gain charts 72, 90
  lift curves 72
  Lift Curves 90
  PRC curve 71
  ROC curve 71, 90
model evolution, monitoring
  about 199
  drift detection method (DDM) 199
  early drift detection method (EEDM) 200
  Kubat 199
  Widmer 199
modeling techniques
  density based algorithm 220
  ensemble algorithms 207
  grid based algorithm 222
  hierarchical clustering 216, 218
  linear algorithm 202
  micro clustering 216, 218
  non-linear algorithms 205
  partition based algorithm 215
models
  clustering analysis 145, 146
  ensemble learning 65
  meta learners 65
  non-linear models 56
  observations 145, 146
model validation techniques
  about 211
  algorithms, versus metrics 214
  controlled permutations 212
  evaluation criteria 212

  holdout evaluation 212
  prequential evaluation 211
most probable explanation (MPE) 256
Multidimensional Scaling (MDS)
  about 104
  advantages 104
  inputs 104
  limitations 104
  outputs 104
  working 104
multi-layered neural network
  about 315
  activation function 314, 316
  inputs 314
  mathematical notation 314
  neuron 314
  structure and mathematical
    notations 315, 316
  training 317
multi-layered perceptron (MLP) 460
multi-layer feed-forward neural
    network 314
multinomial distribution 253
multiple algorithms, comparing
  ANOVA test 75
  Friedman's test 76
multivariate feature analysis
  about 34
  parallel plots 34
  ScatterPlot Matrix 34
  scatter plots 34
multivariate feature selection
  about 49
  correlation-based feature selection (CFS) 50
  minimal redundancy maximal relevance
    (mRMR) 50
multi-view SSL 158

N

Naïve Bayes (NB)
  about 54, 460
  advantages 54
  algorithm input 54
  algorithm output 54
  limitation 54
  working 54

advantages 64
algorithm input 61
algorithm output 61
limitations 64
working 61-63
Syntactic features 394, 395
Syntactic Language Models (SLM) 395
Synthetic Minority Oversampling
    Technique (SMOTE) 40

T

tasks 383
term frequency-inverse document frequency
    (TF-IDF) 398
Term Frequency (TF) 397, 402
text categorization 384
text clustering
  about 384, 409
  evaluation 415
  feature transformation 409
  reduction 409
  selection 409
  techniques 409
text mining
  categorization/classification 403, 404
  clustering 409
  Deep Learning 420-424
  named entity recognition (NER) 416
  NLP 420-424
  topic modeling 405
  topics 403
text processing components
  about 388
  dimensionality reduction 400
  document collection 389
  feature extraction/generation 393
  feature representation 396
  feature selection 400
  lemmatization 391
  local-global dictionary 392
  similarity 396
  standardization 389
  stop words removal 390
  tokenization 390
  vocabulary 392
text summarization 387

time-series forecasting 11
tokenization
  about 390
  input 390
  output 390
  working 390
tools
  about 135, 424
  KNIME 425
  Mallet 424
tools, machine learning
  DeepLearning4J 23
  Elki 23
  GraphX 24
  H2O 24
  JCLAL 23
  KEEL 23
  Knime 22
  Mallet 22
  MOA/SAMOA 24
  Neo4j 24
  OpenMarkov 24
  RapidMiner 22
  Smile 25
  Spark-MLlib 23
  Weka 22
topic modeling
  about 405
  business problem 427
  data collection 428
  data sampling 428
  dimensionality reduction 430
  evaluation 431
  feature analysis 430
  machine learning, mapping 427
  models 431
  probabilistic latent semantic analysis
      (PLSA) 405
  results 431
  text processing results, analysis 432
  transformation 428, 429
  with mallet 426
training phases
  adaptive phase 116
  competitive phase 115
  cooperation phase 115
transaction data 13

transductive graph label propagation
  about 161
  advantages 163
  input 162
  limitations 163
  output 162
  working 162
transductive SVM (TSVM)
  about 163
  advantages 164
  input 163
  limitations 164
  output 163
  working 163, 164
transformations 388
tree augmented networks (TAN)
  about 251, 293
  advantages and limitations 294
  input and output 294
  working 294
Tunedit
  about 25
  URL 25

U

UCI repository
  reference link 180
UC Irvine (UCI) database
  about 25
  URL 25
uncertainty sampling
  about 174
  advantages 175
  label entropy sampling 175
  least confident sampling 174
  limitations 175
  smallest margin sampling 175
  working 174
undersampling 40
univariate feature analysis
  about 33
  categorical features 33
  continuous features 33, 34
univariate feature selection
  information theoretic approach 47
  statistical approach 48

unnormalized measure 255
unstructured data
  about 13
  mining, issues 388
unsupervised learning
  about 10
  assumptions 192
  mathematical notations 192, 193
  outlier detection, used 229
  specific issues 99
usage 424
US Forest Service (USFS) 460
US Geological Survey (USGS) 460

V

validation
  techniques 45
variable elimination (VE) algorithm 264
variance 493
vector
  about 483
  scalar product 484
vector space model (VSM)
  about 396
  binary 397
  inverse document frequency (IDF) 398
  term frequency-inverse document
    frequency (TF-IDF) 398
  Term Frequency (TF) 397
version space sampling
  about 175
  Query by disagreement (QBD) 175
very fast decision trees (VFDT)
  about 205
  advantages 207
  limitations 207
  output 206
Very Fast K-means Algorithm (VFKM) 216
visualization analysis
  about 33
  multivariate feature analysis 34
  univariate feature analysis 33
V-Measure
  about 226
  completeness 226, 227
  homogeneity 226

CPSIA information can be obtained
at www.ICGtesting.com
Printed in the USA
LVHW020504180723
752608LV00004B/312

9 781785 880